Eduard Sachau, Muhammad ibn Ahmad Biruni

**Alberuni's India**

an account of the religion, philosophy, literature, geography, chronology,

astronomy, customs, laws and astrology of India, about A.D. 1030

Eduard Sachau, Muhammad ibn Ahmad Biruni

**Alberuni's India**
*an account of the religion, philosophy, literature, geography, chronology, astronomy, customs, laws and astrology of India, about A.D. 1030*

ISBN/EAN: 9783337080464

Printed in Europe, USA, Canada, Australia, Japan

Cover: Foto ©ninafisch / pixelio.de

More available books at **www.hansebooks.com**

# TRÜBNER'S ORIENTAL SERIES.

"A knowledge of the commonplace, at least, of Oriental literature, philosophy, and religion is as necessary to the general reader of the present day as an acquaintance with the Latin and Greek classics was a generation or so ago. Immense strides have been made within the present century in these branches of learning; Sanskrit has been brought within the range of accurate philology, and its invaluable ancient literature thoroughly investigated; the language and sacred books of the Zoroastrians have been laid bare; Egyptian, Assyrian, and other records of the remote past have been deciphered, and a group of scholars speak of still more recondite Accadian and Hittite monuments; but the results of all the scholarship that has been devoted to these subjects have been almost inaccessible to the public because they were contained for the most part in learned or expensive works, or scattered throughout the numbers of scientific periodicals. Messrs. TRÜBNER & Co., in a spirit of enterprise which does them infinite credit, have determined to supply the constantly-increasing want, and to give in a popular, or, at least, a comprehensive form, all this mass of knowledge to the world."—*Times.*

---

Second Edition, post 8vo, pp. xxxii.—748, with Map, cloth, price 21s.

## THE INDIAN EMPIRE: ITS PEOPLE, HISTORY, AND PRODUCTS.

By the HON. SIR W. W. HUNTER, K.C.S.I., C.S.I., C.I.E., LL.D.,

Member of the Viceroy's Legislative Council,

Director-General of Statistics to the Government of India.

Being a Revised Edition, brought up to date, and incorporating the general results of the Census of 1881.

"It forms a volume of more than 700 pages, and is a marvellous combination of literary condensation and research. It gives a complete account of the Indian Empire, its history, peoples, and products, and forms the worthy outcome of seventeen years of labour with exceptional opportunities for rendering that labour fruitful. Nothing could be more lucid than Sir William Hunter's expositions of the economic and political condition of India at the present time, or more interesting than his scholarly history of the India of the past."—*The Times.*

*THE FOLLOWING WORKS HAVE ALREADY APPEARED:—*

Third Edition, post 8vo, cloth, pp. xvi.—428, price 16s.

## ESSAYS ON THE SACRED LANGUAGE, WRITINGS, AND RELIGION OF THE PARSIS.

BY MARTIN HAUG, PH.D.,

Late of the Universities of Tübingen, Göttingen, and Bonn; Superintendent of Sanskrit Studies, and Professor of Sanskrit in the Poona College.

EDITED AND ENLARGED BY DR. E. W. WEST.

To which is added a Biographical Memoir of the late Dr. HAUG by Prof. E. P. EVANS.

I. History of the Researches into the Sacred Writings and Religion of the Parsis, from the Earliest Times down to the Present.
II. Languages of the Parsi Scriptures.
III. The Zend-Avesta, or the Scripture of the Parsis.
IV. The Zoroastrian Religion, as to its Origin and Development.

"'Essays on the Sacred Language, Writings, and Religion of the Parsis,' by the late Dr. Martin Haug, edited by Dr. E. W. West. The author intended, on his return from India, to expand the materials contained in this work into a comprehensive account of the Zoroastrian religion, but the design was frustrated by his untimely death. We have, however, in a concise and readable form, a history of the researches into the sacred writings and religion of the Parsis from the earliest times down to the present—a dissertation on the languages of the Parsi Scriptures, a translation of the Zend-Avesta, or the Scripture of the Parsis, and a dissertation on the Zoroastrian religion, with especial reference to its origin and development."—*Times.*

---

Post 8vo, cloth, pp. viii.—176, price 7s. 6d.

## TEXTS FROM THE BUDDHIST CANON

### COMMONLY KNOWN AS "DHAMMAPADA."

*With Accompanying Narratives.*

Translated from the Chinese by S. BEAL, B.A., Professor of Chinese, University College, London.

The Dhammapada, as hitherto known by the Pali Text Edition, as edited by Fausböll, by Max Müller's English, and Albrecht Weber's German translations, consists only of twenty-six chapters or sections, whilst the Chinese version, or rather recension, as now translated by Mr. Beal, consists of thirty-nine sections. The students of Pali who possess Fausböll's text, or either of the above-named translations, will therefore needs want Mr. Beal's English rendering of the Chinese version; the thirteen above-named additional sections not being accessible to them in any other form; for, even if they understand Chinese, the Chinese original would be unobtainable by them.

"Mr. Beal's rendering of the Chinese translation is a most valuable aid to the critical study of the work. It contains authentic texts gathered from ancient canonical books, and generally connected with some incident in the history of Buddha. Their great interest, however, consists in the light which they throw upon everyday life in India at the remote period at which they were written, and upon the method of teaching adopted by the founder of the religion. The method employed was principally parable, and the simplicity of the tales and the excellence of the morals inculcated, as well as the strange hold which they have retained upon the minds of millions of people, make them a very remarkable study."—*Times.*

"Mr. Beal, by making it accessible in an English dress, has added to the great services he has already rendered to the comparative study of religious history."—*Academy.*

"Valuable as exhibiting the doctrine of the Buddhists in its purest, least adulterated form, it brings the modern reader face to face with that simple creed and rule of conduct which won its way over the minds of myriads, and which is now nominally professed by 145 millions, who have overlaid its austere simplicity with innumerable ceremonies, forgotten its maxims, perverted its teaching, and so inverted its leading principle that a religion whose founder denied a God, now worships that founder as a god himself."—*Scotsman.*

Second Edition, post 8vo, cloth, pp. xxiv.—360, price 10s. 6d.

## THE HISTORY OF INDIAN LITERATURE.

By ALBRECHT WEBER.

Translated from the Second German Edition by JOHN MANN, M.A., and THÉODOR ZACHARIAE, Ph.D., with the sanction of the Author.

Dr. BUHLER, Inspector of Schools in India, writes:—"When I was Professor of Oriental Languages in Elphinstone College, I frequently felt the want of such a work to which I could refer the students."

Professor COWELL, of Cambridge, writes:—"It will be especially useful to the students in our Indian colleges and universities. I used to long for such a book when I was teaching in Calcutta. Hindu students are intensely interested in the history of Sanskrit literature, and this volume will supply them with all they want on the subject."

Professor WHITNEY, Yale College, Newhaven, Conn., U.S.A., writes:—"I was one of the class to whom the work was originally given in the form of academic lectures. At their first appearance they were by far the most learned and able treatment of their subject; and with their recent additions they still maintain decidedly the same rank."

"Is perhaps the most comprehensive and lucid survey of Sanskrit literature extant. The essays contained in the volume were originally delivered as academic lectures, and at the time of their first publication were acknowledged to be by far the most learned and able treatment of the subject. They have now been brought up to date by the addition of all the most important results of recent research."—*Times.*

---

Post 8vo, cloth, pp. xii.—198, accompanied by Two Language Maps, price 7s. 6d.

## A SKETCH OF THE MODERN LANGUAGES OF THE EAST INDIES.

By ROBERT N. CUST.

The Author has attempted to fill up a vacuum, the inconvenience of which pressed itself on his notice. Much had been written about the languages of the East Indies, but the extent of our present knowledge had not even been brought to a focus. It occurred to him that it might be of use to others to publish in an arranged form the notes which he had collected for his own edification.

"Supplies a deficiency which has long been felt."—*Times.*

"The book before us is then a valuable contribution to philological science. It passes under review a vast number of languages, and it gives, or professes to give, in every case the sum and substance of the opinions and judgments of the best-informed writers."—*Saturday Review.*

---

Second Corrected Edition, post 8vo, pp. xii.—116, cloth, price 5s.

## THE BIRTH OF THE WAR-GOD.

A Poem. By KALIDASA.

Translated from the Sanskrit into English Verse by RALPH T. H. GRIFFITH, M.A.

"A very spirited rendering of the *Kumárasambhava*, which was first published twenty-six years ago, and which we are glad to see made once more accessible."—*Times.*

"Mr. Griffith's very spirited rendering is well known to most who are at all interested in Indian literature, or enjoy the tenderness of feeling and rich creative imagination of its author."—*Indian Antiquary.*

"We are very glad to welcome a second edition of Professor Griffith's admirable translation. Few translations deserve a second edition better."—*Athenæum.*

Post 8vo, pp. 432, cloth, price 16s.

## A CLASSICAL DICTIONARY OF HINDU MYTHOLOGY AND RELIGION, GEOGRAPHY, HISTORY, AND LITERATURE.

By JOHN DOWSON, M.R.A.S.,
Late Professor of Hindustani, Staff College.

"This not only forms an indispensable book of reference to students of Indian literature, but is also of great general interest, as it gives in a concise and easily accessible form all that need be known about the personages of Hindu mythology whose names are so familiar, but of whom so little is known outside the limited circle of *savants*."—*Times*.

"It is no slight gain when such subjects are treated fairly and fully in a moderate space; and we need only add that the few wants which we may hope to see supplied in new editions detract but little from the general excellence of Mr. Dowson's work."—*Saturday Review*.

---

Post 8vo, with View of Mecca, pp. cxii.—172, cloth, price 9s.

## SELECTIONS FROM THE KORAN.

By EDWARD WILLIAM LANE,
Translator of "The Thousand and One Nights;" &c., &c.

A New Edition, Revised and Enlarged, with an Introduction by
STANLEY LANE POOLE.

". . . Has been long esteemed in this country as the compilation of one of the greatest Arabic scholars of the time, the late Mr. Lane, the well-known translator of the 'Arabian Nights.' . . . The present editor has enhanced the value of his relative's work by divesting the text of a great deal of extraneous matter introduced by way of comment, and prefixing an introduction."—*Times*.

"Mr. Poole is both a generous and a learned biographer. . . . Mr. Poole tells us the facts . . . so far as it is possible for industry and criticism to ascertain them, and for literary skill to present them in a condensed and readable form."—*Englishman, Calcutta*.

---

Post 8vo, pp. vi.—368, cloth, price 14s.

## MODERN INDIA AND THE INDIANS,

BEING A SERIES OF IMPRESSIONS, NOTES, AND ESSAYS.

By MONIER WILLIAMS, D.C.L.,
Hon. LL.D. of the University of Calcutta, Hon. Member of the Bombay Asiatic Society, Boden Professor of Sanskrit in the University of Oxford.

Third Edition, revised and augmented by considerable Additions, with Illustrations and a Map.

"In this volume we have the thoughtful impressions of a thoughtful man on some of the most important questions connected with our Indian Empire. . . . An enlightened observant man, travelling among an enlightened observant people, Professor Monier Williams has brought before the public in a pleasant form more of the manners and customs of the Queen's Indian subjects than we ever remember to have seen in any one work. He not only deserves the thanks of every Englishman for this able contribution to the study of Modern India—a subject with which we should be specially familiar—but he deserves the thanks of every Indian, Parsee or Hindu, Buddhist and Moslem, for his clear exposition of their manners, their creeds, and their necessities."—*Times*.

---

Post 8vo, pp. xliv.—376, cloth, price 14s.

## METRICAL TRANSLATIONS FROM SANSKRIT WRITERS.

With an Introduction, many Prose Versions, and Parallel Passages from Classical Authors.

By J. MUIR, C.I.E., D.C.L., LL.D., Ph.D.

". . . An agreeable introduction to Hindu poetry."—*Times*.

". . . A volume which may be taken as a fair illustration alike of the religious and moral sentiments and of the legendary lore of the best Sanskrit writers."—*Edinburgh Daily Review*.

Second Edition, post 8vo, pp. xxvi.—244, cloth, price 10s. 6d.

# THE GULISTAN;

## OR, ROSE GARDEN OF SHEKH MUSHLIU'D-DIN SADI OF SHIRAZ.

Translated for the First Time into Prose and Verse, with an Introductory Preface, and a Life of the Author, from the Atish Kadah,

BY EDWARD B. EASTWICK, C.B., M.A., F.R.S., M.R.A.S.

"It is a very fair rendering of the original."—*Times.*

"The new edition has long been desired, and will be welcomed by all who take any interest in Oriental poetry. The *Gulistan* is a typical Persian verse-book of the highest order. Mr. Eastwick's rhymed translation . . . has long established itself in a secure position as the best version of Sadi's finest work."—*Academy.*

"It is both faithfully and gracefully executed."—*Tablet.*

---

In Two Volumes, post 8vo, pp. viii.—408 and viii.—348, cloth, price 28s.

# MISCELLANEOUS ESSAYS RELATING TO INDIAN SUBJECTS.

BY BRIAN HOUGHTON HODGSON, ESQ., F.R.S.,

Late of the Bengal Civil Service; Corresponding Member of the Institute; Chevalier of the Legion of Honour; late British Minister at the Court of Nepal, &c., &c.

*CONTENTS OF VOL. I.*

SECTION I.—On the Kocch, Bódó, and Dhimál Tribes.—Part I. Vocabulary.—Part II. Grammar.—Part III. Their Origin, Location, Numbers, Creed, Customs, Character, and Condition, with a General Description of the Climate they dwell in.—Appendix.

SECTION II.—On Himalayan Ethnology.—I. Comparative Vocabulary of the Languages of the Broken Tribes of Népál.—II. Vocabulary of the Dialects of the Kiranti Language.—III. Grammatical Analysis of the Váyu Language. The Váyu Grammar.—IV. Analysis of the Báhing Dialect of the Kiranti Language. The Báhing Grammar.—V. On the Váyu or Háyu Tribe of the Central Himaláya.—VI. On the Kiranti Tribe of the Central Himaláya.

*CONTENTS OF VOL. II.*

SECTION III.—On the Aborigines of North-Eastern India. Comparative Vocabulary of the Tibetan, Bódó, and Gáró Tongues.

SECTION IV.—Aborigines of the North-Eastern Frontier.

SECTION V.—Aborigines of the Eastern Frontier.

SECTION VI.—The Indo-Chinese Borderers, and their connection with the Himalayans and Tibetans. Comparative Vocabulary of Indo-Chinese Borderers in Arakan. Comparative Vocabulary of Indo-Chinese Borderers in Tenasserim.

SECTION VII.—The Mongolian Affinities of the Caucasians.—Comparison and Analysis of Caucasian and Mongolian Words.

SECTION VIII.—Physical Type of Tibetans.

SECTION IX.—The Aborigines of Central India.—Comparative Vocabulary of the Aboriginal Languages of Central India.—Aborigines of the Eastern Ghats.—Vocabulary of some of the Dialects of the Hill and Wandering Tribes in the Northern Sircars.—Aborigines of the Nilgiris, with Remarks on their Affinities.—Supplement to the Nilgirian Vocabularies.—The Aborigines of Southern India and Ceylon.

SECTION X.—Route of Nepalese Mission to Pekin, with Remarks on the Water-Shed and Plateau of Tibet.

SECTION XI.—Route from Káthmándú, the Capital of Nepál, to Darjeeling in Sikim.—Memorandum relative to the Seven Cosis of Nepál.

SECTION XII.—Some Accounts of the Systems of Law and Police as recognised in the State of Nepál.

SECTION XIII.—The Native Method of making the Paper denominated Hindustan, Népálese.

SECTION XIV.—Pre-eminence of the Vernaculars; or, the Anglicists Answered; Being Letters on the Education of the People of India.

"For the study of the less-known races of India Mr. Brian Hodgson's 'Miscellaneous Essays' will be found very valuable both to the philologist and the ethnologist."

Third Edition, Two Vols., post 8vo, pp. viii.—268 and viii.—326, cloth, price 21s.

## THE LIFE OR LEGEND OF GAUDAMA,

THE BUDDHA OF THE BURMESE. With Annotations.

The Ways to Neibban, and Notice on the Phongyies or Burmese Monks.

BY THE RIGHT REV. P. BIGANDET,

Bishop of Ramatha, Vicar-Apostolic of Ava and Pegu.

"The work is furnished with copious notes, which not only illustrate the subject-matter, but form a perfect encyclopædia of Buddhist lore."—*Times.*

"A work which will furnish European students of Buddhism with a most valuable help in the prosecution of their investigations."—*Edinburgh Daily Review.*

"Bishop Bigandet's invaluable work."—*Indian Antiquary.*

"Viewed in this light, its importance is sufficient to place students of the subject under a deep obligation to its author."—*Calcutta Review.*

"This work is one of the greatest authorities upon Buddhism."—*Dublin Review.*

---

Post 8vo, pp. xxiv.—420, cloth, price 18s.

## CHINESE BUDDHISM.

A VOLUME OF SKETCHES, HISTORICAL AND CRITICAL.

BY J. EDKINS, D.D.

Author of "China's Place in Philology," "Religion in China," &c., &c.

"It contains a vast deal of important information on the subject, such as is only to be gained by long-continued study on the spot."—*Athenæum.*

"Upon the whole, we know of no work comparable to it for the extent of its original research, and the simplicity with which this complicated system of philosophy, religion, literature, and ritual is set forth."—*British Quarterly Review.*

"The whole volume is replete with learning. . . . It deserves most careful study from all interested in the history of the religions of the world, and expressly of those who are concerned in the propagation of Christianity. Dr. Edkins notices in terms of just condemnation the exaggerated praise bestowed upon Buddhism by recent English writers."—*Record.*

---

Post 8vo, pp. 496, cloth, price 10s. 6d.

## LINGUISTIC AND ORIENTAL ESSAYS.

WRITTEN FROM THE YEAR 1846 TO 1878.

BY ROBERT NEEDHAM CUST,

Late Member of Her Majesty's Indian Civil Service; Hon. Secretary to the Royal Asiatic Society;
and Author of "The Modern Languages of the East Indies."

"We know none who has described Indian life, especially the life of the natives, with so much learning, sympathy, and literary talent."—*Academy.*

"They seem to us to be full of suggestive and original remarks."—*St. James's Gazette.*

"His book contains a vast amount of information. The result of thirty-five years of inquiry, reflection, and speculation, and that on subjects as full of fascination as of food for thought."—*Tablet.*

"Exhibit such a thorough acquaintance with the history and antiquities of India as to entitle him to speak as one having authority."—*Edinburgh Daily Review.*

"The author speaks with the authority of personal experience. . . . It is this constant association with the country and the people which gives such a vividness to many of the pages."—*Athenæum.*

Post 8vo, pp. civ.—348, cloth, price 18s.

## BUDDHIST BIRTH STORIES; or, Jataka Tales.

### The Oldest Collection of Folk-lore Extant:

### BEING THE JATAKATTHAVANNANA,

### For the first time Edited in the original Pāli.

### BY V. FAUSBOLL;

### And Translated by T. W. RHYS DAVIDS.

### Translation. Volume I.

"These are tales supposed to have been told by the Buddha of what he had seen and heard in his previous births. They are probably the nearest representatives of the original Aryan stories from which sprang the folk-lore of Europe as well as India. The introduction contains a most interesting disquisition on the migrations of these fables, tracing their reappearance in the various groups of folk-lore legends. Among other old friends, we meet with a version of the Judgment of Solomon."—*Times.*

"It is now some years since Mr. Rhys Davids asserted his right to be heard on this subject by his able article on Buddhism in the new edition of the 'Encyclopædia Britannica.'"—*Leeds Mercury.*

"All who are interested in Buddhist literature ought to feel deeply indebted to Mr. Rhys Davids. His well-established reputation as a Pali scholar is a sufficient guarantee for the fidelity of his version, and the style of his translations is deserving of high praise."—*Academy.*

"No more competent expositor of Buddhism could be found than Mr. Rhys Davids. In the Jātaka book we have, then, a priceless record of the earliest imaginative literature of our race; and . . . it presents to us a nearly complete picture of the social life and customs and popular beliefs of the common people of Aryan tribes, closely related to ourselves, just as they were passing through the first stages of civilisation."—*St. James's Gazette.*

---

Post 8vo, pp. xxviii.—362, cloth, price 14s.

## A TALMUDIC MISCELLANY;

### OR, A THOUSAND AND ONE EXTRACTS FROM THE TALMUD, THE MIDRASHIM, AND THE KABBALAH.

### Compiled and Translated by PAUL ISAAC HERSHON,

### Author of "Genesis According to the Talmud," &c.

### With Notes and Copious Indexes.

"To obtain in so concise and handy a form as this volume a general idea of the Talmud is a boon to Christians at least."—*Times.*

"Its peculiar and popular character will make it attractive to general readers. Mr. Hershon is a very competent scholar. . . . Contains samples of the good, bad, and indifferent, and especially extracts that throw light upon the Scriptures."—*British Quarterly Review.*

"Will convey to English readers a more complete and truthful notion of the Talmud than any other work that has yet appeared."—*Daily News.*

"Without overlooking in the slightest the several attractions of the previous volumes of the 'Oriental Series,' we have no hesitation in saying that this surpasses them all in interest."—*Edinburgh Daily Review.*

"Mr. Hershon has . . . thus given English readers what is, we believe, a fair set of specimens which they can test for themselves."—*The Record.*

"This book is by far the best fitted in the present state of knowledge to enable the general reader to gain a fair and unbiassed conception of the multifarious contents of the wonderful miscellany which can only be truly understood—so Jewish pride asserts—by the life-long devotion of scholars of the Chosen People."—*Inquirer.*

"The value and importance of this volume consist in the fact that scarcely a single extract is given in its pages but throws some light, direct or refracted, upon those Scriptures which are the common heritage of Jew and Christian alike."—*John Bull.*

"It is a capital specimen of Hebrew scholarship; a monument of learned, loving, light-giving labour."—*Jewish Herald.*

Post 8vo, pp. xii.—228, cloth, price 7s. 6d.

## THE CLASSICAL POETRY OF THE JAPANESE.

By BASIL HALL CHAMBERLAIN,

Author of "Yeigo Heñkaku Shirañ."

"A very curious volume. The author has manifestly devoted much labour to the task of studying the poetical literature of the Japanese, and rendering characteristic specimens into English verse."—*Daily News.*

"Mr. Chamberlain's volume is, so far as we are aware, the first attempt which has been made to interpret the literature of the Japanese to the Western world. It is to the classical poetry of Old Japan that we must turn for indigenous Japanese thought, and in the volume before us we have a selection from that poetry rendered into graceful English verse."—*Tablet.*

"It is undoubtedly one of the best translations of lyric literature which has appeared during the close of the last year."—*Celestial Empire.*

"Mr. Chamberlain set himself a difficult task when he undertook to reproduce Japanese poetry in an English form. But he has evidently laboured *con amore*, and his efforts are successful to a degree."—*London and China Express.*

---

Post 8vo, pp. xii.—164, cloth, price 10s. 6d.

## THE HISTORY OF ESARHADDON (Son of Sennacherib),

KING OF ASSYRIA, B.C. 681-668.

Translated from the Cuneiform Inscriptions upon Cylinders and Tablets in the British Museum Collection; together with a Grammatical Analysis of each Word, Explanations of the Ideographs by Extracts from the Bi-Lingual Syllabaries, and List of Eponyms, &c.

By ERNEST A. BUDGE, B.A., M.R.A.S.,

Assyrian Exhibitioner, Christ's College, Cambridge.

"Students of scriptural archæology will also appreciate the 'History of Esarhaddon.'"—*Times.*

"There is much to attract the scholar in this volume. It does not pretend to popularise studies which are yet in their infancy. Its primary object is to translate, but it does not assume to be more than tentative, and it offers both to the professed Assyriologist and to the ordinary non-Assyriological Semitic scholar the means of controlling its results."—*Academy.*

"Mr. Budge's book is, of course, mainly addressed to Assyrian scholars and students. They are not, it is to be feared, a very numerous class. But the more thanks are due to him on that account for the way in which he has acquitted himself in his laborious task."—*Tablet.*

Post 8vo, pp. 448, cloth, price 21s.

## THE MESNEVI

(Usually known as The Mesneviyi Sherif, or Holy Mesnevi)

OF

MEVLANA (OUR LORD) JELALU 'D-DIN MUHAMMED ER-RUMI.

Book the First.

*Together with some Account of the Life and Acts of the Author, of his Ancestors, and of his Descendants.*

Illustrated by a Selection of Characteristic Anecdotes, as Collected by their Historian,

Mevlana Shemsu-'d-Din Ahmed, el Eflaki, el 'Arifi.

Translated, and the Poetry Versified, in English,

By JAMES W. REDHOUSE, M.R.A.S., &c.

"A complete treasury of occult Oriental lore."—*Saturday Review.*

"This book will be a very valuable help to the reader ignorant of Persia, who is desirous of obtaining an insight into a very important department of the literature extant in that language."—*Tablet.*

Post 8vo, pp. xvi.—280, cloth, price 6s.

## EASTERN PROVERBS AND EMBLEMS

### ILLUSTRATING OLD TRUTHS.

BY REV. J. LONG,

Member of the Bengal Asiatic Society, F.R.G.S.

"We regard the book as valuable, and wish for it a wide circulation and attentive reading."—*Record.*

"Altogether, it is quite a feast of good things."—*Globe.*

"It is full of interesting matter."—*Antiquary.*

---

Post 8vo, pp. viii.—270, cloth, price 7s. 6d.

## INDIAN POETRY;

Containing a New Edition of the "Indian Song of Songs," from the Sanscrit of the "Gita Govinda" of Jayadeva; Two Books from "The Iliad of India" (Mahabharata), "Proverbial Wisdom" from the Shlokas of the Hitopadesa, and other Oriental Poems.

BY EDWIN ARNOLD, C.S.I., Author of "The Light of Asia."

"In this new volume of Messrs. Trübner's Oriental Series, Mr. Edwin Arnold does good service by illustrating, through the medium of his musical English melodies, the power of Indian poetry to stir European emotions. The 'Indian Song of Songs' is not unknown to scholars. Mr. Arnold will have introduced it among popular English poems. Nothing could be more graceful and delicate than the shades by which Krishna is portrayed in the gradual process of being weaned by the love of

'Beautiful Radha, jasmine-bosomed Radha,'

from the allurements of the forest nymphs, in whom the five senses are typified."—*Times.*

"No other English poet has ever thrown his genius and his art so thoroughly into the work of translating Eastern ideas as Mr. Arnold has done in his splendid paraphrases of language contained in these mighty epics."—*Daily Telegraph.*

"The poem abounds with imagery of Eastern luxuriousness and sensuousness; the air seems laden with the spicy odours of the tropics, and the verse has a richness and a melody sufficient to captivate the senses of the dullest."—*Standard.*

"The translator, while producing a very enjoyable poem, has adhered with tolerable fidelity to the original text."—*Overland Mail.*

"We certainly wish Mr. Arnold success in his attempt 'to popularise Indian classics,' that being, as his preface tells us, the goal towards which he bends his efforts."—*Allen's Indian Mail.*

---

Post 8vo, pp. xvi.—296, cloth, price 10s. 6d.

## THE MIND OF MENCIUS;

### OR, POLITICAL ECONOMY FOUNDED UPON MORAL PHILOSOPHY.

A SYSTEMATIC DIGEST OF THE DOCTRINES OF THE CHINESE PHILOSOPHER MENCIUS.

Translated from the Original Text and Classified, with Comments and Explanations,

By the REV. ERNST FABER, Rhenish Mission Society.

Translated from the German, with Additional Notes,

By the REV. A. B. HUTCHINSON, C.M.S., Church Mission, Hong Kong.

"Mr. Faber is already well known in the field of Chinese studies by his digest of the doctrines of Confucius. The value of this work will be perceived when it is remembered that at no time since relations commenced between China and the West has the former been so powerful—we had almost said aggressive—as now. For those who will give it careful study, Mr. Faber's work is one of the most valuable of the excellent series to which it belongs."—*Nature.*

Post 8vo, pp. 336, cloth, price 16s.

## THE RELIGIONS OF INDIA.

BY A. BARTH.

Translated from the French with the authority and assistance of the Author.

The author has, at the request of the publishers, considerably enlarged the work for the translator, and has added the literature of the subject to date; the translation may, therefore, be looked upon as an equivalent of a new and improved edition of the original.

"Is not only a valuable manual of the religions of India, which marks a distinct step in the treatment of the subject, but also a useful work of reference."—*Academy.*

"This volume is a reproduction, with corrections and additions, of an article contributed by the learned author two years ago to the 'Encyclopédie des Sciences Religieuses.' It attracted much notice when it first appeared, and is generally admitted to present the best summary extant of the vast subject with which it deals."—*Tablet.*

"This is not only on the whole the best but the only manual of the religions of India, apart from Buddhism, which we have in English. The present work . . . shows not only great knowledge of the facts and power of clear exposition, but also great insight into the inner history and the deeper meaning of the great religion, for it is in reality only one, which it proposes to describe."—*Modern Review.*

"The merit of the work has been emphatically recognised by the most authoritative Orientalists, both in this country and on the continent of Europe. But probably there are few Indianists (if we may use the word) who would not derive a good deal of information from it, and especially from the extensive bibliography provided in the notes."—*Dublin Review.*

"Such a sketch M. Barth has drawn with a master-hand."—*Critic (New York).*

---

Post 8vo, pp. viii.—152, cloth, price 6s.

## HINDU PHILOSOPHY.

THE SĀNKHYA KĀRIKA OF IS'WARA KRISHNA.

An Exposition of the System of Kapila, with an Appendix on the Nyāya and Vais'eshika Systems.

BY JOHN DAVIES, M.A. (Cantab.), M.R.A.S.

The system of Kapila contains nearly all that India has produced in the department of pure philosophy.

"The non-Orientalist . . . finds in Mr. Davies a patient and learned guide who leads him into the intricacies of the philosophy of India, and supplies him with a clue, that he may not be lost in them. In the preface he states that the system of Kapila is the 'earliest attempt on record to give an answer, from reason alone, to the mysterious questions which arise in every thoughtful mind about the origin of the world, the nature and relations of man and his future destiny,' and in his learned and able notes he exhibits 'the connection of the Sankhya system with the philosophy of Spinoza,' and 'the connection of the system of Kapila with that of Schopenhauer and Von Hartmann.'"—*Foreign Church Chronicle.*

"Mr. Davies's volume on Hindu Philosophy is an undoubted gain to all students of the development of thought. The system of Kapila, which is here given in a translation from the Sānkhya Kārikā, is the only contribution of India to pure philosophy. . . . Presents many points of deep interest to the student of comparative philosophy, and without Mr. Davies's lucid interpretation it would be difficult to appreciate these points in any adequate manner."—*Saturday Review.*

"We welcome Mr. Davies's book as a valuable addition to our philosophical library."—*Notes and Queries.*

Post 8vo, pp. x.—130, cloth, price 6s.

## A MANUAL OF HINDU PANTHEISM. VEDÂNTASÂRA.

Translated, with copious Annotations,

BY MAJOR G. A. JACOB,

Bombay Staff Corps; Inspector of Army Schools.

The design of this little work is to provide for missionaries, and for others who, like them, have little leisure for original research, an accurate summary of the doctrines of the Vedânta.

"The modest title of Major Jacob's work conveys but an inadequate idea of the vast amount of research embodied in his notes to the text of the Vedantasara. So copious, indeed, are these, and so much collateral matter do they bring to bear on the subject, that the diligent student will rise from their perusal with a fairly adequate view of Hindû philosophy generally. His work . . . is one of the best of its kind that we have seen."—*Calcutta Review.*

---

Post 8vo, pp. xii.—154, cloth, price 7s. 6d.

## TSUNI—| | GOAM:

THE SUPREME BEING OF THE KHOI-KHOI.

BY THEOPHILUS HAHN, Ph.D.,

Custodian of the Grey Collection, Cape Town; Corresponding Member of the Geogr. Society, Dresden; Corresponding Member of the Anthropological Society, Vienna, &c., &c.

"The first instalment of Dr. Hahn's labours will be of interest, not at the Cape only, but in every University of Europe. It is, in fact, a most valuable contribution to the comparative study of religion and mythology. Accounts of their religion and mythology were scattered about in various books; these have been carefully collected by Dr. Hahn and printed in his second chapter, enriched and improved by what he has been able to collect himself."—*Prof. Max Müller in the Nineteenth Century.*

"It is full of good things."—*St. James's Gazette.*

---

In Four Volumes. Post 8vo, Vol. I., pp. xii.—392, cloth, price 12s. 6d., Vol. II., pp. vi.—408, cloth, price 12s. 6d., Vol. III., pp. viii.—414, cloth, price 12s. 6d., Vol. IV., pp. viii.—340, cloth, price 10s. 6d.

## A COMPREHENSIVE COMMENTARY TO THE QURAN.

TO WHICH IS PREFIXED SALE'S PRELIMINARY DISCOURSE, WITH ADDITIONAL NOTES AND EMENDATIONS.

Together with a Complete Index to the Text, Preliminary Discourse, and Notes.

By Rev. E. M. WHERRY, M.A., Lodiana.

"As Mr. Wherry's book is intended for missionaries in India, it is no doubt well that they should be prepared to meet, if they can, the ordinary arguments and interpretations, and for this purpose Mr. Wherry's additions will prove useful."—*Saturday Review.*

Second Edition. Post 8vo, pp. vi.—208, cloth, price 8s. 6d.

## THE BHAGAVAD-GÎTÂ.

Translated, with Introduction and Notes.

By JOHN DAVIES, M.A. (Cantab.)

"Let us add that his translation of the Bhagavad Gîtâ is, as we judge, the best that has as yet appeared in English, and that his Philological Notes are of quite peculiar value."—*Dublin Review.*

---

Post 8vo, pp. 96, cloth, price 5s.

## THE QUATRAINS OF OMAR KHAYYAM.

Translated by E. H. WHINFIELD, M.A.,

Barrister-at-Law, late H.M. Bengal Civil Service.

---

Post 8vo, pp. xxxii.—336, cloth, price 10s. 6d.

## THE QUATRAINS OF OMAR KHAYYAM.

The Persian Text, with an English Verse Translation.

By E. H. WHINFIELD, late of the Bengal Civil Service.

"Mr. Whinfield has executed a difficult task with considerable success, and his version contains much that will be new to those who only know Mr. Fitzgerald's delightful selection."—*Academy.*

"The most prominent features in the Quatrains are their profound agnosticism, combined with a fatalism based more on philosophic than religious grounds, their Epicureanism and the spirit of universal tolerance and charity which animates them."—*Calcutta Review.*

---

Post 8vo, pp. xxiv.—268, cloth, price 9s.

## THE PHILOSOPHY OF THE UPANISHADS AND ANCIENT INDIAN METAPHYSICS.

As exhibited in a series of Articles contributed to the *Calcutta Review.*

By ARCHIBALD EDWARD GOUGH, M.A., Lincoln College, Oxford; Principal of the Calcutta Madrasa.

"For practical purposes this is perhaps the most important of the works that have thus far appeared in 'Trübner's Oriental Series.' . . . We cannot doubt that for all who may take it up the work must be one of profound interest."—*Saturday Review.*

---

In Two Volumes. Vol. I., post 8vo, pp. xxiv.—230, cloth, price 7s. 6d.

## A COMPARATIVE HISTORY OF THE EGYPTIAN AND MESOPOTAMIAN RELIGIONS.

By Dr. C. P. TIELE.

Vol. I.—History of the Egyptian Religion.

Translated from the Dutch with the Assistance of the Author.

By JAMES BALLINGAL.

"It places in the hands of the English readers a history of Egyptian Religion which is very complete, which is based on the best materials, and which has been illustrated by the latest results of research. In this volume there is a great deal of information, as well as independent investigation, for the trustworthiness of which Dr. Tiele's name is in itself a guarantee; and the description of the successive religions under the Old Kingdom, the Middle Kingdom, and the New Kingdom, is given in a manner which is scholarly and minute."—*Scotsman.*

Post 8vo, pp. xii.—302, cloth, price 8s. 6d.

## YUSUF AND ZULAIKHA.

A POEM BY JAMI.

Translated from the Persian into English Verse.

BY RALPH T. H. GRIFFITH.

"Mr. Griffith, who has done already good service as translator into verse from the Sanskrit, has done further good work in this translation from the Persian, and he has evidently shown not a little skill in his rendering the quaint and very oriental style of his author into our more prosaic, less figurative, language. . . . The work, besides its intrinsic merits, is of importance as being one of the most popular and famous poems of Persia, and that which is read in all the independent native schools of India where Persian is taught."—*Scotsman*.

---

Post 8vo, pp. viii.—266, cloth, price 9s.

## LINGUISTIC ESSAYS.

BY CARL ABEL.

"An entirely novel method of dealing with philosophical questions and impart a real human interest to the otherwise dry technicalities of the science."—*Standard*.

"Dr. Abel is an opponent from whom it is pleasant to differ, for he writes with enthusiasm and temper, and his mastery over the English language fits him to be a champion of unpopular doctrines."—*Athenæum*.

---

Post 8vo, pp. ix.—281, cloth, price 10s. 6d.

## THE SARVA-DARSANA-SAMGRAHA;

OR, REVIEW OF THE DIFFERENT SYSTEMS OF HINDU PHILOSOPHY.

BY MADHAVA ACHARYA.

Translated by E. B. COWELL, M.A., Professor of Sanskrit in the University of Cambridge, and A. E. GOUGH, M.A., Professor of Philosophy in the Presidency College, Calcutta.

This work is an interesting specimen of Hindu critical ability. The author successively passes in review the sixteen philosophical systems current in the fourteenth century in the South of India; and he gives what appears to him to be their most important tenets.

"The translation is trustworthy throughout. A protracted sojourn in India, where there is a living tradition, has familiarised the translators with Indian thought."—*Athenæum*.

---

Post 8vo, pp. lxv.—368, cloth, price 14s.

## TIBETAN TALES DERIVED FROM INDIAN SOURCES.

Translated from the Tibetan of the KAH-GYUR.

BY F. ANTON VON SCHIEFNER.

Done into English from the German, with an Introduction,

BY W. R. S. RALSTON, M.A.

"Mr. Ralston, whose name is so familiar to all lovers of Russian folk-lore, has supplied some interesting Western analogies and parallels, drawn, for the most part, from Slavonic sources, to the Eastern folk-tales, culled from the Kahgyur, one of the divisions of the Tibetan sacred books."—*Academy*.

"The translation . . . could scarcely have fallen into better hands. An Introduction . . . gives the leading facts in the lives of those scholars who have given their attention to gaining a knowledge of the Tibetan literature and language."—*Calcutta Review*.

"Ought to interest all who care for the East, for amusing stories, or for comparative folk-lore."—*Pall Mall Gazette*.

Post 8vo, pp. xvi.—224, cloth, price 9s.

## UDÂNAVARGA.

A COLLECTION OF VERSES FROM THE BUDDHIST CANON.

Compiled by DHARMATRÂTA.

BEING THE NORTHERN BUDDHIST VERSION OF DHAMMAPADA.

Translated from the Tibetan of Bkah-hgyur, with Notes, and Extracts from the Commentary of Pradjnavarman,

By W. WOODVILLE ROCKHILL.

"Mr. Rockhill's present work is the first from which assistance will be gained for a more accurate understanding of the Pali text; it is, in fact, as yet the only term of comparison available to us. The 'Udanavarga,' the Thibetan version, was originally discovered by the late M. Schiefner, who published the Tibetan text, and had intended adding a translation, an intention frustrated by his death, but which has been carried out by Mr. Rockhill. . . . Mr. Rockhill may be congratulated for having well accomplished a difficult task."—*Saturday Review.*

---

In Two Volumes, post 8vo, pp. xxiv.—566, cloth, accompanied by a Language Map, price 18s.

## A SKETCH OF THE MODERN LANGUAGES OF AFRICA.

BY ROBERT NEEDHAM CUST,

Barrister-at-Law, and late of Her Majesty's Indian Civil Service.

"Any one at all interested in African languages cannot do better than get Mr. Cust's book. It is encyclopædic in its scope, and the reader gets a start clear away in any particular language, and is left free to add to the initial sum of knowledge there collected."—*Natal Mercury.*

"Mr. Cust has contrived to produce a work of value to linguistic students."—*Nature.*

---

Third Edition. Post 8vo, pp. xv.-250, cloth, price 7s. 6d.

## OUTLINES OF THE HISTORY OF RELIGION TO THE SPREAD OF THE UNIVERSAL RELIGIONS.

BY C. P. TIELE,

Doctor of Theology, Professor of the History of Religions in the University of Leyden.

Translated from the Dutch by J. ESTLIN CARPENTER, M.A.

"Few books of its size contain the result of so much wide thinking, able and laborious study, or enable the reader to gain a better bird's-eye view of the latest results of investigations into the religious history of nations. As Professor Tiele modestly says, 'In this little book are outlines—pencil sketches, I might say—nothing more.' But there are some men whose sketches from a thumb-nail are of far more worth than an enormous canvas covered with the crude painting of others, and it is easy to see that these pages, full of information, these sentences, cut and perhaps also dry, short and clear, condense the fruits of long and thorough research."—*Scotsman.*

Post 8vo, pp. xii.—312, with Maps and Plan, cloth, price 14s.

## A HISTORY OF BURMA.

Including Burma Proper, Pegu, Taungu, Tenasserim, and Arakan. From the Earliest Time to the End of the First War with British India.

By Lieut.-Gen. Sir ARTHUR P. PHAYRE, G.C.M.G., K.C.S.I., and C.B., Membre Correspondant de la Société Académique Indo-Chinoise de France.

"Sir Arthur Phayre's contribution to Trübner's Oriental Series supplies a recognised want, and its appearance has been looked forward to for many years. . . . . General Phayre deserves great credit for the patience and industry which has resulted in this History of Burma."—*Saturday Review.*

---

Third Edition. Post 8vo, pp. 276, cloth, price 7s. 6d.

## RELIGION IN CHINA.

By JOSEPH EDKINS, D.D., Peking.

Containing a Brief Account of the Three Religions of the Chinese, with Observations on the Prospects of Christian Conversion amongst that People.

"Dr. Edkins has been most careful in noting the varied and often complex phases of opinion, so as to give an account of considerable value of the subject."—*Scotsman.*

"As a missionary, it has been part of Dr. Edkins' duty to study the existing religions in China, and his long residence in the country has enabled him to acquire an intimate knowledge of them as they at present exist."—*Saturday Review.*

"Dr. Edkins' valuable work, of which this is a second and revised edition, has, from the time that it was published, been the standard authority upon the subject of which it treats."—*Nonconformist.*

"Dr. Edkins . . . may now be fairly regarded as among the first authorities on Chinese religion and language."—*British Quarterly Review.*

---

Post 8vo, pp. x.-274, cloth, price 9s.

## THE LIFE OF THE BUDDHA AND THE EARLY HISTORY OF HIS ORDER.

Derived from Tibetan Works in the Bkah-hgyur and Bstan-hgyur. Followed by notices on the Early History of Tibet and Khoten.

Translated by W. W. ROCKHILL, Second Secretary U.S. Legation in China.

"The volume bears testimony to the diligence and fulness with which the author has consulted and tested the ancient documents bearing upon his remarkable subject."—*Times.*

"Will be appreciated by those who devote themselves to those Buddhist studies which have of late years taken in these Western regions so remarkable a development. Its matter possesses a special interest as being derived from ancient Tibetan works, some portions of which, here analysed and translated, have not yet attracted the attention of scholars. The volume is rich in ancient stories bearing upon the world's renovation and the origin of castes, as recorded in these venerable authorities."—*Daily News.*

---

Third Edition. Post 8vo, pp. viii.-464, cloth, price 16s.

## THE SANKHYA APHORISMS OF KAPILA,

With Illustrative Extracts from the Commentaries.

Translated by J. R. BALLANTYNE, LL.D., late Principal of the Benares College.

Edited by FITZEDWARD HALL.

The work displays a vast expenditure of labour and scholarship, for which students of Hindoo philosophy have every reason to be grateful to Dr. Hall and the publishers."—*Calcutta Review.*

In Two Volumes, post 8vo, pp. xii.-318 and vi.-312, cloth, price 21s.

# MISCELLANEOUS PAPERS RELATING TO INDO-CHINA.

Reprinted from "Dalrymple's Oriental Repertory," "Asiatic Researches," and the "Journal of the Asiatic Society of Bengal."

*CONTENTS OF VOL. I.*

I.—Some Accounts of Quedah. By Michael Topping.

II.—Report made to the Chief and Council of Balambangan, by Lieut. James Barton, of his several Surveys.

III.—Substance of a Letter to the Court of Directors from Mr. John Jesse, dated July 20, 1775, at Borneo Proper.

IV.—Formation of the Establishment of Poolo Peenang.

V.—The Gold of Limong. By John Macdonald.

VI.—On Three Natural Productions of Sumatra. By John Macdonald.

VII.—On the Traces of the Hindu Language and Literature extant amongst the Malays. By William Marsden.

VIII.—Some Account of the Elastic Gum Vine of Prince-Wales Island. By James Howison.

IX.—A Botanical Description of Urceola Elastica, or Caoutchouc Vine of Sumatra and Pulo-Pinang. By William Roxburgh, M.D.

X.—An Account of the Inhabitants of the Poggy, or Nassau Islands, lying off Sumatra. By John Crisp.

XI.—Remarks on the Species of Pepper which are found on Prince-Wales Island. By William Hunter, M.D.

XII.—On the Languages and Literature of the Indo-Chinese Nations. By J. Leyden, M.D.

XIII.—Some Account of an Orang-Outang of remarkable height found on the Island of Sumatra. By Clarke Abel, M.D.

XIV.—Observations on the Geological Appearances and General Features of Portions of the Malayan Peninsula. By Captain James Low.

XV.—Short Sketch of the Geology of Pulo-Pinang and the Neighbouring Islands. By T. Ware.

XVI.—Climate of Singapore.

XVII.—Inscription on the Jetty at Singapore.

XVIII.—Extract of a Letter from Colonel J. Low.

XIX.—Inscription at Singapore.

XX.—An Account of Several Inscriptions found in Province Wellesley. By Lieut.-Col. James Low.

XXI.—Note on the Inscriptions from Singapore and Province Wellesley. By J. W. Laidlay.

XXII.—On an Inscription from Keddah. By Lieut.-Col. Low.

XXIII.—A Notice of the Alphabets of the Philippine Islands.

XXIV.—Succinct Review of the Observations of the Tides in the Indian Archipelago.

XXV.—Report on the Tin of the Province of Mergui. By Capt. G. B. Tremenheere.

XXVI.—Report on the Manganese of Mergui Province. By Capt. G. B. Tremenheere.

XXVII.—Paragraphs to be added to Capt. G. B. Tremenheere's Report.

XXVIII.—Second Report on the Tin of Mergui. By Capt. G. B. Tremenheere.

XXIX.—Analysis of Iron Ores from Tavoy and Mergui, and of Limestone from Mergui. By Dr. A. Ure.

XXX.—Report of a Visit to the Pakchan River, and of some Tin Localities in the Southern Portion of the Tenasserim Provinces. By Capt. G. B. Tremenheere.

XXXI.—Report on a Route from the Mouth of the Pakchan to Krau, and thence across the Isthmus of Krau to the Gulf of Siam. By Capt. Al. Fraser and Capt. J. G. Forlong.

XXXII.—Report, &c., from Capt. G. B. Tremenheere on the Price of Mergui Tin Ore.

XXXIII.—Remarks on the Different Species of Orang-utan. By E. Blyth.

XXXIV.—Further Remarks. By E. Blyth.

## MISCELLANEOUS PAPERS RELATING TO INDO-CHINA—continued.

*CONTENTS OF VOL. II.*

XXXV.—Catalogue of Mammalia inhabiting the Malayan Peninsula and Islands. By Theodore Cantor, M.D.

XXXVI.—On the Local and Relative Geology of Singapore. By J. R. Logan.

XXXVII.—Catalogue of Reptiles inhabiting the Malayan Peninsula and Islands. By Theodore Cantor, M.D.

XXXVIII.—Some Account of the Botanical Collection brought from the Eastward, in 1841, by Dr. Cantor. By the late W. Griffith.

XXXIX.—On the Flat-Horned Taurine Cattle of S.E. Asia. By E. Blyth.

XL.—Note, by Major-General G. B. Tremenheere.

General Index.

Index of Vernacular Terms.

Index of Zoological Genera and Sub-Genera occurring in Vol. II.

"The papers treat of almost every aspect of Indo-China—its philology, economy, geography, geology—and constitute a very material and important contribution to our accessible information regarding that country and its people."—*Contemporary Review.*

---

Post 8vo, pp. xii.-72, cloth, price 5s.

## THE SATAKAS OF BHARTRIHARI.

Translated from the Sanskrit

By the Rev. B. HALE WORTHAM, M.R.A.S.,

Rector of Eggesford, North Devon.

"A very interesting addition to Trübner's Oriental Series."—*Saturday Review.*

"Many of the Maxims in the book have a Biblical ring and beauty of expression."—*St. James' Gazette.*

---

Post 8vo, pp. xii.-180, cloth, price 6s.

## ANCIENT PROVERBS AND MAXIMS FROM BURMESE SOURCES;

OR, THE NITI LITERATURE OF BURMA.

BY JAMES GRAY,

Author of "Elements of Pali Grammar," "Translation of the Dhammapada," &c.

The Sanscrit-Pâli word Nîti is equivalent to "conduct" in its abstract, and "guide" in its concrete signification. As applied to books, it is a general term for a treatise which includes maxims, pithy sayings, and didactic stories, intended as a guide to such matters of every-day life as form the character of an individual and influence him in his relations to his fellow-men. Treatises of this kind have been popular in all ages, and have served as a most effective medium of instruction.

---

Post 8vo, pp. xxxii. and 330, cloth, price 7s. 6d.

## MASNAVI I MA' NAVI:

THE SPIRITUAL COUPLETS OF MAULANA JALALU-'D-DIN MUHAMMAD I RUMI.

Translated and Abridged by E. H. WHINFIELD, M.A., Late of H.M. Bengal Civil Service.

Post 8vo, pp. viii. and 346, cloth, price 10s. 6d.

## MANAVA-DHARMA-CASTRA: THE CODE OF MANU.

ORIGINAL SANSKRIT TEXT, WITH CRITICAL NOTES.
BY J. JOLLY, Ph.D.,

Professor of Sanskrit in the University of Wurzburg; late Tagore Professor of Law in the University of Calcutta.

The date assigned by Sir William Jones to this Code—the well-known Great Law Book of the Hindus—is 1250-500 B.C., although the rules and precepts contained in it had probably existed as tradition for countless ages before. There has been no reliable edition of the Text for Students for many years past, and it is believed, therefore, that Prof. Jolly's work will supply a want long felt.

---

Post 8vo, pp. 215, cloth, price 7s. 6d.

## LEAVES FROM MY CHINESE SCRAP-BOOK.

BY FREDERIC HENRY BALFOUR,

Author of "Waifs and Strays from the Far East," "Taoist Texts," "Idiomatic Phrases in the Peking Colloquial," &c. &c.

---

Post 8vo, pp. xvi.-548, with Six Maps, cloth, price 21s.

## LINGUISTIC AND ORIENTAL ESSAYS.

WRITTEN FROM THE YEAR 1847 TO 1887. *Second Series.*

BY ROBERT NEEDHAM CUST, LL.D.,

Barrister-at-Law; Honorary Secretary of the Royal Asiatic Society; Late Member of Her Majesty's Indian Civil Service.

---

In Two Volumes, post 8vo, pp. x.-308 and vi.-314, cloth, price 25s.

## MISCELLANEOUS PAPERS RELATING TO INDO-CHINA.

Edited by R. ROST, Ph.D., &c. &c.,
Librarian to the India Office.

SECOND SERIES.

Reprinted for the Straits Branch of the Royal Asiatic Society from the Malayan "Miscellanies," the "Transactions and Journal" of the Batavian Society, and the "Journals" of the Asiatic Society of Bengal, and the Royal Geographical and Royal Asiatic Societies.

---

Post 8vo, pp. xii.-512, price 16s.

## FOLK-TALES OF KASHMIR.

By the REV. J. HINTON KNOWLES, F.R.G.S., M.R.A.S, &c.

(C.M.S.) Missionary to the Kashmiris.

1000—9/11/88.

# TRÜBNER'S

# ORIENTAL SERIES.

# ALBERUNI'S INDIA.

*AN ACCOUNT OF THE RELIGION, PHILOSOPHY, LITERATURE,*
*GEOGRAPHY, CHRONOLOGY, ASTRONOMY, CUSTOMS,*
*LAWS AND ASTROLOGY OF INDIA*
*ABOUT A.D. 1030.*

शिव।

**An English Edition, with Notes and Indices.**

BY

DR. EDWARD C. SACHAU,

Professor in the Royal University of Berlin, and Principal of the Seminary for Oriental Languages; Member of the Royal Academy of Berlin, and Corresponding Member of the Imperial Academy of Vienna; Honorary Member of the Asiatic Society of Great Britain and Ireland, London, and of the American Oriental Society, Cambridge, U.S.A.

*IN TWO VOLUMES.*

VOL. II.

LONDON:
TRÜBNER & CO., LUDGATE HILL.
1888.

Ballantyne Press
BALLANTYNE, HANSON AND CO.
EDINBURGH AND LONDON

# ALBÊRÛNÎ'S INDIA.

## CHAPTER XLIX.

### A SUMMARY DESCRIPTION OF THE ERAS.

THE eras serve to fix certain moments of time which are mentioned in some historical or astronomical connection. The Hindus do not consider it wearisome to reckon with huge numbers, but rather enjoy it. Still, in practical use, they are compelled to replace them by smaller (more handy) ones.

Page 203. Enumeration of some of the eras of the Hindus.

Of their eras we mention—

1. The beginning of the existence of Brahman.

2. The beginning of the day of the present nychthemeron of Brahman, *i.e.* the beginning of the *kalpa*.

3. The beginning of the seventh *manvantara*, in which we are now.

4. The beginning of the twenty-eighth *caturyuga*, in which we are now.

5. The beginning of the fourth *yuga* of the present *caturyuga*, called *kalikâla*, *i.e.* the time of Kali. The whole *yuga* is called after him, though, accurately speaking, *his* time falls only in the last part of the *yuga*. Notwithstanding, the Hindus mean by *kalikâla* the beginning of the *kaliyuga*.

6. *Pâṇḍava-kâla*, *i.e.* the time of the life and the wars of Bhârata.

All these eras vie with each other in antiquity, the

one going back to a still more remote beginning than the other, and the sums of years which they afford go beyond hundreds, thousands, and higher orders of numbers. Therefore not only astronomers, but also other people, think it wearisome and unpractical to use them.

The author adopts the year 400 of Yazdajird as a test-year.

In order to give an idea of these eras, we shall use as a first gauge or point of comparison that Hindu year the great bulk of which coincides with the *year 400 of Yazdajird*. This number consists only of hundreds, not of units and tens, and by this peculiarity it is distinguished from all other years that might possibly be chosen. Besides, it is a memorable time; for the breaking of the strongest pillar of the religion, the decease of the pattern of a prince, Maḥmûd, the lion of the world, the wonder of his time—may God have mercy upon him!—took place only a short time, less than a year, before it. The Hindu year precedes the Naurôz or new year's day of this year only by twelve days, and the death of the prince occurred precisely ten complete Persian months before it.

Page 204.

Now, presupposing this our gauge as known, we shall compute the years for this point of junction, which is the beginning of the corresponding Hindu year, for the end of all years which come into question coincides with it, and the Naurôz of the year 400 of Yazdajird falls only a little latter (viz. twelve days).

How much of the life of Brahman has elapsed according to the *Vishṇu-Dharma.*

The book *Vishṇu-Dharma* says: "Vajra asked Mârkaṇḍeya how much of the life of Brahman had elapsed; whereupon the sage answered: 'That which has elapsed is 8 years, 5 months, 4 days, 6 *manvantaras*, 7 *saṁdhi*, 27 *caturyugas*, and 3 *yugas* of the twenty-eighth *caturyuga*, and 10 *divya-years* up to the time of the *aśvamedha* which thou hast offered.' He who knows the details of this statement and comprehends them duly is a *sage* man, and *the sage* is he who serves the only Lord and strives to reach the neighbourhood of his place, which is called *Paramapada*."

Presupposing this statement to be known, and referring the reader to our explanation of the various measures of time which we have given in former chapters, we offer the following analysis.

Of the life of Brahman there have elapsed before our gauge 26,215,732,948,132 of our years. Of the nychthemeron of Brahman, *i.e.* of the *kalpa of the day*, there have elapsed 1,972,948,132, and of the seventh *manvantara* 120,532,132.

The latter is also the date of the imprisoning of the King Bali, for it happened in the first *caturyuga* of the seventh *manvantara*.

In all chronological dates which we have mentioned already and shall still mention, we only reckon with *complete* years, for the Hindus are in the habit of disregarding *fractions* of a year.

The time of Râma according to *Vishṇu-Dharma*.

Further, the *Vishṇu-Dharma* says: "Mârkaṇḍeya says, in answer to a question of Vajra, 'I have already lived as long as 6 *kalpas* and 6 *manvantaras* of the seventh *kalpa*, 23 *tretâyugas* of the seventh *manvantara*. In the twenty-fourth *tretâyuga* Râma killed Râvaṇa, and Lakshmaṇa, the brother of Râma, killed Kumbhakarṇa, the brother of Râvaṇa. The two subjugated all the Râkshasas. At that time Vâlmiki, the Rishi, composed the story of Râma and Râmâyaṇa and eternalised it in his books. It was I who told it to Yudhishṭhira, the son of Pâṇḍu, in the forest of Kâmyakavana.'"

The author of the *Vishṇu-Dharma* reckons here with *tretâyugas*, first, because the events which he mentions occurred in a certain *tretâyuga*, and secondly, because it is more convenient to reckon with a simple unit than with such a unit as requires to be explained by reference to its single quarters. Besides, the latter part of the *tretâyuga* is a more suitable time for the events mentioned than its beginning, because it is so much nearer to the age of evil-doing (v. i. pp. 379, 380). No doubt, the date of Râma and Râmâyaṇa is known among the

Hindus, but I for my part have not been able to ascertain it.

Twenty-three *caturyugas* are 99,360,000 years, and, together with the time from the beginning of a *caturyuga* till the end of the *tretâyuga*, 102,384,000 years.

If we subtract this number of years from the number of years of the seventh *manvantara* that have elapsed before our gauge-year, viz. 120,532,132 (v. p. 3), we get the remainder of 18,148,132 years, *i.e.* so many years before our gauge-year as the conjectural date of Râma; and this may suffice, as long as it is not supported by a trustworthy tradition. The here-mentioned year corresponds to the 3,892,132d year of the 28th *caturyuga*.

How much time has elapsed before of the present *kalpa*, according to Pulisa and Brahmagupta.

All these computations rest on the measures adopted by Brahmagupta. He and Pulisa agree in this, that the number of *kalpas* which have elapsed of the life of Brahman before the present *kalpa* is 6068 (equal to 8 years, 5 months, 4 days of Brahman). But they differ from each other in converting this number into *caturyugas*. According to Pulisa, it is equal to 6,116,544; according to Brahmagupta, only to 6,068,000 *caturyugas*. Therefore, if we adopt the system of Pulisa, reckoning 1 *manvantara* as 72 *caturyugas* without *saṁdhi*, 1 *kalpa* as 1008 *caturyugas*, and each *yuga* as the fourth part of a *caturyuga*, that which has elapsed of the life of Brahman before our gauge-year is the sum of 26,425,456,204,132 (!) years, and of the *kalpa* there have elapsed 1,986,124,132 years, of the *manvantara* 119,884,132 years, and of the *caturyuga* 3,244,132 years.

Page 205.

How much time has elapsed of the current *kaliyuga*.

Regarding the time which has elapsed since the beginning of the *kaliyuga*, there exists no difference amounting to whole years. According to both Brahmagupta and Pulisa, of the *kaliyuga* there have elapsed before our gauge-year 4132 years, and between the wars of Bhârata and our gauge-year there have elapsed 3479 years. The year 4132 before the gauge-year is the epoch of the *kalikâla*, and the year 3479 before the gauge-year is the epoch of the *Pâṇḍavakâla*.

The Hindus have an era called *Kâlayavana*, regarding which I have not been able to obtain full information. They place its epoch in the end of the last *dvâparayuga*. The here-mentioned Yavana (JMN) severely oppressed both their country and their religion. The era Kâlayavana.

To date by the here-mentioned eras requires in any case vast numbers, since their epochs go back to a most remote antiquity. For this reason people have given up using them, and have adopted instead the eras of—

(1.) *Śrî Harsha*.
(2.) *Vikramâditya*.
(3.) *Śaka*.
(4.) *Valabha*, and
(5.) *Gupta*.

The Hindus believe regarding Śrî Harsha that he used to examine the soil in order to see what of hidden treasures was in its interior, as far down as the seventh earth; that, in fact, he found such treasures; and that, in consequence, he could dispense with oppressing his subjects (by taxes, &c.) His era is used in Mathurâ and the country of Kanoj. Between Śrî Harsha and Vikramâditya there is an interval of 400 years, as I have been told by some of the inhabitants of that region. However, in the Kashmîrian calendar I have read that Śrî Harsha was 664 years later than Vikramâditya. In face of this discrepancy I am in perfect uncertainty, which to the present moment has not yet been cleared up by any trustworthy information. Era of Śrî Harsha.

Those who use the era of Vikramâditya live in the southern and western parts of India. It is used in the following way: 342 are multiplied by 3, which gives Era of Vikramâditya.

the product 1026. To this number you add the years which have elapsed of the current *shashṭyabda* or sexagesimal *samvatsara*, and the sum is the corresponding year of the era of Vikramâditya. In the book *Srûdhava* by Mahâdeva I find as his name *Candrabîja*.

As regards this method of calculation, we must first say that it is rather awkward and unnatural, for if they began with 1026 as the basis of the calculation, as they begin—without any apparent necessity—with 342, this would serve the same purpose. And, secondly, admitting that the method is correct as long as there is only *one shashṭyabda* in the date, how are we to reckon if there is a number of *shashṭyabdas*?

The Śakakâla.

The epoch of the era of Śaka or Śakakâla falls 135 years later than that of Vikramâditya. The here-mentioned Śaka tyrannised over their country between the river Sindh and the ocean, after he had made Âryavarta in the midst of this realm his dwelling-place. He interdicted the Hindus from considering and representing themselves as anything but Śakas. Some maintain that he was a Śûdra from the city of Almanṣûra; others maintain that he was not a Hindu at all, and that he had come to India from the west. The Hindus had much to suffer from him, till at last they received help from the east, when Vikramâditya marched against him, put him to flight and killed him in the region of Karûr, between Multân and the castle of Lônî. Now this date became famous, as people rejoiced in the news of the death of the tyrant, and was used as the epoch of an era, especially by the astronomers. They honour the conqueror by adding Śrî to his name, so as to say Śrî Vikramâditya. Since there is a long interval between the era which is called the era of Vikramâditya (v. p. 5) and the killing of Śaka, we think that that Vikramâditya from whom the era has got its name is not identical with that one who killed Śaka, but only a namesake of his.

The era of Valabha is called so from Valabha, the ruler of the town Valabhî, nearly 30 *yojanas* south of Anhilvâra. The epoch of this era falls 241 years later than the epoch of the Śaka era. People use it in this way. They first put down the year of the Śakakâla, and then subtract from it the cube of 6 and the square of 5 (216 + 25 = 241). The remainder is the year of the Valabha era. The history of Valabha is given in its proper place (cf. chap. xvii.) Era of Valabha. Page 206.

As regards the Guptakâla, people say that the Guptas were wicked powerful people, and that when they ceased to exist this date was used as the epoch of an era. It seems that Valabha was the last of them, because the epoch of the era of the Guptas falls, like that of the Valabha era, 241 years later than the Śakakâla. Guptakâla.

The *era of the astronomers* begins 587 years later than the Śakakâla. On this era is based the canon *Khaṇḍakhâdyaka* by Brahmagupta, which among Muhammadans is known as *Al-arkand*. Era of the astronomers.

Now, the year 400 of Yazdajird, which we have chosen as a gauge, corresponds to the following years of the Indian eras:— Comparison of the epochs of the Indian eras with the test-year.

(1) To the year 1488 of the era of Śrî Harsha,
(2) To the year 1088 of the era of Vikramâditya,
(3) To the year 953 of the Śakakâla,
(4) To the year 712 of the Valabha era, which is identical with the Guptakâla,
(5) To the year 366 of the era of the canon *Khaṇḍakhâdyaka*,
(6) To the year 526 of the era of the canon *Pañcasiddhântikâ* by Varâhamihira,
(7) To the year 132 of the era of the canon *Karaṇasâra*; and
(8) To the year 65 of the era of the canon *Karaṇatilaka*.

The eras of the here-mentioned *canones* are such as the authors of them considered the most suitable to be used as cardinal points in astronomical and other calculations, whence calculation may conveniently extend forward or backward. Perhaps the epochs of these eras fall within the time when the authors in question themselves lived, but it is also possible that they fall within a time anterior to their lifetime.

On the popular mode of dating by *centennia* or *samvatsaras*.

Common people in India date by the years of a *centennium*, which they call *samvatsara*. If a *centennium* is finished, they drop it, and simply begin to date by a new one. This era is called *lokakâla*, *i.e.* the era of the nation at large. But of this era people give such totally different accounts, that I have no means of making out the truth. In a similar manner they also differ among themselves regarding the beginning of the year. On the latter subject I shall communicate what I have heard myself, hoping meanwhile that one day we shall be able to discover a rule in this apparent confusion.

Different beginnings of the year.

Those who use the Śaka era, the astronomers, begin the year with the month Caitra, whilst the inhabitants of Kanir, which is conterminous with Kashmîr, begin it with the month Bhâdrapada. The same people count our gauge-year (400 Yazdajird) as the eighty-fourth year of an era of theirs.

All the people who inhabit the country between Bardarî and Mârîgala begin the year with the month Kârttika, and they count the gauge-year as the 110th year of an era of theirs. The author of the Kashmirian calendar maintains that the latter year corresponds to the sixth year of a new *centennium*, and this, indeed, is the usage of the people of Kashmîr.

The people living in the country Nirahara, behind Mârîgala, as far as the utmost frontiers of Tâkeshar and Lohâvar, begin the year with the month Mârgaśirsha, and reckon our gauge-year as the 108th year of their era. The people of *Lanbaga*, *i.e.* Lamghân, follow their example. I have been told by people of Multân that this system is peculiar to the people of Sindh and Kanoj, and that they used to begin the year with the new moon of Mârgaśirsha, but that the people of Multân only a few years ago had given up this system, and had adopted the system of the people of Kashmir, and followed their example in beginning the year with the new moon of Caitra.

Popular mode of dating in use among the Hindus, and criticisms thereon.

I have already before excused myself on account of the imperfection of the information given in this chapter. For we cannot offer a strictly scientific account of the eras to which it is devoted, simply because in them we have to reckon with periods of time far exceeding a *centennium*, (and because all tradition of events farther back than a hundred years is confused (v. p. 8).) So I have myself seen the roundabout way in which they compute the year of the destruction of Somanâth in the year of the Hijra 416, or 947 Śakakâla. First, they write down the number 242, then under it 606, then under this 99. The sum of these numbers is 947, or the year of the Śakakâla.

Now I am inclined to think that the 242 years have elapsed before the beginning of their centennial system, and that they have adopted the latter together with the Guptakâla; further, that the number 606 represents complete *samvatsaras* or centennials, each of which they must reckon as 101 years; lastly, that the 99 years represent that time which has elapsed of the current *centennium*. Page 207.

That this, indeed, is the nature of the calculation is confirmed by a leaf of a canon composed by Durlabha of Multân, which I have found by chance. Here the author says: "First write 848 and add to it the *laukika-kâla*, *i.e.* the era of the people, and the sum is the Śakakâla."

If we write first the year of the Śakakâla corresponding to our gauge-year, viz. 953, and subtract 848 from it, the remainder, 105, is the year of the *laukika-kâla*, whilst the destruction of Somanâth falls in the ninety-eighth year of the *centennium* or *laukika-kâla*.

Durlabha says, besides, that the year begins with the month Mârgaśîrsha, but that the astronomers of Multân begin it with Caitra.

Origin of the dynasty of the Shâhs of Kâbul.

The Hindus had kings residing in Kâbul, Turks who were said to be of Tibetan origin. The first of them, Barhatakin, came into the country and entered a cave in Kâbul, which none could enter except by creeping on hands and knees. The cave had water, and besides he deposited there victuals for a certain number of days. It is still known in our time, and is called *Var*. People who consider the name of Barhatakin as a good omen enter the cave and bring out some of its water with great trouble.

Certain troops of peasants were working before the door of the cave. Tricks of this kind can only be carried out and become notorious, if their author has made a secret arrangement with somebody else — in fact, with confederates. Now these had induced persons to work there continually day and night in turns, so that the place was never empty of people.

Some days after he had entered the cave, he began to creep out of it in the presence of the people, who looked on him as a new-born baby. He wore Turkish dress, a short tunic open in front, a high hat, boots and arms. Now people honoured him as a being of miraculous origin, who had been destined to be king, and in fact he brought those countries under his sway and ruled them under the title of a *shâhiya of Kâbul*. The rule remained among his descendants for generations, the number of which is said to be about sixty.

Unfortunately the Hindus do not pay much attention to the historical order of things, they are very careless in relating the chronological succession of their kings, and when they are pressed for information and are at a loss, not knowing what to say, they invariably take to tale-telling. But for this, we should communicate to the reader the traditions which we have received from some people among them. I have been told that the pedigree of this royal family, written on silk, exists in the fortress *Nagarkot*, and I much desired to make myself acquainted with it, but the thing was impossible for various reasons.

The story of Kanik.

One of this series of kings was Kanik, the same who is said to have built the *vihâra* (Buddhistic monastery) of Purushâvar. It is called, after him, *Kanik-caitya*. People relate that the king of Kanoj had presented to him, among other gifts, a gorgeous and most singular piece of cloth. Now Kanik wanted to have dresses made out of it for himself, but his tailor had not the courage to make them, for he said, "There is (in the embroidery) the figure of a human foot, and whatever trouble I may take, the foot will always lie between the shoulders." And that means the same as we have already mentioned in the story of Bali, the son of Virocana (*i.e.* a sign of subjugation, cf. i. p. 397). Now Kanik felt convinced that the ruler of Kanoj had thereby intended to vilify and disgrace him, and in hot haste he set out with his troops marching against him.

When the *râî* heard this, he was greatly perplexed, for he had no power to resist Kanik. Therefore he consulted his Vazîr, and the latter said, "You have roused a man who was quiet before, and have done unbecoming things. Now cut off my nose and lips, let me be mutilated, that I may find a cunning device; for there is no possibility of an open resistance." The *râî* did with him as he had proposed, and then he went off to the frontiers of the realm.

There he was found by the hostile army, was recognised and brought before Kanik, who asked what was the matter with him. The Vazîr said, "I tried to dissuade *him* from opposing you, and sincerely advised him to be obedient to you. He, however, conceived a suspicion against me and ordered me to be mutilated. Since then he has gone, of his own accord, to a place which a man can only reach by a very long journey when he marches on the highroad, but which he may easily reach by undergoing the trouble of crossing an intervening desert, supposing that he can carry with himself water for so and so many days." Thereupon Kanik answered: "The latter is easily done." He ordered water to be carried along, and engaged the Vazîr to show him the road. The Vazîr marched before the king and led him into a boundless desert. After the number of days had elapsed and the road did not come to an end, the king asked the Vazîr what was now to be done. Then the Vazîr said, "No blame attaches to me that I tried to save my master and to destroy his enemy. The nearest road leading out of this desert is that on which you have come. Now do with me as you like, for none will leave this desert alive."

Then Kanik got on his horse and rode round a depression in the soil. In the centre of it he thrust his spear into the earth, and lo! water poured from it in sufficient quantity for the army to drink from and to draw from for the march back. Upon this the Vazîr said, "I had not directed my cunning scheme against powerful angels, but against feeble men. As things stand thus, accept my intercession for the prince, my benefactor, and pardon him." Kanik answered, "I
Page 208. march back from this place. Thy wish is granted to thee. Thy master has already received what is due to him." Kanik returned out of the desert, and the Vazîr went back to his master, the *râî* of Kanoj. There he

found that on the same day when Kanik had thrust his spear into the earth, both the hands and feet had fallen off the body of the *râî*.

End of the Tibetan dynasty, and origin of the Brahman dynasty.

The last king of this race was *Lagatûrmân*, and his Vazír was Kallar, a Brahman. The latter had been fortunate, in so far as he had found by accident hidden treasures, which gave him much influence and power. In consequence, the last king of this Tibetan house, after it had held the royal power for so long a period, let it by degrees slip from his hands. Besides, Lagatûrmân had bad manners and a worse behaviour, on account of which people complained of him greatly to the Vazir. Now the Vazir put him in chains and imprisoned him for correction, but then he himself found ruling sweet, his riches enabled him to carry out his plans, and so he occupied the royal throne. After him ruled the Brahman kings Sâmand (Sâmanta), Kamalû, Bhim (Bhîma), Jaipâl (Jayapâla), Ânandapâla, Tarojanapâla (Trilocanapâla). The latter was killed A.H. 412 (A.D. 1021), and his son Bhîmapâla five years later (A.D. 1026).

This Hindu Shâhiya dynasty is now extinct, and of the whole house there is no longer the slightest remnant in existence. We must say that, in all their grandeur, they never slackened in the ardent desire of doing that which is good and right, that they were men of noble sentiment and noble bearing. I admire the following passage in a letter of Ânandapâla, which he wrote to the prince Maḥmûd, when the relations between them were already strained to the utmost: "I have learned that the Turks have rebelled against you and are spreading in Khurâsân. If you wish, I shall come to you with 5000 horsemen, 10,000 foot-soldiers, and 100 elephants, or, if you wish, I shall send you my son with double the number. In acting thus, I do not speculate on the impression which this will make on you. I have been conquered by *you*, and therefore I do not wish that another man should conquer you."

The same prince cherished the bitterest hatred against the Muhammadans from the time when his son was made a prisoner, whilst his son Tarojanapâla (Trilocanapâla) was the very opposite of his father.

## CHAPTER L.

### HOW MANY STAR-CYCLES THERE ARE BOTH IN A "KALPA" AND IN A "CATURYUGA."

It is one of the conditions of a *kalpa* that in it the planets, with their apsides and nodes, must unite in 0° of Aries, *i.e.* in the point of the vernal equinox. Therefore each planet makes within a *kalpa* a certain number of complete revolutions or cycles.

These star-cycles as known through *the canon* of Alfazârî and Ya'ḳûb Ibn Ṭâriḳ, were derived from a Hindu who came to Bagdad as a member of the political mission which Sindh sent to the Khalif Almansûr, A.H. 154 (= A.D. 771). If we compare these secondary statements with the primary statements of the Hindus, we discover discrepancies, the cause of which is not known to me. Is their origin due to the translation of Alfazârî and Ya'ḳûb? or to the dictation of that Hindu? or to the fact that afterwards these computations have been corrected by Brahmagupta, or some one else? For, certainly, any scholar who becomes aware of mistakes in astronomical computations and takes an interest in the subject, will endeavour to correct them, as, *e.g.* Muḥammad Ibn Isḥâḳ of Sarakhs has done. For he had discovered in the computation of Saturn a falling back behind real time (*i.e.*, that Saturn, according to this computation, revolved slower than it did in reality). Now he assiduously studied the subject, till at last he was convinced that his fault did not originate

*The tradition of Alfazârî and Ya'ḳûb Ibn Ṭâriḳ.*

*Muḥammad Ibn Isḥâḳ of Sarakhs.*

from the *equation* (*i.e.* from the correction of the places of the stars, the computation of their mean places). Then he added to the cycles of Saturn one cycle more, and compared his calculation with the actual motion of the planet, till at last he found the calculation of the cycles completely to agree with astronomical observation. In accordance with this correction he states the star-cycles in his *canon*.

Âryabhaṭa quoted by Brahmagupta.

Brahmagupta relates a different theory regarding the cycles of the apsides and nodes of the moon, on the authority of Âryabhaṭa. We quote this from Brahmagupta, for we could not read it in the original work of Âryabhaṭa, but only in a quotation in the work of Brahmagupta.

Number of the rotations of the planets in a *kalpa*. Page 209.

The following table contains all these traditions, which will facilitate the study of them, if God will!

| The planets. | Number of their revolutions in a Kalpa. | Number of the revolutions of their apsides. | Number of the revolutions of their nodes. |
|---|---|---|---|
| Sun | 4,320,000,000 | 480 | Has no node. |
| Moon. Brahmagupta | 57,753,300,000 | 488,105,858 | 232,311,168 |
| Moon. The translation of Alfazârî | 57,753,300,000 | 488,105,858 | 232,312,138 |
| Moon. Âryabhaṭa | 57,753,300,000 | 488,219,000 | 232,316,000 |
| Moon. The anomalistic revolution of the moon according to Brahmagupta | 57,753,300,000 | 57,265,194,142 | The anomalistic revolution of the moon is here treated as if it were the apsis, being the difference between the motion of the moon and that of the apsis. (See the *notes*.) |
| Mars | 2,296,828,522 | 292 | 267 |
| Mercury | 17,936,998,984 | 332 | 521 |
| Jupiter | 364,226,455 | 855 | 63 |
| Venus | 7,022,389,492 | 653 | 893 |
| Saturn. Brahmagupta | 146,567,298 | 41 | 584 |
| Saturn. The translation of Alfazârî | 146,569,284 | 41 | 584 |
| Saturn. The correction of Alsarakhsî | 146,569,238 | 41 | 584 |
| The fixed stars | 120,000 according to the translation of Alfazârî. | | |

The computation of these cycles rests on the mean motion of the planets. As a *caturyuga* is, according to Brahmagupta, the one-thousandth part of a *kalpa*, we have only to divide these cycles by 1000, and the quotient is the number of the star-cycles in one *caturyuga*. *Cycles of the planets in a caturyuga and kaliyuga.*

Likewise, if we divide the cycles of the table by 10,000, the quotient is the number of the star-cycles in a *kaliyuga*, for this is one-tenth of a *caturyuga*. The fractions which may occur in those quotients are raised to wholes, to *caturyugas* or *kaliyugas*, by being multiplied by a number equal to the denominator of the fraction.

The following table represents the star-cycles specially in a *caturyuga* and *kaliyuga*, not those in a *manvantara*. Although the *manvantaras* are nothing but multiplications of whole *caturyugas*, still it is difficult to reckon with them on account of the *saṁdhi* which is attached both to the beginning and to the end of them.

Page 213.

| The names of the planets. | Their revolutions in a Caturyuga. | Their revolutions in a Kaliyuga. |
|---|---|---|
| Sun | 4,320,000 | 432,000 |
| His apsis | $0\frac{12}{25}$ | $0\frac{60}{1250}$ |
| Moon | 57,753,300 | 5,775,330 |
| Her apsis — Brahmagupta | $488,105\frac{429}{500}$ | $48,810\frac{2929}{5000}$ |
| Her apsis — Âryabhaṭa | 488,219 | $48,821\frac{9}{10}$ |
| Her anomalistic revolution | $57,265,194\frac{71}{500}$ | $5,726,519\frac{2071}{5000}$ |
| Her node — Brahmagupta | $232,311\frac{21}{125}$ | $23,231\frac{292}{2500}$ |
| Her node — The translation of Alfazârî | $232,312\frac{63}{500}$ | $23,231\frac{1063}{5000}$ |
| Her node — Âryabhaṭa | 232,316 | $23,231\frac{3}{5}$ |
| Mars | $2,296,828\frac{261}{500}$ | $229,682\frac{4261}{5000}$ |
| His apsis | $0\frac{73}{250}$ | $0\frac{73}{2500}$ |
| His node | $0\frac{267}{1000}$ | $0\frac{267}{10000}$ |
| Mercury | $17,936,998\frac{123}{125}$ | $1,793,699\frac{1123}{1250}$ |
| His apsis | $0\frac{83}{250}$ | $0\frac{83}{2500}$ |
| His node | $0\frac{521}{1000}$ | $0\frac{521}{10000}$ |
| Jupiter | $364,220\frac{91}{200}$ | $36,422\frac{1291}{2000}$ |
| His apsis | $0\frac{171}{200}$ | $0\frac{171}{2000}$ |
| His node | $0\frac{63}{1000}$ | $0\frac{63}{10000}$ |

| The names of the planets. | Their revolutions in a Caturyuga. | Their revolutions in a Kaliyuga. |
|---|---|---|
| Venus | $7,022,389\frac{123}{250}$ | $702,238\frac{2373}{2500}$ |
| Her apsis | $0\frac{653}{1000}$ | $0\frac{653}{10000}$ |
| Her node | $0\frac{893}{1000}$ | $0\frac{893}{10000}$ |
| Saturn | $146,567\frac{149}{600}$ | $14,656\frac{3649}{6000}$ |
| His apsis | $0\frac{41}{1000}$ | $0\frac{41}{10000}$ |
| His node | $0\frac{73}{125}$ | $0\frac{73}{1250}$ |
| Saturn: The translation of Alfazârî | $146,569\frac{71}{400}$ | $14,656\frac{2231}{2500}$ |
| Saturn: The correction of Alsarakhsî | $146,569\frac{119}{300}$ | $14,656\frac{4619}{3000}$ |
| The fixed stars | 120 | 12 |

Page 211. Star-cycles of a *kalpa* and *caturyuga*, according to Pulisa.

After we have stated how many of the star-cycles of a *kalpa* fall in a *caturyuga* and in a *kaliyuga*, according to Brahmagupta, we shall now derive from the number of star-cycles of a *caturyuga* according to Pulisa the number of star-cycles of a *kalpa*, first reckoning a *kalpa* = 1000 *caturyugas*, and, secondly, reckoning it as 1008 *caturyugas*. These numbers are contained in the following table:—

*The Yugas according to Pulisa.*

| The names of the planets. | Number of their revolutions in a Caturyuga. | Number of their revolutions in a Kalpa of 1000 Caturyugas. | Number of their revolutions in a Kalpa of 1008 Caturyugas. |
|---|---|---|---|
| Sun | 4,320,000 | 4,320,000,000 | 4,354,560,000 |
| Moon | 57,753,336 | 57,753,336,000 | 58,215,362,688 |
| Her apsis | 488,219 | 488,219,000 | 492,124,752 |
| Her node | 232,226 | 232,226,000 | 234,083,808 |
| Mars | 2,296,824 | 2,296,824,000 | 2,315,198,592 |
| Mercury | 17,937,000 | 17,937,000,000 | 18,080,496,000 |
| Jupiter | 364,220 | 364,220,000 | 367,133,760 |
| Venus | 7,022,388 | 7,022,388,000 | 7,078,567,104 |
| Saturn | 146,564 | 146,564,000 | 147,736,512 |

Transformation of the word Âryabhaṭa among the Arabs.

We meet in this context with a curious circumstance. Evidently Alfazârî and Ya'ḳûb sometimes heard from their Hindu master expressions to this effect, that his calculation of the star-cycles was that of *the great Siddhânta, whilst Âryabhaṭa reckoned with one-thousandth part of it.* They apparently did not understand him properly, and imagined that *âryabhaṭa* (Arab. *ârjabhad*) meant *a thousandth part.* The Hindus pronounce the *ḍ* of this word something between a *d* and an *r*. So the consonant became changed to an *r*, and people wrote *ârjabhar*. Afterwards it was still more mutilated, the first *r* being changed to a *z*, and so people wrote *âzjabhar*. If the word in this garb wanders back to the Hindus, they will not recognise it.

Star-cycles according to Abû-alḥasan of Al'ahwâz.

Further, Abû-alḥasan of Al'ahwâz mentions the revolutions of the planets in *the years of al-arjabhar, i.e.* in *caturyugas*. I shall represent them in the table such as I have found them, for I guess that they are directly derived from the dictation of that Hindu. Possibly, therefore, they give us the theory of Âryabhaṭa. Some of these numbers agree with the star-cycles in a *caturyuga*, which we have mentioned on the authority of Brahmagupta; others differ from them, and agree with the theory of Pulisa; and a third class of numbers differs from those of both Brahmagupta and Pulisa, as the examination of the whole table will show. Page 212.

| The names of the planets. | Their Yugas as parts of a Caturyuga according to Abû-alḥasan Al'ahwâz |
|---|---|
| Sun . . . . . | 4,320,000 |
| Moon . . . . . | 57,753,336 |
| Her apsis . . | 488,219 |
| Her node . . | 232,226 |
| Mars . . . . . | 2,296,828 |
| Mercury . . . | 17,937,020 |
| Jupiter . . . | 364,224 |
| Venus . . . . | 7,022,388 |
| Saturn . . . | 146,564 |

# CHAPTER LI.

## AN EXPLANATION OF THE TERMS "ADHIMÂSA," "ÛNARÂTRA," AND THE "AHARGAṆAS," AS REPRESENTING DIFFERENT SUMS OF DAYS.

On the leap month.

THE months of the Hindus are lunar, their years solar; therefore their new year's day must in each solar year fall by so much earlier as the lunar year is shorter than the solar (roughly speaking, by eleven days). If this precession makes up one complete month, they act in the same way as the Jews, who make the year a leap year of thirteen months by reckoning the month Adar twice, and in a similar way to the heathen Arabs, who in a so-called *annus procrastinationis* postponed the new year's day, thereby extending the preceding year to the duration of thirteen months.

The Hindus call the year in which a month is repeated in the common language *malamâsa*. *Mala* means the dirt that clings to the hand. As such dirt is thrown away, thus the leap month is thrown away out of the calculation, and the number of the months of a year remains twelve. However, in the literature the leap month is called *adhimâsa*.

That month is repeated within which (it being considered as a solar month) two lunar months finish. If the end of the lunar month coincides with the beginning of the solar month, if, in fact, the former ends before any part of the latter has elapsed, this month is repeated, because the end of the lunar month, although it has not yet run into the new solar month, still does no longer form part of the preceding month.

If a month is repeated, the first time it has its ordinary name, whilst the second time they add before the name the word *durâ* to distinguish between them. If, *e.g.* the month Âshâḍha is repeated, the first is called Âshâḍha, the second *Durâshâḍha*. The first month is that which is disregarded in the calculation. The Hindus consider it as unlucky, and do not celebrate any of the festivals in it which they celebrate in the other months. The most unlucky time in this month is that day on which the lunation reaches its end. Page 213.

The author of the *Vishṇu-Dharma* says: "*Candra* (*mâna*) is smaller than *sâvana*, *i.e.* the lunar year is smaller than the civil year, by six days, *i.e.* *ûnarâtra*. *Ûna* means *decrease*, *deficiency*. *Saura* is greater than *candra* by eleven days, which gives in two years and seven months the supernumerary *adhimâsa* month. This whole month is unlucky, and nothing must be done in it." Quotation from the *Vishṇu-Dharma*.

This is a rough description of the matter. We shall now describe it accurately.

The lunar year has 360 lunar days, the solar year has $371\frac{31}{480}$ lunar days. This difference sums up to the thirty days of an *adhimâsa* in the course of $976\frac{4176}{47799}$ lunar days, *i.e.* in 32 months, or in 2 years, 8 months, 16 days, *plus* the fraction: $\frac{4176}{47799}$ lunar day, which is nearly = 5 minutes, 15 seconds.

As the religious reason of this theory of intercalation the Hindus mention a passage of the *Veda*, which they have read to us, to the following tenor: "If the day of conjunction, *i.e.* the first lunar day of the month, passes without the sun's marching from one zodiacal sign to the other, and if this takes place on the following day, the preceding month falls out of the calculation." Quotation from the *Veda*.

The meaning of this passage is not correct, and the fault must have risen with the man who recited and Criticisms thereon.

translated the passage to me. For a month has thirty lunar days, and a twelfth part of the solar year has $30\frac{5311}{5760}$ lunar days. This fraction, reckoned in day-minutes, is equal to $55^{i}\ 19^{ii}\ 22^{iii}\ 30^{iv}$. If we now, for example, suppose a conjunction or new moon to take place at 0° of a zodiacal sign, we add this fraction to the time of the conjunction, and thereby we find the times of the sun's entering the signs successively. As now the difference between a lunar and a solar month is only a fraction of a day, the sun's entering a new sign may naturally take place on any of the days of the month. It may even happen that the sun enters two consecutive signs on the same month-day (*e.g.* on the second or third of two consecutive months). This is the case if in one month the sun enters a sign before $4^{i}\ 40^{ii}\ 37^{iii}\ 30^{iv}$ have elapsed of it; for the next following entering a sign falls later by $55^{i}\ 19^{ii}\ 23^{iii}\ 30^{iv}$, and both these fractions (*i.e.* less than $4^{i}\ 40^{ii}\ 37^{iii}\ 30^{iv}$ *plus* the last-mentioned fraction) added together are not sufficient to make up one complete day. Therefore the quotation from the *Veda* is not correct.

Proposed explanation of the Vedic passage.

I suppose, however, that it may have the following correct meaning:—If a month elapses in which the sun does not march from one sign to another, this month is disregarded in the calculation. For if the sun enters a sign on the 29th of a month, when at least $4^{i}\ 40^{ii}\ 37^{iii}\ 30^{iv}$ have elapsed of it, this entering takes place before the beginning of the succeeding month, and therefore the latter month is without an entering of the sun into a new sign, because the next following entering falls on the first of the next but one or third month. If you compute the consecutive enterings, beginning with a conjunction taking place in 0° of a certain sign, you

Page 214.

find that in the thirty-third month the sun enters a new sign at $30^{i}\ 20^{ii}$ of the twenty-ninth day, and that he enters the next following sign at $25^{i}\ 39^{ii}\ 22^{iii}\ 30^{iv}$ of the first day of the thirty-fifth month.

Hence also becomes evident why this month, which is disregarded in the calculation, is considered as unlucky. The reason is that the month misses just that moment which is particularly adapted to earn in it a heavenly reward, viz. the moment of the sun's entering a new sign.

As regards *adhimâsa*, the word means *the first month*, for AD means *beginning* (*i.e. âdi*). In the books of Ya'ḳûb Ibn Ṭâriḳ and of Alfazârî this name is written *padamâsa*. *Pada* (in the orig. *P–Dh*) means *end*, and it is possible that the Hindus call the leap month by both names; but the reader must be aware that these two authors frequently misspell or disfigure the Indian words, and that there is no reliance on their tradition. I only mention this because Pulisa explains the latter of the *two* months, which are called by the same name, as the supernumerary one.

Explanation of the terms *universal* or *partial* months and days.

The month, as the time from one conjunction to the following, is one revolution of the moon, which revolves through the ecliptic, but in a course distant from that of the sun. This is the difference between the motions of the two heavenly luminaries, whilst the direction in which they move is the same. If we subtract the revolutions of the sun, *i.e.* the solar cycles of a *kalpa*, from its lunar cycles, the remainder shows how many more lunar months a *kalpa* has than solar months. All months or days which we reckon as parts of whole *kalpas* we call here *universal*, and all months or days which we reckon as parts of a part of a *kalpa*, *e.g.* of a *caturyuga*, we call *partial*, for the purpose of simplifying the terminology.

Universal *adhimâsa* months.

The year has twelve solar months, and likewise twelve lunar months. The lunar year is complete with twelve months, whilst the solar year, in consequence of the difference of the two year kinds, has, with the addition of the *adhimâsa*, thirteen months. Now evidently the difference between the universal solar and lunar months is represented by these supernumerary months, by which a single year is extended to thirteen months. These, therefore, are the *universal adhimâsa* months.

The *universal* solar months of a *kalpa* are 51,840,000,000; the *universal* lunar months of a *kalpa* are 53.433.300,000. The difference between them or the *adhimâsa* months is 1,593,300,000.

Multiplying each of these numbers by 30, we get days, viz. solar days of a *kalpa*, 1,555,200,000,000; lunar days, 1,602,999,000,000; the days of the *adhimâsa* months, 47,799,000,000.

In order to reduce these numbers to smaller ones we divide them by a common divisor, viz. 9,000,000. Thus we get as the sum of the days of the solar months 172,800; as the sum of the days of the lunar months, 178,111; and as the sum of the days of the *adhimâsa* months, 5311.

How many solar, lunar, and civil days are required for the formation of an *adhimâsa* month.

If we further divide the *universal solar, civil,* and *lunar* days of a *kalpa*, each kind of them separately, by the *universal adhimâsa* months, the quotient represents the number of days within which a whole *adhimâsa* month sums up, viz. in $976\frac{464}{5311}$ solar days, in $1006\frac{464}{5311}$ lunar days, and in $990\frac{3663}{10622}$ civil days.

This whole computation rests on the measures which Brahmagupta adopts regarding a *kalpa* and the star-cycles in a *kalpa*.

The computation of *adhimâsa* according to Pulisa. Page 215.

According to the theory of Pulisa regarding the *caturyuga*, a *caturyuga* has 51,840,000 solar months, 53,433,336 lunar months, 1,593,336 *adhimâsa* months. Accordingly a *caturyuga* has 1,555,200,000 solar days, 1,603,000,080 lunar days, 47,800,080 days of *adhimâsa* months.

If we reduce the numbers of the months by the common divisor of 24, we get 2,160,000 solar months, 2,226,389 lunar months, 66,389 *adhimâsa* months. If we divide the numbers of the day by the common divisor of 720, we get 2,160,000 solar days, 2,226,389 lunar days, 66,389 days of the *adhimâsa* months. If we, lastly, divide the *universal* solar, lunar, and civil days of a *caturyuga*, each kind separately, by the universal *adhimâsa* months of a *caturyuga*, the quotient represents the numbers of days within which a whole *adhimâsa* month sums up, viz. in $976\frac{4336}{66389}$ solar days, in $1006\frac{4336}{66389}$ lunar days, and in $990\frac{21465}{66389}$ civil days.

These are the elements of the computation of the *adhimâsa*, which we have worked out for the benefit of the following investigations.

Explanation of the term *ûnarâtra*.

Regarding the cause which necessitates the *ûnarâtra*, lit. *the days of the decrease*, we have to consider the following.

If we have one year or a certain number of years, and reckon for each of them twelve months, we get the corresponding number of solar months, and by multiplying the latter by 30, the corresponding number of solar days. It is evident that the number of the lunar months or days of the same period is the same, *plus* an increase which forms one or several *adhimâsa* months. If we reduce this increase to *adhimâsa* months due to the period of time in question, according to the relation between the universal solar months and the universal *adhimâsa* months, and add this to the months or days of the years in question, the sum represents the *partial* lunar days, *i.e.* those which correspond to the given number of years.

This, however, is not what is wanted. What we want is the number of *civil* days of the given number of years which are *less* than the lunar days; for one *civil* day is greater than one *lunar* day. Therefore, in order to find that which is sought, we must subtract something from the number of lunar days, and this element which must be subtracted is called *ûnarâtra*.

The *ûnarâtra* of the *partial* lunar days stands in the same relation to the *universal* lunar days as the universal civil days are less than the universal lunar days. The universal lunar days of a *kalpa* are 1,602,999,000,000. This number is larger than the number of universal civil days by 25,082,550,000, which represents the universal *ûnarâtra*.

Both these numbers may be diminished by the common divisor of 450,000. Thus we get 3,562,220 universal lunar days, and 55,739 universal *ûnarâtra* days.

Computation of the *ûnarâtra* according to Pulisa.

According to Pulisa, a *caturyuga* has 1,603,000,080 lunar days, and 25,082,280 *ûnarâtra* days. The common divisor by which both numbers may be reduced is 360. Thus we get 4,452,778 lunar days and 69,673 *ûnarâtra* days.

These are the rules for the computation of the *ûnarâtra*, which we shall hereafter want for the computation of the *ahargaṇa*. The word means *sum of days*; for *âh* means *day*, and *argaṇa*, *sum*.

Criticisms on Ya'kûb Ibn Târiḳ.

Ya'ḳûb Ibn Târiḳ has made a mistake in the computation of the solar days; for he maintains that you get them by subtracting the solar cycles of a *kalpa* from the civil days of a *kalpa*, *i.e.* the *universal* civil days. But this is not the case. We get the solar days by multiplying the solar cycles of a *kalpa* by 12, in order to reduce them to months, and the product by 30, in order to reduce them to days, or by multiplying the number of cycles by 360.

Page 216.

In the computation of the lunar days he has first taken the right course, multiplying the lunar months of a *kalpa* by 30, but afterwards he again falls into a mistake in the computation of the days of the *ûnarâtra*. For he maintains that you get them by subtracting the solar days from the lunar days, whilst the correct thing is to subtract the *civil* days from the lunar days.

# CHAPTER LII.

## ON THE CALCULATION OF "AHARGAṆA" IN GENERAL, THAT IS, THE RESOLUTION OF YEARS AND MONTHS INTO DAYS, AND, VICE VERSÂ, THE COMPOSITION OF YEARS AND MONTHS OUT OF DAYS.

General rule how to find the *sâvanâhargaṇa*.

THE general method of resolution is as follows:—The complete years are multiplied by 12; to the product are added the months which have elapsed of the current year, [and this sum is multiplied by 30;] to this product are added the days which have elapsed of the current month. The sum represents the *saurâhargaṇa*, *i.e.* the sum of the partial solar days.

You write down the number in two places. In the one place you multiply it by 5311, *i.e.* the number which represents the *universal adhimâsa* months. The product you divide by 172,800, *i.e.* the number which represents the *universal* solar months. The quotient you get, as far as it contains complete days, is added to the number in *the second place*, and the sum represents the *candrâhargaṇa*, *i.e.* the sum of the partial lunar days.

The latter number is again written down in two different places. In the one place you multiply it by 55,739, *i.e.* the number which represents the *universal ûnarâtra* days, and divide the product by 3,562,220, *i.e.* the number which represents the universal lunar days. The quotient you get, as far as it represents complete days, is subtracted from the number written in the second place, and the remainder is the *sâvanâhargaṇa*, *i.e.* the sum of *civil* days which we wanted to find.

More detailed rule for the same purpose.

However, the reader must know that this computation applies to dates in which there are only complete *adhimâsa* and *ûnarâtra* days, without any fraction. If, therefore, a given number of years commences with the beginning of a *kalpa*, or a *caturyuga*, or a *kaliyuga*, this computation is correct. But if the given years begin with some other time, it may by chance happen that this computation is correct, but possibly, too, it may result in proving the existence of *adhimâsa* time, and in that case the computation would not be correct. Also the reverse of these two eventualities may take place. However, if it is known with what particular moment in the *kalpa*, *caturyuga*, or *kaliyuga* a given number of years commences, we use a special method of computation, which we shall hereafter illustrate by some examples.

The latter method carried out for Śakakâla 953.

We shall carry out this method for the beginning of the Indian year Śakakâla 953, the same year which we use as the gauge-year in all these computations.

First we compute the time from the beginning of the life of Brahman, according to the rules of Brahmagupta. We have already mentioned that 6068 *kalpas* have elapsed before the present one. Multiplying this by the well-known number of the days of a *kalpa* (1,577,916,450,000 civil days, *vide* i. p. 368), we get 9,574,797,018,600,000 as the sum of the days of 6068 *kalpas*.

Dividing this number by 7, we get 5 as a remainder, and reckoning five days backwards from the Saturday which is the last day of the preceding *kalpa*, we get Tuesday as the first day of the life of Brahman.

We have already mentioned the sum of the days of a *caturyuga* (1,577,916,450 days, v. i. p. 370), and have explained that a *kritayuga* is equal to four-tenths of it, *i.e.* 631,166,580 days. A *manvantara* has seventy-one

Page 217.

times as much, *i.e.* 112,032,067,950 days. The days of

six *manvantaras* and their *saṁdhi*, consisting of seven *kṛitayuga*, are 676,610,573,760. If we divide this number by 7, we get a remainder of 2. Therefore the six *manvantaras* end with a Monday, and the seventh begins with a Tuesday.

Of the seventh *manvantara* there have already elapsed twenty-seven *caturyugas*, *i.e.* 42,603.744,150 days. If we divide this number by 7, we get a remainder of 2. Therefore the twenty-eighth *caturyuga* begins with a Thursday.

The days of the *yugas* which have elapsed of the present *caturyuga* are 1,420,124,805. The division by 7 gives the remainder 1. Therefore the *kaliyuga* begins with a Friday.

Now, returning to our gauge-year, we remark that the years which have elapsed of the *kalpa* up to that year are 1,972,948,132. Multiplying them by 12, we get as the number of their months 23,675,377,584. In the date which we have adopted as gauge-year there is no month, but only complete years; therefore we have nothing to add to this number.

By multiplying this number by 30 we get days, viz. 710,261,327,520. As there are no days in the normal date, we have no days to add to this number. If, therefore, we had multiplied the number of years by 360, we should have got the same result, viz. the *partial* solar days.

Multiply this number by 5311 and divide the product by 172,800. The quotient is the number of the *adhimâsa* days, viz. 21,829,849,018$\frac{103}{120}$. If, in multiplying and dividing, we had used the months, we should have found the *adhimâsa* months, and, multiplied by 30, they would be equal to the here-mentioned number of *adhimâsa* days.

If we further add the *adhimâsa* days to the *partial* solar days, we get the sum of 732,091,176,538, *i.e.* the *partial* lunar days. Multiplying them by 55,739, and dividing the product by 3,562,220, we get the *partial ûnarâtra* days, viz., $11{,}455{,}224{,}575\frac{1{,}747{,}541}{1{,}781{,}110}$.

This sum of days without the fraction is subtracted from the *partial* lunar days, and the remainder, 720,635,951,963, represents the number of the *civil* days of our gauge-date.

Dividing it by 7, we get as remainder 4, which means that the last of these days is a Wednesday. Therefore the Indian year commences with a Thursday.

If we further want to find the *adhimâsa* time, we divide the *adhimâsa* days by 30, and the quotient is the number of the *adhimâsas* which have elapsed, viz. 727,661,633, *plus* a remainder of 28 days, 51 minutes, 30 seconds, for the current year. This is the time which has already elapsed of the *adhimâsa* month of the current year. To become a complete month, it only wants 1 day, 8 minutes, 30 seconds more.

**The same calculation applied to a *caturyuga* according to the theory of Pulisa.**

We have here used the solar and lunar days, the *adhimâsa* and *ûnarâtra* days, to find a certain past portion of a *kalpa*. We shall now do the same to find the past portion of a *caturyuga*, and we may use the same elements for the computation of a *caturyuga* which we have used for that of a *kalpa*, for both methods lead to the same result, as long as we adhere to one and the same theory (*e.g.* that of Brahmagupta), and do not mix up different chronological systems, and as long as each *guṇakâra* and its *bhâgabhâra*, which we here mention together, correspond to each other in the two computations.

The former term means a *multiplicator* in all kinds of calculations. In our (Arabic) astronomical handbooks, as well as those of the Persians, the word occurs in the form *guncâr*. The second term means each *divisor*. It occurs in the astronomical handbooks in the form *bahcâr*.

It would be useless if we were to exemplify this computation on a *caturyuga* according to the theory of Brahmagupta, as according to him a *caturyuga* is simply one-thousandth of a *kalpa*. We should only have to shorten the above-mentioned numbers by three ciphers, and in every other respect get the same results. Therefore we shall now give this computation according to the theory of Pulisa, which, though applying to the *caturyuga*, is similar to the method of computation used for a *kalpa*.

Page 218.

According to Pulisa, in the moment of the beginning of the gauge-year, there have elapsed of the years of the *caturyuga* 3,244,132, which are equal to 1,167,887,520 solar days. If we multiply the number of months which corresponds to this number of days with the number of the *adhimâsa* months of a *caturyuga* or a corresponding multiplicator, and divide the product by the number of the solar months of a *caturyuga*, or a corresponding divisor, we get as the number of *adhimâsa* months $1,196,525\frac{44837}{45000}$.

Further, the past 3,244,132 years of the *caturyuga* are 1,203,783,270 lunar days. Multiplying them by the number of the *ûnarâtra* days of a *caturyuga*, and dividing the product by the lunar days of a *caturyuga*, we get as the number of *ûnarâtra* days $18,835,700\frac{598,055}{2,226,389}$. Accordingly, the *civil* days which have elapsed since the beginning of the *caturyuga* are 1,184,947,570, and this it was which we wanted to find.

A similar method of computation taken from the *Pulisa-siddhânta*.

We shall here communicate a passage from the *Pulisa-siddhânta*, describing a similar method of computation, for the purpose of rendering the whole subject clearer to the mind of the reader, and fixing it there more thoroughly. Pulisa says: "We first mark the *kalpas* which have elapsed of the life of Brahman before the present *kalpa*, i.e. 6068. We multiply this number by the number of the *caturyugas* of a *kalpa*, i.e. 1008. Thus we get the product 6,116,544. This number we multiply by the number of the *yugas* of a *caturyuga*, i.e. 4, and get the product 24,466,176. This number we multiply by the number of years of a *yuga*, *i.e.* 1,080,000, and get the product 26,423,470,080,000. These are the years which have elapsed before the present *kalpa*.

We further multiply the latter number by 12, so as to get months, viz. 317,081,640,960,000. We write down this number in two different places.

In the one place, we multiply it by the number of the *adhimâsa* months of a *caturyuga*, *i.e.* 1,593,336, or a corresponding number which has been mentioned in the preceding, and we divide the product by the number of the solar months of a *caturyuga*, *i.e.* 51,840,000. The quotient is the number of *adhimâsa* months, viz. 9,745,709,750,784.

This number we add to the number written in the second place, and get the sum of 326,827,350,710,784. Multiplying this number by 30, we get the product 9,804,820,521,323,520, viz. lunar days.

This number is again written down in two different places. In the one place we multiply it by the *ûnarâtra* of a *caturyuga*, *i.e.* the difference between civil and lunar days, and divide the product by the lunar days of a *caturyuga*. Thus we get as quotient 153,416,869,240,320, *i.e.* *ûnarâtra* days.

We subtract this number from that one written in the second place, and we get as remainder 9,651,403,652,083,200, *i.e.* the days which have elapsed of the life of Brahman before the present *kalpa*, or the days of 6068 *kalpas*, each *kalpa* having 1,590,541,142,400 days. Dividing this sum of days by 7, we get no remainder. This period of time ends with a Saturday, and the present *kalpa* commences with a *Sunday*. This shows that the beginning of the life of Brahman too was a Sunday.

Of the current *kalpa* there have elapsed six *manvantaras*, each of 72 *caturyugas*, and each *caturyuga* of
Page 219. 4,320,000 years. Therefore six *manvantaras* have 1,866,240,000 years. This number we compute in the

same way as we have done in the preceding example. Thereby we find as the number of days of six complete *manvantaras*, 681,660,489,600. Dividing this number by 7, we get as remainder 6. Therefore the elapsed *manvantaras* end with a Friday, and the seventh *manvantara* begins with a *Saturday*.

Of the current *manvantara* there have elapsed 27 *caturyugas*, which, according to the preceding method of computation, represent the number of 42,603,780,600 days. The twenty-seventh *caturyuga* ends with a *Monday*, and the twenty-eighth begins with a Tuesday.

Of the current *caturyuga* there have elapsed three *yugas*, or 3,240,000 years. These represent, according to the preceding method of computation, the number of 1,183,438,350 days. Therefore these three *yugas* end with a Thursday, and *kaliyuga* commences with a Friday.

Accordingly, the sum of days which have elapsed of the *kalpa* is 725,447,708,550, and the sum of days which have elapsed between the beginning of the life of Brahman and the beginning of the present *kaliyuga* is 9,652,129,099,791,750.

The method of *ahargaṇa* employed by Âryabhaṭa.

To judge from the quotations from Âryabhaṭa, as we have not seen a book of his, he seems to reckon in the following manner :—

The sum of days of a *caturyuga* is 1,577,917,500. The time between the beginning of the *kalpa* and the beginning of the *kaliyuga* is 725,447,570,625 days. The time between the beginning of the *kalpa* and our gauge-date is 725,449,079,845. The number of days which have elapsed of the life of Brahman before the present *kalpa* is 9,651,401,817,120,000.

This is the correct method for the resolution of years into days, and all other measures of time are to be treated in accordance with this.

We have already pointed out (on p. 26) a mistake

The *ahargaṇa* as given by Ya'ḳûb Ibn Ṭârik.

of Ya'ḳûb Ibn Ṭârik in the calculation of the universal solar and *ûnarâtra* days. As he translated from the Indian language a calculation the reasons of which he did not understand, it would have been his duty to examine it, and to check the various numbers of it one by the other. He mentions in his book also the method of *ahargaṇa*, *i.e.* the resolution of years, but his description is not correct; for he says:—

"Multiply the months of the given number of years by the number of the *adhimâsa* months which have elapsed up to the time in question, according to the well-known rules of *adhimâsa*. Divide the product by the solar months. The quotient is the number of complete *adhimâsa* months *plus* its fractions which have elapsed up to the date in question."

The mistake is here so evident that even a copyist would notice it; how much more a mathematician who makes a computation according to this method; for he multiplies by the *partial adhimâsa* instead of the *universal*.

A second method given by Ya'ḳûb.

Besides, Ya'ḳûb mentions in his book another and perfectly correct method of resolution, which is this: "When you have found the number of months of the years, multiply them by the number of the lunar months, and divide the product by the solar months. The quotient is the number of *adhimâsa* months together with the number of the months of the years in question.

"This number you multiply by 30, and you add to the product the days which have elapsed of the current month. The sum represents the lunar days.

"If, instead of this, the first number of months were multiplied by 30, and the past portion of the month were added to the product, the sum would represent the partial solar days; and if this number were further computed according to the preceding method, we should get the *adhimâsa* days together with the solar days."

The rationale of this calculation is the following:—If we multiply, as we have done, by the number of the universal *adhimâsa* months, and divide the product by the universal solar months, the quotient represents the portion of *adhimâsa* time by which we have multiplied. As, now, the lunar months are the sum of solar and *adhimâsa* months, we multiply by them (the lunar months) and the division remains the same. The quotient is the sum of that number which is multiplied and that one which is sought for, *i.e.* the lunar days.

Explication of the last-mentioned method.

We have already mentioned in the preceding part that by multiplying the lunar days by the universal *ûnarâtra* days, and by dividing the product by the universal lunar days, we get the portion of *ûnarâtra* days which belongs to the number of lunar days in question. However, the *civil* days in a *kalpa* are less than the lunar days by the amount of the *ûnarâtra* days. Now the lunar days we have stand in the same relation to the lunar days *minus* their due portion of *ûnarâtra* days as the whole number of lunar days (of a *kalpa*) to the whole number of lunar days (of a *kalpa*) *minus* the complete number of *ûnarâtra* days (of a *kalpa*); and the latter number are the *universal civil* days. If we, therefore, multiply the number of lunar days we have by the universal civil days, and divide the product by the universal lunar days, we get as quotient the number of civil days of the date in question, and that it was which we wanted to find. Instead of multiplying by the whole sum of civil days (of a *kalpa*), we multiply by 3,506,481, and instead of dividing by the whole number of lunar days (of a *kalpa*), we divide by 3,562,220.

Page 220.

The Hindus have still another method of calculation. It is the following:—"They multiply the elapsed years of the *kalpa* by 12, and add to the product the complete months which have elapsed of the current year. The sum they write down above the number 69,120,

Another method of *ahargaṇa* of the Hindus.

(*Lacuna.*)

and the number they get is subtracted from the number written down in the middle place. The double of the remainder they divide by 65. Then the quotient represents the partial *adhimâsa* months. This number they add to that one which is written down in the uppermost place. They multiply the sum by 30, and add to the product the days which have elapsed of the current month. The sum represents the partial solar days. This number is written down in two different places, one under the other. They multiply the lower number by 11, and write the product under it. Then they divide it by 403,963, and add the quotient to the middle number. They divide the sum by 703, and the quotient represents the partial *ûnarâtra* days. This number they subtract from the number written in the uppermost place, and the remainder is the number of civil days which we want to find."

Explication of the latter method.

The rationale of this computation is the following:—If we divide the universal solar months by the universal *adhimâsa* months, we get as the measure of one *adhimâsa* month $32\frac{8544}{15933}$ solar months. The double of this is $65\frac{1155}{15933}$ solar months. If we divide by this number the double of the months of the given years, the quotient is the number of the partial *adhimâsas*. However, if we divide by wholes *plus* a fraction, and want to subtract from the number which is divided a certain portion, the remainder being divided by the wholes only, and the two subtracted portions being equal portions of the wholes to which they belong, the whole divisor stands in the same relation to its fraction as the divided number to the subtracted portion.

The latter method applied to the gauge-year.

If we make this computation for our gauge-year, we get the fraction of $\frac{1155}{1,055,805}$, and dividing both numbers by 15, we get $\frac{77}{70,387}$.

It would also be possible here to reckon by single *adhimâsas* instead of double ones, and in that case it would not be necessary to double the remainder. But the inventor of this method seems to have preferred the reduplication in order to get smaller numbers; for if we reckon with single *adhimâsas*, we get the fraction of $\frac{8544}{518400}$, which may be reduced by 96 as a common divisor. Thereby we get 89 as the multiplicator, and 5400 as the divisor. In this the inventor of the method has shown his sagacity, for the reason for his computation is the intention of getting partial lunar days and smaller multiplicators.

Method for the computation of the *ûnarâtra* days according to Brahmagupta. Page 221.

His method (*i.e.* Brahmagupta's) for the computation of the *ûnarâtra* days is the following:—

If we divide the universal lunar days by the universal *ûnarâtra* days, we get as quotient 63 and a fraction, which may be reduced by the common divisor 450,000. Thus we get $63\frac{30,663}{33,759}$ lunar days as the period of time within which one *ûnarâtra* day sums up. If we change this fraction into eleventh parts, we get $\frac{9}{11}$ and a remainder of $\frac{33,642}{33,759}$, which, if expressed in minutes, is equal to 0′ 59″ 54‴.

Since this fraction is very near to one whole, people have neglected it, and use, in a rough way, $\frac{10}{11}$ instead. Therefore, according to the Hindus, one *ûnarâtra* day sums up in $63\frac{10}{11}$ or $\frac{703}{11}$ lunar days.

If we now multiply the number of *ûnarâtra* days, which corresponds to the number of lunar days by $63\frac{30,663}{33,759}$, the product is less than that which we get by multiplying by $63\frac{10}{11}$. If we, therefore, want to divide the lunar days by $\frac{703}{11}$, on the supposition that the quotient is equal to the first number, a certain portion must be added to the lunar days, and this portion he (the author of *Pulisa-Siddhânta*) had not computed accurately, but only approximatively. For if we multiply the universal *ûnarâtra* days by 703, we get the product 17,633,032,650,000, which is more than eleven times the universal lunar days. And if we multiply the universal lunar days by 11, we get the product 17,632,989,000,000.

The difference between the two numbers is 43,650,000. If we divide by this number the product of eleven times the universal lunar days, we get as quotient 403,963.

Criticisms of this method.

This is the number used by the inventor of the method. If there were not a small remainder beyond the last-mentioned quotient (403,963 + a fraction), his method would be perfectly correct. However, there remains a fraction of $\frac{405}{4365}$ or $\frac{9}{97}$, and this is the amount which is neglected. If he uses this divisor without the fraction, and divides by it the product of eleven times the partial lunar days, the quotient would be by so much larger as the dividendum has increased. The other details of the calculation do not require comment.

Method for finding the *adhimâsa* for the years of a *kalpa*, *caturyuga*, or *kaliyuga*.

Because the majority of the Hindus, in reckoning their years, require the *adhimâsa*, they give the preference to this method, and are particularly painstaking in describing the methods for the computation of the *adhimâsa*, disregarding the methods for the computation of the *ûnarâtra* days and the *sum of the days* (*ahargaṇa*). One of their methods of finding the *adhimâsa* for the years of a *kalpa* or *caturyuga* or *kaliyuga* is this:—

They write down the years in three different places. They multiply the upper number by 10, the middle by 2481, and the lower by 7739. Then they divide the middle and lower numbers by 9600, and the quotients are days for the middle number and *avama* for the lower number.

The sum of these two quotients is added to the number in the upper place. The sum represents the number of the complete *adhimâsa* days which have elapsed, and the sum of that which remains in the other two places is the fraction of the current *adhimâsa*. Dividing the days by 30, they get months.

Ya'ḳûb Ibn Ṭâriḳ states this method quite correctly. We shall, as an example, carry out this computation for our gauge-year. The years of the *kalpa* which have elapsed

The latter method applied to the gauge-year.

till the moment of the gauge-date are 1,972,948,132. We write down this number in three different places. The upper number we multiply by ten, by which it gets a cipher more at the right side. The middle number we multiply by 2481 and get the product 4,894,884,315,492. The lower number we multiply by 7739, and get the product 15,268,645,593,548. The latter two numbers we divide by 9600; thereby we get for the *middle* number as quotient 509,883,782 and a remainder of 8292, and for the lower number a quotient of 1,590,483,915 and a remainder of 9548. The sum of these two remainders is 17,840. This fraction (*i.e.* $\frac{17,840}{9600}$) is reckoned as one whole. Thereby the sum of the numbers in all three places is raised to 21,829,849,018, *i.e. adhimâsa* days, *plus* $\frac{103}{120}$ day of the current *adhimâsa* day (*i.e.* which is now in course of summing up).

Page 222.

Reducing these days to months, we get 727,661,633 months and a remainder of twenty-eight days, which is called *Sh-D-D.* This is the interval between the beginning of the month Caitra, which is not omitted in the series of months, and the moment of the vernal equinox.

Further, adding the quotient which we have got for the middle number to the years of the *kalpa*, we get the sum of 2,482,831,914. Dividing this number by 7, we get the remainder 3. Therefore the sun has, in the year in question, entered Aries on a Tuesday.

Explanatory note to the latter method.

The two numbers which are used as multiplicators for the numbers in the middle and lower places are to be explained in the following manner:—

Dividing the *civil* days of a *kalpa* by the solar cycles of a *kalpa*, we get as quotient the number of days which compose a year, *i.e.* $365\frac{1,116,450,000}{4,320,000,000}$. Reducing this fraction by the common divisor of 450,000, we get $365\frac{2481}{9600}$. The fraction may be further reduced by being divided by 3, but people leave it as it is, in order that this fraction and the other fractions which occur in the further course of this computation should have the same denominator.

Dividing the universal *ûnarâtra* days by the solar years of a *kalpa*, the quotient is the number of *ûnarâtra* days which belong to a solar year, viz. $5\frac{3,482,550,000}{4,320,000,000}$ days. Reducing this fraction by the common divisor of 450,000, we get $5\frac{7739}{9600}$ days. The fraction may further be reduced by being divided by 3.

The measures of solar and lunar years are about 360 days, as are also the *civil* years of sun and moon, the one being a little larger, the other a little shorter. The one of these measures, the lunar year, is used in this computation, whilst the other measure, the solar year, is sought for. The sum of the two quotients (of the middle and lower number) is the difference between the two kinds of years. The upper number is multiplied by the sum of the complete days, and the middle and lower numbers are multiplied by each of the two fractions.

Simplification of the same method.

If we want to abbreviate the computation, and do not, like the Hindus, wish to find the mean motions of sun and moon, we add the two multiplicators of the middle and lower numbers together. This gives the sum of 10,220.

To this sum we add, for the upper place, the product of the divisor × 10 = 96,000, and we get $\frac{106,220}{9600}$. Reducing this fraction by the half, we get $\frac{5311}{480}$.

In this chapter (p. 27) we have already explained that by multiplying the days by 5311, and dividing the product by 172,800, we get the number of the *adhimâsas*. If we now multiply the number of years instead of the days, the product is $\frac{1}{360}$ of the product which we should get when multiplying by the number of days. If we, therefore, want to have the same quotient which we get by the first division, we must divide by $\frac{1}{360}$ of the divisor by which we divided in the first case, viz. 480 (for 360 × 480 = 172,800).

Page 223.

Similar to this method is that one prescribed by Pulisa: "Write down the number of the partial months in two different places. In the one place multiply it by 1111, and divide the product by 67,500. Subtract the quotient from the number in the other place, and divide the remainder by 32. The quotient is the number of the *adhimâsa* months, and the fraction in the quotient, if there is one, represents that part of an *adhimâsa* month which is in course of formation. Multiplying this amount by 30, and dividing the product by 32, the quotient represents the days and day-fractions of the current *adhimâsa* month."

A second method for finding the *adhimâsa*, according to Pulisa.

The rationale of this method is the following:—

If you divide the solar months of a *caturyuga* by the *adhimâsa* months of a *caturyuga*, in accordance with the theory of Pulisa, you get as quotient $32\frac{35,552}{66,389}$. If you divide the months by this number, you get the complete *adhimâsa* months of the past portion of the *caturyuga* or *kalpa*. Pulisa, however, wanted to divide by wholes alone, without any fractions. Therefore he had to subtract something from the dividendum, as has already been explained in a similar case (p. 36). We have found, in applying the computation to our gauge-year, as the fraction of the divisor, $\frac{35,552}{2,160,000}$, which may be reduced by being divided by 32. Thereby we get $\frac{1111}{67,500}$.

Explication of the method of Pulisa.

Pulisa has, in this calculation, reckoned by the solar days into which a date is resolved, instead of by months. For he says: "You write this number of days in two different places. In the one place you multiply it by 271 and divide the product by 4,050,000. The quotient you subtract from the number in the other place and divide the remainder by 976. The quotient is the number of *adhimâsa* months, days, and day-fractions."

Further quotation from Pulisa.

Further he says: "The reason of this is, that by dividing the days of a *caturyuga* by the *adhimâsa* months, you get as quotient 976 days and a remainder of 104,064. The common divisor for this number and for the divisor is 384. Reducing the fraction thereby, we get $\frac{271}{2,030,000}$ days."

Criticisms on the passage from Pulisa.

Here, however, I suspect either the copyist or the translator, for Pulisa was too good a scholar to commit similar blunders. The matter is this:—

Those days which are divided by the *adhimâsa* months are of necessity *solar* days. The quotient contains wholes and fractions, as has been stated. Both denominator and numerator have as common divisor the number 24. Reducing the fraction thereby, we get $\frac{4336}{66,389}$.

If we apply this rule to the months, and reduce the number of *adhimâsa* months to fractions, we get 47,800,000 as denominator. A divisor common to both this denominator and its numerator is 16. Reducing the fraction thereby, we get $\frac{271}{2,800,000}$.

If we now multiply the number which Pulisa adopts as devisor by the just-mentioned common divisor, *i.e.* 384, we get the product 1,555,200,000, viz. solar days in a *caturyuga*. But it is quite impossible that this number should, in this part of the calculation, be used as a divisor. If we want to base this method on the rules of Brahmagupta, dividing the universal solar months by the *adhimâsa* months, the result will be, according to the method employed by him, double the amount of the *adhimâsa*.

Method for the computation of the ûnarâtra days.

Further, a similar method may be used for the computation of the *ûnarâtra* days.

Write down the partial lunar days in two different places. In the one place, multiply the number by 50,663, and divide the product by 3,562,220. Subtract the quotient from the number in the other place, and divide the remainder by 63 without any fraction.

Page 224.

In the further very lengthy speculations of the

Hindus there is no use at all, especially as they require the *avama*, i.e. the remainder of the partial *ûnarâtra*, for the remainders which we get by the two divisions have two different denominators.

Rule how to construct a chronological date from a certain given number of days. The converse of the *ahargaṇa*.

He who is perfectly acquainted with the preceding rules of resolution will also be able to carry out the opposite function, the composition, if a certain amount of past days of a *kalpa* or *caturyuga* be given. To make sure, however, we shall now repeat the necessary rules.

If we want to find the years, the days being given, the latter must necessarily be *civil* days, i.e. the difference between the lunar days and the *ûnarâtra* days. This difference (i.e. the *civil* days) stands in the same relation to their *ûnarâtra* as the difference between the universal lunar days and the universal *ûnarâtra* days, viz. 1,577,916,450,000, to the universal *ûnarâtra* days. The latter number (i.e. 1,577,916,450,000) is represented by 3,506,481. If we multiply the given days by 55,739, and divide the product by 3,506,481, the quotient represents the partial *ûnarâtra* days. Adding hereto the civil days, we get the number of lunar days, viz. the sum of the partial solar and the partial *adhimâsa* days. These lunar days stand in the same relation to the *adhimâsa* days which belong to them as the sum of the universal solar and *adhimâsa* days, viz. 160,299,900,000, to the universal *adhimâsa* days, which number (i.e. 160,299,900,000) is represented by the number 178,111.

If you, further, multiply the partial lunar days by 5311, and divide the product by 178,111, the quotient is the number of the partial *adhimâsa* days. Subtracting them from the lunar days, the remainder is the number of solar days. Thereupon you reduce the days to months by dividing them by 30, and the months to years by dividing them by 12. This is what we want to find.

*E.g.* the partial civil days which have elapsed up to

Application of the rule to the gauge-year.

our gauge-year are 720,635,951,963. This number is given, and what we want to find is, how many Indian years and months are equal to this sum of days.

First, we multiply the number by 55,739, and divide the product by 3,506,481. The quotient is 11,455,224,575 *ûnarâtra* days.

We add this number to the civil days. The sum is 732,091,176,538 lunar days. We multiply them by 5311, and divide the product by 178,111. The quotient is the number of *adhimâsa* days, viz. 21,829,849,018.

We subtract them from the lunar days and get the remainder of 710,261,327,520, *i.e.* partial solar days. We divide these by 30 and get the quotient of 23,675,377,584, *i.e.* solar months. Dividing them by 12, we get Indian years, viz. 1,972,948,132, the same number of years of which our gauge-date consists, as we have already mentioned in a previous passage.

Rule for the same purpose given by Ya'kûb Ibn Târik.

Ya'kûb Ibn Târik has a note to the same effect: "Multiply the given civil days by the universal lunar days and divide the product by the universal civil days. Write down the quotient in two different places. In the one place multiply the number by the universal *adhimâsa* days and divide the product by the universal lunar days. The quotient gives the *adhimâsa* months. Multiply them by 30 and subtract the product from the number in the other place. The remainder is the number of partial solar days. You further reduce them to months and years."

Explanation of the latter method.

The rationale of this calculation is the following:— We have already mentioned that the given number of days are the difference between the lunar days and their *ûnarâtra*, as the universal civil days are the difference between the universal lunar days and their universal *ûnarâtra*. These two measures stand in a constant relation to each other. Therefore we get the partial lunar days which are marked in two different places. Now, these are equal to the sum of the solar

Page 225.

and *adhimâsa* days, as the general lunar days are equal to the sum of universal solar days and universal *adhimâsa* days. Therefore the partial and the universal *adhimâsa* days stand in the same relation to each other as the two numbers written in two different places, there being no difference, whether they both mean months or days.

Ya'kûb's method for the computation of the partial *ûnarâtra* days.

The following rule of Ya'kûb for the computation of the partial *ûnarâtra* days by means of the partial *adhimâsa* months is found in all the manuscripts of his book:—

"The past *adhimâsa*, together with the fractions of the current *adhimâsa*, are multiplied by the universal *ûnarâtra* days, and the product is divided by the universal solar months. The quotient is added to the *adhimâsa*. The sum is the number of the past *ûnarâtras*."

Criticism thereon.

This rule does not, as I think, show that its author knew the subject thoroughly, nor that he had much confidence either in analogy or experiment. For the *adhimâsa* months which have passed of the *caturyuga* up to our gauge-date are, according to the theory of Pulisa, $1,196,525\frac{44837}{65000}$. Multiplying this number by the *ûnarâtra* of the *caturyuga*, we get the product $30,011,600,068,426\frac{51}{125}$. Dividing this number by the solar months, we get the quotient 578,927. Adding this to the *adhimâsa*, we get the sum 1,775,452. And this is not what we wanted to find. On the contrary, the number of *ûnarâtra* days is 18,835,700. Nor is the product of the multiplication of this number by 30 that which we wanted to find. On the contrary, it is 53,263,560. Both numbers are far away from the truth.

# CHAPTER LIII.

## ON THE AHARGAṆA, OR THE RESOLUTION OF YEARS INTO MONTHS, ACCORDING TO SPECIAL RULES WHICH ARE ADOPTED IN THE CALENDARS FOR CERTAIN DATES OR MOMENTS OF TIME.

Method of *ahargaṇa* as applied to special dates.

NOT all the eras which in the calendars are resolved into days have epochs falling at such moments of time when just an *adhimâsa* or *ûnarâtra* happens to be complete. Therefore the authors of the calendars require for the calculation of *adhimâsa* and *ûnarâtra* certain numbers which either must be added or subtracted if the calculation is to proceed in good order. We shall communicate to the reader whatever of these rules we happened to learn by the study of their calendars or astronomical handbooks.

First, we mention the rule of the *Khaṇḍakhâdyaka*, because this calendar is the best known of all, and preferred by the astronomers to all others.

Method of the Khaṇḍakhâdyaka.

Brahmagupta says: "Take the year of the *Śakakâla*, subtract therefrom 587, multiply the remainder by 12, and add to the product the complete months which have elapsed of the year in question. Multiply the sum by 30, and add to the product the days which have elapsed of the current month. The sum represents the partial solar days.

"Write down this number in three different places. Add 5 both to the middle and lower numbers, and divide the lowest one by 14,945. Subtract the quotient from the middle number, and disregard the remainder which you have got by the division. Divide the middle number by 976. The quotient is the number of complete *adhimâsa* months, and the remainder is that which has elapsed of the current *adhimâsa* month.

"Multiply these months by 30, and add the product to the upper number. The sum is the number of the partial lunar days. Let them stand in the upper place, and write the same number in the middle place. Multiply it by 11, and add thereto 497. Write this sum in the lower place. Then divide the sum by 111,573. Subtract the quotient from the middle number, and disregard the remainder (which you get by the division). Further, divide the middle number by 703, and the quotient represents the *ûnarâtra* days, the remainder the *avamas*. Subtract the *ûnarâtra* days from the upper number. The remainder is the number of civil days." Page 226.

This is the *ahargaṇa* of the *Khaṇḍakhâdyaka*. Dividing the number by 7, the remainder indicates the weekday on which the date in question falls.

Application of this method to the gauge-year.

We exemplify this rule in the case of our gauge-year. The corresponding year of the *Śakakâla* is 953. We subtract therefrom 587, and get the remainder 366. We multiply it by the product of 12 × 30, since the date is without months and days. The product is 131,760, *i.e.* solar days.

We write down this number in three different places. We add 5 to the middle and lower numbers, whereby we get 131,765 in both places. We divide the lower number by 14,945. The quotient is 8, which we subtract from the middle number, and here we get the remainder 131,757. Then we disregard the remainder in which the division has resulted.

Further, we divide the middle number by 976. The quotient 134 represents the number of months. There is besides a remainder of $\frac{973}{976}$. Multiplying the months by 30, we get the product 4020, which we add to the solar days. Thereby we get lunar days, viz. 135.780. We write down this number below the three numbers, multiply it by 11, and add 497 to the product. Thus we get the sum 1,494,077. We write this number below the four numbers, and divide it by 111,573. The quotient is 13, and the remainder, *i.e.* 43,628, is disregarded. We subtract the quotient from the middle number. Thus we get the remainder, 1,494.064. We divide it by 703. The quotient is 2125, and the remainder, *i.e. avama*, is $\frac{189}{703}$. We subtract the quotient from the lunar days, and get the remainder 133,655. These are the civil days which we want to find. Dividing them by 7, we get 4 as remainder. Therefore the 1st of the month Caitra of the gauge-year falls on a Wednesday.

The epoch of the era of Yazdajird precedes the epoch of this era (v. era nr. 5, p. 7) by 11,968 days. Therefore the sum of the days of the era of Yazdajird up to our gauge-date is 145,623 days. Dividing them by the Persian year and months, we get as the corresponding Persian date *the year of Yazdajird* 399, *the* 18*th Isfandârmadh.* Before the *adhimâsa* month becomes complete with 30 days, there must still elapse five *ghaṭî*, *i.e.* two hours. In consequence, the year is a leap year, and Caitra is the month which is reckoned twice in it.

Method of the Arabic book *Al-arkand.*

The following is the method of the canon or calendar *Al-arkand*, according to a bad translation: "If you want to know the *Arkand*, i.e. *ahargaṇa*, take 90, multiply it by 6, add to the product 8, and the years of the realm of Sindh, *i.e.* the time till the month Ṣafar, A.H. 117, which corresponds to the Caitra of the year 109. Subtract therefrom 587, and the remainder represents the years of the *Shakh*.

An easier method is the following: "Take the complete years of the *Aera Yazdagirdi*, and subtract therefrom 33. The remainder represents the years of the *Shakh*. Or you may also begin with the original ninety years of the *Arkand*. Multiply them by 6, and add 14 to the product. Add to the sum the years of the *Aera Yazdajirdi*, and subtract therefrom 587. The remainder represents the years of the *Shakh*."

I believe that the here-mentioned *Shakh* is identical with *Śaka*. However, the result of this calculation does not lead us to the *Śaka era*, but to the *Gupta era*, which here is resolved into days. If the author of the *Arkand* began with 90, multiplied them by 6, added thereto 8, which would give 548, and did not change this number by an increase of years, the matter would come to the same result, and would be more easy and simple.

Critical notes on the latter method.

The first of the month Ṣafar, which the author of the latter method mentions, coincides with the eighth Daimâh of the year 103 of Yazdajird. Therefore he makes the month Caitra depend upon the new moon of Daimâh. However, the Persian months have since that time been in advance of real time, because the day-quarters (after the 365 complete days) have no longer been intercalated. According to the author, the era of the realm of Sindh which he mentions must precede the era of Yazdajird by six years. Accordingly, the years of this era for our gauge-year would be 405. These together with the years of the Arkand, with which the author begins, viz. 548, represent the sum of 953 years as the year of the *Śakakâla*. By the subtraction of that amount which the author has mentioned, it is changed into the corresponding year of the *Guptakâla*.

Page 227.

The other details of this method of resolution or *ahargaṇa* are identical with those of the method of the *Khaṇḍakhâdyaka*, as we have described it. Sometimes you find in a manuscript such a reading as prescribes the division by 1000 instead of by 976, but this is simply a mistake of the manuscripts, as such a method is without any foundation.

Next follows the method of Vijayanandin in his

**Method of the canon *Karaṇatilaka*.**

canon called *Karaṇatilaka:* "Take the years of the Śakakâla, subtract therefrom 888, multiply the remainder by 12, and add to the product the complete months of the current year which have elapsed. Write down the sum in two different places. Multiply the one number by 900, add 661 to the product, and divide the sum by 29,282. The quotient represents *adhimâsa* months. Add it to the number in the second place, multiply the sum by 30, and add to the product the days which have elapsed of the current month. The sum represents the lunar days. Write down this number in two different places. Multiply the one number by 3300, add to the product 64,106, divide the sum by 210,902. The quotient represents the *ûnarâtra* days, and the remainder the *avamas*. Subtract the *ûnarâtra* days from the lunar days. The remainder is the *ahargaṇa*, being reckoned from midnight as the beginning."

**Application of this method to the gauge-year.**

We exemplify this method in the use of our gauge-year. We subtract from the corresponding year of the Śakakâla (953) 888, and there remains 65. This number of years is equal to 780 months. We write down this number in two different places. In the one place we multiply it by 900, add thereto 661, and divide the product by 29,282. The quotient gives $23\frac{29175}{29282}$ *adhimâsa* months.

The multiplicator is 30. By being multiplied by it, the months are changed into days. The product, however, is again multiplied by 30. The divisor is the product of the multiplication of 976 *plus* the following fraction by 30, the effect of which is that both numbers belong to the same kind (*i.e.* that both represent days). Further, we add the resulting number of months to those months which we have previously found. By multiplying the sum by 30, we get the product of 24,060 (*read* 24,090), *i.e.* lunar days.

We write them down in two different places. The one number we multiply by 3300 and get the product

79,398,000 (*read* 79,497,000). Adding thereto 64,106 (*read* 69,601), we get the sum 79,462,104 (*read* 79,566,601). By dividing it by 210,902, we get the quotient 376 (*read* 307), *i.e.* *ûnarâtra* days, and a remainder of $\frac{162952}{210902}$ (*read* $\frac{56547}{210902}$), *i.e.* the *avamas*. We subtract the *ûnarâtra* days from the lunar days, written in the second place, and the remainder is the *civil ahargaṇa*, *i.e.* the sum of the civil days, viz. 23,684 (*read* 23,713).

Method of the *Pañca-Siddhântikâ*.

The method of the *Pañca-Siddhântikâ* of Varâhamihira is the following: "Take the years of the *Śakakâla*, subtract therefrom 427. Change the remainder into months by multiplying it by 12. Write down that number in two different places. Multiply the one number by 7 and divide the product by 228. The quotient is the number of *adhimâsa* months. Add them to the number written down in the second place, multiply the sum by 30, and add to the product the days which have elapsed of the current month. Write down the sum in two different places. Multiply the lower number by 11, add to the product 514, and divide the sum by 703. Subtract the quotient from the number written in the upper place. The remainder you get is the number of the civil days." Page 228.

This, Varâhamihira says, is the method of the Siddhânta of the Greeks.

Application of this method to the gauge-year.

We exemplify this method in one of our gauge-years. From the years of the Śakakâla we subtract 427. The remainder, *i.e.* 526 years, is equal to 6312 months. The corresponding number of *adhimâsa* months is 193 and a remainder of $\frac{13}{19}$. The sum of these months together with the other months is 6505, which are equal to 195,150 lunar days.

The additions which occur in this method are required on account of the fractions of time which adhere to the epoch of the era in question. The multiplication by 7 is for the purpose of reducing the number to seventh parts.

The divisor is the number of sevenths of the time of one *adhimâsa*, which he reckons as 32 months, 17 days, 8 *ghaṭî*, and about 34 *cashaka*.

Further, we write down the lunar days in two different places. The lower number we multiply by 11, and add to the product 514. The sum is 2,147,164. Dividing it by 703, we get the quotient 3054, *i.e.* the *ûnarâtra* days, and a remainder of $\frac{202}{703}$. We subtract the days from the number in the second place, and get the remainder 192,096, *i.e.* the civil days of the date on which we base the chronological computations of this book.

The theory of Varâhamihira comes very near that of Brahmagupta; for here the fraction at the end of the number of the *adhimâsa* days of the gauge-date is $\frac{15}{16}$, whilst in the calculations which we have made, starting from the beginning of the *kalpa*, we found it to be $\frac{103}{120}$, which is nearly equal to $\frac{15}{17}$ (*cf.* p. 29).

Method of the Arabic canon *Al-harkan*.

In a Muhammadan canon or calendar called *the canon Al-harkan* we find the same method of calculation, but applied to and starting from another era, the epoch of which must fall 40,081 (days) after that of the era of Yazdajird. According to this book, the beginning of the Indian year falls on Sunday the 21st of Daimâh of the year 110 of Yazdajird. The method may be tested in the following manner:—

"Take seventy-two years, change them into months by multiplying them by 12, which gives the product 864. Add thereto the months which have elapsed between the 1st of Sha'bân of the year 197, and the 1st of the month in which you happen to be. Write down the sum in two different places. Multiply the lower number by 7 and divide the product by 228. Add the quotient to the upper number and multiply the sum by 30. Add to the product the number of days which have elapsed of the month in which you are. Write down this number in two different places.

Add 38 to the lower number and multiply the sum by 11. Divide the product by 703, and subtract the quotient from the upper number. The remainder in the upper place is the number of the civil days, and the remainder in the lower place is the number of the *avamas*. Add 1 to the number of days and divide the sum by 7. The remainder shows the day of the week on which the date in question falls."

This method would be correct if the months of the seventy-two years with which the calculation begins were lunar. However, they are solar months, in which nearly twenty-seven months must be intercalated, so that these seventy-two years are more than 864 months.

Application of the method to the gauge-date.

We shall again exemplify this method in the case of our gauge-date, *i.e.* the beginning of Rabîʿ I., A.H. 422. Between the above-mentioned 1st of Shaʿbân and the latter date there have elapsed 2695 months. Adding these to the number of months adopted by the author of the method (864), you get the sum of 3559 months. Write down this number in two places. Multiply the one by 7, and divide the product by 228. The quotient represents the *adhimâsa* months, viz. 109. Page 229. Add them to the number in the other place, and you get the sum 3668. Multiply it by 30, and you get the product 110,040. Write down this number in two different places. Add to the lower number 38, and you get 110,078. Multiply it by 11 and divide the product by 703. The quotient is 1722 and a remainder of 292, *i.e.* the *avamas*. Subtract the quotient from the upper number, and the remainder, 108,318, represents the civil days.

Emendation of the method.

This method is to be amended in the following way: You must know that between the epoch of the era here used and the first of Shaʿbân, here adopted as a date, there have elapsed 25,958 days, *i.e.* 876 Arabic months, or seventy-three years and two months. If we further add to this number the months which have elapsed between that 1st Sha'bân and the 1st Rabî' I. of the gauge-year, we get the sum of 3571, and, together with the *adhimâsa* months, 3680 months, *i.e.* 110,400 days. The corresponding number of *ûnarâtra* days is 1727, and a remainder of 319 *avamas*. Subtracting these days, we get the remainder 108,673. If we now subtract 1 and divide the remainder by 7, the computation is correct, for the remainder is 4, *i.e.* the day of the gauge-date is a Wednesday, as has above (p. 48) been stated.

Method of Durlabha of Multân.

The method of Durlabha, a native of Multân, is the following:—He takes 848 years and adds thereto the Laukika-kâla. The sum is the Śakakâla. He subtracts therefrom 854, and changes the remainder of years into months. He writes them down together with the past months of the current year in three different places. The lower number he multiplies by 77, and divides the product by 69,120. The quotient he subtracts from the middle number, doubles the remainder, and adds thereto 29. The sum he divides by 65, so as to get *adhimâsa* months. He adds them to the upper number and multiplies the sum by 30. He writes down the product together with the past days of the current month in two different places. He multiplies the lower number by 11 and adds to the product 686. The sum he writes underneath. He divides it by 403,963, and adds the quotient to the middle number. He divides the sum by 703. The quotient represents the *ûnarâtra* days. He subtracts them from the upper number. The remainder is the civil *ahargaṇa*, *i.e.* the sum of the civil days of the date in question.

We have already in a former place mentioned the outlines of this method. After the author, Durlabha, had adopted it for a particular date, he made some additions, whilst the bulk of it is unchanged. However, the Karaṇasâra forbids introducing any innovations which in the method of *ahargaṇa* deviate to some other process. Unfortunately that which we possess of the book is badly translated. What we are able to quote from it is the following:—

He subtracts 821 from the years of the Śakakâla. The remainder is the *basis*. This would be the year 132 for our gauge-year. He writes down this number in three different places. He multiplies the first number by 132 degrees. The product gives the number 17,424 for our gauge-date. He multiplies the second number by 46 minutes, and gets the product 6072. He multiplies the third number by 34, and gets the product 4488. He divides it by 50, and the quotient represents minutes, seconds, &c., viz. 89′ 46″. Then he adds to the sum of degrees in the upper place 112, changing the seconds to minutes, the minutes to degrees, the degrees to circles. Thus he gets 48 circles 358° 41′ 46″. This is the mean place of the moon when the sun enters Aries.

Further, he divides the degrees of the mean place of the moon by 12. The quotient represents days. The remainder of the division he multiplies by 60, and adds thereto the minutes of the mean place of the moon. He divides the sum by 12, and the quotient represents Page 230. *ghaṭîs* and minor portions of time. Thus we get 27° 23′ 29″, *i.e.* *adhimâsa* days. No doubt this number represents the past portion of the *adhimâsa* month, which is at present in the course of formation.

The author, in regard to the manner in which the measure of the *adhimâsa* month is found, makes the following remark:—

He divides the lunar number which we have mentioned, viz. 132° 46′ 34″, by 12. Thereby he gets as the *portio anni* 11° 3′ 52″ 50‴, and as the *portio mensis* 0° 55′ 19″ 24‴ 10$^{\text{iv}}$. By means of the latter *portio* he computes the duration of the time in which 30 days sum up as 2 years, 8 months, 16 days, 4 *ghaṭî*, 45 *cashaka*. Then he multiplies the *basis* by 29 and gets the product 3828. He adds thereto 20, and divides the sum by 36. The quotient represents the *ûnarâtra* days, viz. $106\frac{8}{9}$.

However, as I have not been able to find the proper explanation of this method, I simply give it as I find it, but I must remark that the amount of *ûnarâtra* days which corresponds to a single *adhimâsa* month is $15\frac{7887}{10622}$.

# CHAPTER LIV.

## ON THE COMPUTATION OF THE MEAN PLACES OF THE PLANETS.

General method for the determination of the mean place of a planet at any given time.

If we know the number of cycles of the planets in a *kalpa* or *caturyuga*, and further know how many cycles have elapsed at a certain moment of time, we also know that the sum-total of the days of the *kalpa* or *caturyuga* stands in the same relation to the sum-total of the cycles as the past days of the *kalpa* or *caturyuga* to the corresponding amount of planetary cycles. The most generally used method is this:—

The past days of the *kalpa* or *caturyuga* are multiplied by the cycles of the planet, or of its apsis, or of its node which it describes in a *kalpa* or *caturyuga*. The product is divided by the sum-total of the days of the *kalpa* or *caturyuga* accordingly as you reckon by the one or the other. The quotient represents complete cycles. These, however, because not wanted, are disregarded.

The remainder which you get by the division is multiplied by 12, and the product is divided by the sum-total of the days of either *kalpa* or *caturyuga* by which we have already once divided. The quotient represents signs of the ecliptic. The remainder of this division is multiplied by 30, and the product divided by the same divisor. The quotient represents degrees. The remainder of this division is multiplied by 60, and is divided by the same divisor. The quotient represents minutes.

This kind of computation may be continued if we want to have seconds and minor values. The quotient represents the place of that planet according to its mean motion, or the place of that apsis or that node which we wanted to find.

Method of Pulisa for the same purpose.

The same is also mentioned by Pulisa, but his method differs, as follows:—"After having found the complete cycles which have elapsed at a certain moment of time, he divides the remainder by 131,493,150. The quotient represents the mean signs of the ecliptic.

"The remainder is divided by 4,383,105. The quotient represents degrees. The fourfold of the remainder is divided by 292,207. The quotient represents minutes. The remainder is multiplied by 60 and the product divided by the last-mentioned divisor. The quotient represents seconds.

"This calculation may be continued, so as to give third parts, fourth parts, and minor values. The quotient thus found is the mean place of the planet which we want to find."

Explanatory notes thereon.

The fact is that Pulisa was obliged to multiply the remainder of the cycles by 12, and to divide the product by the days of a *caturyuga*, because his whole computation is based on the *caturyuga*. But instead of doing this, he divided by the quotient which you get if you divide the number of days of a *caturyuga* by 12. This quotient is the first number he mentions, viz. 131,493,150.

Further, he was obliged to multiply the remainder of the signs of the ecliptic by 30, and to divide the product by the first divisor; but instead of doing this, he divided by the quotient which you get if you divide the first number by 30. This quotient is the second number, viz. 4,383,105.

According to the same analogy, he wanted to divide the remainder of the degrees by the quotient which you get if you divide the second number by 60. However, making this division, he got as quotient 73,051 and a remainder of $\frac{3}{4}$. Therefore he multiplied the whole by 4, in order that the fractions should be raised to wholes. For the same reason he also multiplies the following remainder by 4; but when he did not get wholes, as has been indicated, he returned to multiplying by 60. Page 231.

If we apply this method to a *kalpa* according to the theory of Brahmagupta, the first number, by which the remainder of the cycles is divided, is 131,493,037,500. The second number, by which the remainder of the signs of the ecliptic is divided, is 4,383,101,250. The third number, by which the remainder of the degrees is divided, is 73,051,687. In the remainder which we get by this division there is the fraction of $\frac{1}{2}$. Therefore we take the double of the number, viz. 146,103,375, and we divide by it the double of the remainder of minutes.

Brahmagupta applies this method to the *kaliyuga* in order to get smaller numbers.

Brahmagupta, however, does not reckon by the *kalpa* and *caturyuga*, on account of the enormous sums of their days, but prefers to them the *kaliyuga*, in order to facilitate the calculation. Applying the preceding method of *ahargaṇa* to the precise date of the *kaliyuga*, we multiply its sum of days by the star-cycles of a *kalpa*. To the product we add the *basis*, *i.e.* the remaining cycles which the planet had at the beginning of the *kaliyuga*. We divide the sum by the civil days of the *kaliyuga*, viz. 157,791,645. The quotient represents the complete cycles of the planet, which are disregarded.

The remainder we compute in the above-described manner, and thereby we find the mean place of the planet.

The here-mentioned *bases* are the following for the single planets:—

For Mars, 4,308,768,000.

For Mercury, 4,288,896,000.

For Jupiter, 4,313,520,000.

For Venus, 4,304,448,000.

For Saturn, 4,305,312,000.

For the Sun's apsis, 933,120,000.

For the Moon's apsis, 1,505,952,000.

For the ascending node, 1,838,592,000 (v. the notes).

At the same moment, *i.e.* at the beginning of the *kaliyuga*, sun and moon stood according to their mean motion in 0° of Aries, and there was neither a *plus* nor a *minus* consisting of an *adhimâsa* month or of *ûnarâtra* days.

Methods of the *Khaṇḍakhâdyaka*, *Karaṇatilaka*, and *Karaṇasâra*.

In the above-mentioned *canones* or calendars we find the following method:—"The *ahargaṇa*, *i.e.* the sum of the days of the date, is, for each planet respectively, multiplied by a certain number, and the product is divided by another number. The quotient represents complete cycles and fractions of cycles, according to mean motion. Sometimes the computation becomes perfect simply by this multiplication and division. Sometimes, in order to get a perfect result, you are compelled once more to divide by a certain number the days of the date, either such as they are, or multiplied by some number. The quotient must then be combined with the result obtained in the first place.

Sometimes, too, certain numbers are adopted, as *e.g.* the *basis*, which must either be added or subtracted for this purpose, in order that the mean motion at the beginning of the era should be computed as beginning with 0° of *Aries*. This is the method of the books *Khaṇḍakhâdyaka* and *Karaṇatilaka*. However, the author of the *Karaṇasâra* computes the mean places of the planets for the vernal equinox, and reckons the *ahargaṇa* from this moment. But these methods are very subtle, and are so numerous, that none of them has obtained any particular authority. Therefore we refrain from reproducing them, as this would detain us too long and be of no use.

The other methods of the computation of the mean places of the planets and similar calculations have nothing to do with the subject of the present book.

## CHAPTER LV.

### ON THE ORDER OF THE PLANETS, THEIR DISTANCES AND SIZES.

Traditional view on the sun being below the moon.

WHEN speaking of the *lokas*, we have already given a quotation from the *Vishṇu-Purâṇa* and from the commentary of Patañjali, according to which the place of the sun is in the order of the planets below that of the moon. This is the traditional view of the Hindus. Compare in particular the following passage of the *Matsya-Purâṇa*:—

"The distance of heaven from the earth is equal to the radius of the earth. The sun is the lowest of all planets. Above him there is the moon, and above the moon are the lunar stations and their stars. Above them is Mercury, then follow Venus, Mars, Jupiter, Saturn, the Great Bear, and above it the pole. The pole is connected with the heaven. The stars cannot be counted by man. Those who impugn this view maintain that the moon at conjunction becomes hidden by the sun, as the light of the lamp becomes invisible in the light of the sun, and she becomes more visible the more she moves away from the sun."

We shall now give some quotations from the books of this school relating to the sun, the moon, and the stars, and we shall combine herewith the views of the astronomers, although of the latter we have only a very slender knowledge.

Popular notions of astronomy.

Page 232.

The *Vâyu-Purâṇa* says: "The sun has globular shape, fiery nature, and 1000 rays, by which he attracts the water; 400 of these are for the rain, 300 for the snow, and 300 for the air." Quotations from *Vâyu-Purâṇa.*

In another passage it says: "Some of them (*i.e.* the rays) are for this purpose, that the *devas* should live in bliss; others for the purpose that men should live in comfort, whilst others are destined for the fathers."

In another passage the author of the *Vâyu-Purâṇa* divides the rays of the sun over the six seasons of the year, saying: "The sun illuminates the earth in that third of the year which commences with 0° of Pisces by 300 rays; he causes rain in the following third by 400 rays, and he causes cold and snow in the remaining third by 300 rays."

Another passage of the same book runs as follows: "The rays of the sun and the wind raise the water from the sea to the sun. Now, if the water dropped down from the sun, it would be hot. Therefore the sun hands the water over to the moon, that it should drop down from the moon cold, and thus refresh the world."

Another passage: "The heat of the sun and his light are one-fourth of the heat and the light of the fire. In the north, the sun falls into the water during the night; therefore he becomes red."

Another passage: "In the beginning there were the earth, water, wind, and heaven. Then Brahman perceived sparks under the earth. He brought them forth and divided them into three parts. One third of them is the common fire, which requires wood and is extinguished by water. Another third is the sun, and the last third is the lightning. In the animals, too, there is fire, which cannot be extinguished by water. The sun attracts the water, the lightning shines through the rain, but the fire in the animals is distributed over the moist substances by which they nourish themselves."

The Hindus seem to believe that the heavenly bodies nourish themselves by the vapours, which also Aristotle mentions as the theory of certain people. Thus the author of the *Vishṇu-Dharma* explains that "the sun nourishes the moon and the stars. If the sun did not exist, there would not be a star, nor angel, nor man."

On the nature of the stars.

The Hindus believe regarding the bodies of all the stars that they have a globular shape, a watery essence, and that they do not shine, whilst the sun alone is of fiery essence, self-shining, and *per accidens* illuminates other stars when they stand opposite to him. They reckon, according to eyesight, among the stars also such luminous bodies as in reality are not stars, but the lights into which those men have been metamorphosed who have received eternal reward from God, and reside in the height of heaven on thrones of crystal. The *Vishṇu-Dharma* says: "The stars are watery, and the rays of the sun illuminate them in the night. Those who by their pious deeds have obtained a place in the height sit there on their thrones, and, when shining, they are reckoned among the stars."

Quotation from the *Vishṇu-Dharma*.

All the stars are called *târa*, which word is derived from *taraṇa*, *i.e.* the passage. The idea is that those saints have *passed* through the wicked world and have reached bliss, and that the stars *pass* through heaven in a circular motion. The word *nakshatra* is limited to the stars of the lunar stations. As, however, all of these are called *fixed stars*, the word *nakshatra* also applies to all the fixed stars; for it means *not increasing and not decreasing*. I for my part am inclined to think that this increasing and decreasing refers to their number and to the distances of the one from the other, but the author of the last-mentioned book (*Vishṇu-Dharma*) combines it with their light. For he adds, "as the moon increases and decreases."

Further, there is a passage in the same book where Mârkaṇḍeya says: "The stars which do not perish before the end of the *kalpa* are equal to a *nikharva*, *i.e.* 100,000,000,000. The number of those which fall down before the end of a *kalpa* is unknown. Only he can know it who dwells in the height during a *kalpa*."

Vajra spoke: "O Mârkaṇḍeya, thou hast lived during six *kalpas*. This is thy seventh *kalpa*. Therefore why dost thou not know them?"

He answered: "If they always remained in the same condition, not changing as long as they exist, I should not be ignorant of them. However, they perpetually raise some pious man and bring another down to the earth. Therefore I do not keep them in my memory."

On the diameters of the planets.

Regarding the diameters of sun and moon and their shadows the *Matsya-Purâṇa* says: "The diameter of the body of the sun is 9000 *yojanas;* the diameter of the moon is the double of it, and the apsis is as much as the two together."

The same occurs in the *Vâyu-Purâṇa*, except that it says with regard to the apsis that it is equal to the sun when it is with the sun, and that it is equal to the moon when it is with the moon.

Another author says: "The apsis is 50,000 *yojanas*."

Regarding the diameters of the planets the *Matsya-Purâṇa* says: "The circumference of Venus is one-sixteenth of the circumference of the moon, that of Page 233 Jupiter three-fourths of the circumference of Venus, that of Saturn or Mars three-fourths of that of Jupiter, that of Mercury three-fourths of that of Mars."

The same statement is also found in the *Vâyu-Purâṇa*.

On the circumference of the fixed stars.

The same two books fix the circumference of the great fixed stars as equal to that of Mercury. The next smaller class have a circumference of 500 *yojanas*, the following classes 400, 300, and 200. But there are no fixed stars with a smaller circumference than 150 *yojanas*.

Thus the *Vâyu-Purâṇa*. But the *Matsya-Purâṇa* says: "The next following classes have a circumference of 400, 300, 200, and 100 *yojanas*. But there is no fixed star with less circumference than a half *yojana*."

The latter statement, however, looks suspicious to me, and is perhaps a fault in the manuscript.

The author of *Vishṇu-Dharma* says, relating the

words of Mârkaṇḍeya: "*Abhijit*, the Falling Eagle; *Ârdrâ*, the Sirius Yemenicus; *Rohiṇî*, or Aldabarân; *Punarvasu*, i.e. the Two Heads of the Twins; *Pushya*, *Revatî*, *Agastya* or Canopus, the Great Bear, the master of *Vâyu*, the master of *Ahirbudhnya*, and the master of *Vasishṭha*, each of these stars has a circumference of five *yojanas*. All the other stars have each only a circumference of four *yojanas*. I do not know those stars, the distance of which is not measurable. They have a circumference between four *yojanas* and two *kuroh*, i.e. two miles. Those which have less circumference than two *kuroh* are not seen by men, but only by the *devas*."

The Hindus have the following theory regarding the magnitude of the stars, which is not traced back to any known authority: "The diameters of the sun and moon are each 67 *yojanas*; that of the apsis is 100; that of Venus 10, of Jupiter 9, of Saturn 8, of Mars 7, of Mercury 7."

Views of the Hindu astronomers on the same subjects.

This is all we have been able to learn of the confused notions of the Hindus regarding these subjects. We shall now pass on to the views of the Hindu astronomers with whom we agree regarding the order of the planets and other topics, viz. that the sun is the middle of the planets, Saturn and the moon their two ends, and that the fixed stars are above the planets. Some of these things have already been mentioned in the preceding chapters.

Quotation from the *Saṁhitâ* of Varâhamihira, chap. iv. 1–3.

Varâhamihira says in the book *Saṁhitâ*: "The moon is always below the sun, who throws his rays upon her, and lits up the one half of her body, whilst the other half remains dark and shadowy like a pot which you place in the sunshine. The one half which faces the sun is lit up, whilst the other half which does not face it remains dark. The moon is watery in her essence, therefore the rays which fall on her are reflected, as they are reflected from the water and the mirror towards the wall. If the moon is in conjunction with the sun, the white part of her turns towards the sun, the black part towards us. Then the white part sinks downward towards us slowly, as the sun marches away from the moon."

Every educated man among the Hindu theologians, and much more so among their astronomers, believes indeed that the moon is below the sun, and even below all the planets.

*Ya'kub Ibn Târik on the distances of the stars.*

The only Hindu traditions we have regarding the distances of the stars are those mentioned by Ya'kub Ibn Târik in his book, *The Composition of the Spheres*, and he had drawn his information from the well-known Hindu scholar who, A.H. 161, accompanied an embassy to Bagdâd. First, he gives a metrological statement: "A finger is equal to six barleycorns which are put one by the side of the other. An arm (yard) is equal to twenty-four fingers. A *farsakh* is equal to 16,000 yards."

Here, however, we must observe that the Hindus do not know the *farsakh*, that it is, as we have already explained, equal to one half a *yojana*.

Further, Ya'kûb says: "The diameter of the earth is 2100 *farsakh*, its circumference $6596\frac{9}{25}$ *farsakh*."

On this basis he has computed the distances of the planets as we exhibit them in the following table.

*Pulisa and Brahmagupta on the same subject.*

However, this statement regarding the size of the earth is by no means generally agreed to by all the Hindus. So, *e.g.* Pulisa reckons its diameter as 1600 *yojanas*, and its circumference as $5026\frac{14}{15}$ *yojanas*, whilst Brahmagupta reckons the former as 1581 *yojanas*, and the latter as 5000 *yojanas*.

If we double thesenumbers, they ought to be equal to the numbers of Ya'kûb; but this is not the case. Now the yard and the mile are respectively identical according to the measurement both of us and of the Hindus. According to our computation the radius of the earth is 3184 miles. Reckoning, according to the custom of our country, 1 *farsakh* = 3 miles, we get 6728 *farsakh*; and reckoning 1 *farsakh* = 16,000 yards, as is mentioned by Ya'kûb, we get 5046 *farsakh*. Reckoning 1 *yojana* = 32,000 yards, we get 2523 *yojanas*.

Page 234.

Distances of the planets from the centre of the earth, and their diameters, according to Ya'kûb Ibn Târik.

The following table is borrowed from the book of Ya'kûb Ibn Târik:—

| The planets. | Their distances from the centre of the earth, and their diameters. | The conventional measures of the distances, differing according to time and place, reckoned in *farsakh*, 1 *farsakh* = 16,000 yards. | Their constant measures, based on the radius of the earth = 1. |
|---|---|---|---|
| | Radius of the earth . | 1,050 | 1 |
| Moon. | The smallest distance . | 37,500 | $35\frac{5}{7}$ |
| | The middle distance . | 48,500 | $46\frac{4}{21}$ |
| | The greatest distance . | 59,000 | $56\frac{4}{21}$ |
| | Diameter of the moon | 5,000 | $4\frac{16}{21}$ |
| Mercury. | The smallest distance . | 64,000 | $60\frac{20}{21}$ |
| | The middle distance . | 164,000 | $156\frac{4}{21}$ |
| | The greatest distance . | 264,000 | $251\frac{3}{7}$ |
| | Diameter of Mercury | 5,000 | $4\frac{16}{21}$ |
| Venus. | The smallest distance . | 269,000 | $256\frac{4}{21}$ |
| | The middle distance . | 709,500 | $675\frac{5}{7}$ |
| | The greatest distance . | 1,150,000 | $1,095\frac{5}{21}$ |
| | Diameter of Venus . | 20,000 | $19\frac{1}{21}$ |
| Sun. | The smallest distance . | 1,170,000 | $1,114\frac{2}{7}$ |
| | The middle distance . | 1,690,000 | $1,609\frac{11}{21}$ |
| | The greatest distance . | 2,210,000 | $2,104\frac{16}{21}$ |
| | Diameter of the Sun . | 20,000 | $19\frac{1}{21}$ |
| Mars. | The smallest distance . | 2,230,000 | $2,123\frac{17}{21}$ |
| | The middle distance . | 5,315,000 | $5,061\frac{19}{21}$ |
| | The greatest distance . | 8,400,000 | 8,000 |
| | Diameter of Mars . | 20,000 | $19\frac{1}{21}$ |
| Jupiter. | The smallest distance . | 8,420,000 | $8,019\frac{1}{21}$ |
| | The middle distance . | 11,410,000 | $10,866\frac{2}{3}$ |
| | The greatest distance . | 14,400,000 | $13,714\frac{2}{7}$ |
| | Diameter of Jupiter . | 20,000 | $19\frac{1}{21}$ |
| Saturn. | The smallest distance . | 14,420,000 | $13,733\frac{1}{3}$ |
| | The middle distance . | 16,220,000 | $15,447\frac{13}{21}$ |
| | The greatest distance . | 18,020,000 | $17,161\frac{19}{21}$ |
| | Diameter of Saturn . | 20,000 | $19\frac{1}{21}$ |
| Zodiacus. | The radius of the outside | 20,000,000 | $19,047\frac{13}{21}$ |
| | The radius of the inside | 19,962,000 | $1,866\frac{2}{3}$ (*sic*) |
| | Its circumference from the outside . . | 125,664,000 | |

Page 235.

This theory differs from that on which Ptolemy has based his computation of the distances of the planets in the *Kitâb-almanshûrât*, and in which he has been followed both by the ancient and the modern astronomers. It is their principle that the greatest distance of a planet is equal to its smallest distance from the next higher planet, and that between the two globes there is not a space void of action. Ptolemy on the distances of the planets. Page 236.

According to this theory, there is between the two globes a space not occupied by either of them, in which there is something like an axis around which the rotation takes place. It seems that they attributed to the æther a certain gravity, in consequence of which they felt the necessity of adopting something which *keeps* or *holds* the inner globe (the planet) in the midst of the outer globe (the æther).

On occultation and the parallax.

It is well known among all astronomers that there is no possibility of distinguishing between the higher and the lower one of two planets except by means of the *occultation* or the increase of the *parallax*. However, the occultation occurs only very seldom, and only the parallax of a single planet, viz. the moon, can be observed. Now the Hindus believe that the motions are equal, but the distances different. The reason why the higher planet moves more slowly than the lower is the greater extension of its sphere (or orbit); and the reason why the lower planet moves more rapidly is that its sphere or orbit is less extended. Thus, *e.g.* one minute in the sphere of Saturn is equal to 262 minutes in the sphere of the moon. Therefore the times in which Saturn and the moon traverse the same space are different, whilst their motions are equal.

I have never found a Hindu treatise on this subject, but only numbers relating thereto scattered in various books—numbers which are corrupt. Somebody objected to Pulisa that he reckoned the circumference of the sphere of each planet as 21,600, and its radius as 3438, whilst Varâhamihira reckoned the sun's distance from the earth as 2,598,900, and the distance of the fixed stars as 321,362,683. Thereupon Pulisa replied that the former numbers were minutes, the latter *yojanas;* whilst in another passage he says that the distance of the fixed stars from the earth is sixty times larger than the distance of the sun. Accordingly he ought to have reckoned the distance of the fixed stars as 155,934,000.

Hindu method for the computation of the distances of the planets.

The Hindu method of the computation of the distances of the planets which we have above mentioned is based on a principle which is unknown to me in the present stage of my knowledge, and as long as I have no facility in translating the books of the Hindus. The principle is this, that the extension of a minute in the orbit of the moon is equal to fifteen *yojanas.* The nature of this principle is not cleared up by the commentaries of Balabhadra, whatsoever trouble he takes. For he says: "People have tried to fix by observation the time of the moon's passing through the horizon, *i.e.* the time between the shining of the first part of her body and the rising of the whole, or the time between the beginning of her setting and the completion of the act of setting. People have found this process to last thirty-two minutes of the circumference of the sphere." However, if it is difficult to fix by observation the degrees, it is much more so to fix the minutes.

Quotations from Balabhadra.

Further, the Hindus have tried to determine by observation the *yojanas* of the diameter of the moon, and have found them to be 480. If you divide them by the minutes of her body, the quotient is 15 *yojanas,* as corresponding to one minute. If you multiply it by the minutes of the circumference, you get the product 324,000. This is the measure of the sphere of the moon which she traverses in each rotation. If you multiply this number by the cycles of the moon in a *kalpa* or *caturyuga,* the product is the distance which the moon traverses in either of them. According to Brahmagupta, this is in a *kalpa* 18.712,069,200,000,000 *yojanas*. Brahmagupta calls this number *the yojanas of the ecliptic.*

Evidently if you divide this number by the cycles of each planet in a *kalpa*, the quotient represents the *yojanas* of one rotation. However, the motion of the planets is, according to the Hindus, as we have already mentioned, in every distance one and the same. Therefore the quotient represents the measure of the path of the sphere of the planet in question.

As further, according to Brahmagupta, the relation of the diameter to the circumference is nearly equal to that of 12,959 : 40,980, you multiply the measure of the path of the sphere of the planet by 12,959, and divide the product by 81,960. The quotient is the radius, or the distance of the planet from the centre of the earth. The radii of the planets, or their distances from the centre of the earth, computed according to Brahmagupta.

We have made this computation for all the planets according to the theory of Brahmagupta, and present the results to the reader in the following table :—

Page 237.

| The planets. | The circumference of the sphere of each planet, reckoned in *yojanas*. | Their radii, which are identical with their distances from the earth's centre, reckoned in *yojanas*. |
|---|---|---|
| Moon . . . | 324,000 | 51,229 |
| Mercury . . | 1,043,210 [illegible] | 164,947 |
| Venus . . . | 2,664,629 [illegible] | 421,315 |
| Sun . . . . | 4,331,497 $\frac{1}{3}$ | 684,869 |
| Mars . . . | 8,146,916 [illegible] | 1,288,139 |
| Jupiter . . | 51,374,821 [illegible] | 8,123,064 |
| Saturn . . | 127,668,787 [illegible] | 20,186,186 |
| The Fixed Stars, their distance from the earth's centre being sixty times the distance of the sun from the same . . | 259,889,850 | 41,092,140 |

The same computation according to the theory of Pulisa.

As Pulisa reckons by *caturyugas*, not by *kalpas*, he multiplies the distance of the path of the sphere of the moon by the lunar cycles of a *caturyuga*, and gets the product 18,712,080,864,000 *yojanas*, which he calls *the yojanas of heaven*. It is the distance which the moon traverses in each *caturyuga*.

Pulisa reckons the relation of the diameter to the circumference as 1250 : 3927. Now, if you multiply the circumference of each planetary sphere by 625 and divide the product by 3927, the quotient is the distance of the planet from the earth's centre. We have made the same computation as the last one according to the view of Pulisa, and present the results in the following table. In computing the radii we have disregarded the fractions smaller than $\frac{1}{2}$, and have reduced larger fractions to wholes. We have, however, not taken the same liberty in the calculation of the circumferences, but have calculated with the utmost accuracy, because they are required in the computations of the revolutions. For if you divide the *yojanas of heaven* in
Page 238.
a *kalpa* or *caturyuga* by the civil days of the one or the other, you get the quotient 11,858 *plus* a remainder, which is $\frac{25,498}{35,419}$ according to Brahmagupta, and $\frac{209,554}{292,207}$ according to Pulisa. This is the distance which the moon every day traverses, and as the motion of all planets is the same, it is the distance which every planet in a day traverses. It stands in the same relation to the *yojanas* of the circumference of its sphere as its motion, which we want to find, to the circumference, the latter being divided into 360 equal parts. If you therefore multiply the path common to all the planets by 360 and divide the product by the *yojanas* of the circumference of the planet in question, the quotient represents its mean daily motion.

| The planets. | The circumferences of the spheres of the planets, reckoned in *yojanas*. | The distances of the planets from the earth's centre, reckoned in *yojanas*. |
|---|---|---|
| Moon . . . . | 324,000 | 51,566 |
| Mercury . . . . | $1,043,211\frac{573}{1993}$ | 166,033 |
| Venus . . . . | $2,664,632\frac{90232}{585199}$ | 424,089 |
| Sun . . . . . | $4,331,500\frac{1}{5}$ | 690,295 (*sic*) |
| Mars . . . . | $8,146,937\frac{18163}{95761}$ | 1,296,624 (!) |
| Jupiter . . . . | $51,375,764\frac{4496}{18211}$ | 8,176,689 (!) |
| Saturn . . . | $127,671,739\frac{22801}{35641}$ | 20,319,542 (!) |
| The Fixed Stars, the sun's distance from the earth's centre being $\frac{1}{60}$th of theirs | 259,890,012 | 41,417,700 (*sic*) |

As, now, the minutes of the diameter of the moon stand in the same relation to the minutes of her circumference, *i.e.* 21,600, as the number of *yojanas* of the diameter, *i.e.* 480, to the *yojanas* of the circumference of the whole sphere, exactly the same method of calculation has been applied to the minutes of the diameter of the sun, which we have found to be equal to 6522 *yojanas* according to Brahmagupta, and equal to 6480 according to Pulisa. Since Pulisa reckons the minutes of the body of the moon as 32, *i.e.* a power of 2, he divides this number in order to get the minutes of the bodies of the planets by 2, till he at last gets 1. Thus he attributes to the body of Venus $\frac{1}{2}$ of 32 minutes, *i.e.* 16; to that of Jupiter $\frac{1}{4}$ of 32 minutes, *i.e.* 8; to that of Mercury $\frac{1}{8}$ of 32 minutes, *i.e.* 4; to that of Saturn $\frac{1}{16}$ of 32 minutes, *i.e.* 2; to that of Mars $\frac{1}{32}$ of of 32 minutes, *i.e.* 1. The diameters of the planets. Page 239.

This precise order seems to have taken his fancy, or he would not have overlooked the fact that the diameter of Venus is, according to observation, not equal to the radius of the moon, nor Mars equal to $\frac{1}{16}$th of Venus.

Method for the computation of the bodies of sun and moon at any given time.

The following is the method of the computation of the bodies of sun and moon at every time, based on their distances from the earth, *i.e.* the true diameter of its orbit, which is found in the computations of the corrections of sun and moon. AB is the diameter of the body of the sun, CD is the diameter of the earth, CDH is the cone of the shadow, HL is its elevation. Further, draw CR parallel to DB. Then is AR the difference between AB and CD, and the normal line CT is the middle distance of the sun, *i.e.* the radius of its orbit derived from *the yojanas of heaven* (v. p. 72). From this the true distance of the sun always differs, sometimes being larger, sometimes smaller. We draw CK, which is of course determined by the parts of the *sine*. It stands in the same relation to CT, this being the *sinus totus* (=radius), as the *yojanas* of CK to the *yojanas* of CT. Hereby the measure of the diameter is reduced to *yojanas*.

The *yojanas* of AB stand in the same relation to the *yojanas* of TC as the minutes of AB to the minutes of TC, the latter being the *sinus totus*. Thereby AB becomes known and determined by the minutes of the sphere, because the *sinus totus* is determined by the measure of the circumference. For this reason Pulisa says: "Multiply the *yojanas* of the radius of the sphere of the sun or the moon by the true distance, and divide the product by the *sinus totus*. By the quotient you get for the sun, divide 22,278,240, and by the quotient you get for the moon, divide 1,650,240. The quotient then represents the minutes of the diameter of the body of either sun or moon."

Quotations from Pulisa, Brahmagupta, and Balabhadra.

The last-mentioned two numbers are products of the multiplication of the *yojanas* of the diameters of sun and moon by 3438, which is the number of the minutes of the *sinus totus*.

Likewise Brahmagupta says: "Multiply the *yojanas* of sun or moon by 3416, *i.e.* the minutes of the *sinus totus*, and divide the product by the *yojanas* of the radius of the sphere of sun or moon." But the latter rule of division is not correct, because, according to it, the measure of the body would not vary (v. p. 74). Therefore the commentator Balabhadra holds the same opinion as Pulisa, viz. that the divisor in this division should be the true distance reduced (to the measure of *yojanas*).

Brahmagupta's method for the computation of the diameter of the shadow.

Brahmagupta gives the following rule for the computation of the diameter of the shadow, which in our *canones* is called *the measure of the sphere of the dragon's head and tail*: "Subtract the *yojanas* of the diameter of the earth, *i.e.* 1581, from the *yojanas* of the diameter of the sun, *i.e.* 6522. There remains 4941, which is kept in memory to be used as divisor. It is represented in the figure by AR. Further multiply the diameter of the earth, which is the double *sinus totus*, by the *yojanas* of the true distance of the sun, which is found by the correction of the sun. Divide the product by the divisor kept in memory. The quotient is the true distance of the shadow's end.

"Evidently the two triangles ARC and CDH are similar to each other. However, the normal line CT does not vary in size, whilst in consequence of the true distance the *appearance* of AB varies, though its size is constantly the same. Now let *this* distance be CK. Draw the lines AJ and RV parallel to each other, and JKV parallel to AB. Then the latter is equal to the divisor kept in memory.

"Draw the line JCM. Then M is the head of the cone of the shadow for that time. The relation of JV, the divisor kept in memory, to KC, the true distance, is the same as that of CD, the diameter of the earth, to ML, which he (Brahmagupta) calls a true distance (of the shadow's end), and it is determined by the minutes of the *sine* (the earth's radius being the *sinus totus*). For KC——" Page 240.

Lacuna in the manuscript copy of Brahmagupta.

Now, however, I suspect that in the following something has fallen out in the manuscript, for the author continues: "Then multiply it (*i.e.* the quotient of CK, by the divisor kept in memory) by the diameter of the earth. The product is the distance between the earth's centre and the end of the shadow. Subtract therefrom the true distance of the moon and multiply the remainder by the diameter of the earth. Divide the product by the true distance of the shadow's end. The quotient is the diameter of the shadow in the sphere of the moon. Further, we suppose the true distance of the moon to be LS, and FX is a part of the lunar sphere, the radius of which is LS. Since we have found LM as determined by the minutes of the *sine*, it stands in the same relation to CD, this being the double *sinus totus*, as MS, measured in minutes of the *sine*, to XZ, measured in minutes of the sine."

Here I suppose Brahmagupta wished to reduce LM, the true distance of the shadow's end, to *yojanas*, which is done by multiplying it by the *yojanas* of the diameter of the earth, and by dividing the product by the double *sinus totus*. The mentioning of this division has fallen out in the manuscript; for without it the multiplication of the corrected distance of the shadow's end by the diameter of the earth is perfectly superfluous, and in no way required by the computation.

Further: "If the number of *yojanas* of LM is known, LS, which is the true distance, must also be reduced to *yojanas*, for the purpose that MS should be determined by the same measure. The measure of the diameter of the shadow which is thus found represents *yojanas*.

Further, Brahmagupta says: "Then multiply the shadow which has been found by the *sinus totus*, and divide the product by the true distance of the moon. The quotient represents the minutes of the shadow which we wanted to find."

Criticisms on Brahmagupta's method.

However, if the shadow which he has found were determined by *yojanas*, he ought to have multiplied it by the double *sinus totus*, and to have divided the product by the *yojanas* of the diameter of the earth, in order to find the minutes of the shadow. But as he has not done so, this shows that, in his computation, he limited himself to determining the true diameter in minutes, without reducing it to *yojanas*.

The author uses the true (*sphuṭa*) diameter without its having been reduced to *yojanas*. Thus he finds that the shadow in the circle, the radius of which is LS, is the true diameter, and this is required for the computation of the circle, the radius of which is the *sinus totus*. The relation of ZX, which he has already found, to SL, the true distance, is the same as the relation of ZX in the measure which is sought to SL, this being the *sinus totus*. On the basis of this equation the reduction (to *yojanas*) must be made.

**Another method of Brahmagupta's for computing the shadow.**

In another passage Brahmagupta says: "The diameter of the earth is 1581, the diameter of the moon 480, the diameter of the sun 6522, the diameter of the shadow 1581. Subtract the *yojanas* of the earth from the *yojanas* of the sun, there remains 4941. Multiply this remainder by the *yojanas* of the true distance of the moon, and divide the product by the *yojanas* of the true distance of the sun. Subtract the quotient you get from 1581, and the remainder is the measure of the shadow in the sphere of the moon. Multiply it by 3416, and divide the product by the *yojanas* of *the middle radius of the sphere of the moon*. The quotient represents the minutes of the diameter of the shadow.

"Evidently if the *yojanas* of the diameter of the earth are subtracted from the *yojanas* of the diameter of the sun, the remainder is AR, *i.e.* JV. Draw the line VCF and let fall the normal line KC on O. Then the relation of the surplus JV to KC, the true distance of the sun, is the same as the relation of ZF to OC, the true distance of the moon. It is indifferent whether these two *mean* diameters are reduced (to *yojanas*) or not, for ZF is, in this case, found as determined by the measure of *yojana*.

"Draw XN as equal to OF. Then ON is necessarily

equal to the diameter of CD, and its sought-for part is ZX. The number which is thus found must be subtracted from the diameter of the earth, and the remainder will be ZX."

The author criticises the corrupt state of his manuscript of Brahmagupta. Page 241.

For such mistakes as occur in this computation, the author, Brahmagupta, is not to be held responsible, but we rather suspect that the fault lies with the manuscript. We, however, cannot go beyond the text we have at our disposal, as we do not know how it may be in a correct copy.

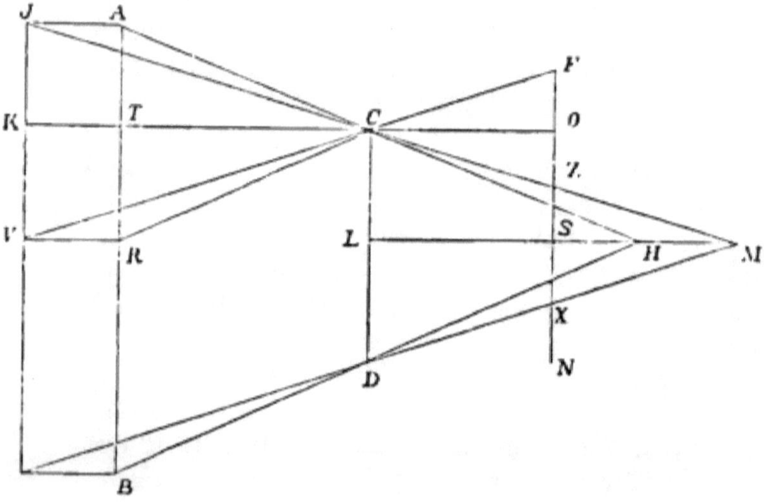


The measure of the shadow adopted by Brahmagupta, from which he orders the reader to subtract, cannot be a *mean* one, for a *mean* measure stands in the midst, between too little and too much. Further, we cannot imagine that this measure should be the greatest of the measures of the shadow, including the *plus* (?); for ZF, which is the *minus*, is the base of a triangle, of which the one side, FC, cuts SL in the direction of the sun, not in the direction of the end of the shadow. Therefore ZF has nothing whatsoever to do with the shadow (conjectural rendering.)

Lastly, there is the possibility that the *minus* belongs to the diameter of the moon. In that case the relation of ZX, which has been determined in *yojanas*, to SL, the *yojanas* of the true distance of the moon, is the same as the relation of ZX reckoned in minutes to SL, this being the *sinus totus* (conjectural rendering.)

By this method is found what Brahmagupta wants to find, quite correctly, without the division by the mean radius of the sphere of the moon, which is derived from the *yojanas of the sphere of heaven* (v. p. 72). (For the last three passages *vide* Notes.)

The computation of the diameters of sun and moon according to other sources.

The methods of the computation of the diameters of sun and moon, as given by the Hindu *canones*, such as the *Khaṇḍakhâdyaka* and *Karaṇasâra*, are the same as are found in the canon of Alkhwârizmî. Also the computation of the diameter of the shadow in the *Khaṇḍakhâdyaka* is similar to that one given by Alkhwârizmî, whilst the *Karaṇasara* has the following method:—"Multiply the *bhukti* of the moon by 4 and the *bhukti* of the sun by 13. Divide the difference between the two products by 30, and the quotient is the diameter of the shadow."

Diameter of the sun and of the shadow according to the *Karaṇatilaka*.

The *Karaṇatilaka* gives the following method for the computation of the diameter of the sun:—"Divide the *bhukti* of the sun by 2, and write down the half in two different places. In the one place divide it by 10, and add the quotient to the number in the second place. The sum is the number of minutes of the diameter of the sun."

In the computation of the diameter of the moon, he first takes the *bhukti* of the moon, adds thereto $\frac{1}{50}$th of it, and divides the number by 25. The quotient is the number of the minutes of the moon's diameter.

In the computation of the diameter of the shadow, he multiplies the *bhukti* of the sun by 3, and from the product he subtracts $\frac{1}{24}$th of it. The remainder he subtracts from the *bhukti* of the moon, and the double of the remainder he divides by 15. The quotient is the number of the minutes of the dragon's head and tail.

If we would indulge in further quotations from the *canones* of the Hindus, we should entirely get away from
Page 242. the subject of the present book. Therefore we restrict ourselves to quote from them only subjects more or less connected with the special subject of this book, which either are noteworthy for their strangeness, or which are unknown among our people (the Muslims) and in our (the Muslim) countries.

# CHAPTER LVI.

## ON THE STATIONS OF THE MOON.

THE Hindus use the lunar stations exactly in the same way as the zodiacal signs. As the ecliptic is, by the zodiacal signs, divided into twelve equal parts, so, by the lunar stations, it is divided into twenty-seven equal parts. Each station occupies $13\frac{1}{3}$ degrees, or 800 minutes of the ecliptic. The planets enter into them and leave them again, and wander to and fro through their northern and southern latitudes. The astrologers attribute to each station a special nature, the quality of foreboding events, and other particular characteristic traits, in the same way as they attribute them to the zodiacal signs. On the twenty-seven lunar stations.

The number 27 rests on the fact that the moon passes through the whole ecliptic in $27\frac{1}{3}$ days, in which number the fraction of $\frac{1}{3}$ may be disregarded. In a similar way, the Arabs determine their lunar stations as beginning with the moon's first becoming visible in the west till her ceasing to be visible in the east. Herein they use the following method:— Lunar stations of the Arabs.

Add to the circumference the amount of the revolution of the sun in a lunar month. Subtract from the sum the march of the moon for the two days called *almiḥâḳ* (*i.e.* the 28th and 29th days of a lunation). Divide the remainder by the march of the moon for one day. The quotient is 27 and a little more than $\frac{2}{3}$, which fraction must be counted as a whole day.

However, the Arabs are illiterate people, who can neither write nor reckon. They only rely upon numbers and eyesight. They have no other medium of research than eyesight, and are not able to determine the lunar stations without the fixed stars in them. If the Hindus want to describe the single stations, they agree with the Arabs regarding certain stars, whilst regarding others they differ from them. On the whole, the Arabs keep near to the moon's path, and use, in describing the stations, only those fixed stars with which the moon either stands in conjunction at certain times, or through the immediate neighbourhood of which she passes.

Whether the Hindus have twenty-seven or twenty-eight lunar stations.

The Hindus do not strictly follow the same line, but also take into account the various positions of one star with reference to the other, *e.g.* one star's standing in opposition or in the zenith of another. Besides, they reckon also the Falling Eagle among the stations, so as to get 28.

It is this which has led our astronomers and the authors of *'anwâ* books astray; for they say that the Hindus have twenty-eight lunar stations, but that they leave out one which is always covered by the rays of the sun. Perhaps they may have heard that the Hindus call that station in which the moon is, the *burning one;* that station which it has just left, *the left one after the embrace;* and that station in which she will enter next, *the smoking one.* Some of our Muslim authors have maintained that the Hindus leave out the station *Al-zubânâ,* and account for it by declaring that the moon's path is *burning* in the end of Libra and the beginning of Scorpio.

All this is derived from one and the same source, viz. their opinion that the Hindus have twenty-eight stations, and that under certain circumstances they drop one. Whilst just the very opposite is the case; they have twenty-seven stations, and under certain circumstances add one.

A Vedic tradition from Brahmagupta.

Brahmagupta says that in the book of the *Veda* there is a tradition, derived from the inhabitants of Mount Meru, to this effect, that they see two suns, two moons, and fifty-four lunar stations, and that they have double the amount of days of ours. Then he tries to refute this theory by the argument that we do not see the fish (*sic*) of the pole revolve twice in a day, but only once. I for my part have no means of arraying this erroneous sentence in a reasonable shape.

The proper method for the computation of the place of a star or of a certain degree of a lunar station is this:— Method for computing the place of any given degree of a lunar station.

Take its distance from 0° Aries in minutes, and divide them by 800. The quotient represents whole stations preceding that station in which the star in question stands.

Then remains to be found the particular place within the station in question. Now, either star or degree is simply determined according to the 800 parts of the station, and reduced by a common denominator, or the degrees are reduced to minutes, or they are multiplied by 60 and the product is divided by 800, in which case the quotient represents that part of the station which the moon has in that moment already traversed, if the station is reckoned as $\frac{1}{60}$.

These methods of computation suit as well the moon as the planets and other stars. The following, however, applies exclusively to the moon:—The product of the multiplication of the remainder (*i.e.* the portion of the incomplete lunar station) by 60 is divided by the *bhukti* of the moon. The quotient shows how much of the lunar *nakshatra* day has elapsed.

The Hindus are very little informed regarding the fixed stars. I never came across any one of them who knew the single stars of the lunar stations from eyesight, and was able to point them out to me with his fingers. I have taken the greatest pains to investigate this subject, and to settle most of it by all sorts of comparisons, and have recorded the results of my research in a treatise *on the determination of the lunar stations.* Of their theories on this subject I shall mention as much as I think suitable in the present context. But before, that I shall give the positions of the stations in longitude and latitude and their numbers, according to the canon *Khaṇḍakhâdyaka*, facilitating the study of the subject by comprehending all details in the following table:— Table of the lunar stations taken from the *Khaṇḍakhâdyaka.*

Page 243.

| The number of the lunar stations. | The names of the lunar stations. | The number of their stars. | Longitude. | | | Latitude. | | Whether northern or southern latitude. | Notes on the stars of which the lunar stations consist. |
|---|---|---|---|---|---|---|---|---|---|
| | | | Zodiacal signs. | Degrees. | Minutes. | Parts. | Minutes. | | |
| 1 | Aśvinî | 2 | 0 | 8 | 0 | 10 | 0 | Northern | Alsharatân. |
| 2 | Bharaṇî | 3 | 0 | 20 | 0 | 12 | 0 | Northern | Albuṭain. |
| 3 | Kṛittikâ | 6 | 1 | 7 | 28 | 5 | 0 | Northern | Althurayyâ. |
| 4 | Rohiṇî | 5 | 1 | 19 | 28 | 5 | 0 | Southern | Aldabarân, together with the stars of the head of Taurus. |
| 5 | Mṛigaśîrsha | 3 | 2 | 3 | 0 | 5 | 0 | Southern | Alhaḳ'a. |
| 6 | Ârdrâ | 1 | 2 | 7 | 0 | 11 | 0 | Southern | Unknown. Most likely identical with Canis Minor. |
| 7 | Punarvasu | 2 | 3 | 3 | 0 | 6 | 0 | Northern | Aldhirâ'. |
| 8 | Pushya | 1 | 3 | 16 | 0 | 0 | 0 | Without any latitude | Alnathra. |
| 9 | Âślesha | 6 | 3 | 18 | 0 | 6 | 0 | Southern | Unknown. Most likely identical with two stars of Cancer and four stars outside of it. |
| 10 | Maghâ | 6 | 4 | 9 | 0 | 0 | 0 | Without any latitude | Aljabha, together with two other stars. |
| 11 | Pûrvaphâlgunî | 2 | 4 | 27 | 0 | 12 | 0 | Northern | Alzubra. |
| 12 | Uttaraphâlgunî | 2 | 5 | 5 | 0 | 13 | 0 | Northern | Alṣarfa, together with the third star of Alḍafîra. |

Page 244.

| | | | | | | | | | |
|---|---|---|---|---|---|---|---|---|---|
| 13 | Hasta | 5 | 5 | 20 | 0 | 11 | 0 | Southern | Consists of the stars of the Crow. |
| 14 | Citrâ | 1 | 6 | 3 | 0 | 2 | 0 | Southern | Alsimâk Al'a'zal. |
| 15 | Svâtî | 1 | 6 | 19 | 0 | 37 | 0 | Northern | Alsimâk Alrâmiḥ. |
| 16 | Viśâkhâ | 2 | 7 | 2 | 5 | 1 | 30 | Southern | Unknown. |
| 17 | Anurâdhâ | 4 | 7 | 14 | 5 | 3 | 0 | Southern | The Crown, together with another star. |
| 18 | Jyeshṭhâ | 3 | 7 | 19 | 5 | 4 | 0 | Southern | The heart of Scorpio, together with the pericardium. |
| 19 | Mûla | 2 | 8 | 1 | 0 | 9 | 30 | Southern | Alshaula. |
| 20 | Pûrvâshadhâ | 4 | 8 | 14 | 0 | 5 | 20 | Southern | Alna'âm Alwârid. |
| 21 | Uttarâshâḍhâ | 4 | 8 | 20 | 0 | 5 | 0 | Southern | Alna'âm Alṣâdir. |
| 22 / 0 | Abhijit | 3 | 8 | 25 | 0 | 62 | 0 | Northern | Alnasr Alwâḳi'. |
| 23 / 22 | Śravaṇa | 3 | 9 | 8 | 0 | 30 | 0 | Northern | Alnasr Alṭâ'ir. |
| 24 / 23 | Dhanishṭhâ | 5 | 9 | 20 | 0 | 36 | 0 | Northern | Unknown. Most likely it is the Dolphin. |
| 25 / 24 | Śatabhishaj | 1 | 10 | 20 | 0 | 0 | 18 | Southern | Unknown. Most likely identical with the upper part of the hip-joint of Aquarius. |
| 26 / 25 | Pûrvabhâdrapadâ | 2 | 10 | 26 | 0 | 24 | 0 | Northern | Unknown. |
| 27 / 26 | Uttarabhâdrapadâ | 2 | 11 | 6 | 0 | 26 | 0 | Northern | Most likely identical with the stars of Al'irs Al'a'zam. |
| 28 / 27 | Revati | 1 | 0 | 0 | 0 | 0 | 0 | Without any latitude | Unknown. Most likely identical with some of the stars of the Cotton Thread between the Two Fishes. |

The notions of the Hindus regarding the stars are not free from confusion. They are only little skilled in practical observation and calculation, and have no understanding of the motions of the fixed stars. So Varâhamihira says in his book *Saṁhitâ:* "In six stations, beginning with Revatî and ending with Mṛigaśiras, observation precedes calculation, so that the moon enters each one of them *earlier* according to eyesight than according to calculation.

On the precession of the equinoxes; quotation from Varâhamihira, chap. iv. 7.

"In twelve stations, beginning with Ârdrâ and ending with Anurâdhâ, the precession is equal to half a station, so that the moon is *in the midst* of a station according to observation, whilst she is in its first part according to calculation.

"In the nine stations, beginning with Jyeshṭhâ and ending with Uttarabhâdrapadâ, observation falls back behind calculation, so that the moon enters each of them according to observation, when, according to calculation, she leaves it in order to enter the following."

The author criticises Varâhamihira's statement.

My remark relating to the confused notions of the Hindus regarding the stars is confirmed, though this is perhaps not apparent to the Hindus themselves, *e.g.* by the note of Varâhamihira regarding *Alsharaṭân* = Aśvinî, one of the first-mentioned six stations; for he says that in it observation precedes calculation. Now the two stars of Aśvinî stand, in our time, in two-thirds of Aries (*i.e.* between 10°–20° Aries), and the time of Varâhamihira precedes our time by about 526 years. Therefore by whatever theory you may compute the motion of the fixed stars (or precession of the equinoxes), the Aśvinî did, in his time, certainly not stand in less than one-third of Aries (*i.e.* they had not come in the precession of the equinoxes farther than to 1°–10° Aries).

Supposing that, in *his* time, Aśvinî really stood in this part of Aries or near it, as is mentioned in the *Khaṇḍakhâdyaka*, which gives the computation of sun and moon in a perfectly correct form, we must state that at that time there was not yet known what is now known, viz. the retrograde motion of the star by the distance of eight degrees. How, therefore, could, in his time, observation precede calculation, since the moon, when standing in conjunction with the two stars, had already traversed nearly two-thirds of the first station? According to the same analogy, also, the other statements of Varâhamihira may be examined.

Each station occupies the same space on the ecliptic.

The stations occupy a smaller or larger space according to their figures, *i.e.* their constellations, not they themselves, for all stations occupy the same space on the ecliptic. This fact does not seem to be known to the Hindus, although we have already related similar notions of theirs regarding the Great Bear. For Brahmagupta says in the *Uttara-khaṇḍakhâdyâka*, *i.e.* the emendation of the *Khaṇḍa-khâdyaka*:—

Quotation from Brahmagupta.

"The measure of some stations exceeds the measure of the mean daily motion of the moon by one half. Accordingly their measure is 19° 45′ 52″ 18‴. There are six stations, viz. Rohiṇî, Punarvasu, Uttaraphalguni, Viśâkhâ, Uttarâshâḍhâ, Uttarabhâdrapadâ. These together occupy the space of 118° 35′ 13″ 48‴. Further six stations are short ones, each of them occupying less than the mean daily motion of the moon by one half. Accordingly their measure is 6° 35′ 17″ 26‴. These are Bharaṇî, Ârdrâ, Âśleshâ, Svâti, Jyeshṭhâ, Śatabhishaj. They together occupy the space of 39° 31′ 44″ 36‴. Of the remaining fifteen stations, each occupies as much as the mean daily motion. Accordingly it occupies the space of 13° 10′ 34″ 52‴. They together occupy the space of 197° 38′ 43″. These three groups of stations together occupy the space of 355° 45′ 41″ 24‴, the remainder of the complete circle 4° 14′ 18″ 36‴, and this is the space of *Abhijit*, *i.e.* the Falling Eagle, which is left out. I have tried to make the investigation of this subject acceptable to the student in my above-mentioned special treatise on the lunar stations (v. p. 83).

Quotation from Varâhamihira, *Saṁhitâ*, ch. iii. 1–3.

The scantiness of the knowledge of the Hindus regarding the motion of the fixed stars is sufficiently illustrated by the following passage from the *Saṁhitâ* of Varâhamihira:—"It has been mentioned in the books of the ancients that the summer solstice took place in the midst of Âśleshâ, and the winter solstice in Dhanishṭhâ. And this is correct for that time. Nowadays the summer solstice takes place in the beginning of Cancer, and the winter solstice in the beginning of Capricornus. If any one doubts this, and maintains that it is as the ancients have said and not as *we* say, let him go out to some level country when he thinks that the summer solstice is near. Let him there draw a circle, and place in its centre some body which stands perpendicular on the plain. Let him mark the end of its shadow by some sign, and continue the line till it reaches the circumference of the circle either in east or west. Let him repeat the same at the same moment of the following day, and make the same observation. When he then finds that the end of the shadow deviates from the first sign towards the south, he must know that the sun has moved towards the north and has not yet reached its solstice. But if he finds that the end of the shadow deviates towards the north, he knows that the sun has already commenced to move southward and has already passed its solstice. If a man continues this kind of observations, and thereby finds the day of the solstice, he will find that our words are true."

Page 246.

The author on the precession of the equinoxes.

This passage shows that Varâhamihira had no knowledge of the motion of the fixed stars towards the east. He considers them, in agreement with the name, as *fixed*, immovable stars, and represents the solstice as moving towards the west. In consequence of this fancy, he has, in the matter of the lunar stations, confounded two things, between which we shall now properly distinguish, in order to remove doubt and to give the matter in a critically emended form.

In the order of the zodiacal signs we begin with that twelfth part of the ecliptic which lies north of the point of intersection of the equator and the ecliptic according to *the second motion*, *i.e.* the precession of the equinoxes. In that case, the summer solstice always occurs at the beginning of the fourth sign, the winter solstice at the beginning of the tenth sign.

In the order of the lunar stations we begin with that twenty-seventh part of the ecliptic which belongs to the first of the first zodiacal sign. In that case the summer solstice falls always on three-fourths of the seventh station (*i.e.* on 600′ of the station), and the winter solstice on one fourth of the twenty-first station (*i.e.* on 200′ of the station). This order of things wil remain the same as long as the world lasts.

If, now, the lunar stations are marked by certain constellations, and are called by names peculiar to these constellations, the stations wander round together with the constellations. The stars of the zodiacal signs and of the stations have, in bygone times, occupied earlier (*i.e.* more western) parts of the ecliptic. From them they have wandered into those which they occupy at present, and in future they will wander into other still more eastern parts of the ecliptic, so that in the course of time they will wander through the whole ecliptic.

According to the Hindus, the stars of the station Âśleshâ stand in 18° of Cancer. Therefore, according to the rate of the precession of the equinoxes adopted by the ancient astronomers, they stood 1800 years before our time in the 0° of the fourth sign, whilst the constellation of Cancer stood in the third sign, in which there was also the solstice. The solstice has kept its place, but the constellations have migrated, just the very opposite of what Varâhamihira has fancied.

## CHAPTER LVII.

### ON THE HELIACAL RISINGS OF THE STARS, AND ON THE CEREMONIES AND RITES WHICH THE HINDUS PRACTISE AT SUCH A MOMENT.

How far a star must be distant from the sun in order to become visible.

THE Hindu method for the computation of the heliacal risings of the stars and the young moon is, as we think, the same as is explained in the *canones* called *Sindhind.* They call the degrees of a star's distance from the sun which are thought necessary for its heliacal rising *kâlâṁśaka.* They are, according to the author of the *Ghurrat-alzîjât*, the following:—13° for Suhail, Alyamâniya, Alwâḳi', Al'ayyûḳ, Alsimâkân, Ḳalb-al'aḳrab; 20° for Albuṭain, Alhaḳ'a, Alnathra, Âśleshâ, Śatabhishaj, Revatî; 14° for the others.

Page 247.

Evidently the stars have, in this respect, been divided into three groups, the first of which seems to comprise the stars reckoned by the Greeks as stars of the first and second magnitude, the second the stars of the third and fourth magnitude, and the third the stars of the fifth and sixth magnitude.

Brahmagupta ought to have given this classification in his emendation of the *Khaṇḍakhâdyaka*, but he has not done so. He expresses himself in general phrases, and simply mentions 14° distance from the sun as necessary for the heliacal risings of all lunar stations.

Quotation from Vijayanandin.

Vijayanandin says: "Some stars are not covered by the rays nor impaired in their shining by the sun, viz. Al'ayyûḳ, Alsimâk, Alrâmiḥ, the two Eagles, Dhanishṭhâ, and Uttarabhâdrapadâ, because they have so much northern latitude, and because also the country (of the observer) has so much latitude. For in the more northern regions they are seen both at the beginning and end of one and the same night, and never disappear."

On the heliacal rising of Canopus.

They have particular methods for the computation of the heliacal rising of Agastya, *i.e.* Suhail or Canopus. They observe it first when the sun enters the station Hasta, and they lose it out of sight when he enters the station Rohiṇî. Pulisa says: "Take double the apsis of the sun. If it is equalled by the corrected place of the sun, this is the time of the heliacal setting of Agastya."

The apsis of the sun is, according to Pulisa, $2\frac{2}{3}$ zodiacal signs. The double of it falls in 10° of Spica, which is the beginning of the station Hasta. Half the apsis falls on 10° of Taurus, which is the beginning of the station-Rohiṇî.

Quotation from Brahmagupta.

Brahmagupta maintains the following in the emendation of the *Khaṇḍakhâdyaka*:—

"The position of Suhail is 27° Orion, its southern latitude 71 parts. The degrees of its distance from the sun necessary for its heliacal rising are 12.

"The position of Mṛigavyâdha, *i.e.* Sirius Yemenicus, is 26° Orion, its southern latitude 40 parts. The degrees of its distance from the sun necessary for its heliacal rising are 13. If you want to find the time of their risings, imagine the sun to be in the place of the star. That amount of the day which has already elapsed is the number of degrees of its distance from the sun necessary for its heliacal rising. Fix the *ascendens* on this particular place. When, then, the sun reaches the degree of this *ascendens*, the star first becomes visible.

"In order to find the time of the heliacal setting of a star, add to the degree of the star six complete zodiacal signs. Subtract from the sum the degrees of its distance from the sun necessary for its heliacal rising, and fix the *ascendens* on the remainder. When, then, the sun enters the degree of the *ascendens*, that is the time of its setting."

On the ceremonies practised at the heliacal rising of certain stars.

The book *Saṁhitâ* mentions certain sacrifices and ceremonies which are practised at the heliacal risings of various stars. We shall now record them, translating also that which is rather chaff than wheat, since we have made it obligatory on ourselves to give the quotations from the books of the Hindus complete and exactly as they are.

Quotation from Varâhamihira's *Saṁhitâ*, ch. xii. preface, and vv. 1–18, on Canopus-Agastya and the sacrifice to him.

Varâhamihira says: "When in the beginning the sun had risen, and in his revolution had come to stand in the zenith of the towering mountain Vindhya, the latter would not recognise his exalted position, and, actuated by haughtiness, moved towards him to hinder his march and to prevent his chariot from passing above it. The Vindhya rose even to the neighbourhood of Paradise and the dwellings of the Vidyâdharas, the spiritual beings. Now the latter hastened to it because it was pleasant and its gardens and meadows were lovely, and dwelt there in joy; their wives going to and fro, and their children playing with each other. When the wind blew against the white garments of their daughters, they flew like waving banners.

In its ravines the wild animals and the lions appear as dark black, in consequence of the multitude of the animals called *bhramara*, which cling to them, liking the dirt of their bodies when they rub each other with the soiled claws. When they attack the rutting elephants, the latter become raving. The monkeys and bears are seen climbing up to the horns of Vindhya and to its lofty peaks; as if by instinct, they took the direction towards heaven. The anchorites are seen at its water-places, satisfied with nourishing themselves by its fruits. The further glorious things of the Vindhya are innumerable.

Page 248.

When, now, Agastya, the son of Varuṇa (*i.e.* Suhail,

the son of the water), had observed all these proceedings of the Vindhya, he offered to be his companion in his aspirations, and asked him to remain in his place until he (Agastya) should return and should have freed him (Vindhya) from the darkness which was on him.

V. 1.—Then Agastya turned towards the ocean, devouring its water, so that it disappeared. There appeared the lower parts of the mountain Vindhya, whilst the *makara* and the water animals were clinging to it. They scratched the mountain till they pierced it and dug mines in it, in which there remained gems and pearls.

V. 2.—The ocean became adorned by them, further by trees which grew up, though it (the water) was feeble, and by serpents rushing to and fro in windings on its surface.

V. 3.—The mountain has, in exchange for the wrong done to it by Suhail, received the ornament which it has acquired, whence the angels got tiaras and crowns made for themselves.

V. 4.—Likewise the ocean has, in exchange for the sinking down of its water into the depth, received the sparkling of the fishes when they move about in it, the appearance of jewels at its bottom, and the rushing to and fro of the serpents and snakes in the remainder of its water. When the fishes rise over it, and the conch-shells and pearl-oysters, you would take the ocean for ponds, the surface of their water being covered with the white lotus in the season of *śarad* and the season of autumn.

V. 5.—You could scarcely distinguish between this water and heaven, because the ocean is adorned with jewels as the heaven is adorned with stars; with many-headed serpents, resembling threads of rays which come from the sun; with crystal in it, resembling the body of the moon, and with a white mist, above which rise the clouds of heaven.

V. 6.—How should I not praise him who did this

great deed, who pointed out to the angels the beauty of the crowns, and made the ocean and the mountain Vindhya a treasure-house for them!

V. 7.—That is Suhail, by whom the water becomes clean from earthly defilement, with which the purity of the heart of the pious man is commingled, clean, I say, from that which overpowers him in the intercourse with the wicked.

V. 8.—Whenever Agastya rises and the water increases in the rivers and valleys during his time, you see the rivers offering to the moon all that is on the surface of their water, the various kinds of white and red lotus and the papyrus; all that swims in them, the ducks and the geese (pelicans ?), as a sacrifice unto him, even as a young girl offers roses and presents when she enters them (the rivers).

V. 9.—We compare the standing of the pairs of red geese on the two shores, and the swimming to and fro of the white ducks in the midst while they sing, to the two lips of a beautiful woman, showing her teeth when she laughs for joy.

V. 10.—Nay, we compare the black lotus, standing between white lotus, and the dashing of the bees against it from desire of the fragrancy of its smell, with the black of her pupil within the white of the ring, moving coquettishly and amorously, being surrounded by the hair of the eyebrows.

V. 11.—When you then see the ponds, when the light of the moon has risen over them, when the moon illuminates their dim waters, and when the white lotus opens which was shut over the bees, you would think them the face of a beautiful woman, who looks with a black eye from a white eyeball.

V. 12.—When a stream of the torrents of Varshakâla has flown to them with serpents, poison, and the impurities, the rising of Suhail above them cleans them from defilement and saves them from injury.

V. 13.—As one moment's thinking of Suhail before the door of a man blots out his sins deserving of punishment, how much more effective will be the fluency of the tongue praising him, when the task is to do away with sin and to acquire heavenly reward! The former Rishis have mentioned what sacrifice is necessary when Suhail rises. I shall make a present to the kings by relating it, and shall make this relation a sacrifice unto Him. So I say: Page 249.

V. 14.—His rising takes place at the moment when some of the light of the sun appears from the east, and the darkness of night is gathered in the west. The beginning of his appearance is difficult to perceive, and not every one who looks at him understands it. Therefore ask the astronomer at that moment about the direction whence it rises.

V. 15, 16.—Towards this direction offer the sacrifice called *argha*, and spread on the earth what you happen to have, roses and fragrant flowers as they grow in the country. Put on them what you think fit, gold, garments, jewels of the sea, and offer incense, saffron, and sandalwood, musk and camphor, together with an ox and a cow, and many dishes and sweetmeats.

V. 17.—Know that he who does this during seven consecutive years with pious intention, strong belief, and confidence, possesses at the end of them the whole earth and the ocean which surrounds it on the four sides, if he is a Kshatriya.

V. 18.—If he is a Brahman, he obtains his wishes, learns the Veda, obtains a beautiful wife, and gets noble children from her. If he is a Vaiśya, he obtains much landed property and acquires a glorious lordship. If he is a Śûdra, he will obtain wealth. All of them obtain health and safety, the cessation of injuries, and the realisation of reward."

This is Varâhamihira's statement regarding the offering

to Suhail. In the same book he gives also the rules regarding Rohiṇi:

Varâhamihira's *Saṁhitâ*, chap. xxiv. 1–37, on Rohiṇî.

"Garga, Vasishṭha, Kâśyapa, and Parâśara told their pupils that Mount Meru is built of planks of gold. Out of them there have risen trees with numerous sweet-swelling flowers and blossoms. The bees already surround them with a humming pleasant to hear, and the nymphs of the Devas wander there to and fro with exhilarating melodies, with pleasant instruments and everlasting joy. This mountain lies in the plain Nandanavana, the park of paradise. So they say. Jupiter was there at a time, and then Nârada the Ṛishi asked him regarding the prognostics of Rohiṇî, upon which Jupiter explained them to him. I shall here relate them as far as necessary.

V. 4.—Let a man in the black days of the month Âshâḍha observe if the moon reaches Rohiṇî. Let him seek to the north or east of the town a high spot. To this spot the Brahman must go who has the charge of the houses of the kings. He is to light there a fire and to draw a diagram of the various planets and lunar stations round it. He is to recite what is necessary for each one of them, and to give each its share of the roses, barley, and oil, and to make each planet propitious by throwing these things into the fire. Round the fire on all four sides there must be as much as possible of jewels and jugs filled with the sweetest water, and whatever else there happens to be at hand at the moment, fruits, drugs, branches of trees, and roots of plants. Further, he is to spread there grass which is cut with a sickle for his night-quarters. Then he is to take the different kinds of seeds and corns, to wash them with water, to put gold in the midst of them, and to deposit them in a jug. He is to place it towards a certain direction, and to prepare *Homa*, i.e. throwing barley and oil into the fire, at the same time reciting certain passages from the *Veda*, which refer to different directions, viz. Varuṇa-mantra, Vâyava-mantra, and Soma-mantra. Page 250.

He raises a *daṇḍa*, *i.e.* a long and high spear, from the top of which hang down two straps, the one as long as the spear, the other thrice as long. He must do all this before the moon reaches Rohiṇî, for this purpose, that when she reaches it, he should be ready to determine the times of the blowing of the wind as well as its directions. He learns this by means of the straps of the spear.

V. 10.—If the wind on that day blows from the centres of the four directions, it is considered propitious; if it blows from the directions between them, it is considered unlucky. If the wind remains steady in the same direction, powerful and without changing, this too is considered propitious. The time of its blowing is measured by the eight parts of the day, and each eighth part is considered as corresponding to the half of a month.

V. 11.—When the moon leaves the station Rohiṇî, you look at the seeds placed in a certain direction. That of them which sprouts will grow plentifully in that year.

V. 12.—When the moon comes near Rohiṇî, you must be on the look-out. If the sky is clear, not affected by any disturbance; if the wind is pure and does not cause a destructive commotion; if the melodies of the animals and birds are pleasant, this is considered propitious. We shall now consider the clouds.

V. 13, 14.—If they float like the branches of the valley (? *baṭn* ?), and out of them the flashes of lightning appear to the eye; if they open as opens the white lotus; if the lightning encircles the cloud like the rays of the sun; if the cloud has the colour of *stibium*, or of bees, or of saffron;

V. 15–19.—If the sky is covered with clouds, and out of them flashes the lightning like gold, if the rainbow shows its round form coloured with something like the red of evening twilight, and with colours like those of the garments of a bride; if the thunder roars like the screaming peacock, or the bird which cannot drink water except from falling rain, which then screams for joy, as the frogs enjoy the full water-places, so as to croak vehemently; if you see the sky raging like the raging of elephants and buffaloes in the thicket, in the various parts of which the fire is blazing; if the clouds move like the limbs of the elephants, if they shine like the shining of pearls, conch-shells, snow, and even as the moonbeams, as though the moon had lent the clouds her lustre and splendour;

V. 20.—All this indicates much rain and blessing by a rich growth.

V. 25.—At the time when the Brahman sits amidst the water-jugs, the falling of stars, the flashing of the lightning, thunderbolts, red glow in the sky, tornado, earthquake, the falling of hail, and the screaming of the wild animals, all these things are considered as unlucky.

V. 26.—If the water decreases in a jug on the north side, either by itself, or by a hole, or by dripping away, there will be no rain in the month Śrâvaṇa. If it decreases in a jug on the east side, there will be no rain in Bhâdrapada. If it decreases in a jug on the south side, there will be no rain in Âśvayuja; and if it decreases in a jug on the west side, there will be no rain in Kârttika. If there is no decrease of water in the jugs, the summer rain will be perfect.

V. 27.—From the jugs they also derive prognostics as to the different castes. The northern jug refers to the Brahman, the eastern to the Kshatriya, the southern to the Vaiśya, and the western to the Śûdra. If the names of people and certain circumstances are inscribed upon the jugs, all that happens to them if, *e.g.* they break or the water in them decreases, is considered as prognosticating something which concerns those persons or circumstances."

"The rules relating to the stations Svâtî and Śravaṇa are similar to those relating to Rohiṇî. When you are in the white days of the month Ashâḍha, when the moon stands in either of the two stations Ashâḍhâ, *i.e.* Pûrva-ashâḍhâ or Uttara-ashâḍhâ, select a spot as you have selected it for Rohiṇî, and take a balance of gold. That is the best. If it is of silver, it is middling. If it is not of silver, make it of wood called *khayar*, which seems to be the *khadira* tree (*i.e.* Acacia catechu), or of the head of an arrow with which already a man has been killed. The smallest measure for the length of its beam is a span. The longer it is, the better; the shorter it is, the less favourable.

*Saṁhitâ*, chap. xxv. v. 1., on Svâtî and Śravaṇa.

Page 251.

*Saṁhitâ*, chap. xxvi. v. 9.

V. 6.—A scale has four strings, each 10 digits long. Its two scales are of linen cloth of the size of 6 digits. Its two weights are of gold.

V. 7, 8.—Weigh by it equal quantities of each matter, water of the wells, of the ponds, and of the rivers, elephants' teeth, the hair of horses, pieces of gold with the names of kings written on them, and pieces of other metal over which the names of other people, or the names of animals, years, days, directions, or countries have been pronounced.

V. 1.—In weighing, turn towards the east; put the weight in the right scale, and the things which are to be weighed in the left. Recite over them and speak to the balance:

V. 2.—'Thou art correct; thou art Deva, and the wife of a Deva. Thou art Sarasvatî, the daughter of Brahman. Thou revealest the right and the truth. Thou art more correct than the soul of correctness.

V. 3.—Thou art like the sun and the planets in their wandering from east to west on one and the same road.

V. 4.—Through thee stands upright the order of the

world, and in thee is united the truth and the correctness of all the angels and Brahmans.

V. 5.—Thou art the daughter of Brahman, and a man of thy house is Kaśyapa.'

V. 1.—This weighing must take place in the evening. Then put the things aside, and repeat their weighing the next morning. That which has increased in weight will flourish and thrive in that year; that which has decreased will be bad and go back.

This weighing, however, is not only to be done in Ashâḍhâ, but also in Rohiṇî and Svâti.

V. 11.—If the year is a leap-year, and the weighing happens to take place in the repeated month, the weighing is in that year twice done.

V. 12.—If the prognostics are identical, what they forebode will happen. If they were not identical, observe the prognostics of Rohiṇî, for it is predominant."

# CHAPTER LVIII.

## HOW EBB AND FLOW FOLLOW EACH OTHER IN THE OCEAN.

Quotation from the *Matsya-Puráṇa.*

WITH regard to the cause why the water of the ocean always remains as it is, we quote the following passage from the *Matsya-Purâṇa*:—"At the beginning there were sixteen mountains, which had wings and could fly and rise up into the air. However, the rays of Indra, the ruler, burned their wings, so that they fell down, deprived of them, somewhere about the ocean, four of them in each point of the compass—in the east, Ṛishabha, Balâhaka, Cakra, Mainâka; in the north, Candra, Kaṅka, Droṇa, Suhma; in the west, Vakra, Vadhra, Nârada, Parvata; in the south, Jîmûta, Draviṇa, Mainâka, Mahâśaila (?). Between the third and the fourth of the eastern mountains there is the fire *Saṁvartaka*, which drinks the water of the ocean. But for this the ocean would fill up, since the rivers perpetually flow to it.

Story of King Aurva.

"This fire was the fire of one of their kings, called *Aurva*. He had inherited the realm from his father, who was killed while he was still an embryo. When he was born and grew up, and heard the history of his father, he became angry against the angels, and drew his sword to kill them, since they had neglected the guardianship of the world, notwithstanding mankind's worshipping them and notwithstanding their being in close contact with the world. Thereupon the angels humiliated themselves before him and tried to conciliate him, so that he ceased from his wrath. Then he spoke to them: 'But what am I to do with the fire of my wrath?' and they advised him to throw it into the ocean. It is this fire which absorbs the waters of the ocean. Others say: 'The water of the streams does not Page 252. increase the ocean, because Indra, the ruler, takes up the ocean in the shape of the cloud, and sends it down as rains.'"

The man in the moon.

Again the *Matsya-Purâṇa* says: "The black part in the moon which is called *Śaśalaksha*, *i.e.* the hare's figure, is the image of the figures of the above-mentioned sixteen mountains reflected by the light of the moon on her body."

The *Vishṇu-Dharma* says: "The moon is called Śaśalaksha, for the globe of her body is watery, reflecting the figure of the earth as a mirror reflects. On the earth there are mountains and trees of different shapes, which are reflected in the moon as a hare's figure. It is also called *Mṛigalâñcana*, *i.e.* the figure of a gazelle, for certain people compare the black part on the moon's face to the figure of a gazelle."

Story of the leprosy of the moon.

The lunar stations they declare to be the daughters of Prajâpati, to whom the moon is married. He was especially attached to Rohiṇi, and preferred her to the others. Now her sisters, urged by jealousy, complained of him to their father Prajâpati. The latter strove to keep peace among them, and admonished him, but without any success. Then he cursed the moon (*Lunus*), in consequence of which his face became leprous. Now the moon repented of his doing, and came penitent to Prajâpati, who spoke to him: "My word is one, and cannot be cancelled; however, I shall cover thy shame for the half of each month." Thereupon the moon spoke to Prajâpati: "But how shall the trace of the sin of the past be wiped off from me?" Prajâpati answered: "By erecting the shape of the *liṅga* of Mahâdeva as an object of thy worship." This he did. The *liṅga* he raised was the stone of Somanâth, for *soma* means the moon and *nâtha* means *master*, so that the whole word means *master of the moon*. The image was destroyed by the Prince Maḥmûd — may God be merciful to him! — A.H. 416. He ordered the upper part to be broken and the remainder to be transported to his residence, Ghaznin, with all its coverings and trappings of gold, jewels, and embroidered garments. Part of it has been thrown into the hippodrome of the town, together with the *Cakrasvâmin*, an idol of bronze, that had been brought from Tâneshar. Another part of the idol from Somanâth lies before the door of the mosque of Ghaznin, on which people rub their feet to clean them from dirt and wet.

The idol of Somanâth.

The *liṅga* is an image of the penis of Mahâdeva. I have heard the following story regarding it :—"A Ṛishi, on seeing Mahâdeva with his wife, became suspicious of him, and cursed him that he should lose his penis. At once his penis dropped, and was as if wiped off. But afterwards the Ṛishi was in a position to establish the signs of his innocence and to confirm them by the necessary proofs. The suspicion which had troubled his mind was removed, and he spoke to him: 'Verily, I shall recompense thee by making the image of the limb which thou hast lost the object of worship for men, who thereby will find the road to God, and come near him.'"

Origin of the Liṅga.

Varâhamihira says about the construction of the *liṅga*: "After having chosen a faultless stone for it, take it as long as the image is intended to be. Divide it into three parts. The lowest part of it is quadrangular, as if it were a cube or quadrangular column. The middle part is octagonal, its surface being divided by four pilasters. The upper third is round, rounded off so as to resemble the gland of a penis.

The construction of the Liṅga according to Varâhamihira. *Bṛihatsaṁhitâ*, chap. lviii. 53.

V. 54.—In erecting the figure, place the quadrangular third within the earth, and for the octagonal third make a cover, which is called *piṇḍa*, quadrangular from without, but so as to fit also on the quadrangular third in the earth. The octagonal form of the inner side is to fit on to the middle third, which projects out

Page 253.]

of the earth. The round third alone remains without cover."

Further he says:—

V. 55.—"If you make the round part too small or too thin, it will hurt the country and bring about evil among the inhabitants of the regions who have constructed it. If it does not go deep enough down into the earth, or if it projects too little out of the earth,

Chapter lx.; v. 6.

this causes people to fall ill. When it is in the course of construction, and is struck by a peg, the ruler and his family will perish. If on the transport it is hit, and the blow leaves a trace on it, the artist will perish, and destruction and diseases will spread in that country."

The worship of the idol of Somanâth.

In the south-west of the Sindh country this idol is frequently met with in the houses destined for the worship of the Hindus, but Somanâth was the most famous of these places. Every day they brought there a jug of Ganges water and a basket of flowers from Kashmîr. They believed that the *liṅga* of Somanâth would cure persons of every inveterate illness and heal every desperate and incurable disease.

The reason why in particular Somanâth has become so famous is that it was a harbour for seafaring people, and a station for those who went to and fro between Sufâla in the country of the Zanj and China.

Popular belief about the cause of the tides.

Now as regards ebb and flow in the Indian Ocean, of which the former is called *bharṇa* (?), the latter *vuhara* (?), we state that, according to the notions of the common Hindus, there is a fire called *Vaḍavânala* in the ocean, which is always blazing. The flow is caused by the fire's drawing breath and its being blown up by the wind, and the ebb is caused by the fire's exhaling the breath and the cessation of its being blown up by the wind.

Mânî has come to a belief like this, after he had heard from the Hindus that there is a demon in the sea whose drawing breath and exhaling breath causes the flow and the ebb.

The educated Hindus determine the daily phases of the tides by the rising and setting of the moon, the monthly phases by the increase and waning of the moon; but the physical cause of both phenomena is not understood by them.

It is flow and ebb to which Somanâth owes its name (*i.e.* master of the moon); for the stone (or *liṅga*) of Somanâth was originally erected on the coast, a little less than three miles west of the mouth of the river Sarsutî, east of the golden fortress Bârôi, which had appeared as a dwelling-place for Vâsudeva, not far from the place where he and his family were killed, and where they were burned. Each time when the moon rises and sets, the water of the ocean rises in the flood so as to cover the place in question. When, then, the moon reaches the meridian of noon and midnight, the water recedes in the ebb, and the place becomes again visible. Thus the moon was perpetually occupied in serving the idol and bathing it. Therefore the place was considered as sacred to the moon. The fortress which contained the idol and its treasures was not ancient, but was built only about a hundred years ago. Origin of the sacredness of Somanâth.

The *Vishṇu-Purâṇa* says: "The greatest height of the water of the flow is 1500 digits." This statement seems rather exaggerated; for if the waves and the mean height of the ocean rose to between sixty to seventy yards, the shores and the bays would be more overflown than has ever been witnessed. Still this is not entirely improbable, as it is not in itself impossible on account of some law of nature. Quotation from the *Vishṇu-Purâṇa.*

The fact that the just-mentioned fortress is said to

The golden fortress Bârôi. Parallel of the Maledives and Laccadives. Page 254.

have appeared out of the ocean is not astonishing for that particular part of the ocean; for the Dîbajât islands (Maledives and Laccadives) originate in a similar manner, rising out of the ocean as sand-downs. They increase, and rise, and extend themselves, and remain in this condition for a certain time. Then they become decrepit as if from old age; the single parts become dissolved, no longer keep together, and disappear in the water as if melting away. The inhabitants of the islands quit that one which apparently dies away, and migrate to a young and fresh one which is about to rise above the ocean. They take their cocoanut palms along with them, colonise the new island, and dwell on it.

That the fortress in question is called *golden* may only be a conventional epithet. Possibly, however, this object is to be taken literally, for the islands of the Zâbaj are called the *Gold Country* (*Suvarṇadvîpa*), because you obtain much gold as deposit if you wash only a little of the earth of that country.

# CHAPTER LIX.

## ON THE SOLAR AND LUNAR ECLIPSES.

It is perfectly known to the Hindu astronomers that the moon is eclipsed by the shadow of the earth, and the sun is eclipsed by the moon. Hereon they have based their computations in the astronomical handbooks and other works.

Varâhamihira says in the *Saṁhitâ*:—

Quotation from Varâhamihira's *Saṁhitâ*, ch. v.

V. 1.—"Some scholars maintain that the *Head* belonged to the Daityas, and that his mother was Siṁhikâ. After the angels had fetched the *amṛita* out of the ocean, they asked Vishṇu to distribute it among them. When he did so, the Head also came, resembling the angels in shape, and associated himself with them. When Vishṇu handed him a portion of the *amṛita*, he took and drank it. But then Vishṇu perceived who it was, hit him with his round *cakra*, and cut off his head. However, the head remained alive on account of the *amṛita* in its mouth, whilst the body died, since it had not yet partaken of the *amṛita*, and the force of the latter had not yet spread through it. Then the Head, humbling itself, spoke: 'For what sin has this been done?' Thereupon he was recompensed by being raised to heaven and by being made one of its inhabitants.

V. 2.—Others say that the Head has a body like sun and moon, but that it is black and dark, and cannot therefore be seen in heaven. Brahman, the first father, ordered that he should never appear in heaven except at the time of an eclipse.

V. 3.—Others say that he has a head like that of a serpent, and a tail like that of a serpent, whilst others say that he has no other body besides the black colour which is seen."

After having finished the relation of these absurdities, Varâhamihira continues:—

V. 4.—"If the Head had a body, it would act by immediate contact, whilst we find that he eclipses from a distance, when between him and the moon there is an interval of six zodiacal signs. Besides, his motion does not increase nor decrease, so that we cannot imagine an eclipse to be caused by his body reaching the spot of the lunar eclipse.

V. 5.—And if a man commits himself to such a view, let him tell us for what purpose the cycles of the Head's rotation have been calculated, and what is the use of their being correct in consequence of the fact that his rotation is a regular one. If the Head is imagined to be a serpent with head and tail, why does it not eclipse from a distance less or more than six zodiacal signs?

V. 6.—His body is there present between head and tail; both hang together by means of the body. Still it does not eclipse sun nor moon nor the fixed stars of the lunar stations, there being an eclipse only if there are two heads opposed to each other.

V. 7.—If the latter were the case, and the moon rose, being eclipsed by one of the two, the sun would necessarily set, being eclipsed by the other. Likewise,
Page 235. if the moon should set eclipsed, the sun would rise eclipsed. And nothing of the kind ever occurs.

V. 8.—As has been mentioned by scholars who enjoy the help of God, an eclipse of the moon is her entering the shadow of the earth, and an eclipse of the sun consists in this that the moon covers and hides the sun from us. Therefore the lunar eclipse will never revolve from the west nor the solar eclipse from the east.

V. 9.—A long shadow stretches away from the earth, in like manner as the shadow of a tree.

V. 10.—When the moon has only little latitude, standing in the seventh sign of its distance from the sun, and if it does not stand too far north or south, in that case the moon enters the shadow of the earth and is eclipsed thereby. The first contact takes place on the side of the east.

V. 11.—When the sun is reached by the moon from the west, the moon covers the sun, as if a portion of a cloud covered him. The amount of the covering differs in different regions.

V. 12.—Because that which covers the moon is large, her light wanes when one-half of it is eclipsed; and because that which covers the sun is not large, the rays are powerful notwithstanding the eclipse.

V. 13.—The nature of the Head has nothing whatever to do with the lunar and solar eclipses. On this subject the scholars in their books agree."

After having described the nature of the two eclipses, as *he* understands them, he complains of those who do not know this, and says: "However, common people are always very loud in proclaiming the Head to be the cause of an eclipse, and they say, 'If the Head did not appear and did not bring about the eclipse, the Brahmans would not at that moment undergo an obligatory washing.'"

Varâhamihira says:—

V. 14.—"The reason of this is that the head humiliated itself after it had been cut off, and received from Brahman a portion of the offering which the Brahmans offer to the fire at the moment of an eclipse.

V. 15.—Therefore he is near the spot of the eclipse, searching for his portion. Therefore at that time people mention him frequently, and consider him as the cause of the eclipse, although he has nothing whatsoever to do with it; for the eclipse depends entirely upon the uniformity and the declination of the orbit of the moon."

Praise of Varâhamihira.

The latter words of Varâhamihira, who, in passages quoted previously, has already revealed himself to us as a man who accurately knows the shape of the world, are odd and surprising. However, he seems sometimes to side with the Brahmans, to whom he belonged, and from whom he could not separate himself. Still he does not deserve to be blamed, as, on the whole, his foot stands firmly on the basis of the truth, and he clearly speaks out the truth. Compare, *e.g.* his statement regarding the *Samdhi*, which we have mentioned above (v. i. 366).

Strictures on Brahmagupta's want of sincerity.

Would to God that all distinguished men followed his example! But look, for instance, at Brahmagupta, who is certainly the most distinguished of their astronomers. For as he was one of the Brahmans who read in their Purâṇas that the sun is lower than the moon, and who therefore require a head biting the sun in order that he should be eclipsed, he shirks the truth and lends his support to imposture, if he did not—and this we think by no means impossible—from intense disgust at them, speak as he spoke simply in order to mock them, or under the compulsion of some mental derangement, like a man whom death is about to rob of his consciousness. The words in question are found in the first chapter of his *Brahmasiddhânta*:—

Quotation from the *Brahmasiddhânta*.

"Some people think that the eclipse is not caused by the Head. This, however, is a foolish idea, for it is *he* in fact who eclipses, and the generality of the inhabitants of the world say that it is the Head who eclipses. (Page 256.) The *Veda*, which is the word of God from the mouth of Brahman, says that the Head eclipses, likewise the book *Smṛiti*, composed by Manu, and the *Saṁhitâ*, composed by Garga the son of Brahman. On the contrary, Varâhamihira, Śrishena, Âryabhaṭa, and Vishṇucandra maintain that the eclipse is not caused by the Head, but by the moon and the shadow of the earth, in direct opposition to all (to the generality of men), and from enmity against the just-mentioned dogma. For if the Head does not cause the eclipse, all the usages of the Brahmans which they practise at the moment of an eclipse, viz. their rubbing themselves with warm oil, and other works of prescribed worship, would be illusory and not be rewarded by heavenly bliss. If a man declares these things to be illusory, he stands outside of the generally acknowledged dogma, and that is not allowed. Manu says in the *Smṛiti:* 'When the Head keeps the sun or moon in eclipse, all waters on earth become pure, and in purity like the water of the Ganges.' The *Veda* says: 'The Head is the son of a woman of the daughters of the Daityas, called *Sainakâ*' (? Siṁhikâ ?). Therefore people practise the well-known works of piety, and therefore those authors must cease to oppose the generality, for everything which is in the *Veda, Smṛiti,* and *Saṁhitâ* is true."

If Brahmagupta, in this respect, is one of those of whom God says (*Koran,* Sûra xxvii. 14), "*They have denied our signs, although their hearts knew them clearly, from wickedness and haughtiness,*" we shall not argue with him, but only whisper into his ear: If people must under circumstances give up opposing the religious codes (as seems to be your case), why then do you order people to be pious if you forget to be so yourself? Why do you, after having spoken such words, then begin to calculate the diameter of the moon in order to explain her eclipsing the sun, and the diameter of the shadow of the earth in order to explain its eclipsing the moon? Why do you compute both eclipses in agreement with the theory of those heretics, and not according to the views of those with whom you think it proper to agree? If the Brahmans are ordered to practise some act of worship or something else at the occurrence of an eclipse, the eclipse is only *the date* of these things, not *their cause.* Thus we Muslims are bound to say certain prayers, and prohibited from saying others, at certain times of the revolution of the sun and his light. These things are simply chronological dates for those acts, nothing more, for the sun has nothing whatever to do with our (Muslim) worship.

Brahmagupta says (ii. 110), "The generality thinks thus." If he thereby means the totality of the inhabitants of the inhabitable world, we can only say that he would be very little able to investigate *their* opinions either by exact research or by means of historical tradition. For India itself is, in comparison to the whole inhabitable world, only a small matter, and the number of those who differ from the Hindus, both in religion and law, is larger than the number of those who agree with them.

Possible excuses for Brahmagupta.

Or if Brahmagupta means *the generality of the Hindus,* we agree that the uneducated among them are much more numerous than the educated; but we also point out that in all our religious codes of divine revelation the uneducated crowd is blamed as being ignorant, always doubting, and ungrateful.

I, for my part, am inclined to the belief that that which made Brahmagupta speak the above-mentioned words (which involve a sin against conscience) was something of a calamitous fate, like that of Socrates, which had befallen him, notwithstanding the abundance of his knowledge and the sharpness of his intel-

Page 257.

lect, and notwithstanding his extreme youth at the time. For he wrote the *Brahmasiddhânta* when he was only thirty years of age. If this indeed is his excuse, we accept it, and herewith drop the matter.

As for the above-mentioned people (the Hindu theologians), from whom you must take care not to differ, how should they be able to understand the astronomical theory regarding the moon's eclipsing the sun, as they, in their Purâṇas, place the moon *above* the sun, and that which is higher cannot cover that which is lower in the sight of those who stand lower than both. Therefore they required some being which devours moon and sun, as the fish devours the bait, and causes them to appear in those shapes in which the eclipsed parts of them in reality appear. However, in each nation there are ignorant people, and leaders still more ignorant than they themselves, who (as the Koran, Sura xxix. 12, says) "*bear their own burdens and other burdens besides them*," and who think they can increase the light of their minds; the fact being that the masters are as ignorant as the pupils.

Quotations from Varâhamihira's *Saṁhitâ*, chap. v. 17, 16, 63.

Very odd is that which Varâhamihira relates of certain ancient writers, to whom we must pay no attention if we do not want to oppose them, viz. that they tried to prognosticate the occurrence of an eclipse by pouring a small amount of water together with the same amount of oil into a large vase with a flat bottom on the eighth of the lunar days. Then they examined the spots where the oil was united and dispersed. The united portion they considered as a prognostication for the beginning of the eclipse, the dispersed portion as a prognostication for its end.

Further, Varâhamihira says that somebody used to think that the conjunction of the planets is the cause of the eclipse (V. 16), whilst others tried to prognosticate an eclipse from unlucky phenomena, as, *e.g.* the falling of stars, comets, halo, darkness, hurricane, landslip, and earthquake. "These things," so he says, "are not always contemporary with an eclipse, nor are they its cause; the nature of an unlucky event is the only thing which these occurrences have in common with an eclipse. A reasonable explanation is totally different from such absurdities."

The same man, knowing only too well the character

of his countrymen, who like to mix up peas with wolf's beans, pearls with dung, says, without quoting any authority for his words (V. 63): "If at the time of an eclipse a violent wind blows, the next eclipse will be six months later. If a star falls down, the next eclipse will be twelve months later. If the air is dusty, it will be eighteen months later. If there is an earthquake, it will be twenty-four months later. If the air is dark, it will be thirty months later. If hail falls, it will be thirty-six months later."

To such things silence is the only proper answer.

On the colours of the eclipses.

I shall not omit to mention that the different kinds of eclipses described in the canon of Alkhwârizmî, though correctly represented, do not agree with the results of actual observation. More correct is a similar view of the Hindus, viz. that the eclipse has the colour of smoke if it covers less than half the body of the moon; that it is coal-black if it completely covers one half of her; that it has a colour between black and red if the eclipse covers more than half of her body; and, lastly, that it is yellow-brown if it covers the whole body of the moon.

# CHAPTER LX.

## ON THE PARVAN.

Page 258.

Explanation of the term *parvan*.

THE intervals between which an eclipse may happen and the number of their lunations are sufficiently demonstrated in the sixth chapter of Almagest. The Hindus call a period of time at the beginning and end of which there occur lunar eclipses, *parvan*. The following information on the subject is taken from the *Saṁhitâ*. Its author, Varâhamihira, says: "Each six months form a *parvan*, in which an eclipse may happen. These eclipses form a cycle of seven, each of which has a particular *dominant* and prognostics, as exhibited in the following table:

Quotation from Varâhamihira's *Saṁhitâ*, chap. v. 19–23.

| Number of the Parvans. | 1 | 2 | 3 | 4 | 5 | 6 | 7 |
|---|---|---|---|---|---|---|---|
| Dominants of the Parvans. | Brahman. | Śaśin, *i.e.* the Moon. | Indra, the Ruler. | Kubera, the Protector of the North. | Varuṇa, the Protector of the Water. | Agni, the Fire, also called Mitrâkhya. | Yama, the Angel of Death. |
| Their prognostics. | Favourable to the Brahmans; the cattle is thriving, the crops are flourishing, and there is general well-being and safety. | The same as in the first Parvan, but rain is scarce in it, and scholars are ill. | The kings become estranged from each other, safety declines, and the autumnal crops are ruined. | There is abundance and wealth; rich people ruin their property. | Not favourable to kings, but favourable to others; the crops are flourishing. | There is much water, fine crops, general well-being and safety; pestilence and mortality are declining. | Rain is scarce, the crops perish, and this leads to famine. |

Rules for the computation of the *parvan* from the *Khaṇḍakhâdyaka*.

The computation of the *parvan* in which you happen to be is the following, according to the *Khaṇḍakhâdyaka:* "Write down the *ahargaṇa*, as computed according to this canon, in two places. Multiply the one by 50, and divide the product by 1296, reckoning a fraction, if it is not less than one-half, as a whole. Add to the quotient 1063. Add the sum to the number written in the second place, and divide the sum by 180. The quotient, as consisting of wholes, means the number of complete *parvans*. Divide it by 7, and the remainder under 7 which you get means the distance of the particular *parvan* from the first one, *i.e.* from that of Brahman. However, the remainder under 180 which you get by the division is the elapsed part of the *parvan* in which

Page 259.

you are. You subtract it from 180. If the remainder is less than 15, a lunar eclipse is possible or necessary; if the remainder is larger, it is impossible. Therefore you must always by a similar method compute that time which has elapsed before the particular *parvan* in which you happen to be."

In another passage of the book we find the following rule: "Take the *kalpa-ahargaṇa, i.e.* the past portion of the days of a *kalpa.* Subtract therefrom 96,031, and write down the remainder in two different places. Subtract from the lower number 84, and divide the sum by 561. Subtract the quotient from the upper number and divide the remainder by 173. The quotient you disregard, but the remainder you divide by 7. The quotient gives *parvans*, beginning with *Brahmâdi*" (sic).

These two methods do not agree with each other. We are under the impression that in the second passage something has either fallen out or been changed by the copyists.

Quotation from Varâhamihira's *Saṃhitâ*, chap. v. 23.

What Varâhamihira says of the astrological portents of the *parvans* does not well suit his deep learning. He says: "If in a certain *parvan* there is no eclipse, but there is one in the other cycle, there are no rains, and there will be much hunger and killing." If in this passage the translator has not made a blunder, we can only say that this description applies to each *parvan* preceding such a one in which there occurs an eclipse.

Stranger still is the following remark of his (V. 24): "If an eclipse occurs earlier than has been calculated, there is little rain and the sword is drawn. If it occurs later than has been calculated, there will be pestilence, and death, and destruction in the corn, the fruit, and flowers. (V. 25.) This is part of what I have found in the books of the ancients and transferred to this place. If a man properly knows how to calculate, it will not happen to him in his calculations that an eclipse falls too early or too late. If the sun is eclipsed Chap. iii. v. 6.
and darkened outside a *parvan*, you must know that an angel called Tvashṭṛi has eclipsed him."

Similar to this is what he says in another passage: "If the turning to the north takes place before the sun Ibid. v. 4. 5.
enters the sign Capricornus, the south and the west will be ruined. If the turning to the south takes place before the sun enters Cancer, the east and the north will be ruined. If the turning coincides with the sun's entering the first degrees of these two signs, or takes place after it, happiness will be common to all four sides, and bliss in them will increase."

Such sentences, understood as they seem intended to be understood, sound like the ravings of a madman, but perhaps there is an esoteric meaning concealed behind them which we do not know.

After this we must continue to speak of the *domini temporum*, for these too are of a cyclical nature, adding such materials as are related to them.

# CHAPTER LXI.

## ON THE DOMINANTS OF THE DIFFERENT MEASURES OF TIME IN BOTH RELIGIOUS AND ASTRONOMICAL RELATIONS, AND ON CONNECTED SUBJECTS.

Which of the different measures of time have dominants and which not.

DURATION, or time in general, only applies to the Creator as being *his* age, and not determinable by a beginning and an end. In fact, it is his eternity. They frequently call it *the soul*, i.e. *purusha*. But as regards common time, which is determinable by motion, the single parts of it apply to beings beside the Creator, and to natural phenomena beside *the soul*. Thus *kalpa* is always used in relation to Brahman, for it is his day and night, and his life is determined by it.

Page 260.

Each *manvantara* has a special dominant called *Manu*, who is described by special qualities, already mentioned in a former chapter. On the other hand, I have never heard anything of dominants of the *caturyugas* or *yugas*.

Varâhamihira says in the *Great Book of Nativities:* "*Abda, i.e.* the year, belongs to Saturn; *Ayana*, half a year, to the sun; *Ṛitu*, the sixth part of a year, to Mercury; *the month*, to Jupiter; *Paksha*, half a month, to Venus; *Vâsara*, the day, to Mars; *Muhûrta*, to the moon."

In the same book he defines the sixth parts of the year in the following manner: "The first, beginning with the winter solstice, belongs to Saturn; the second, to Venus; the third, to Mars; the fourth, to the Moon the fifth, to Mercury; the sixth, to Jupiter."

We have already, in former chapters, described the dominants of the hours, of the *muhûrtas*, of the halves of the lunar days, of the single days in the white and black halves of the month, of the *parvans* of the eclipses, and of the single *manvantaras*. What there is more of the same kind we shall give in this place.

Computation of the dominant of the year according to the Khaṇḍakhâdyaka.

In computing the *dominant of the year*, the Hindus use another method than the Western nations, who compute it, according to certain well-known rules, from the *ascendens* or horoscope of a year. The dominant of the year as well as the dominant of the month are the rulers of certain periodically recurring parts of time, and are by a certain calculation derived from the *dominants of the hours* and the *dominants of the days*.

If you want to find the dominant of the year, compute the sum of days of the date in question according to the rules of the canon *Khaṇḍakhâdyaka*, which is the most universally used among them. Subtract therefrom 2201, and divide the remainder by 360. Multiply the quotient by 3, and add to the product always 3. Divide the sum by 7. The remainder, a number under 7, you count off on the week-days, beginning with Sunday. The dominant of that day you come to is at the same time *the dominant of the year*. The remainders you get by the division are the days of his rule which have already elapsed. These, together with the days of his rule which have not yet elapsed, give the sum of 360.

It is the same whether we reckon as we have just explained, or add to the here-mentioned sum of days 319, instead of subtracting from it.

How to find the dominant of the month.

If you want to find the *dominant of the month*, subtract 71 from the sum of days of the date in question, and divide the remainder by 30. Double the quotient and add 1. The sum divide by 7, and the remainder count off on the week-days, beginning with Sunday. The dominant of the day you come to is at the same time the dominant of the month. The remainder you get by the division is that part of his rule which has already elapsed. This, together with that part of his rule which has not yet elapsed, gives the sum of 30 days.

It is the same whether you reckon as we have just explained, or add 19 to the days of the date, instead of subtracting from them, and then add 2 instead of 1 to the double of the sum.

It is useless here to speak of the dominant of the day, for you find it by dividing the sum of the days of a date by 7; or to speak of the dominant of the hour, for you find it by dividing the revolving sphere by 15. Those, however, who use the ὥραι καιρικαί divide by 15 the distance between the degree of the sun and the degree of the *ascendens*, it being measured by equal degrees.

Page 261.

Quotation from *Mahâdeva*.

The book *Srûdhara* of *Mahâdeva* says: "Each of the thirds of the day and night has a dominant. The dominant of the first third of day and night is Brahman, that of the second Vishnu, and that of the third Rudra." This division is based on the order of the three primeval forces (*satva, rajas, tamas*).

The *Nâgas* in connection with the planets.

The Hindus have still another custom, viz. that of mentioning together with the dominant of the year one of the *Nâgas* or serpents, which have certain names as they are used in connection with one or other of the planets. We have united them in the following table:—

| Table of the serpents. | | |
|---|---|---|
| The dominant of the year. | The names of the serpents which accompany the *Dominus Anni*, given in two different forms. | |
| Sun. | Suka (? Vâsuki), | Nanda. |
| Moon. | Pushkara, | Citrâṅgada. |
| Mars. | Piṇḍâraka, Bharma (?), | Takshaka. |
| Mercury. | Cabrahasta (?), | Karkoṭa. |
| Jupiter. | Elâpatra, | Padma. |
| Venus. | Karkoṭaka, | Mahâpadma. |
| Saturn. | Cakshabbhadra (?), | Śaṅkha. |

The Hindus combine the planets with the sun because they depend upon the sun, and the fixed stars with the moon because the stars of her stations belong to them. It is known among Hindu as well as Muslim astrologers that the planets exercise the rule over the zodiacal signs. Therefore they assume certain angelic beings as the dominants of the planets, who are exhibited in the following table, taken from the *Vishṇu-dharma*:— The dominants of the planets according to *Vishṇu-dharma.*

Table of the dominants of the planets.

| The planets and the two nodes. | Their dominants. |
|---|---|
| Sun. | Agni. |
| Moon. | Vyâna (?). |
| Mars | *Kalmâsha* (?). |
| Mercury. | Vishṇu. |
| Jupiter. | Śukra. |
| Venus. | Gaurî. |
| Saturn. | Prajâpati. |
| The Head. | Gaṇapati (?). |
| The Tail. | Viśvakarman. |

The same book attributes also to the lunar stations as to the planets certain dominants, who are contained in the following table:— The dominants of the lunar stations.

Page 262.

| The Lunar Stations. | Their dominants. |
|---|---|
| Kṛittikâ. | Agni. |
| Rohiṇî. | Keśvara. |
| Mṛigaśîrsha. | Indu, *i.e.* the moon. |
| Ârdrâ. | Rudra. |
| Punarvasu. | Aditi. |
| Pushya. | Guru, *i.e.* Jupiter. |
| Âśleshâ. | Sarpâs. |
| Maghâ. | Pitaras. |
| Pûrvaphalgunî. | Bhaga. |
| Uttaraphalgunî. | Aryaman. |
| Hasta. | Savitṛi, *i.e.* Savitâ. |
| Citrâ. | Tvashṭṛi. |
| Svâtî. | Vâyu. |
| Viśâkhâ. | Indrâgnî. |

| The Lunar Stations. | Their dominants. |
|---|---|
| Anurâdhâ. | Mitra. |
| Jyeshṭhâ. | Śakra. |
| Mûla. | Nirṛiti. |
| Pûrvâshâḍhâ. | Âpas. |
| Uttarâshâḍhâ. | Viśvê[devâs]. |
| Abhijit. | Brahman. |
| Śravaṇa. | Vishṇu. |
| Dhanishṭâ. | Vasavas. |
| Śatabhishaj. | Varuṇa. |
| Pûrvabhâdrapadâ. | [Aja ekapâd]. |
| Uttarabhâdrapadâ. | Ahir budhnya. |
| Revatî. | Pûshan. |
| Aśvinî. | Aśvin (?). |
| Bharaṇî. | Yama. |

# CHAPTER LXII.

## ON THE SIXTY YEARS-SAMVATSARA, ALSO CALLED "SHASHṬYABDA."

Page 263.

*Explanation of the terms samvatsara and shashṭyabda.*

THE word *samvatsara*, which means *the years*, is a technical term for cycles of years constructed on the basis of the revolutions of Jupiter and the sun, the heliacal rising of the former being reckoned as the beginning. It revolves in sixty years, and is therefore called *shashṭyabda, i.e.* sixty years.

*A year is presided over by that month in which the heliacal rising of Jupiter occurs.*

We have already mentioned that the names of the lunar stations are, by the names of the months, divided into groups, each month having a namesake in the corresponding group of stations. We have represented these things in a table, in order to facilitate the subject (v. i. 218). Knowing the station in which the heliacal rising of Jupiter occurs, and looking up this station in the just-mentioned table, you find at the left of it the name of the month which rules over the year in question. You bring the year in connection with the month, and say, *e.g. the year of Caitra, the year of Vaiśâkha*, &c. For each of these years there exist astrological rules which are well known in their literature.

*How to find the lunar station of Jupiter's heliacal rising. Quotation from Varâhamihira's Saṁhitâ, chap. viii. 20, 21.*

For the computation of the lunar station in which the heliacal rising of Jupiter occurs, Varâhamihira gives the following rule in his *Saṁhitâ* :—

"Take the Śakakâla, multiply it by 11, and multiply the product by 4. You may do this, or you may also multiply the Śakakâla by 44. Add 8589 to the product and divide the sum by 3750. The quotient represents years, months, days, &c.

"Add them to the Śakakâla, and divide the sum by 60. The quotient represents great sexagenarian *yugas*, *i.e.* complete *shashṭyabdas*, which, as not being necessary, are disregarded. Divide the remainder by 5, and the quotient represents small, complete five-year *yugas*. That which remains being less than one *yuga*, is called *samvatsara*, *i.e.* the year.

"V. 22.—Write down the latter number in two different places. Multiply the one by 9, and add to the product $\frac{1}{12}$ of the number in the other place. Take of the sum the fourth part, and this number represents complete lunar stations, its fractions representing part of the next following current station. Count off this number of the stations, beginning with Dhanishṭhâ. The station you arrive at is that one in which the heliacal rising of Jupiter takes place." Thereby you know the month of the years, as has above been explained.

Smaller cycles as contained in the cycle of sixty years.

The great *yugas* begin with the heliacal rising of Jupiter in the beginning of the station Dhanishṭhâ and the beginning of the month Mâgha. The small *yugas* have within the great ones a certain order, being divided into groups which comprehend certain numbers of years, and each of which has a special dominant. This division is represented by the following table.

If you know what number in the great *yuga* the year in question occupies, and you look up this number among the numbers of the years in the upper part of the table, you find under it, in the corresponding columns, both the name of the year and the name of its dominant.

Page 264.

| The number of each year of the sixty-years cycle. | Numbers with the unit 1. | Numbers with the unit 6. | Numbers with the unit 2. | Numbers with the unit 7. | Numbers with the unit 3. | Numbers with the unit 8. | Numbers with the unit 4. | Numbers with the unit 9. | Numbers with the unit 5. | Numbers without a unit. |
|---|---|---|---|---|---|---|---|---|---|---|
| | 1<br>11<br>21<br>31<br>41<br>51 | 6<br>16<br>26<br>36<br>46<br>56 | 2<br>12<br>22<br>32<br>42<br>52 | 7<br>17<br>27<br>37<br>47<br>57 | 3<br>13<br>23<br>33<br>43<br>53 | 8<br>18<br>28<br>38<br>48<br>58 | 4<br>14<br>24<br>34<br>44<br>54 | 9<br>19<br>29<br>39<br>49<br>59 | 5<br>15<br>25<br>35<br>45<br>55 | 10<br>20<br>30<br>40<br>50<br>60 |
| The names which each dozen of years has in common. | Samvatsara. | | Parivatsara. | | Idâvatsara. | | Anuvatsara. | | Udvatsara. | |
| Their dominants. | Agni, *i.e.* the fire. | | Arka, *i.e.* the sun. | | Śîtamayûkhamâlin, *i.e.* having a cold ray, viz. the moon. | | Prajâpati, the father of the lunar stations. | | Śailasutâpati, *i.e.* the husband of the daughter of the mountain, viz. Mahâdeva. | |

The names of the single years of a *saṁvatsara*.

Further, every single one of the sixty years has a name of its own, and the *yugas*, too, have names which are the names of their dominants. All these names are exhibited in the following table.

This table is to be used in the same way as the preceding one, as you find the name of each year of the whole cycle (of sixty years) under the corresponding number. It would be a lengthy affair if we were to explain the meanings of the single names and their prognostics. All this is found in the book *Saṁhitâ*.

Page 205.

| | | | | | |
|---|---|---|---|---|---|
| I.—Lustrum. Favourable. Its lord is Manu, *i.e.* Nârâyaṇa | 1. Prabhava. | 2. Vibhava. | 3. Śukla. | 4. Pramoda. | 5. Prajâpati. |
| II.—Lustrum. Favourable. Its lord Surejya, *i.e.* Jupiter | 6. Aṅgiras. | 7. Śrîmukha. | 8. Bhâva. | 9. Yuvan. | 10. Dhâtṛi. |
| III.—Lustrum. Favourable. Its lord Balabhit, *i.e.* Indra | 11. Îśvara. | 12. Bahudhânya. | 13. Pramâthin. | 14. Vikrama. | 15. Visha. (Vṛishabha ?) |
| IV.—Lustrum. Favourable. Its lord Hutâśa, *i.e.* the fire | 16. Citrabhânu. | 17. Subhânu. | 18 Pârthiva (?). | 19. Târaṇa. | 20. Vyaya. |
| V.—Lustrum. Indifferent. Its lord Tvashṭṛi, the lord of the lunar station Citrâ | 21. Sarvajit | 22. Sarvadhârin. | 23. Virodhin. | 24. Vikṛita. | 25. Khara. |
| VI.—Lustrum. Indifferent. Its lord Proshṭhapada, the lord of the lunar station Uttarabhâdrapadâ | 26. Nandana. | 27. Vijaya. | 28. Jaya. | 29. Manmatha. | 30. Cadur (!). |

Page 266

| | | | | | |
|---|---|---|---|---|---|
| VII.—Lustrum. Indifferent. Its lord Pitáras, *i.e.* the fathers . . . . . . | 31. Hemalamba. | 32. Vilambin. | 33. Vikârin. | 34. Śarvarî (?). | 35. Plava. |
| VIII.—Lustrum. Indifferent. Its lord is Śiva, *i.e.* the creatures . . . . . . | 36. Śokakṛit. | 37. Śubhakṛit. | 38. Krodhin. | 39. Viśvâvasu. | 40. Parâvasu. |
| IX.—Lustrum. Unlucky. Its lord Soma, *i.e.* the moon | 41. Plavaṅga. | 42. Kîlaka. | 43. Saumya. | 44. Sâdhâraṇa. | 45. Rodhakṛit. |
| X.—Lustrum. Unlucky. Its lord Śakrânala, *i.e.* Indra and the fire together . . . . | 46. Paridhâvin. | 47. Pramâdin. | 48. Vikrama. | 49. Râkshasa. | 50. Anala. |
| XI.—Lustrum. Unlucky. Its lord Aśvin, the lord of the lunar station Aśvinî . . . | 51. Piṅgala. | 52. Kâlayukta. | 53. Siddhârtha. | 54. Raudra. | 55. Durmati. |
| XII.—Lustrum. Unlucky. Its lord Bhaga, the lord of the lunar station Pûrvaphalgunî . | 56. Dundubhi. | 57. Aṅgâra. | 58. Raktâksha (?). | 59. Krodha. | 60. Kshaya. |

This is the method for the determination of the years of the *shashṭyabda*, as recorded in their books. However, I have seen Hindus who subtract 3 from the era of Vikramâditya, and divide the remainder by 60. The remainder they count off from the beginning of the great *yuga*. This method is not worth anything. By-the-bye, it is the same whether you reckon in the manner mentioned, or add 12 to the Śakakâla. Page 267.

The *samvatsaras* of the people of Kanoj.

I have come across some people from the country of Kanoj who told me that, with them, the cycle of *samvatsaras* has 1248 years, each single one of the twelve *samvatsaras* having 104 years. According to this statement we must subtract 554 from the Śakakâla, and with the remainder compare the following diagram. In the corresponding column you see in which *samvatsara* the year in question lies, and how many years of the *samvatsara* have already elapsed:—

| | | | | | | |
|---|---|---|---|---|---|---|
| The years | 1. | 105. | 209. | 313. | 417. | 521. |
| Their names | Rukmâksha. (?) | Pilumant. (?) | Kadara. | Kâlavṛinta. | Naumand. (?) | Meru. |
| The years | 625. | 729. | 833. | 937. | 1041. | 1145. |
| Their names | Barbara. | Jambu. | Kṛiti. | Sarpa. | Hindhu. | Sindhu. |

When I heard, among these pretended names of *samvatsaras*, names of nations, trees, and mountains, I conceived a suspicion of my reporters, more particularly as their chief business was indeed to practise hocus-pocus and deception (as jugglers?); and a dyed beard proves its bearer to be a liar. I used great care in examining every single one of them, in repeating the same questions at different times, in a different order and context. But lo! what different answers did I get! God is all-wise!

# CHAPTER LXIII.

## ON THAT WHICH ESPECIALLY CONCERNS THE BRAHMANS, AND WHAT THEY ARE OBLIGED TO DO DURING THEIR WHOLE LIFE.

First period in the Brahman's life.

THE life of the Brahman, after seven years of it have passed, is divided into four parts. The first part begins with the eighth year, when the Brahmans come to him to instruct him, to teach him his duties, and to enjoin him to adhere to them and to embrace them as long as he lives. Then they bind a girdle round his waist and invest him with a pair of *yajnopavîtas*, i.e. one strong cord consisting of nine single cords which are twisted together, and with a third *yajnopavîta*, a single one made from cloth. This girdle runs from the left shoulder to the right hip. Further, he is presented with a stick which he has to wear, and with a seal-ring of a certain grass, called *darbha*, which he wears on the ring-finger of the right hand. This seal-ring is also called *pavitra*. The object of his wearing the ring on the ring-finger of his right hand is this, that it should be a good omen and a blessing for all those who receive gifts from that hand. The obligation of wearing the ring is not quite so stringent as that of wearing the *yajnopavîta*, for from the latter he is not to separate himself under any circumstances whatever. If he takes it off while eating or fulfilling some want of nature, he thereby commits a sin which cannot be Page 263. wiped off save by some work of expiation, fasting, or almsgiving.

This first period of the Brahman's life extends till the twenty-fifth year of his age, or, according to the *Vishṇu-Purâṇa*, till his forty-eighth year. His duty is to practise abstinence, to make the earth his bed, to begin with the learning of the Veda and of its explanation, of the science of theology and law, all this being taught to him by a master whom he serves day and night. He washes himself thrice a day, and performs a sacrifice to the fire both at the beginning and end of the day. After the sacrifice he worships his master. He fasts a day and he breaks fast a day, but he is never allowed to eat meat. He dwells in the house of the master, which he only leaves in order to ask for a gift and to beg in not more than five houses once a day, either at noon or in the evening. Whatever alms he receives he places before his master to choose from it what he likes. Then the master allows him to take the remainder. Thus the pupil nourishes himself from the remains of the dishes of his master. Further, he fetches the wood for the fire, wood of two kinds of trees, *palâśa* (*Butea frondosa*) and *darbha*, in order to perform the sacrifice; for the Hindus highly venerate the fire, and offer flowers to it. It is the same case with all other nations. They always thought that the sacrifice was accepted by the deity if the fire came down upon it, and no other worship has been able to draw them away from it, neither the worship of idols nor that of stars, cows, asses, or images. Therefore Bashshâr Ibn Burd says: "Since there is fire, it is worshipped."

Second period in the Brahman's life.

The second period of their life extends from the twenty-fifth year till the fiftieth, or, according to the *Vishṇu-Purâṇa*, till the seventieth. The master allows him to marry. He marries, establishes a household, and intends to have descendants, but he cohabits with his wife only once in a month after she has become clean of the menstruation. He is not allowed to marry a woman above twelve years of age. He gains his sustenance *either* by the fee he

obtains for teaching Brahmans and Kshatriyas, not as a payment, but as a present, *or* by presents which he receives from some one because he performs for him the sacrifices to the fire, *or* by asking a gift from the kings and nobles, there being no importunate pressing on his part, and no unwillingness on the part of the giver. There is always a Brahman in the houses of those people, who there administers the affairs of religion and the works of piety. He is called *purohita*. Lastly, the Brahman lives from what he gathers on the earth or from the trees. He may try his fortune in the trade of clothes and betel-nuts, but it is preferable that he should not trade himself, and that a Vaiśya should do the business for him, because originally trade is forbidden on account of the deceiving and lying which are mixed up with it. Trading is permitted to him only in case of dire necessity, when he has no other means of sustenance. The Brahmans are not, like the other castes, bound to pay taxes and to perform services to the kings. Further, he is not allowed continually to busy himself with horses and cows, with the care for the cattle, nor with gaining by usury. The blue colour
Page 259. is impure for him, so that if it touches his body, he is obliged to wash himself. Lastly, he must always beat the drum before the fire, and recite for it the prescribed holy texts.

The third period.

The third period of the life of the Brahman extends from the fiftieth year to the seventy-fifth, or, according to the *Vishṇu-Purâṇa*, till the ninetieth. He practises abstinence, leaves his household, and hands it as well as his wife over to his children, if the latter does not prefer to accompany him into the life in the wilderness. He dwells outside civilisation, and leads the same life again which he led in the first period. He does not take shelter under a roof, nor wear any other dress but some bark of a tree, simply sufficient to cover his loins. He sleeps on the earth without any bed, and only nourishes himself by fruit, vegetables, and roots. He lets the hair grow long, and does not anoint himself with oil.

The fourth period extends till the end of life. He wears a red garment and holds a stick in his hand. He is always given to meditation; he strips the mind of friendship and enmity, and roots out desire, and lust, and wrath. He does not converse with anybody at all. When walking to a place of a particular merit, in order to gain a heavenly reward, he does not stop on the road in a village longer than a day, nor in a city longer than five days. If any one gives him something, he does not leave a remainder of it for the following day. He has no other business but that of caring for the path which leads to salvation, and for reaching *moksha*, whence there is no return to this world.

The fourth period.

The universal duties of the Brahman throughout his whole life are works of piety, giving alms and receiving them. For that which the Brahmans give reverts to the *pitaras* (is in reality a benefit to the *Fathers*). He must continually read, perform the sacrifices, take care of the fire which he lights, offer before it, worship it, and preserve it from being extinguished, that he may be burned by it after his death. It is called *homa*.

The duties of Brahmans in general.

Every day he must wash himself thrice: at the *saṁdhi* of rising, *i.e.* morning dawn, at the *saṁdhi* of setting, *i.e.* evening twilight, and between them in the middle of the day. The first washing is on account of sleep, because the openings of the body have become lax during it. Washing is a cleansing from accidental impurity and a preparation for prayer.

Their prayer consists of praise, glorification, and prostration according to their peculiar manner, viz. prostrating themselves on the two thumbs, whilst the two palms of the hands are joined, and they turn their faces towards the sun. For the sun is their *kibla*, wherever he may be, except when in the south. For they do not perform any work of piety with the face turned southward; only when occupied with something evil and unlucky they turn themselves towards the south.

The time when the sun declines from the meridian (the afternoon) is well suited for acquiring in it a heavenly reward. Therefore at this time the Brahman must be clean.

The evening is the time of supper and of prayer. The Brahman may take his supper and pray without having previously washed himself. Therefore, evidently, the rule as to the third washing is not as stringent as that relating to the first and second washings.

A nightly washing is obligatory for the Brahman only at the times of eclipses, that he should be prepared to perform the rules and sacrifices prescribed for that occasion.

The Brahman, as long as he lives, eats only twice a day, at noon and at nightfall; and when he wants to take his meal, he begins by putting aside as much as
Page 270. is sufficient for one or two men as alms, especially for strange Brahmans who happen to come at evening-time asking for something. To neglect *their* maintenance would be a great sin. Further, he puts something aside for the cattle, the birds, and the fire. Over the remainder he says prayers and eats it. The remainder of his dish he places outside his house, and does not any more come near it, as it is no longer allowable for him, being destined for the chance passer-by who wants it, be he a man, bird, dog, or something else.

The Brahman must have a water-vessel for himself. If another one uses it, it is broken. The same remark applies to his eating-instruments. I have seen Brahmans who allowed their relatives to eat with them from the same plate, but most of them disapprove of this.

He is obliged to dwell between the river Sindh in the north and the river Carmaṇvatî in the south. He is not allowed to cross either of these frontiers so as to enter the country of the Turks or of the Karṇâṭa. Further, he must live between the ocean in the east and west. People say that he is not allowed to stay in a country in which the grass which he wears on the ring-finger does not grow, nor the black-haired gazelles graze. This is a description for the whole country within the just-mentioned boundaries. If he passes beyond them he commits a sin.

In a country where not the whole spot in the house which is prepared for people to eat upon it is plastered with clay, where they, on the contrary, prepare a separate tablecloth for each person eating by pouring water over a spot and plastering it with the dung of cows, the shape of the Brahman's tablecloth must be square. Those who have the custom of preparing such tablecloths give the following as the cause of this custom:—The spot of eating is soiled by the eating. If the eating is finished, the spot is washed and plastered to become clean again. If, now, the soiled spot is not distinguished by a separate mark, you would suppose also the other spots to be soiled, since they are similar to and cannot be distinguished from each other.

Five vegetables are forbidden to them by the religious code:—Onions, garlic, a kind of gourd, the root of a plant like the carrots called *krncn* (?), and another vegetable which grows round their tanks called *nâlî*.

# CHAPTER LXIV.

## ON THE RITES AND CUSTOMS WHICH THE OTHER CASTES, BESIDES THE BRAHMANS, PRACTISE DURING THEIR LIFETIME.

Duties of the single castes.

THE Kshatriya reads the Veda and learns it, but does not teach it. He offers to the fire and acts according to the rules of the Purâṇas. In places where, as we have mentioned (v. p. 135), a tablecloth is prepared for eating, he makes it angular. He rules the people and defends them, for he is created for this task. He girds himself with a single cord of the threefold *yajnopavîta*, and a single other cord of cotton. This takes place after he has finished the twelfth year of his life.

It is the duty of the Vaiśya to practise agriculture and to cultivate the land, to tend the cattle and to remove the needs of the Brahmans. He is only allowed to gird himself with a single *yajnopavîta*, which is made of two cords.

The Śûdra is like a servant to the Brahman, taking care of his affairs and serving him. If, though being poor in the extreme, he still desires not to be without a *yajnopavîta*, he girds himself only with the linen one. Every action which is considered as the privilege of a Brahman, such as saying prayers, the recitation of the Veda, and offering sacrifices to the fire, is forbidden to him, to such a degree that when, *e.g.* a Śûdra or a Vaiśya is proved to have recited the Veda, he is accused by the Brahmans before the ruler, and the latter will order his tongue to be cut off. However, the meditation on God,

Page 271.

works of piety, and almsgiving are not forbidden to him.

Every man who takes to some occupation which is not allowed to his caste, as, *e.g.* a Brahman to trade, a Śûdra to agriculture, commits a sin or crime, which they consider only a little less than the crime of theft.

The following is one of the traditions of the Hindus:—In the days of King Râma human life was very long, always of a well-defined and well-known length. Thus a child never died before its father. Then, however, it happened that the son of a Brahman died while the father was still alive. Now the Brahman brought his child to the door of the king and spoke to him: "This innovation has sprung up in thy days for no other reason but this, that there is something rotten in the state of the country, and because a certain Vazir commits in thy realm what he commits." Then Râma began to inquire into the cause of this, and finally they pointed out to him a Caṇḍâla who took the greatest pains in performing worship and in self-torment. The king rode to him and found him on the banks of the Ganges, hanging on something with his head downward. The king bent his bow, shot at him, and pierced his bowels. Then he spoke: "That is it! I kill thee on account of a good action which thou art not allowed to do." When he returned home, he found the son of the Brahman, who had been deposited before his door, alive.

Story of King Râma, the *Caṇḍâla* and the Brahman.

All other men except the Caṇḍâla, as far as they are not Hindus, are called *mleccha, i.e.* unclean, all those who kill men and slaughter animals and eat the flesh of cows.

All these things originate in the difference of the classes or castes, one set of people treating the others as fools. This apart, all men are equal to each other, as Vâsudeva says regarding him who seeks salvation: "In the judgment of the intelligent man, the Brahman

Philosophic opinion about all things being equal.

and the Caṇḍâla are equal, the friend and the foe, the faithful and the deceitful, nay, even the serpent and the weasel. If to the eyes of intelligence all things are equal, to ignorance they appear as separated and different."

Vâsudeva speaks to Arjuṇa: "If the civilisation of the world is that which is intended, and if the direction of it cannot proceed without our fighting for the purpose of suppressing evil, it is the duty of us who are the intelligent to act and to fight, not in order to bring to an end that which is deficient within us, but because it is necessary for the purpose of healing what is ill and banishing destructive elements. Then the ignorant imitate us in acting, as the children imitate their elders, without their knowing the real aim and purport of actions. For their nature has an aversion to intellectual methods, and they use force only in order to act in accordance with the influences of lust and passion on their senses. In all this, the intelligent and educated man is directly the contrary of them."

# CHAPTER LXV.

## ON THE SACRIFICES.

MOST of the Veda treats of the sacrifices to the fire, and describes each one of them. They are different in extent, so that certain of them can only be performed by the greatest of their kings. So, *e.g.* the *aśvamedha*. Aśvamedha. A mare is let freely to wander about in the country grazing, without anybody's hindering her. Soldiers follow her, drive her, and cry out before her: "She is the king of the world. He who does not agree, let him come forward." The Brahmans walk behind her and perform sacrifices to the fire where she casts dung. When she thus has wandered about through all parts Page 277. of the world, she becomes food for the Brahmans and for him whose property she is.

Further, the sacrifices differ in duration, so that only he could perform certain of them who lives a very long life; and such long lives do no longer occur in this our age. Therefore most of them have been abolished, and only few of them remain and are practised nowadays.

According to the Hindus, the fire eats everything. On fire-offerings in general. Therefore it becomes defiled, if anything unclean is mixed up with it, as, *e.g.* water. Accordingly they are very punctilious regarding fire and water if they are in the hands of non-Hindus, because they are defiled by being touched by them.

That which the fire eats for its share, reverts to the Devas, because the fire comes out of their mouths.

What the Brahmans present to the fire to eat is oil and different cereals—wheat, barley, and rice—which they throw into the fire. Further, they recite the prescribed texts of the Veda in case they offer on their own behalf. However, if they offer in the name of somebody else, they do not recite anything.

Story of the fire becoming leprous from *Vishṇu-Dharma.*

The *Vishṇu-Dharma* mentions the following tradition:—Once upon a time there was a man of the class of the Daityas, powerful and brave, the ruler of a wide realm called Hiraṇyâksha. He had a daughter of the name of Dkish (?), who was always bent upon worship and trying herself by fasting and abstinence. Thereby she had earned as reward a place in heaven. She was married to Mahâdeva. When he, then, was alone with her and did with her according to the custom of the Devas, *i.e.* cohabiting very long and transferring the *semen* very slowly, the fire became aware of it and became jealous, fearing lest the two might procreate a fire similar to themselves. Therefore it determined to defile and to ruin them.

When Mahâdeva saw the fire, his forehead became covered with sweat from the violence of his wrath, so that some of it dropped down to the earth. The earth drank it, and became in consequence pregnant with Mars, *i.e. Skanda*, the commander of the army of the Devas.

Rudra, the destroyer, seized a drop of the *semen* of Mahâdeva and threw it away. It was scattered in the interior of the earth, and represents all atom-like substances (?).

The fire, however, became leprous, and felt so much ashamed and confounded that it plunged down into *pâtâla, i.e.* the lowest earth. As, now, the Devas missed the fire, they went out to search for it.

First, the frogs pointed it out to them. The fire, on seeing the Devas, left its place and concealed itself in the tree *aśvattha*, laying a curse on the frogs, that they should have a horrid croaking and be odious to all others.

Next, the parrots betrayed to the Devas the hiding-place of the fire. Thereupon the fire cursed them, that their tongues should be turned topsy-turvy, that their root should be where its tip ought to be. But the Devas spoke to them: "If your tongue is turned topsy-turvy, you shall speak in human dwellings and eat delicate things."

The fire fled from the *aśvattha* tree to the tree *śamî*. Thereupon the elephant gave a hint to the Devas regarding its hiding-place. Now it cursed the elephant that his tongue should be turned topsy-turvy. But then the Devas spoke to him: "If your tongue is turned topsy-turvy, you shall participate with man in his victuals and understand his speech."

At last they hit upon the fire, but the fire refused to stay with them because it was leprous. Now the Devas restored it to health, and freed it from the leprosy. The Devas brought back to them the fire with all honour and made it a mediator between themselves and mankind, receiving from the latter the shares which they offer to the Devas, and making these shares reach them.

# CHAPTER LXVI.

## ON PILGRIMAGE AND THE VISITING OF SACRED PLACES.

Page 273. PILGRIMAGES are not obligatory to the Hindus, but facultative and meritorious. A man sets off to wander to some holy region, to some much venerated idol or to some of the holy rivers. He worships in them, worships the idol, makes presents to it, recites many hymns and prayers, fasts, and gives alms to the Brahmans, the priests, and others. He shaves the hair of his head and beard, and returns home.

The holy much venerated ponds are in the cold mountains round Meru. The following information regarding them is found in both the *Vâyu* and the *Matsya Purâṇas*:—

An extract on holy ponds from the *Vâyu* and *Matsya Purâṇas*.

"At the foot of Meru there is Arhata (?), a very great pond, described as shining like the moon. In it originates the river Zanba (? Jambu), which is very pure, flowing over the purest gold.

"Near the mountain Śveta there is the pond Uttaramânasa, and around it twelve other ponds, each of them like a lake. Thence come the two rivers Sâṇḍî (?) and Maddhyandâ (?), which flow to Kimpurusha.

"Near the mountain Nîla there is the pond *pyṇd* (pitanda ?) adorned with lotuses.

"Near the mountain Nishadha there is the pond Vishṇupada, whence comes the river Sarasvatî, *i.e.*, Sarsuti. Besides, the river Gandharvî comes from there.

"In the mountain Kailâsa there is the pond Manda, as large as a sea, whence comes the river Mandâkini.

"North-east of Kailâsa there is the mountain Candraparvata, and at its foot the pond Âcûd (?), whence comes the river Âcûd.

"South-east of Kailâsa there is the mountain Lohita, and at its foot a pond called Lohita. Thence comes the river Lohitanadî.

"South of Kailâsa there is the mountain Sarayuśatî (?), and at its foot the pond Mânasa. Thence comes the river Sarayû.

"West of Kailâsa there is the mountain Aruṇa, always covered with snow, which cannot be ascended. At its foot is the pond Śailôdâ, whence comes the river Śailôdâ.

"North of Kailâsa there is the mountain Gaura (?), and at its foot the pond C-n-d-sara (?), *i.e.* having golden sand. Near this pond the King Bhagîratha led his anchorite life.

"His story is as follows:—A king of the Hindus called Sagara had 60,000 sons, all of them bad, mean fellows. Once they happened to lose a horse. They at once searched for it, and in searching they continually ran about so violently that in consequence the surface of the earth broke in. They found the horse in the interior of the earth standing before a man who was looking down with deep-sunken eyes. When they came near him he smote them with his look, in consequence of which they were burned on the spot and went to hell on account of their wicked actions. Story of Bhagîratha.

"The collapsed part of the earth became a sea, the great ocean. A king of the descendants of that king, called Bhagîratha, on hearing the history of his ancestors, was much affected thereby. He went to the above-mentioned pond, the bottom of which was polished gold, and stayed there, fasting all day and worshipping during the nights. Finally, Mahâdeva asked him what he wanted; upon which he answered, Page 264.

'I want the river Ganges which flows in Paradise,' knowing that to any one over whom its water flows all his sins are pardoned. Mahâdeva granted him his desire. However, the Milky Way was the bed of the Ganges, and the Ganges was very haughty, for nobody had ever been able to stand against it. Now Mahâdeva took the Ganges and put it on his head. When the Ganges could not move away, he became very angry and made a great uproar. However, Mahâdeva held him firmly, so that it was not possible for anybody to plunge into it. Then he took part of the Ganges and gave it to Bhagîratha, and this king made the middle one of its seven branches flow over the bones of his ancestors, whereby they became liberated from punishment. Therefore the Hindus throw the burned bones of their dead into the Ganges. The Ganges was also called by the name of that king who brought him to earth, *i.e.* Bhagîratha."

On the construction of holy ponds.

We have already quoted Hindu traditions to the effect that in the Dvipas there are rivers as holy as the Ganges. In every place to which some particular holiness is ascribed, the Hindus construct ponds intended for the ablutions. In this they have attained to a very high degree of art, so that our people (the Muslims), when they see them, wonder at them, and are unable to describe them, much less to construct anything like them. They build them of great stones of an enormous bulk, joined to each other by sharp and strong cramp-irons, in the form of steps (or terraces) like so many ledges; and these terraces run all around the pond, reaching to a height of more than a man's stature. On the surface of the stones between two terraces they construct staircases rising like pinnacles. Thus the first steps or terraces are like roads (leading round the pond), and the pinnacles are steps (leading up and down). If ever so many people descend to the pond whilst others ascend, they do not meet each other, and the road is never blocked up, because there are so many terraces, and the ascending person can always turn aside to another terrace than that on which the descending people go. By this arrangement all troublesome thronging is avoided.

On single holy ponds.

In Multân there is a pond in which the Hindus worship by bathing themselves, if they are not prevented.

The *Saṁhitâ* of Varâhamihira relates that in Tâneshar there is a pond which the Hindus visit from afar to bathe in its water. Regarding the cause of this custom they relate the following:—The waters of all the other holy ponds visit this particular pond at the time of an eclipse. Therefore, if a man washes in it, it is as if he had washed in every single one of all of them. Then Varâhamihira continues: "People say, if it were not the head (apsis) which causes the eclipse of sun and moon, the other ponds would not visit this pond."

The ponds become particularly famous for holiness either because some important event has happened at them, or because there is some passage in the holy text or tradition which refers to them. We have already quoted words spoken by Śaunaka. Venus had related them to him on the authority of Brahman, to whom they had originally been addressed. In this text King Bali also is mentioned, and what he would do till the time when Nârâyaṇa would plunge him down to the lowest earth. In the same text occurs the following passage:—"I do that to him only for this purpose that the equality between men, which he desires to realise, shall be done away with, that men shall be different in their conditions of life, and that on this difference the order of the world is to be based; further, that people shall turn away from *his* worship and worship *me* and believe in *me*. The mutual assistance of civilised people presupposes a certain difference

On the inequality of created beings and the origin of patriotism. A tradition from Śaunaka.

Page 275.

among them, in consequence of which the one requires the other. According to the same principle, God has created the world as containing many differences in itself. So the single countries differ from each other, one being cold, the other warm; one having good soil, water, and air, the other having bitter salt soil, dirty and bad smelling water, and unhealthy air. There are still more differences of this kind; in some cases advantages of all kinds being numerous, in others few. In some parts there are periodically returning physical disasters; in others they are entirely unknown. All these things induce civilised people carefully to select the places where they want to build towns.

That which makes people do these things is usage and custom. However, religious commands are much more powerful, and influence much more the nature of man than usages and customs. The bases of the latter are investigated, explored, and accordingly either kept or abandoned, whilst the bases of the religious commands are left as they are, not inquired into, adhered to by the majority simply on *trust*. They do not argue over them, as the inhabitants of some sterile region do not argue over it, since they are born in it and do not know anything else, for they love the country as their fatherland, and find it difficult to leave it. If, now, besides physical differences, the countries differ from each other also in law and religion, there is so much attachment to it in the hearts of those who live in them that it can never be rooted out."

On Benares as an asylum.

The Hindus have some places which are venerated for reasons connected with their law and religion, *e.g.* Benares (Bârânasi). For their anchorites wander to it and stay there for ever, as the dwellers of the Ka'ba stay for ever in Mekka. They want to live there to the end of their lives, that their reward after death should be the better for it. They say that a murderer is held responsible for his crime and punished with a punishment due to his guilt, except in case he enters the city of Benares, where he obtains pardon. Regarding the cause of the holiness of this asylum they relate the following story:—

"Brahman was in shape four-headed. Now there happened some quarrel between him and Śaṁkara, *i.e.* Mahâdeva, and the succeeding fight had this result, that one of the heads of Brahman was torn off. At that time it was the custom that the victor took the head of the slain adversary in his hand and let it hang down from his hand as an act of ignominy to the dead and as a sign of his own bravery. Further, a bridle was put into the mouth (?). Thus the head of Brahman was dishonoured by the hand of Mahâdeva, who took it always with him wherever he went and whatever he did. He never once separated himself from it when he entered the towns, till at last he came to Benares. After he had entered Benares the head dropped from his hand and disappeared."

On the holy ponds of Pûkara, Tâneshar, Mâhûra, Kashmîr, and Multân.

A similar place is Pûkara, the story of which is this: Brahman once was occupied in offering there to the fire, when a pig came out of the fire. Therefore they represent his image there as that of a pig. Outside the town, in three places, they have constructed ponds which stand in high veneration, and are places of worship.

Another place of the kind is Tâneshar, also called *Kurukshetra*, *i.e.* the land of Kuru, who was a peasant, a pious, holy man, who worked miracles by divine power. Therefore the country was called after him, and venerated for his sake. Besides, Tâneshar is the theatre of the exploits of Vâsudeva in the wars of Bhârata and of the destruction of the evil-doers. It is for this reason that people visit the place.

Mâhûra, too, is a holy place, crowded with Brahmans.

Page 276. It is venerated because Vâsudeva was there born and brought up, in a place in the neighbourhood called *Nandagola*.

Nowadays the Hindus also visit Kashmîr. Lastly, they used to visit Mûltân before its idol-temple was destroyed.

# CHAPTER LXVII.

## ON ALMS, AND HOW A MAN MUST SPEND WHAT HE EARNS.

IT is obligatory with them every day to give alms as much as possible. They do not let money become a year or even a month old, for this would be a draft on an unknown future, of which a man does not know whether he reaches it or not.

With regard to that which he earns by the crops or from the cattle, he is bound first to pay to the ruler of the country the tax which attaches to the soil or the pasture-ground. Further, he pays him one-sixth of the income in recognition of the protection which he affords to the subjects, their property, and their families. The same obligation rests also on the common people, but they will always lie and cheat in the declarations about their property. Further, trading businesses, too, pay a tribute for the same reason. Only the Brahmans are exempt from all these taxes.

As to the way in which the remainder of the income, after the taxes have been deducted, is to be employed, there are different opinions. Some destine one-ninth of it for alms. For they divide it into three parts. One of them is kept in reserve to guarantee the heart against anxiety. The second is spent on trade to bring profit, and one-third of the third portion (*i.e.* one-ninth of the whole) is spent on alms, whilst the two other thirds are spent according to the same rule.

Others divide this income into four portions. One-fourth is destined for common expenses, the second for liberal works of a noble mind, the third for alms, and the fourth for being kept in reserve, *i.e.* not more of it than the common expenses for three years. If the quarter which is to be reserved exceeds this amount, only this amount is reserved, whilst the remainder is spent as alms.

Usury or taking percentages is forbidden. The sin which a man commits thereby corresponds to the amount by which the percentages have increased the capital stock. Only to the Śûdra is it allowed to take percentages, as long as his profit is not more than one-fiftieth of the capital (*i.e.* he is not to take more than two per cent.).

## CHAPTER LXVIII.

### ON WHAT IS ALLOWED AND FORBIDDEN IN EATING AND DRINKING.

ORIGINALLY killing in general was forbidden to them, as it is to the Christians and Manichæans. People, however, have the desire for meat, and will always fling aside every order to the contrary. Therefore the here-mentioned law applies in particular only to the Brahmans, because they are the guardians of the religion, and because it forbids them to give way to their lusts. The same rule applies to those members of the Christian clergy who are in rank above the bishops, viz. the metropolitans, the *catholici*, and the patriarchs, not to the lower grades, such as presbyter and deacon, except in the case that a man who holds one of these degrees is at the same time a monk.

List of animals lawful and unlawful to be eaten.

As matters stand thus, it is allowed to kill animals by means of strangulation, but only certain animals, others being excluded. The meat of such animals, the killing of which is allowed, is forbidden in case they die a sudden death. Animals the killing of which is allowed are sheep, goats, gazelles, hares, rhinoceroses (*gandha*), the buffaloes, fish, water and land birds, as sparrows, ring-doves, francolins, doves, peacocks, and other animals Page 277. which are not loathsome to man nor noxious.

That which is forbidden are cows, horses, mules, asses, camels, elephants, tame poultry, crows, parrots, nightingales, all kinds of eggs and wine. The latter is allowed to the Śûdra. He may drink it, but dare not sell it, as he is not allowed to sell meat.

Why the meat of cows was forbidden.

Some Hindus say that in the time before Bhârata it was allowed to eat the meat of cows, and that there then existed sacrifices part of which was the killing of cows. After that time, however, it had been forbidden on account of the weakness of men, who were too weak to fulfil their duties, as also the Veda, which originally was only one, was afterwards divided into four parts, simply for the purpose of facilitating the study of it to men. This theory, however, is very little substantiated, as the prohibition of the meat of cows is not an alleviating and less strict measure, but, on the contrary, one which is more severe and more restrictive than the former law.

Other Hindus told me that the Brahmans used to suffer from the eating of cows' meat. For their country is hot, the inner parts of the bodies are cold, the natural warmth becomes feeble in them, and the power of digestion is so weak that they must strengthen it by eating the leaves of *betel* after dinner, and by chewing the betel-nut. The hot betel inflames the heat of the body, the chalk on the betel-leaves dries up everything wet, and the betel-nut acts as an astringent on the teeth, the gums, and the stomach. As this is the case, they forbade eating cows' meat, because it is essentially thick and cold.

I, for my part, am uncertain, and hesitate in the question of the origin of this custom between two different views.

(*Lacuna in the manuscript.*)

As for the economical reason, we must keep in mind that the cow is the animal which serves man in travelling by carrying his loads, in agriculture in the works of ploughing and sowing, in the household by the milk and the product made thereof. Further, man makes use of its dung, and in winter-time even of its breath.

Therefore it was forbidden to eat cows' meat; as also Alḥajjâj forbade it, when people complained to him that Babylonia became more and more desert.

That all things are equal from a philosophical point of view.

I have been told the following passage is from an Indian book: "All things are one, and whether allowed or forbidden, equal. They differ only in weakness and power. The wolf has the power to tear the sheep; therefore the sheep is the wolf's food, for the former cannot oppose the latter, and is his prey." I have found in Hindu books passages to the same effect. However, such views come to the intelligent man only by knowledge, when in it he has attained to such a degree that a Brahman and a Caṇḍâla are equal to him. If he is in this state, all other things also are equal to him, in so far as he abstains from them. It is the same if they are all allowed to him, for he can dispense with them, or if they are forbidden to him, for he does not desire them. As to those, however, who require these things, being in the yoke of ignorance, something is allowed to them, something forbidden, and thereby a wall is erected between the two kinds of things.

# CHAPTER LXIX.

## ON MATRIMONY, THE MENSTRUAL COURSES, EMBRYOS, AND CHILDBED.

Necessity of matrimony. No nation can exist without a regular married life, for it prevents the uproar of passions abhorred by the cultivated mind, and it removes all those causes which excite the animal to a fury always leading to harm. Considering the life of the animals by pairs, how the one member of the pair helps the other, and how the lust of other animals of the same species is kept aloof from them, you cannot help declaring matrimony to be a necessary institution; whilst disorderly cohabitation or harlotry on the part of man is a shameful proceeding, that does not even attain to the standing of the development of animals, which in every other respect stand far below him.

Page 278.

Law of marriage. Every nation has particular customs of marriage, and especially those who claim to have a religion and law of divine origin. The Hindus marry at a very young age; therefore the parents arrange the marriage for their sons. On that occasion the Brahmans perform the rites of the sacrifices, and they as well as others receive alms. The implements of the wedding rejoicings are brought forward. No gift is settled between them. The man gives only a present to the wife, as he thinks fit, and a marriage gift in advance, which he has no right to claim back, but the wife may give it back to him of her own will. Husband and wife can only be separated by death, as they have no divorce.

A man may marry one to four wives. He is not allowed to take more than four; but if one of his wives die, he may take another one to complete the legitimate number. However, he must not go beyond it.

If a wife loses her husband by death, she cannot marry another man. She has only to chose between two things—either to remain a widow as long as she lives or to burn herself; and the latter eventuality is considered the preferable, because as a widow she is ill-treated as long as she lives. As regards the wives of the kings, they are in the habit of burning them, whether they wish it or not, by which they desire to prevent any of them by chance committing something unworthy of the illustrious husband. They make an exception only for women of advanced years and for those who have children; for the son is the responsible protector of his mother. The widow.

According to their marriage law it is better to marry a stranger than a relative. The more distant the relationship of a woman with regard to her husband the better. It is absolutely forbidden to marry related women both of the direct *descending* line, viz. a granddaughter or great-granddaughter, and of the direct *ascending* line, viz. a mother, grandmother, or great-grandmother. It is also forbidden to marry collateral relations, viz. a sister, a niece, a maternal or paternal aunt and their daughters, except in case the couple of relations who want to marry each other be removed from each other by five consecutive generations. In that case the prohibition is waived, but, notwithstanding, such a marriage is an object of dislike to them. Forbidden degrees of marriage.

Some Hindus think that the number of the wives depends upon the caste; that, accordingly, a Brahman may take four, a Kshatriya three, a Vaisya two wives, and a Śûdra one. Every man of a caste may marry a woman of his own caste or one of the castes or caste Number of wives.

below his; but nobody is allowed to marry a woman of a caste superior to his own.

*Partus sequitur ventrem.*

The child belongs to the caste of the mother, not to that of the father. Thus, *e.g.* if the wife of a Brahman is a Brahman, her child also is a Brahman; if she is a Śûdra, her child is a Śûdra. In our time, however, the Brahmans, although it is allowed to them, never marry any woman except one of their own caste.

Duration of the menstrual courses.

The longest duration of the menstrual courses which has been observed is sixteen days, but in reality they last only during the first four days, and then the husband is not allowed to cohabit with his wife, nor even to come near her in the house, because during this time she is impure. After the four days have elapsed and she has washed, she is pure again, and the husband may cohabit with her, even if the blood has not yet entirely disappeared; for this blood is not considered as that of the menstrual courses, but as the same substance-matter of which the embryos consist.

On pregnancy and childbed. Page 279.

It is the duty (of the Brahman), if he wants to cohabit with a wife to get a child, to perform a sacrifice to the fire called *garbhâdhâna;* but he does not perform it, because it requires the presence of the woman, and therefore he feels ashamed to do so. In consequence he postpones the sacrifice and unites it with the next following one, which is due in the fourth month of the pregnancy, called *sîmantonnayanam.* After the wife has given birth to the child, a third sacrifice is performed between the birth and the moment when the mother begins to nourish the child. It is called *jâtakarman.*

The child receives a name after the days of the childbed have elapsed. The sacrifice for the occasion of the name-giving is called *nâmakarman.*

As long as the woman is in childbed, she does not touch any vessel, and nothing is eaten in her house, nor does the Brahman light there a fire. These days are eight for the Brahman, twelve for the Kshatriya, fifteen for the Vaiśya, and thirty for the Śûdra. For the low-caste people which are not reckoned among any caste, no term is fixed.

The longest duration of the suckling of the child is three years, but there is no obligation in this matter. The sacrifice on the occasion of the first cutting of the child's hair is offered in the third, the perforation of the ear takes place in the seventh and eighth years.

On the causes of prostitution.

People think with regard to harlotry that it is allowed with them. Thus, when Kâbul was conquered by the Muslims and the Ispahbad of Kâbul adopted Islâm, he stipulated that he should not be bound to eat cows' meat nor to commit sodomy (which proves that he abhorred the one as much as the other). In reality, the matter is not as people think, but it is rather this, that the Hindus are not very severe in punishing whoredom. The fault, however, in this lies with the kings, not with the nation. But for this, no Brahman or priest would suffer in their idol-temples the women who sing, dance, and play. The kings make them an attraction for their cities, a bait of pleasure for their subjects, for no other but financial reasons. By the revenues which they derive from the business both as fines and taxes, they want to recover the expenses which their treasury has to spend on the army.

In a similar way the Buyide prince 'Aḍud-aldaula acted, who besides also had a second aim in view, viz. that of protecting his subjects against the passions of his unmarried soldiers.

# CHAPTER LXX.

## ON LAWSUITS.

On procedure.

THE judge demands from the suitor a document written against the accused person in a well-known writing which is thought suitable for writs of the kind, and in the document the well-established proof of the justice of his suit. In case there is no written document, the contest is settled by means of witnesses without a written document.

Number of witnesses.

The witnesses must not be less than four, but there may be more. Only in case the justice of the deposition of a witness is perfectly established and certain before the judge, he may admit it, and decide the question alone on the basis of the deposition of this sole witness. However, he does not admit prying about in secret, deriving arguments from mere signs or indications in public, concluding by analogy from one thing which seems established about another, and using all sorts of tricks to elicit the truth, as 'Iyâs Ibn Mu'âwiya used to do.

If the suitor is not able to prove his claim, the defendant must swear, but he may also tender the oath to the suitor by saying, "Swear thou that thy claim is true, and I will give thee what thou claimest."

Different kinds of oaths and ordeals.

There are many kinds of the oath, in accordance with the value of the object of the claim. If the object is of no great importance, and the suitor agrees that the accused person shall swear, the latter simply swears before five learned Brahmans in the following words:

"If I lie, he shall have as recompense as much of my goods as is equal to the eightfold of the amount of his claim."

A higher sort of oath is this: The accused person is invited to drink the *bísh* (*visha* ?) called *brahmaṇa* (?). It is one of the worst kinds; but if he speaks the truth, the drink does not do him any harm.

A still higher sort of ordeal is this: They bring the man to a deep and rapidly flowing river, or to a deep well with much water. Then he speaks to the water: "Since thou belongest to the pure angels, and knowest both what is secret and public, kill me if I lie, and preserve me if I speak the truth." Then five men take him between them and throw him into the water. If he has spoken the truth, he will not drown and die. Page 280.

A still higher sort is the following: The judge sends both claimant and defendant to the temple of the most venerated idol of the town or realm. There the defendant has to fast during that day. On the following day he dresses in new garments, and posts himself together with the claimant in that temple. Then the priests pour water over the idol and give it him to drink. If he, then, has not spoken the truth, he at once vomits blood.

A still higher sort is the following: The defendant is placed on the scale of a balance, and is weighed; whereupon he is taken off the scale, and the scale is left as it is. Then he invokes as witnesses for the truth of his deposition the spiritual beings, the angels, the heavenly beings, one after the other, and all which he speaks he writes down on a piece of paper, and fastens it to his head. He is a second time placed in the scale of the balance. In case he has spoken the truth, he now weighs more than the first time.

There is also a still higher sort. It is the following: They take butter and sesame-oil in equal quantities, and boil them in a kettle. Then they throw a leaf into it, which by getting flaccid and burned is to them a sign of the boiling of the mixture. When the boiling is at its height, they throw a piece of gold into the kettle and order the defendant to fetch it out with his hand. If he has spoken the truth, he fetches it out.

The highest kind of ordeal is the following: They make a piece of iron so hot that it is near melting, and put it with a pair of tongs on the hand of the defendant, there being nothing between his hand and the iron save a broad leaf of some plant, and under it some few and scattered corns of rice in the husks. They order him to carry it seven paces, and then he may throw it to the ground.

# CHAPTER LXXI.

## ON PUNISHMENTS AND EXPIATIONS.

In this regard the manners and customs of the Hindus resemble those of the Christians, for they are, like those of the latter, based on the principles of virtue and abstinence from wickedness, such as never to kill under any circumstance whatsoever, to give to him who has stripped you of your coat also your shirt, to offer to him who has beaten your cheek the other cheek also, to bless your enemy and to pray for him. Upon my life, this is a noble philosophy; but the people of this world are not all philosophers. Most of them are ignorant and erring, who cannot be kept on the straight road save by the sword and the whip. And, indeed, ever since Constantine the Victorious became a Christian, both sword and whip have ever been employed, for without them it would be impossible to rule.

The Brahmans originally the rulers of the nation.

India has developed in a similar way. For the Hindus relate that originally the affairs of government and war were in the hands of the Brahmans, but the country became disorganised, since they ruled according to the philosophic principles of their religious codes, which proved impossible when opposed to the mischievous and perverse elements of the populace. They were even near losing also the administration of their religious affairs. Therefore they humiliated themselves before the lord of their religion. Whereupon Brahman intrusted them exclusively with the functions which they now have, whilst he intrusted the Kshatriyas with the Page 231.

duties of ruling and fighting. Ever since the Brahmans live by asking and begging, and the penal code is exercised under the control of the kings, not under that of the scholars.

Law of murder.

The law about murder is this: If the murderer is a Brahman, and the murdered person a member of another caste, he is only bound to do expiation consisting of fasting, prayers, and almsgiving.

If the murdered person is a Brahman, the Brahman murderer has to answer for it in a future life; for he is not allowed to do expiation, because expiation wipes off the sin from the sinner, whilst nothing can wipe off any of the mortal crimes from a Brahman, of which the greatest are: the murder of a Brahman, called *vajra-brahmahatyâ*; further, the killing of a cow, the drinking of wine, whoredom, especially with the wife of one's own father and teacher. However, the kings do not for any of these crimes kill a Brahman or Kshatriya, but they confiscate his property and banish him from their country.

If a man of a caste under those of the Brahman and Kshatriya kills a man of the same caste, he has to do expiation, but besides the kings inflict upon him a punishment in order to establish an example.

Law of theft.

The law of theft directs that the punishment of the thief should be in accordance with the value of the stolen object. Accordingly, sometimes a punishment of extreme or of middling severity is necessary, sometimes a course of correction and imposing a payment, sometimes only exposing to public shame and ridicule. If the object is very great, the kings blind a Brahman and mutilate him, cutting off his left hand and right foot, or the right hand and left foot, whilst they mutilate a Kshatriya without blinding him, and kill thieves of the other castes.

Punishment of an adulteress.

An adulteress is driven out of the house of the husband and banished.

I have repeatedly been told that when Hindu slaves

(in Muslim countries) escape and return to their country and religion, the Hindus order that they should fast by way of expiation, then they bury them in the dung, stale, and milk of cows for a certain number of days, till they get into a state of fermentation. Then they drag them out of the dirt and give them similar dirt to eat, and more of the like.

Hindu prisoners of war, how treated after returning to their country.

I have asked the Brahmans if this is true, but they deny it, and maintain that there is no expiation possible for such an individual, and that he is never allowed to return into those conditions of life in which he was before he was carried off as a prisoner. And how should that be possible? If a Brahman eats in the house of a Śûdra for sundry days, he is expelled from his caste and can never regain it.

# CHAPTER LXXII.

## ON INHERITANCE, AND WHAT CLAIM THE DECEASED PERSON HAS ON IT.

Law of inheritance. THE chief rule of their law of inheritance is this, that the women do not inherit, except the daughter. She gets the fourth part of the share of a son, according to a passage in the book *Manu*. If she is not married, the money is spent on her till the time of her marriage, and her dowry is bought by means of her share. Afterwards she has no more income from the house of her father.

If a widow does not burn herself, but prefers to remain alive, the heir of her deceased husband has to provide her with nourishment and clothing as long as she lives.

The debts of the deceased must be paid by his heir, either out of his share or of the stock of his own property, no regard being had whether the deceased has left any property or not. Likewise he must bear the just-mentioned expenses for the widow in any case whatsoever.

As regards the rule about the male heirs, evidently the descendants, *i.e.* the son and grandson, have a nearer claim to the inheritance than the ascendants, *i.e.* the father and grandfather. Page 282. Further, as regards the single relatives among the descendants as well as the ascendants, the nearer a man is related, the more claim he has on inheriting. Thus a son has a nearer claim than a grandson, a father than a grandfather.

The collateral relations, as, *e.g.* the brothers, have less claim, and inherit only in case there is nobody who has a better claim. Hence it is evident that the son of a daughter has more claim than the son of a sister, and that the son of a brother has more claim than either of them.

If there are several claimants of the same degree of relationship, as, *e.g.*, sons or brothers, they all get equal shares. A hermaphrodite is reckoned as a male being.

If the deceased leaves no heir, the inheritance falls to the treasury of the king, except in the case that the deceased person was a Brahman. In that case the king has no right to meddle with the inheritance, but it is exclusively spent on almsgiving.

Duties of the heir towards the deceased.

The duty of the heir towards the deceased in the first year consists in his giving sixteen banquets, where every guest in addition to his food receives alms also, viz. on the fifteenth and sixteenth days after death; further, once a month during the whole year. The banquet in the sixth month must be more rich and more liberal than the others. Further, on the last but one day of the year, which banquet is devoted to the deceased and his ancestors; and finally, on the last day of the year. With the end of the year the duties towards the deceased have been fulfilled.

If the heir is a son, he must during the whole year wear mourning dress; he must mourn and have no intercourse with women, if he is a legitimate child and of a good stock. Besides, you must know that nourishment is forbidden to the heirs for one single day in the first part of the mourning-year.

Besides the almsgiving at the just-mentioned sixteen banquets, the heirs must make, above the door of the house, something like a shelf projecting from the wall in the open air, on which they have every day to place a dish of something cooked and a vessel of water, till the end of ten days after the death. For possibly the spirit of the deceased has not yet found its rest, but moves still to and fro around the house, hungry and thirsty.

Parallel from Plato.

A similar view is indicated by Plato in *Phaedo*, where he speaks of the soul circling round the graves, because possibly it still retains some vestiges of the love for the body. Further he says: "People have said regarding the soul that it is its habit to combine something coherent out of the single limbs of the body, which is its dwelling in this as well as in the future world, when it leaves the body, and is by the death of the body separated from it."

On the tenth of the last-mentioned days, the heir spends, in the name of the deceased, much food and cold water. After the eleventh day, the heir sends every day sufficient food for a single person and a *dirham* to the house of the Brahman, and continues doing this during all the days of the mourning-year without any interruption until its end.

## CHAPTER LXXIII.

### ABOUT WHAT IS DUE TO THE BODIES OF THE DEAD AND OF THE LIVING (*i.e.* ABOUT BURYING AND SUICIDE).

In the most ancient times the bodies of the dead were exposed to the air by being thrown on the fields without any covering; also sick people were exposed on the fields and in the mountains, and were left there. If they died there, they had the fate just mentioned; but if they recovered, they returned to their dwellings. Primitive burial-customs.

Thereupon there appeared a legislator who ordered people to expose their dead to the wind. In consequence they constructed roofed buildings with walls of rails, through which the wind blew, passing over the dead, as something similar is the case in the grave-towers of the Zoroastrians. Page 283.

After they had practised this custom for a long time, Nârâyaṇa prescribed to them to hand the dead over to the fire, and ever since they are in the habit of burning them, so that nothing remains of them, and every defilement, dirt, and smell is annihilated at once, so as scarcely to leave any trace behind.

Nowadays the Slavonians, too, burn their dead, whilst the ancient Greeks seem to have had both customs, that of burning and that of burying. Socrates speaks in the book *Phaedo*, after Crito had asked him in what manner he wanted to be buried: "As you wish, when you make arrangements for me. I shall not flee from you." Then he spoke to those around him: "Give to Crito regarding myself the opposite guarantee of that Greek parallels.

which he has given to the judges regarding myself; for he guaranteed to them that I should stay, whilst you now must guarantee that I shall not stay after death. I shall go away, that the look of my body may be tolerable to Crito when it is *burned* or *buried*, that he may not be in agony, and not say: 'Socrates is carried away, or is burned or buried.' Thou, O Crito, be at ease about the burial of my body. Do as thou likest, and specially in accordance with the laws."

Galenus says in his commentary to the apothegms of Hippocrates: "It is generally known that Asclepius was raised to the angels in a column of fire, the like of which is also related with regard to Dionysos, Heracles, and others, who laboured for the benefit of mankind. People say that God did thus with them in order to destroy the mortal and earthly part of them by the fire, and afterwards to attract to himself the immortal part of them, and to raise their souls to heaven."

In these words, too, there is a reference to the burning as a Greek custom, but it seems to have been in use only for the great men among them.

In a similar way the Hindus express themselves. There is a point in man by which he is what he is. This point becomes free when the mixed elements of the body are dissolved and scattered by combustion.

Fire and the sunbeam as the nearest roads to God.

Regarding this return (of the immortal soul to God), the Hindus think that partly it is effected by the rays of the sun, the soul attaching itself to them and ascending with them, partly by the flame of the fire, which raises it (to God). Some Hindu used to pray that God would make his road to himself as a straight line, because this is the nearest road, and that there is no other road upwards save the fire or the ray.

Similar to this is the practice of the Ghuzz Turks with reference to a drowned person; for they place the body on a bier in the river, and make a cord hang down from his foot, throwing the end of the cord into the water. By means of this cord the spirit of the deceased is to raise himself for resurrection.

The belief of the Hindus on this head was confirmed by the words of Vâsudeva, which he spoke regarding the sign of him who is liberated from the fetters (of bodily existence). "His death takes place during *uttarâyana* (*i.e.* the northern revolution of the sun from the winter solstice to the summer solstice), during the white half of the month, *between lighted lamps*, *i.e.* between conjunction and opposition (new moon and full moon), in the seasons of winter and spring."

A similar view is recognised in the following words of Mânî: "The other religious bodies blame us because we worship sun and moon, and represent them as an image. But they do not know their real natures; they do not know that sun and moon are our path, the door whence we march forth into the world of our existence (into heaven), as this has been declared by Jesus." So he maintains. Quotation from Mânî. Page 284.

People relate that Buddha had ordered the bodies of the dead to be thrown into flowing water. Therefore his followers, the Shamanians, throw their dead into the rivers.

According to the Hindus, the body of the dead has the claim upon his heirs that they are to wash, embalm, wrap it in a shroud, and then to burn it with as much sandal and other wood as they can get. Part of his burned bones are brought to the Ganges and thrown into it, that the Ganges should flow over them, as it has flowed over the burned bones of the children of Sagara, thereby forcing them from hell and bringing them into paradise. The remainder of the ashes is thrown into some brook of running water. On the spot where the body has been burned they raise a monument similar to a milestone, plastered with gypsum. Hindu manner of burial.

The bodies of children under three years are not burned.

Those who fulfil these duties towards the dead afterwards wash themselves as well as their dresses during two days, because they have become unclean by touching the dead.

Those who cannot afford to burn their dead will either throw them somewhere on the open field or into running water.

Modes of suicide.

Now as regards the right of the body of the living, the Hindus would not think of burning it save in the case of a widow who chooses to follow her husband, or in the case of those who are tired of their life, who are distressed over some incurable disease of their body, some irremovable bodily defect, or old age and infirmity. This, however, no man of distinction does, but only Vaiśyas and Śûdras, especially at those times which are prized as the most suitable for a man to acquire in them, for a future repetition of life, a better form and condition than that in which he happens to have been born and to live. Burning oneself is forbidden to Brahmans and Kshatriyas by a special law. Therefore these, if they want to kill themselves, do so at the time of an eclipse in some other manner, or they hire somebody to drown them in the Ganges, keeping them under water till they are dead.

The tree of Prayâga.

At the junction of the two rivers, Yamunâ and Ganges, there is a great tree called *Prayâga*, a tree of the species called *vaṭa*. It is peculiar to this kind of tree that its branches send forth two species of twigs, some directed upward, as is the case with all other trees, and others directed downward like roots, but without leaves. If such a twig enters into the soil, it is like a supporting column to the branch whence it has grown. Nature has arranged this on purpose, since the branches of this tree are of an enormous extent (and require to be supported). Here the Brahmans and Kshatriyas are in the habit of committing suicide by climbing up the tree and throwing themselves into the Ganges.

Johannes Grammaticus relates that certain people in ancient Greek heathendom, "whom I call the *worshippers of the devil*"—so he says—used to beat their limbs with swords, and to throw themselves into the fire, without feeling any pain therefrom. Greek parallels.

As we have related this as a view of the Hindus not to commit suicide, so also Socrates speaks: "Likewise it does not become a man to kill himself before the gods give him a cause in the shape of some compulsion or *dire necessity*, like that in which we now are."

Further he says: "We human beings are, as it were, in a prison. It does not behove us to flee nor to free ourselves from it, because the gods take notice of us, since we, the human beings, are servants to them."

# CHAPTER LXXIV.

## ON FASTING, AND THE VARIOUS KINDS OF IT.

FASTING is with the Hindus voluntary and supererogatory. Fasting is abstaining from food for a certain length of time, which may be different in duration and in the manner in which it is carried out.

Page 285.

Various methods of fasting.

The ordinary middle process, by which all the conditions of fasting are realised, is this: A man determines the day on which he will fast, and keeps in mind the name of that being whose benevolence he wishes to gain thereby and for whose sake he will fast, be it a god, or an angel, or some other being. Then he proceeds, prepares (and takes) his food on the day before the fast-day at noon, cleans his teeth by rubbing, and fixes his thoughts on the fasting of the following day. From that moment he abstains from food. On the morning of the fast-day he again rubs his teeth, washes himself, and performs the duties of the day. He takes water in his hand, and sprinkles it into all four directions, he pronounces with his tongue the name of the deity for whom he fasts, and remains in this condition till the day after the fast-day. After the sun has risen, he is at liberty to break the fast at that moment if he likes, or, if he prefers, he may postpone it till noon.

This kind is called *upavâsa, i.e.* the fasting; for the not-eating from one noon to the following is called *ekanakta*, not fasting.

Another kind, called *kṛicchra*, is this: A man takes his food on some day at noon, and on the following day in the evening. On the third day he eats nothing except what by chance is given him without his asking for it. On the fourth day he fasts.

Another kind, called *parâka*, is this: A man takes his food at noon on three consecutive days. Then he transfers his eating-hour to the evening during three further consecutive days. Then he fasts uninterruptedly during three consecutive days without breaking fast.

Another kind, called *candrâyaṇa*, is this: A man fasts on the day of full moon; on the following day he takes only a mouthful, on the third day he takes double this amount, on the fourth day the threefold of it, &c., &c., going on thus till the day of new moon. On that day he fasts; on the following days he again diminishes his food by one mouthful a day, till he again fasts on the day of full moon.

Another kind, called *mâsavâsa* (*mâsopavâsa*), is this: A man uninterruptedly fasts all the days of a month without ever breaking fast.

**Reward of the fasting in the single months.**

The Hindus explain accurately what reward the latter fasting in every single month will bring to a man for a new life of his after he has died. They say:

If a man fasts all the days of Caitra, he obtains wealth and joy over the nobility of his children.

If he fasts Vaiśâkha, he will be a lord over his tribe and great in his army.

If he fasts Jyaishṭha, he will be a favourite of the women.

If he fasts Âshâḍha, he will obtain wealth.

If he fasts Śrâvaṇa, he obtains wisdom.

If he fasts Bhâdrapada, he obtains health and valour, riches and cattle.

If he fasts Âśvayuja, he will always be victorious over his enemies.

If he fasts Kârttika, he will be grand in the eyes of people and will obtain his wishes.

If he fasts Mârgaśîrsha, he will be born in the most beautiful and fertile country.

If he fasts Pausha, he obtains a high reputation.

If he fasts Mâgha, he obtains innumerable wealth.

If he fasts Phâlguna, he will be beloved.

He, however, who fasts during all the months of the year, only twelve times breaking the fast, will reside in paradise 10,000 years, and will thence return to life as the member of a noble, high, and respected family.

Page 286. The book *Vishṇu-Dharma* relates that Maitreyî, the wife of Yâjnavalkya, asked her husband what man is to do in order to save his children from calamities and bodily defects, upon which he answered: "If a man begins on the day Duvê, in the month Pausha, *i.e.* the second day of each of the two halves of the month, and fasts four consecutive days, washing himself on the first with water, on the second with sesame oil, on the third with galangale, and on the fourth with a mixture of various balms; if he further on each day gives alms and recites praises over the names of the angels; if he continue to do all this during each month till the end of the year, his children will in the following life be free from calamities and defects, and he will obtain what he wishes; for also *Dilîpa*, *Dushyanta*, and *Yayâti* obtained their wishes for having acted thus."

# CHAPTER LXXV.

## ON THE DETERMINATION OF THE FAST-DAYS.

The eighth and eleventh days of each half of a month are fast-days.

THE reader must know in general that the eighth and eleventh days of the white half of every month are fast-days, except in the case of the leap month, for it is disregarded, being considered unlucky.

The eleventh is specially holy to Vâsudeva, because on having taken possession of Mâhûra, the inhabitants of which formerly used to worship Indra one day in each month, he induced them to transfer this worship to the eleventh, that it should be performed in his name. As the people did so, Indra became angry and poured rains over them like deluges, in order to destroy both them and their cattle. Vâsudeva, however, raised a mountain by his hand and protected them thereby. The water collected round them, but not above them, and the image of Indra fled. The people commemorated this event by a monument on a mountain in the neighbourhood of Mâhûra. Therefore they fast on this day in the state of the most punctilious cleanness, and they stay awake all the night, considering this as an obligatory performance, though in reality it is not obligatory.

On single fast-days throughout the year.

The book *Vishṇu-Dharma* says: "When the moon is in Rohiṇî, the fourth of her stations, on the eighth day of the black half, it is a fast-day called *Jayantî*. Giving alms on this day is an expiation for all sins."

Evidently this condition of the fast-day does not in general apply to all months, but in particular only to Bhâdrapada, since Vâsudeva was born in this month and on this day, whilst the moon stood in the station Rohiṇî. The two conditions, viz. the moon's standing in Rohiṇî and that the day is the eighth of the black half, can happen only once in so and so many years, for various reasons, *e.g.* the intercalation of the year, and because the civil years do not keep pace with lunar time, either getting in advance of it or falling behind.

The same book says: "When the moon stands in Punarvasu, the seventh of her stations, on the eleventh day of the white half of the month, this is a fast-day, called *Atj* (? *Aṭṭâṭaja*). If a man does works of piety on this day, he will be enabled to obtain whatever he wishes, as has been the case with *Sagara*, *Kakutstha*, and *Dandahamâr* (?), who obtained royalty because they had done so.

The sixth day of Caitra is a fast-day holy to the sun.

In the month Âshâḍha, when the moon stands in Anurâdhâ, the seventeenth of her signs, there is a fast-day holy to Vâsudeva called *Devasînî* (?), *i.e.* Deva is sleeping, because it is the beginning of the four months during which Vâsudeva slept. Others add this condition, that the day must be the eleventh of the month.

It is evident that such a day does not occur in every year. The followers of Vâsudeva abstain on this day from meat, fish, sweetmeats, and cohabitation with the women, and take food only once a day. They make
Page 287. the earth their bed without any covering, and do not use a bedstead raised above the earth.

People say that these four months are the night of the angels, to which must be added a month at the beginning as evening twilight, and a month at the end as morning dawn. However, the sun stands then near 0° of Cancer, which is noon in the *day of the angels*, and I do not see in what way this moon is connected with the two Saṁdhis.

The day of full moon in the month Śrâvaṇa is a fast-day holy to Somanâtha.

When in the month Âśvayuja the moon stands in Alsharaṭân (the lunar station) and the sun is in Virgo, it is a fast-day.

The eighth of the same month is a fast-day holy to Bhagavatî. Fasting is broken when the moon rises.

The fifth day of Bhâdrapada is a fast-day holy to the sun, called *shaṭ*. They anoint the solar rays, and in particular those rays which enter through the windows, with various kinds of balsamic ointments, and place upon them odoriferous plants and flowers.

When in this month the moon stands in Rohiṇî, it is a fast-day for the birth of Vâsudeva. Others add, besides, the condition that the day must be the eighth of the black half. We have already pointed out that such a day does not occur in every year, but only in certain ones of a larger number of years.

When in the month Kârttika the moon stands in Revatî, the last of her stations, it is a fast-day in commemoration of the waking up of Vâsudeva. It is called *deotthînî, i.e.* the rising of the Deva. Others add, besides, the condition that it must be the eleventh of the white half. On that day they soil themselves with the dung of cows, and break fasting by feeding upon a mixture of cow's milk, urine, and dung. This day is the first of the five days which are called *Bhîshma pañcarâtri*. They fast during them in honour of Vâsudeva. On the second of them the Brahmans break fasting, after them the others.

On the sixth day of Pausha is a fasting in honour of the sun.

On the third day of Mâgha there is a fasting for the women, not for the men. It is called Gaur-t-r (*gaurî-tṛitîyâ?*), and lasts the whole day and night. On the following morning they make presents to the nearest relatives of their husbands.

## CHAPTER LXXVI.

### ON THE FESTIVALS AND FESTIVE DAYS.

YÂTRÂ means travelling under auspicious circumstances. Therefore a feast is called *yâtrâ*. Most of the Hindu festivals are celebrated by women and children only.

The 2nd Caitra. The 2nd of the month Caitra is a festival to the people of Kashmir, called *Agdûs* (?), and celebrated on account of a victory gained by their king, Muttai, over the Turks. According to their account he ruled over the whole world. But this is exactly what they say of most of their kings. However, they are incautious enough to assign him to a time not much anterior to our time, which leads to their lie being found out. It is, of course, not impossible that a Hindu should rule (over a huge empire), as Greeks, Romans, Babylonians, and Persians have done, but all the times not much anterior to our own are well known. (If, therefore, such had been the case, we should know it.) Perhaps the here mentioned king ruled over the whole of India, and they know of no other country but India and of no other nations but themselves.

11th Caitra. On the 11th there is a festival called *Hindolî-caitra*, when they meet in the *devagriha*, or temple of Vâsudeva, and swing his image to and fro, as had been done with him when he was an infant in the cradle. They perform the same in their houses during the whole day and make merry.

Full moon's day. On the full moon's day of Caitra there is a feast called *Bahand* (*vasanta?*), a festival for the women, when they put on their ornaments and demand presents from their husbands.

The 22nd is a festival called *caitra-cashati*, a day of merriment holy to Bhagavatî, when people use to wash and to give alms. 22nd Caitra.

The 3rd Vaiśâkha is a festival for the women called *Gaur-t-r* (*gaurî-tritîyâ?*), holy to Gaurî, the daughter of the mountain Himavant, the wife of Mahâdeva. They wash and dress gaily, they worship the image of Gaurî and light lamps before it, they offer perfumes, abstain from eating, and play with swings. On the following day they give alms and eat. 3rd Vaiśâkha. Page 286.

On the 10th Vaiśâkha all the Brahmans whom the kings have invited proceed forth to the open fields, and there they light great fires for the sacrifices during five days till full moon. They make the fires in sixteen different spots and in four different groups. In each group a Brahman performs the sacrifice, so that there are *four* performing priests as there are *four* Vedas. On the 16th they return home.

In this month occurs the vernal equinox, called *vasanta*. They determine the day by calculation and make it a festival, when people invite the Brahmans. Vernal equinox.

On the 1st Jyaishṭha, or new moon's day, they celebrate a festival and throw the firstfruits of all seeds into the water in order to gain thereby a favourable prognostic. 1st Jyaishṭha.

The full moon's day of this month is a festival to the women, called *rûpa-panca* (?). Full moon's day.

All the days of the month Âshâḍha are devoted to alms-giving. It is also called *âhârî*. During this time the household is provided with new vessels. Âshâḍha.

On the full moon's day of Srâvaṇa they give banquets to the Brahmans. 15th Srâvaṇa.

On the 8th Âśvayuja, when the moon stands in the nineteenth station, Mûla, begins the sucking of the sugar cane. It is a festival holy to *Mahânavamî*, the 8th Âśvayuja.

sister of Mahâdeva, when they offer the firstfruits of sugar and all other things to her image which is called Bhagavatî. They give much alms before it and kill kids. He who does not possess anything to offer, stands upright by the side of the idol, without ever sitting down, and will sometimes pounce upon whomsoever he meets and kill him.

15th Âśvayuja. On the 15th, when the moon stands in the last of her stations, Revatî, there is the festival *Puhât* (?), when they wrangle with each other and play with the animals. It is holy to Vâsudeva, because his uncle Kaṁsa had ordered him into his presence for the purpose of wrangling.

16th Âśvayuja. On the 16th there is a festival, when they give alms to the Brahmans.

23rd Âśvayuja. On the 23rd is the festival Aśoka, also called *âhoî*, when the moon stands in the seventh station, Punarvasu. It is a day of merriment and of wrangling.

Bhâdrapadâ, new moon. In the month Bhâdrapadâ, when the moon stands in the tenth station, Maghâ, they celebrate a festival which they call *pitṛipaksha, i.e.* the half of the month of the Fathers, because the moon's entering this station falls near the time of new moon. They distribute alms during fifteen days in the name of the Fathers.

3rd Bhâdrapadâ. On the 3rd Bhâdrapadâ is the festival *Harbâlî* (?), for the women. It is their custom that a number of days before they sow all kinds of seeds in baskets, and they bring the baskets forward on this day after they have commenced growing. They throw roses and perfumes on them and play with each other during the whole night. On the following morning they bring them to the ponds, wash them, wash themselves, and give alms.

6th Bhâdrapadâ. On the 6th of this month, which is called *Gâihat* (?), when people give food to those who are in prison.

8th Bhâdrapadâ. On the 8th, when the moonlight has reached half of its development, they have a festival called *dhruva-*

*griha* (?); they wash themselves and eat well growing grain-fruit that their children should be healthy. The women celebrate this festival when they are pregnant and desire to have children.

The 11th Bhâdrapadâ is called *Parvatî* (?). This is the name of a thread which the priest makes from materials presented to him for the purpose. One part of it he dyes with crocus, the other he leaves as it is. He gives the thread the same length as the statue of Vâsudeva is high. Then he throws it over his neck, so that it hangs down to his feet. It is a much venerated festival. 11th Bhâdrapadâ. Page 289.

The 16th, the first day of the black half, is the first of seven days which are called *karâra* (?), when they adorn the children nicely and give a treat to them. They play with various animals. On the seventh day the men adorn themselves and celebrate a festival. And during the rest of the month they always adorn the children towards the end of the day, give alms to the Brahmans, and do works of piety. 16th Bhâdrapadâ.

When the moon stands in her fourth station, Rohiṇî, they call this time *Gûnâlahid* (?), celebrating a festival during three days and making merry by playing with each other, from joy over the birth of Vâsudeva.

Jîvaśarman relates that the people of Kashmîr celebrate a festival on the 26th and 27th of this month, on account of certain pieces of wood called *gana* (?), which the water of the river Vitastâ (Jailam) carries, in those two days, through the capital, *Adhishṭhâna*. People maintain that it is Mahâdeva who sends them. It is peculiar to these pieces of wood, so they say, that nobody is able to seize them, however much he may desire it, that they always evade his grasp and move away. 26th, 27th, Bhâdrapadâ.

However, the people of Kashmîr, with whom I have conversed on the subject, give a different statement as to the place and the time, and maintain that the thing occurs in a pond called *Kûdaishahr* (?), to the left of the source of the just-mentioned river (Vitastâ-Jailam), in the middle of the month Vaiśâkha. The latter version is the more likely, as about this time the waters begin to increase. The matter reminds one of the wood in the river of Jurjân, which appears at the time when the water swells in its source.

The same Jivaśarman relates that in the country of Svât, opposite the district of *Kîrî* (?), there is a valley in which fifty-three streams unite. It is called *Tranjâi* (cf. Sindhi *trêvanjâha*). In those two days the water of this valley becomes white, in consequence of Mahâdeva's washing in it, as people believe.

1st Kârttika.

The 1st Kârttika, or new moon's day, when the sun marches in Libra, is called *Dibâlî*. Then people bathe, dress festively, make presents to each other of betel-leaves and areca-nuts; they ride to the temples to give alms and play merrily with each other till noon. In the night they light a great number of lamps in every place so that the air is perfectly clear. The cause of this festival is that Lakshmî, the wife of Vâsudeva, once a year on this day liberates Bali, the son of Virocana, who is a prisoner in the seventh earth, and allows him to go out into the world. Therefore the festival is called *Balirâjya*, *i.e.* the principality of Bali. The Hindus maintain that this time was a time of luck in the Kṛitayuga, and they are happy because the feast-day in question resembles that time in the Kṛitayuga.

In the same month, when full moon is perfect, they give banquets and adorn their women during all the days of the black half.

3rd Mârgaśirsha.

The 3rd Mârgaśirsha, called *Guvâna-bâtrîj* (—— *tritiyâ ?*), is a feast of the women, sacred to Gaurî. They meet in the houses of the rich among them; they put several silver statues of the goddess on a throne, and perfume it and play with each other the whole day. On the following morning they give alms.

On full moon's day of the same month there is another festival of the women. 15th Mârgaśirsha. Page 290.

On most of the days of the month Pausha they prepare great quantities of *pûhaval* (?), *i.e.* a sweet dish which they eat. Pausha.

On the eighth day of the white half of Pausha, which is called *Ashṭaka*, they make gatherings of the Brahmans, present them with dishes prepared from the plant *Atriplex hortensis*, i.e. *sarmaḳ* in Arabic (= orache), and show attentions to them. 8th Pausha

On the eighth day of the black half, which is called *Sâkârtam*, they eat turnips.

The 3rd Mâgha, called *Mâhatrîj* (*Mâgha-tṛitîyâ* ?), is a feast for the women, and sacred to Gaurî. They meet in the houses of the most prominent among them before the image of Gaurî, place before it various sorts of costly dresses, pleasant perfumes, and nice dishes. In each meeting-place they put 108 jugs full of water, and after the water has become cool, they wash with it four times at the four quarters of that night. On the following day they give alms, they give banquets and receive guests. The women's washing with cold water is common to all the days of this month. 3rd Mâgha.

On the last day of this month, *i.e.* the 29th, when there is only a remainder of 3 day-minutes, *i.e.* $1\frac{1}{5}$ hour, all the Hindus enter the water and duck under in it seven times. 29th Mâgha.

On the full moon's day of this month, called *câmdâha* (?), they light lamps on all high places. 15th Mâgha.

On the 23rd, which is called *mânsartaku*, and also *mâhâtan*, they receive guests and feed them on meat and large black peas. 23rd Mâgha.

On the 8th Phâlguna, called *pûrârtaku*, they prepare for the Brahmans various dishes from flour and butter. 8th Phâlguna.

The full moon's day of Phâlguna is a feast to the women, called *Odâd* (?), or also *dhola* (i.e. *dola*), when 15th Phâlguna.

they make fire on places lower than those on which they make it on the festival *câmâha*, and they throw the fire out of the village.

16th Phâlguna.

On the following night, *i.e.* that of the 16th, called *Śivarâtri*, they worship Mahâdeva during the whole night; they remain awake, and do not lie down to sleep, and offer to him perfumes and flowers.

23rd Phâlguna.

On the 23rd, which is called *pûyattan* (?), they eat rice with butter and sugar.

A festival in Mûltân.

The Hindus of Mûltân have a festival which is called *Sâmbapurayâtrâ;* they celebrate it in honour of the sun, and worship him. It is determined in this way: They first take the *ahargaṇa*, according to the rules of Khaṇḍakhâdyaka, and subtract 98,040 therefrom. They divide the remainder by 365, and disregard the quotient. If the division does not give a remainder, the quotient is the date of the festival in question. If there is a remainder, it represents the days which have elapsed since the festival, and by subtracting these days from 365 you find the date of the same festival in the next following year.

# CHAPTER LXXVII.

## ON DAYS WHICH ARE HELD IN SPECIAL VENERATION, ON LUCKY AND UNLUCKY TIMES, AND ON SUCH TIMES AS ARE PARTICULARLY FAVOURABLE FOR ACQUIRING IN THEM BLISS IN HEAVEN.

THE single days enjoy different degrees of veneration according to certain qualities which they attribute to them. They distinguish, *e.g.*, the Sunday, because it is the day of the sun and the beginning of the week, as the Friday is distinguished in Islam.

The days of new moon and full moon.

To the distinguished days further belong *amâvâsyâ* and *pûrṇimâ*, *i.e.* the days of conjunction (new moon) and opposition (full moon), because they are the limits of the wane and the increase of the moonlight. In accordance with the belief of the Hindus regarding this increase and wane, the Brahmans sacrifice continually to the fire in order to earn heavenly reward. They let the portions of the angels accumulate, which are the offerings thrown into the fire at moonlight during the whole time from new moon to full moon. Then they begin distributing these portions over the angels in the time from full moon to new moon, till at the time of new moon nothing any more remains of them. We have already mentioned that new moon and full moon are noon and midnight of the nychthemeron of the Fathers. Therefore the uninterrupted almsgiving on these two days is always done in honour of the Fathers.

Page 291.

**The four days on which the four *yugas* are said to have commenced.**

Four other days are held in special veneration, because, according to the Hindus, with them the single *yugas* of the present *caturyuga* have commenced, viz. :—

The 3rd Vaiśâkha, called *kshairîtâ* (?), on which the Kṛitayuga is believed to have commenced.

The 9th Kârttika, the beginning of the Tretâyuga.

The 15th Mâgha, the beginning of the Dvâpara-yuga.

The 13th of Âśvayuja, the beginning of the Kali-yuga.

According to my opinion, these days are festivals, sacred to the *yugas*, instituted for the purpose of alms-giving or for the performance of some rites and ceremonies, as, *e.g.*, the commemoration-days in the year of the Christians. However, we must deny that the four *yugas* could really have commenced on the days here mentioned.

**Criticisms thereon.**

With regard to the Kṛitayuga, the matter is perfectly clear, because its beginning is the beginning of the solar and lunar cycles, there being no fraction in the date, since it is, at the same time, the beginning of the *caturyuga*. It is the first of the month Caitra, at the same time the date of the vernal equinox, and on the same day also the other *yugas* commence. For, according to Brahmagupta, a *caturyuga* contains :—

| | |
|---|---|
| Civil days . . . . . . . | 1,577,916,450 |
| Solar months . . . . . . | 51,840,000 |
| Leap months . . . . . . | 1,593,300 |
| Lunar days . . . . . . . | 1,602,999,000 |
| *Ûnarâtra* days . . . . . | 25,082,550 |

These are the elements on which the resolution of chronological dates into days, or the composition of them out of days, is based. All these numbers may be divided by 10, and the divisors are wholes without any fraction. Now the beginnings of the single *yugas* depend upon the beginning of the *caturyuga*.

According to Pulisa the *caturyuga* contains:—

| | |
|---|---|
| Civil days | 1,577,917,800 |
| Solar months | 51,840,000 |
| Leap months | 1,593,336 |
| Lunar days | 1,603,000,010 |
| *Ûnarâtra* days | 25,082,280 |

All these numbers may be divided by 4, and the divisors are wholly without any fraction. According to this computation, also, the beginnings of the single *yugas* are the same as the beginning of the *caturyuga*, *i.e.* the first of the month Caitra and the day of the vernal equinox. However, this day falls on different week days.

Hence it is evident that their theory about the above-mentioned four days being the beginnings of the four *yugas*, is without any foundation at all; that they could never arrive at such a result unless by resorting to very artificial ways of interpretation.

The days called *puṇyakâla*.

The times which are specially favourable to earn a heavenly reward in them are called *puṇyakâla*. Balabhadra says in his commentary to the Khaṇḍakhâdyaka:—"If the *yogin*, *i.e.* the ascetic who understands the creator, who chooses the good and eschews the bad, continued his manner of life during one thousand years, his reward would not be equal to that of a man who gives alms on *puṇyakâla* and fulfils the duties of the day, *i.e.* washing and anointing himself, saying prayers and praises."

No doubt, most of the feast-days enumerated in the preceding belong to this kind of days, for they are (Page 292.) devoted to almsgiving and banqueting. If people did not expect to gain thereby a reward in heaven, they would not approve of the rejoicings and merriments which are characteristic of these days.

Notwithstanding the nature of the *puṇyakâla* is such as here explained, some of them are considered as lucky, others as unlucky days.

Those days are lucky when the planets migrate from one sign into the other, especially the sun. These times are called *saṁkrânti*. The most propitious of them are the days of the equinoxes and solstices, and of these the most propitious is the day of the vernal equinox. It is called *bikhû* or *shibû* (*vishuva*), as the two sounds *sh* and *kh* may be exchanged for each other, and may also, by a *metathesis*, change their place.

Saṁkrânti.

As, however, a planet's entering a new sign does not require more than a moment of time, and, during it, people must offer to the fire the offering *sânta* (?) with oil and corn, the Hindus have given a greater extent to these times, making them *begin* with the moment when the eastern edge of the body of the sun touches the first part of the sign; reckoning as their *middle* the moment when the sun's centre reaches the first part of the sign, which is in astronomy considered as the time of the migration (of the planet from one sign to the other), and reckoning as the *end* that moment when the western edge of the sun's body touches the first part of the sign. This process lasts, in the case of the sun, nearly two hours.

For the purpose of finding the times in the week when the sun migrates from one sign to another, they have several methods, one of which was dictated to me by Samaya (?). It is this:—

Method for calculating the moment of *saṁkrânti*.

Subtract from the Śakakâla 847, multiply the remainder by 180, and divide the product by 143. The quotient you get represents days, minutes, and seconds. This number is the basis.

If you want to know at what time in the year in question the sun enters any one of the twelve signs, you look out the sign in the following table. Take the number which you find side by side with the sign in question, and add it to the basis, days to days, minutes to minutes, seconds to seconds. If the wholes amount to 7 or more, disregard them, and with the remainder count off the week-days, beginning with the beginning of Sunday. That time you arrive at is the moment of *saṁkrânti*.

| The Zodiacal Signs. | What must be added to the *Basis*. | | |
|---|---|---|---|
| | Days. | Ghaṭî. | Cashaka. |
| Aries | 3 | 19 | 0 |
| Taurus | 6 | 17 | 0 |
| Gemini | 2 | 43 | 0 |
| Cancer | 6 | 21 | 0 |
| Leo | 2 | 49 | 0 |
| Virgo | 5 | 49 | 0 |
| Libra | 1 | 14 | 0 |
| Scorpio | 3 | 6 | 30 |
| Arcitenens | 4 | 34 | 30 |
| Capricornus | 5 | 54 | 0 |
| Amphora | 0 | 30 | 0 |
| Pisces | 2 | 11 | 20 |

*On the length of the solar year according to Brahmagupta, Pulisa, and Âryabhaṭa.*

The beginning of consecutive solar years in the week differs by 1 day and the fraction at the end of the year. This amount, reduced to fractions of one kind, is the multiplicator (180), used in the preceding computation in order to find the *surplus* of each year (*i.e.* the amount by which its beginning wanders onward through the week).

The divisor (143) is the denominator of the fraction (which is accordingly $\frac{180}{143}$).

Accordingly the fraction at the end of the solar year is, in this computation, reckoned as $\frac{37}{143}$, which implies as the length of the solar year, 365 days 15′ 31″ 28‴ $6^{iv}$. To raise this fraction of a day to one whole day, $\frac{106}{143}$ of a day are required. I do not know whose theory this is.

If we divide the days of a *caturyuga* by the number of its solar years, according to the theory of Brahmagupta, we get as the length of the solar year, 365 days 30′ 22″ 30‴ $0^{iv}$. In this case the multiplicator or *guṇakâra* is 4027, and the divisor or *bhâgakâra* is 3200 (*i.e.* 1 day 30′ 22″ 30‴ $0^{iv}$ are equal to $\frac{4027}{3200}$).

*Page 293.*

Reckoning according to the theory of Pulisa, we find as the length of the solar year 365 days 15′ 31″ 30‴ 0$^{iv}$. Accordingly, the *guṇakâra* would be 1007, the *bhâgahâra* 800 (*i.e.* 1 day 15′ 31″ 30‴ 0$^{iv}$ are equal to $\frac{1007}{800}$).

According to Âryabhaṭa, the length of the solar year is 365 days 15′ 31″ 15‴. In that case the *guṇakâra* is 725 and the *bhâgahâra* is 572 (*i.e.* 1 day 15′ 31″ 15‴ are equal to $\frac{725}{572}$).

Another method for finding the *saṁkrânti*.

Another method for finding the moment of *saṁkrânti* has been dictated to me by Auliatta (?), the son of *Sahâwî* (?), and is based on the system of Pulisa. It is this:

Subtract from the Śakakâla 918, multiply the remainder by 1007, add to the product 79, and divide the sum by 800. Divide the quotient by 7. The remainder you get is the *basis*. What now must for each sign be added to the *basis*, as has already been mentioned (ii. 188), is indicated by the following table opposite to each sign:—

| The Zodiacal Signs. | What must be added to the *Basis*. | | The Zodiacal Signs. | What must be added to the *Basis*. | |
|---|---|---|---|---|---|
| | Days. | Ghaṭî. | | Days. | Ghaṭî. |
| Aries . . . | 1 | 35 | Libra . . . | 6 | 31 |
| Taurus . . | 4 | 33 | Scorpio . . | 1 | 23 |
| Gemini . . | 0 | 39 | Arcitenens . . | 2 | 11 |
| Cancer . . | 4 | 34 | Capricornus . | 4 | 10 |
| Leo . . . | 1 | 6 | Amphora . . | 5 | 34 |
| Virgo . . . | 4 | 6 | Pisces . . . | 0 | 28 |

*Shaḍaśîtimukha.*

Varâhamihira maintains in the *Pañcasiddhântikâ* that the *shaḍaśîtimukha* is in the same degree propitious as the time of *saṁkrânti* for acquiring in it infinite heavenly reward. This is the moment of the sun's entering:—The 18th degree of Gemini; the 14th degree of Virgo; the 26th degree of Arcitenens; and the 28th degree of Pisces.

The moment of the sun's entering the fixed signs

is four times as propitious as the moment of his entering the other signs. For each of these times they compute the beginning and the end by means of the radius of the sun in the same way as they compute the minutes of the sun's or moon's entering and leaving the shadow at an eclipse. This method is well known in their *canones*. We, however, communicate here only those of their methods of calculation which we think remarkable, or which, as far as we know, have not yet been explained before Muslim ears, as Muslims know of the methods of the Hindus only those which are found in the Sind-hind.

Times of eclipses.

Most propitious times are, further, the times of solar and lunar eclipses. At that time, according to their belief, all the waters of the earth become as pure as that of the Ganges. They exaggerate the veneration of these times to such a degree that many of them commit suicide, wishing to die at such a time as promises them heavenly bliss. However, this is only done by Vaiśyas and Śûdras, whilst it is forbidden to Brahmans and Kshatriyas, who in consequence do not commit suicide (*vide*, however, ii. 170).

*Parvan* and *yoga*.

Further, the times of *Parvan* are propitious, *i.e.* those times in which an eclipse may take place. And even if there is no eclipse at such a time, it is considered quite as propitious as the time of an eclipse itself.

The times of the *yogas* are as propitious as those of the eclipses. We have devoted a special chapter to them (chap. lxxix.).

Unlucky days.

If it happens within the course of one civil day that the moon revolves in the latter part of some station, then enters the following station, proceeds through the whole of it and enters a third station, so that in one single day she stands in three consecutive stations, such a day is called *trihaspaka* (?), and also *triharkasha* (?). It is an unlucky day, boding evil, and it is counted among the *puṇyakâla*. (See ii. 187.) Page 294.

The same applies to that civil day which comprehends a complete lunar day, whose beginning, besides, falls in the latter part of the preceding lunar day, and whose end falls in the beginning of the following lunar day. Such a day is called *trahagattata* (?). It is unlucky, but favourable to earn in it a heavenly reward.

When the days of *ûnarâtra*, i.e. *the days of the decrease* (see ii. 25), sum up so as to form one complete day, it is unlucky and reckoned among the *puṇyakâla*. This takes place according to Brahmagupta in $62\frac{50663}{55739}$ civil days, $62\frac{183}{55739}$ solar days, $63\frac{50663}{55739}$ lunar days.

According to Pulisa, it takes place in $62\frac{63279}{69073}$ civil days, $63\frac{63279}{69073}$ lunar days, $62\frac{714}{69073}$ solar days.

The moment when a complete leap-month without any fraction is summed up, is unlucky, and is not reckoned among the *puṇyakâla*. According to Brahmagupta, this takes place in $990\frac{36663}{106622}$ civil days, $976\frac{4641}{5311}$ solar days, $1006\frac{4641}{5311}$ lunar days.

Times of earthquakes.

Times which are considered as unlucky, to which no merit whatsoever is attributed, are, *e.g.*, the times of earthquakes. Then the Hindus beat with the pots of their households against the earth and break them, in order to get a good omen and to banish the mishap. As times of a similar ill nature, the book *Saṁhitâ* further enumerates the moments of landslips, the falling of stars, red glow in the sky, the combustion of the earth by lightning, the appearance of comets, the occurrence of events contrary both to nature and custom, the entering of the wild beasts into the villages, rainfall when it is not the season for it, the trees putting forth leaves when it is not the season for it, when the nature of one season of the year seems transferred to another, and more of the like.

The book *Srûdhara*, attributed to Mahâdeva, says the following:

"The *burning* days, *i.e.* the unlucky ones—for thus they call them—are: Quotation from the book *Srî-dhara* of Mahâdeva.

"The second days of the white and black halves of the months Caitra and Pausha;

"The fourth days of the two halves of the months Jyaishṭha and Phâlguna;

"The sixth days of the two halves of the months Śrâvaṇa and Vaiśâkha;

"The eighth days of the two halves of the months Âshâḍha and Âśvayuja;

"The tenth days of the two halves of the months Mârgaśirsha and Bhâdrapada;

"The twelfth days of the two halves of the month Kârttika."

# CHAPTER LXXVIII.

## ON THE KARAṆAS.

Explanation of *karaṇa*. WE have already spoken of the lunar days called *tithi*, and have explained that each lunar day is shorter than a civil day, because the lunar month has thirty lunar days, but only a little more than twenty-nine and a half civil days.

As the Hindus call these *tithis* nychthemera, they also call the former half of a *tithi* day, the latter half night. Each of these halves has a separate name, and they all of them (*i.e.* all the halves of the lunar days of the lunar month) are called *karaṇas.*

Fixed and movable *karaṇas.* Some of the names of the *karaṇas* occur only once in a month and are not repeated, viz. four of them about the time of new moon, which are called *the fixed ones*, because they occur only once in the month, and because they always fall on the same day and night of the month.

Others of them revolve and occur eight times in a month. They are called *the movable ones*, because of their revolving, and because each one of them may as well fall on a day as on a night. They are seven in number, and the seventh or last of them is an unlucky day, by which they frighten their children, the simple mention of which makes the hairs on the head of their boys stand on end. We have given an exhaustive
Page 295. description of the *karaṇas* in another book of ours. They are mentioned in every Indian book on astronomy and mathematics.

If you want to know the *karaṇas*, first determine the lunar days, and find out in what part of them the date in question falls, which is done in this way:— Rule how to find the *karaṇas*.

Subtract the corrected place of the sun from the corrected place of the moon. The remainder is the distance between them. If it is less than six zodiacal signs, the date falls in the white half of the month; if it is more, it falls in the black half.

Reduce this number to minutes, and divide the product by 720. The quotient represents *tithis*, *i.e.* complete lunar days. If you get by the division a remainder, multiply it by 60 and divide the product by the mean *bhukti*. The quotient represents *ghaṭīs* and minor fractions, *i.e.* that portion of the current day which has already elapsed.

This is the method of the *canones* of the Hindus. The distance between the corrected places of sun and moon must be divided by the mean *bhukti*. This, however, is impossible for many of the days. Therefore they divide this distance by the difference between the daily revolutions of sun and moon, which they reckon for the moon as 13 degrees, for the sun as 1 degree.

It is a favourite method in rules of this kind, especially in Indian ones, to reckon by the mean motion of sun and moon. The mean motion of the sun is subtracted from the mean motion of the moon, and the remainder is divided by 732, which is the difference between their two middle *bhuktis*. The quotient then represents days and *ghaṭīs*.

The word *buht* is of Indian origin. In the Indian language it is *bhukti* (= the daily motion of a planet). If the corrected motion is meant, it is called *bhukti sphuṭa*. If the mean motion is meant, it is called *bhukti madhyama*, and if the *buht* which renders equal is meant, it is called *bhuktyantara*, *i.e.* the difference between the two *bhuktis*. Explanation of *bhukti*.

Names of the lunar days of the half of a month.

The lunar days of the month have special names, which we exhibit in the following diagram. If you know the lunar day in which you are, you find, by the side of the number of the day, its name, and opposite it the *karaṇa* in which you are. If that which has elapsed of the current day is less than half a day, the *karaṇa* is a diurnal one; if that which has elapsed of it is more than half a day, it is a nocturnal one. This is the diagram:—

| The white half. | | | | The black half. | | | | The *karaṇas* are common to both halves. | |
|---|---|---|---|---|---|---|---|---|---|
| The number of the days. | Their names. | The number of the days. | Their names. | The number of the days. | Their names. | The number of the days. | Their names. | In daytime. | In the night. |
| 1 | Amâvâsyâ. | 0 | 0 | 0 | 0 | 0 | 0 | Catushpada. | Nâga. |
| 2 | Barkhu. | 0 | 0 | 0 | 0 | 0 | 0 | Kinstughna. | Bava. |
| 3 | Biya. | 10 | Navin. | 17 | Barkhu. | 24 | Atin. | Bâlava. | Kaulava. |
| 4 | Triya.; | 11 | Dahîn. | 18 | Biya. | 25 | Navin. | Taitila. | Gara. |
| 5 | Caut. | 12 | Yâhî. | 19 | Triya. | 26 | Dahîn. | Baṇij. | Vishṭi. |
| 6 | Pancî. | 13 | Duvâhî. | 20 | Caut. | 27 | Yâhi. | Bava. | Bâlava. |
| 7 | Sat. | 14 | Trohî. | 21 | Pancî. | 28 | Duvâhî. | Kaulava. | Taitila. |
| 8 | Satîn. | 15 | Caudahî. | 22 | Sat. | 29 | Trohî. | Gara. | Baṇij. |
| 9 | Atin. | 16 | { Pûrnimâ pancâhî. } | 23 | Satîn. | 0 | 0 | Vishṭi. | Bava. |
| 0 | 0 | 0 | 0 | 0 | 0 | 30 | Caudahî. | Vishṭi. | Śakuni. |

Table of *karaṇas* with their dominants and prognostics.

The Hindus attribute to some of the *karaṇas* dominants, as is their custom. Further they give rules showing what during each *karaṇa* must be done or not, rules which are similar to collections of astrological prognostics (as to lucky or unlucky days, &c.). If we give here a second diagram of the *karaṇas*, we thereby simply mean to confirm what we have said already, and to repeat a subject which is unknown among us. Thus it is rendered easy to learn the subject, because learning is the fruit of repetition.

THE FOUR FIXED *KARAṆAS.*

Page 296.

| In which half of the month they fall. | Their names. | Their dominants. | The prognostics of the *karaṇas*, and for what thing each of them is favourable. |
|---|---|---|---|
| In the black half. | Śakuni. | Kali. | Favourable for the action of medicines, of drugs against the bite of serpents, of incantations, of learning, of council-holding, and of reciting holy texts before the idols. |
| In the white half. | Catushpada. | The zodiacal sign Taurus. | Favourable for placing a king on a throne, giving alms in the name of the Fathers, for making use of four-footed animals in agriculture. |
| | Nâga. | The snake. | Favourable for weddings, laying a foundation-stone, examining the state of snake-bitten persons, for frightening people and seizing them. |
| | Kinstughna. | The wind. | Ruins all actions and is favourable only for things connected with marriage, for the construction of parasols, the piercing of the ears, and for works of piety. |

## THE SEVEN MOVABLE *KARAṆAS*.

| In which half of the month they fall. | Their names. | Their dominants. | The pronostics of the *karaṇas*, and for what thing each of them is favourable. |
|---|---|---|---|
| Both in the white and the black halves. | Bava. | Śukra. | When there is a *saṁkrânti* in this *karaṇa*, it is *sitting*, and the fruits will, during it, suffer some mishap. It is favourable for travelling, for beginning with things which are intended to last long, for cleaning oneself, for compounding the drugs which make the women fat, and for the sacrifices which the Brahmans offer to the fire. |
| | Bâlava. | Brahman. | When there is a *saṁkrânti* in it, it is *sitting*, not good for the fruits. It is favourable for the affairs of future life, and for acquiring a heavenly reward. |
| | Kaulava. | Mitra. | When there is a *saṁkrânti* in it, it is *standing*. All that is sown in it will prosper and drop with succulence. It is favourable for making friendships with people. |
| | Taitila. | Aryaman. | When there is a *saṁkrânti* in it, it is *stretched on the ground*. It indicates that the prices will sink, and is favourable for the kneading of aromatic unguents and the compounding of perfumes. |
| | Gara. | Parvata. | When there is a *saṁkrânti* in it, it is *stretched on the ground*. It indicates that the prices will be depressed, and is favourable for sowing and laying the foundation-stone of a building. |
| | Baṇij. | Śrî. | When there is a *saṁkrânti* in it, it is *standing*. All corn will prosper (*lacuna*), and is favourable for commerce. |
| | Vishṭi. | Marut. | When there is a *saṁkrânti* in it, it is *stretched on the ground*. It indicates that the prices will be insufficient. It is not favourable for anything save the crushing of the sugar-cane. It is considered as unlucky and is not good for travelling. |

Rule for the computation of the *karaṇas*.

Page 297.

If you want to find the *karaṇas* by computation, subtract the corrected place of the sun from that of the moon, reduce the remainder to minutes and divide the number of them by 360. The quotient represents complete *karaṇas*.

What remains after the division is multiplied by 60, and divided by the *bhuktyantara*. The quotient represents how much has elapsed of the current *karaṇa*. Every unit of the number is equal to half a *ghaṭî*.

We now return to the complete *karaṇas*. If they are two or less, you are in the second *karaṇa*. In that case you add one to the number and count the sum off, beginning with *catushpada*.

If the number of *karaṇas* is 59, you are in *śakuni*.

If it is less than 59 and more than two, add one to them and divide the sum by seven. The remainder, if it is not more than seven, count off, beginning with the beginning of the cycle of the *movable karaṇas*, *i.e.* with *bava*. Thereby you will arrive at the name of the current *karaṇa* in which you happen to be.

The *karaṇas* as borrowed by Alkindî and other Arab authors.

Wishing to remind the reader of something relating to the *karaṇas* which he perhaps has forgotten, we must tell him that Alkindî and others like him have hit upon the system of the *karaṇas*, but one which was not sufficiently explained. They did not comprehend the method of those who use the *karaṇas*. At one time they trace them back to Indian, another time to Babylonian origin, declaring all the time that they are altered on purpose and corrupted by the inadvertence of the copyists. They have invented a calculation for them which proceeds in a better order than even the original method itself. But thereby the thing has become something totally different from what it originally was. Their method is this: they count half days, beginning with new moon. The first twelve hours they regard as belonging to the sun, as *burning*, *i.e.* unlucky, the next twelve hours as belonging to Venus, the following twelve hours as belonging to Mercury, and so on according to the order of the planets. Whenever the order returns to the sun, they call his twelve hours *the hours of Albist*, i.e. *vishṭi.*

However, the Hindus do not measure the *karaṇas* by civil, but by lunar days, nor do they begin with those *burning* hours following upon new moon. According to the calculation of Alkindî, people begin, after new moon, with Jupiter; in that case the periods of the sun are not *burning*. On the other hand, if they begin, according to the method of the Hindus, after new moon with the sun, the hours of *vishṭi* belong to Mercury. Therefore, each method, that of the Hindus and that of Alkindî, must be treated separately.

Because *vishṭi* recurs eight times in a month, and because the points of the compass are eight, we shall exhibit in the eight fields of the following table their ἀστρολογούμενα regarding the *karaṇas*, observations the like of which are made by all astrologers regarding the shapes of the planets and regarding those stars which rise in the single third parts of the zodiacal signs.

Page 298.

| Their numbers. | In what part of the month they fall. | Names of the *vishṭis.* | The directions in which they rise. | DESCRIPTION OF THE SINGLE "VISHṬIS." | Their names according to the book *Srîdhara.* |
|---|---|---|---|---|---|
| I. | In the night of the 5th *tithi.* | | East. | It has three eyes. The hair on its head is like growing sugar-cane. In one hand it has an iron hook, in the other a black serpent. It is strong and violent like running water. It has a long tongue. Its day is only good for war, and those actions in which there is deception and falsification. | Vadavâmukha. |

| Their numbers. | In what part of the month they fall. | Names of the *vishṭis*. | The directions in which they rise. | DESCRIPTION OF THE SINGLE "VISHṬIS." | Their names according to the book *Srûdhava*. |
|---|---|---|---|---|---|
| II. | In the day of the 9th *tithi*. | ... | Aiśâna. | It is green, and has a sword in its hand. Its place is in the lightning, thundering, stormy, and cold cloud. Its time is favourable for tearing out fattening herbs, for drinking medicine, for commerce, and for casting gold in a mould. | Blv (?). |
| III. | In the night of the 12th *tithi*. | Ghora. | North. | It has a black face, thick lips, bushy eyebrows, long hair of the head. It is long, and rides during its day. In the hand it has a sword, it is intent upon devouring men, it emits fire from its mouth, and says *bâ bâ bâ*. Its time is only good for fighting, for killing miscreants, for curing ill people, and for fetching serpents out of their holes. | Ghora. |
| IV. | In the day of the 16th *tithi*. | ... | Vâyava. | It has five faces and ten eyes. Its time is favourable for punishing rebels, for dividing the army into single corps. During it a man must not turn with his face towards the direction where it rises. | Krâla (?). |
| V. | In the night of the 19th *tithi*. | ... | West. | It is like a smoky flame. It has three heads, in each three eyes turned upside down. Its hair is standing on end. It sits on the head of a human being, it screams like thunder. It is angry, devours men. It holds in one hand a knife, in the other an axe. | Jwâla (?). |

| Their numbers. | In what part of the month they fall. | Names of the *vishṭis.* | The directions in which they rise. | DESCRIPTION OF THE SINGLE "VISHṬIS." | Their names according to the *Srîdhara.* |
|---|---|---|---|---|---|
| VI. | In the day of the 23d *tithi.* | ... | Nairṛita. | It is white, has three eyes, and rides on an elephant, which always remains the same. In the one hand he has a huge rock, in the other a *vajra* of iron, which it throws. It destroys the cattle over which it rises. He who makes war coming from the direction whence it rises will be victorious. A man must not turn with his face towards it when tearing out fattening herbs, digging out treasures, and trying to satisfy the wants of life. | |
| VII. | In the night of the 26th *tithi.* | ... | South. | It has the colour of crystal. In one hand it holds a three-fold *paraśvadha*, and in the other a rosary. It looks towards heaven, and says *hâ hâ hâ.* It rides on an ox. Its time is favourable for handing over the children to the schools, for concluding peace, giving alms, and works of piety. | Kâlarâtri. |
| VIII. | In the day of the 30th *tithi.* | ... | Âgneya. | It is pistachio-coloured like a parrot. It looks like something globular, and has three eyes. In one hand it has a mace with an iron hook, in the other a sharp discus. It sits on its throne, frightening people, and saying *sâ sâ sâ.* Its time is not favourable for beginning anything. It is only good for doing service to relations and for house-work. | ... |

# CHAPTER LXXIX.

## ON THE YOGAS.

Page 299. THESE are times which the Hindus think to be most unlucky and during which they abstain from all action. They are numerous. We shall here mention them.

Explanation of *vyatîpâta* and *vaidhṛita*.

There are two *yogas* regarding which all Hindus agree, viz.:—

(1.) The moment when sun and moon together stand on two circles, which are, as it were, *seizing* each other, *i.e.* each pair of circles, the declinations of which, on one and the same side (of either solstice), are equal. This *yoga* is called *vyatîpâta*.

(2.) The moment when sun and moon stand together on two *equal* circles, *i.e.* each pair of circles, the declinations of which, on different sides (of either solstice), are equal. This is called *vaidhṛita*.

It is the *signum* of the former that in it the sum of the corrected places of sun and moon represents in any case the distance of six zodiacal signs from 0° of Aries, while it is the *signum* for the latter that the same sum represents the distance of twelve signs. If you compute the corrected places of sun and moon for a certain time and add them together, the sum is either of these *signa*, *i.e.* either of these two *yogas*.

If, however, the sum is less than the amount of the *signum* or larger, in that case the time of equality (*i.e.* the time when the sum is equal to either of the *signa*) is computed by means of the difference between this sum and the term in question, and by means of the sum of the two *bhukti* of sun and moon instead of the *bhuktyantara*, in the same manner as in the *canones* the time of full moon and opposition is computed.

On middle time.

If you know the distance of the moment from noon or midnight, whether you correct the places of sun and moon according to the one or the other, its time is called the *middle* one. For if the moon followed the ecliptic as accurately as the sun, this time would be that which we want to find. However, the moon deviates from the ecliptic. Therefore, she does not at that time stand on the circle of the sun or on the circle which, as far as observation goes, is equal to it. For this reason the places of sun and moon and the dragon's head and tail are computed for the *middle* time.

Method for computing *vyatipâta* and *vaidhṛita*.

According to this time they compute the declinations of sun and moon. If they are equal, this is the time which is sought for. If not, you consider the declination of the moon.

If, in computing it, you have added her latitude to the declination of the degree which she occupies, you subtract the latitude of the moon from the declination of the sun. However, if, in computing it, you have subtracted her latitude from the degree which the moon occupies, you add her latitude to the declination of the sun. The result is reduced to arcs by the tables of the *kardajât* of declination, and these arcs are kept in memory. They are the same which are used in the canon *Karaṇatilaka*.

Further, you observe the moon at the *middle* time. If she stands in some of the *odd* quarters of the ecliptic, *i.e.* the vernal and autumnal ones, whilst her declination is less than the declination of the sun, in that case the time of the two declinations equalling each other—and that is what we want to find—falls *after* the *middle*, *i.e.* the future one; but if the declination of the moon is larger than that of the sun, it falls *before* the *middle*, *i.e.* the past one.

If the moon stands in the *even* quarters of the ecliptic (*i.e.* the summer and winter quarters), just the reverse takes place.

Another method by Pulisa.

Pulisa adds together the declinations of sun and moon in *vyatîpâta*, if they stand on different sides of the solstice, and in *vaidhṛita*, if they stand on the same side of the solstice. Further, he takes the difference between the declinations of sun and moon in *vyatîpâta*, if they stand on the same side, and in *vaidhṛita*, if they stand on different sides. This is the first value which is kept in memory, *i.e.* the *middle* time.

Further, he reduces the minutes of the days to *mâshas*, supposing that they are less than one-fourth of a day. Then he computes their motions by means of the *bhukti* of sun and moon and the dragon's head and tail, and he computes their places according to the amount of *middle* time, which they occupy, in the past and the future. This is the second value which is kept in memory.

By this method he manages to find out the condition of the past and the future, and compares it with the *middle* time. If the time of the two declinations equalling each other for both sun and moon is past or future, in that case the *difference* between the two values kept in memory is the *portio divisionis* (divisor); but if it is past for the one and future for the other, the *sum* of the two values kept in memory is the *portio divisionis*.

Page 300.

Further, he multiplies the minutes of the days, which have been found, by the first value kept in memory, and divides the product by the *portio divisionis*. The quotient represents the minutes of the distance from the *middle* time which minutes may either be past or future. Thus the time of the two declinations equalling each other becomes known.

The author of the canon *Karaṇatilaka* makes us return to the arc of the declination which has been

Another method by the author of the *Karapatilaka*.

kept in memory. If the corrected place of the moon is less than three zodiacal signs, it is that which we want; if it is between three and six signs, he subtracts it from six signs, and if it is between six and nine signs, he adds six signs thereto; if it is more than nine signs, he subtracts it from twelve signs. Thereby he gets the second place of the moon, and this he compares with the moon's place at the time of the correction. If the second place of the moon is *less* than the first, the time of the two declinations equalling each other is future; if it is *more* than the first, the time of their equalling each other is past.

Further, he multiplies the difference between the two places of the moon by the *bhukti* of the sun, and divides the product by the *bhukti* of the moon. The quotient he adds to the place of the sun at the time of the correction, if the second place of the moon is larger than the first; but he subtracts it from the sun's place, if the second place of the moon is less than the first. Thereby he finds the place of the sun for the time when the two declinations are equal to each other.

For the purpose of finding it, he divides the difference between the two places of the moon by the *bhukti* of the moon. The quotient gives minutes of days, indicative of the distance. By means of them he computes the places of sun and moon, of the dragon's head and tail, and of the two declinations. If the latter are equal, it is that which we want to find. If they are not equal, the author repeats the calculation so long till they are equal and till the correct time has been found.

Thereupon he computes the measure of sun and moon. However, he disregards half of the sum of them, so that in the further calculation he uses only the one half of their measures. He multiplies it by 60 and divides the product by the *bhuktyantara*. The quotient represents the minutes of the *falling* (*pâta ?*)

The correct time, which has been found, is marked in three different places. From the first number he subtracts the minutes of the *falling*, and to the last number he adds them. Then the first number is the time of the beginning of *vyatîpâta* or *vaidhṛita*, whichever of the two you want to compute. The second number is the time of its middle, and the third number the time of its end.

The author's books on the subject.

We have given a detailed account of the bases on which these methods rest in a special book of ours, called *Khayâl-alkusûfaini* (*i.e.* the image of the two eclipses), and have given an accurate description of them in the canon which we have composed for *Syâvabala* (?), the Kashmîrian, and to which we have given the title *The Arabic Khaṇḍakhâdyaka*.

About the *yogas* being unlucky.

Bhaṭṭila (?) thinks the whole day of either of these two *yogas* to be unlucky, whilst Varâhamihira thinks only that duration of them to be unlucky which is found by the computation. He compares the unlucky portion of the day to the wound of a gazelle shot with a poisoned arrow. The disease does not go beyond the environs of the poisoned shot; if it is cut out, the injury is removed.

According to what Pulisa mentions of Parâśara, the Hindus assume a number of *vyatîpâtas* in the lunar stations, but all of them are computed by the same method which he has given. For the calculation does not increase in its kind; only the single specimens of it become more numerous.

Quotation from Bhaṭṭila(?) on unlucky times.

The Brahman Bhaṭṭila (?) says in his canon:—

"Here there are 8 times, which have certain gauge-measures. If the sum of the corrected places of sun and moon is equal to them, they are unlucky. They are:

"1. *Bak-shûta* (?). Its gauge-measure is 4 zodiacal signs.

"2. *Gaṇḍânta*. Its gauge-measure is 4 signs and $13\frac{1}{2}$ degrees.

"3. *Lâṭa* (?), or the general *vyatipâta*. Its gauge-measure is 6 signs.

"4. *Câsa* (?). Its gauge-measure is 6 signs and $6\frac{2}{3}$ degrees.

"5. *Barh* (?), also called *barhvyatipâta*. Its gauge-measure is 7 signs and $16\frac{2}{3}$ degrees.

"6. *Kâladaṇḍa*. Its gauge-measure is 8 signs and $13\frac{1}{3}$ degrees.

"7. *Vyâkshâta* (?). Its gauge-measure is 9 signs and $23\frac{1}{3}$ degrees.

"8. *Vaidhṛita*. Its gauge-measure is 12 signs."

These *yogas* are well known, but they cannot all be traced back to a rule in the same way as the 3d and 8th ones. Therefore they have no certain duration determined by minutes of the *falling*, but only by general estimates. Thus the duration of *vyâkshâta* (?) and of *bakshûta* (?) is one *muhûrta*, according to the statement of Varâhamihira, the duration of *Gaṇḍânta* and of *Barh* (?) two *muhûrtas*.

The Hindus propound this subject at great length and with much detail, but to no purpose. We have given an account of it in the above-mentioned book. (See ii. 208.)

The canon *Karaṇatilaka* mentions twenty-seven *yogas*, which are computed in the following manner: Twenty-seven *yogas* according to the *Karaṇatilaka*.

Add the corrected place of the sun to that of the moon, reduce the whole sum to minutes, and divide the number by 800. The quotient represents complete *yogas*. Multiply the remainder by 60, and divide the product by the sum of the *bhuktis* of sun and moon. The quotient represents the minutes of days and minor fractions, viz. that time which has elapsed of the current *yoga*. Page 301.

We have copied the names and qualities of the *yogas* from Śripâla, and exhibit them in the following table:—

TABLE OF THE TWENTY-SEVEN "YOGAS."

| The number. | Their names. | Whether good or bad. | The number. | Their names. | Whether good or bad. | The number. | Their names. | Whether good or bad. |
|---|---|---|---|---|---|---|---|---|
| 1 | Vishkambha. | Good. | 10 | Gaṇḍa. | Bad. | 19 | Parigha. | Bad. |
| 2 | Prîti. | Good. | 11 | Vṛiddhi. | Good. | 20 | Śiva. | Good. |
| 3 | Râjakama (?) | Bad. | 12 | Dhruva. | Good. | 21 | Siddha. | Good. |
| 4 | Saubhâgya. | Good. | 13 | Vyâghâta (?) | Bad. | 22 | Sâdhya. | Middling. |
| 5 | Śobhana. | Good. | 14 | Harshaṇa. | Good. | 23 | Śubha. | Good. |
| 6 | Atigaṇḍa. | Bad. | 15 | Vajra. | Bad. | 24 | Śukra. | Good. |
| 7 | Sukarman. | Good. | 16 | Siddhi. | Good. | 25 | Brahman. | Good. |
| 8 | Dhṛiti. | Good. | 17 | K-n-n-âta (?) | Bad. | 26 | Indra. | Good. |
| 9 | Śûla. | Bad. | 18 | Varîyas. | Bad. | 27 | Vaidhṛiti. | Bad. |

# CHAPTER LXXX.

## ON THE INTRODUCTORY PRINCIPLES OF HINDU ASTROLOGY, WITH A SHORT DESCRIPTION OF THEIR METHODS OF ASTROLOGICAL CALCULATIONS.

Indian astrology unknown among Muhammadans.

OUR fellow-believers in these (Muslim) countries are not acquainted with the Hindu methods of astrology, and have never had an opportunity of studying an Indian book on the subject. In consequence, they imagine that Hindu astrology is the same as theirs and relate all sorts of things as being of Indian origin, of which we have not found a single trace with the Hindus themselves. As in the preceding part of this our book we have given something of everything, we shall also give as much of their astrological doctrine as will enable the reader to discuss questions of a similar nature with them. If we were to give an exhaustive representation of the subject, this task would detain us Page 302. very long, even if we limited ourselves to delineate only the leading principles and avoided all details.

First, the reader must know that in most of their prognostics they simply rely on means like auguring from the flight of birds and physiognomy, that they do not—as they ought to do—draw conclusions, regarding the affairs of the sublunary world, from the seconds (*sic*) of the stars, which are the events of the celestial sphere.

On the planets.

Regarding the number seven as that of the planets, there is no difference between us and them. They call them *graha*. Some of them are throughout lucky, viz.

Jupiter, Venus and the Moon, which are called *saumyagraha*. Other three are throughout unlucky, viz. Saturn, Mars, and the Sun, which are called *krûragraha*. Among the latter, they also count the dragon's head, though in reality it is not a star. The nature of one planet is variable and depends upon the nature of that planet with which it is combined, whether it be lucky or unlucky. This is Mercury. However, alone by itself, it is lucky.

The following table represents the natures of the seven planets and everything else concerning them:—

| *Names of the planets.* | *Sun.* | *Moon.* | *Mars.* | *Mercury.* | *Jupiter.* | *Venus.* | *Saturn.* |
|---|---|---|---|---|---|---|---|
| Whether they are lucky or unlucky. | Unlucky. | Lucky, but depending upon the planet near her. Middling in the first, lucky in the second, and unlucky in the last ten days of the month. | Unlucky. | Lucky, when it is alone. Else depending upon the nature of the planet near it. | Lucky. | Lucky. | Unlucky. |
| What elements they indicate. | | ... | Fire. | Earth. | Heaven. | Water. | Wind. |
| Whether they indicate male or female beings. | Male. | Female. | Male. | Neither male nor female. | Male. | Female. | Neither male nor female. |
| Whether they indicate day or night. | Day. | Night. | Night. | Day and night together. | Day. | Day. | Night. |
| What point of the compass they indicate. | East. | North-west. | South. | North. | North-east. | Between east and west. | West. |
| What colour they indicate. | Bronze-colour. | White. | Light red. | Pistachio-green. | Gold-colour. | Many colours. | Black. |
| What time they indicate. | Ayana. | Muhûrta. | Day. | *Ritu*, *i.e.* a sixth part of the year. | Month. | *Paksha*, *i.e.* half a month. | Year. |

Page 303.

| *Names of the planets.* | *Sun.* | *Moon.* | *Mars.* | *Mercury.* | *Jupiter.* | *Venus.* | *Saturn.* |
|---|---|---|---|---|---|---|---|
| What season they indicate. | o | Varsha. | Grîshma. | Śarad. | Hemanta. | Vasanta. | Śiśira. |
| What taste they indicate. | Bitter. | Saltish. | | A mixture of all tastes. | Sweet. | ... | ... |
| What material they indicate. | Bronze. | Crystal. | Gold. | Small pearls. | Silver, or if the constellation is very strong, gold. | Pearl. | Iron. |
| What dress and clothes they indicate. | Thick. | New. | Burned. | Wet from water. | Between new and shabby. | Whole. | Burned. |
| What angel they indicate. | Nema (?). | Ambu, the water. | Agni, the fire. | Brahman. | Mahâdeva. | Indra. | ... |
| What caste they indicate. | Kshatriyas and commanders. | Vaiśyas and commanders. | Kshatriyas and generals. | Śûdras and princes. | Brahmans and ministers. | Brahmans and ministers. | |
| Which Veda they indicate. | o | o | Sâmaveda. | Atharvaṇa-veda. | Ṛigveda. | Yajurveda. | o |
| The months of pregnancy. | The fourth month, in which the bones become hard. | The fifth month, in which the skin appears. | The second month, in which the embyro attains consistency. | The seventh month, in which the child becomes complete, and receives the memory. | The third month, in which the limbs begin to branch off. | The first month, in which the semen and the menstrual blood become mixed. | The sixth month, when the hair grows. |

| | | | | | | | |
|---|---|---|---|---|---|---|---|
| Character as based on the three primary forces. | Satya. | Satya. | Tamas. | Rajas. | Satya. | Rajas. | Tamas. |
| Mitra. { Friendly planets. | Jupiter, Mars, Moon. | Sun, Mercury. | Jupiter, Sun, Moon. | Sun, Venus. | Sun, Moon, Mars. | Saturn, Mercury. | Venus, Mercury. |
| Śatru. { Hostile planets. | Saturn, Venus. | There is no planet hostile to her. | Mercury. | Moon. | Venus, Mercury. | Sun, Moon. | Mars, Sun, Moon. |
| Vi-miśra. { Indifferent planets. | Mercury. | Saturn, Jupiter, Mars, Venus. | Venus, Saturn. | Saturn, Jupiter, Mars. | Saturn. | Jupiter, Mars. | Jupiter. |
| What parts of the body they indicate. | The breath and the bones. | The root of the tongue and the blood. | The flesh and brain. | Voice and skin. | Intellect and fat. | Semen. | Sinews, flesh, and pain. |
| The scale of their magnitude. | 1 | 2 | 6 | 5 | 4 | 25 (!) | 7 |
| Years of *shaḍâya*. | 19 | 25 | 15 | 12 | 15 | 21 | 20 |
| Years of *nai-s argka*. | 20 | 1 | 2 | 9 | 18 | 20 | 50 |

Explanatory notes to the preceding table.

The column of this table which indicates the order of the size and power of the planets, serves for the following purpose:—Sometimes two planets indicate exactly the same thing, exercise the same influence, and stand in the same relation to the event in question. In this case, the preference is given to that planet which, in the column in question, is described as the larger or the more powerful of the two.

The months of pregnancy.

The column relating to the months of pregnancy is to be completed by the remark that they consider the eighth month as standing under the influence of a horoscope which causes abortion. According to them, the embryo takes, in this month, the fine substances of the food. If it takes all of them and is then born, it will remain alive; but if it is born before that, it will die from some deficiency in its formation. The ninth month stands under the influence of the moon, the tenth under that of the sun. They do not speak of a longer duration of pregnancy, but if it happens to last longer, they believe that, during this time, some injury is brought about by the wind. At the time of the horoscope of abortion, which they determine by tradition, not by calculation, they observe the conditions and influences of the planets and give their decision accordingly as this or that planet happens to preside over the month in question.

Page 304.

Friendship and enmity of the planets.

The question as to the friendship and enmity of the planets among each other, as well as the influence of the *dominus domûs*, is of great importance in their astrology. Sometimes it may happen that, at a particular moment of time, this *dominium* entirely loses its original character. Further on we shall give a rule as to the computation of the *dominium* and its single years.

The zodiacal signs.

There is no difference between us and the Hindus regarding the number twelve as the number of the signs of the ecliptic, nor regarding the manner in which the *dominium* of the planets is distributed over them.

The following table shows what qualities are peculiar to each zodiacal sign as a whole:—

Page 305.

| *The Zodiacal Signs.* | *Aries.* | *Taurus.* | *Gemini.* | *Cancer.* | *Leo.* | *Virgo.* | *Libra.* | *Scorpio.* | *Arcitenens.* | *Capricornus.* | *Amphora.* | *Pisces.* |
|---|---|---|---|---|---|---|---|---|---|---|---|---|
| Their dominants. | Mars. | Venus. | Mercury. | Moon. | Sun. | Mercury. | Venus. | Mars. | Jupiter. | Saturn. | Saturn. | Jupiter. |
| Altitudes: Degrees. | 10 | 3 | 0 | 0 | 0 | 15 | 20 | 0 | 0 | 28 | 0 | 27 |
| Altitudes: Altitude. | Sun. | Moon. | 0 | Jupiter. | 0 | Mercury. | Saturn. | 0 | 0 | Mars. | 0 | Venus. |
| Dominants of the *mûlatrikoṇa*. | Mars. | Moon. | 0 | 0 | Sun. | Mercury. | Venus. | 0 | Jupiter. | 0 | Saturn. | 0 |
| Whether male or female. | Male. | Female. | Male. | Female. | Male. | Female. | Male. | Female. | Male. | Female. | Male. | Female. |
| Whether lucky or unlucky. | Unlucky. | Lucky. | Unlucky. | Lucky. | Unlucky. | Lucky. | Unlucky. | Lucky. | Unlucky. | Lucky. | Unlucky. | Lucky. |
| The colours. | Reddish. | White. | Green. | Yellowish. | Gray. | Many coloured. | Black. | Golden. | ... | Striped white and black. | Brown. | Dust-coloured. |
| The directions. | Due east. | S.S.E. | W.S.W. | N.N.W. | E.N.E. | Due south. | Due west. | Due north. | E.S.E. | S.S.W. | W.N.W. | N.N.E. |
| In what manner they rise. | Stretched on the ground. | Stretched on the ground. | Lying on the side. | Stretched on the ground. | Standing erect. | Standing erect. | Standing erect. | Standing erect. | Stretched on the ground. | Stretched on the ground. | Standing erect. | Standing erect. |

| The Zodiacal Signs. | Aries. | Taurus. | Gemini. | Cancer. | Leo. | Virgo. | Libra. | Scorpio. | Arcitenens. | Capricornus. | Amphora. | Pisces. |
|---|---|---|---|---|---|---|---|---|---|---|---|---|
| Whether turning, fixed or double-bodied. | Moving. | Resting. | Moving and resting together. | Moving. | Resting. | Moving and resting together. | Moving. | Resting. | Moving and resting together. | Moving. | Resting. | Moving and resting together. |
| Whether at night, or during day, according to some people. | At night. | At night. | At night. | At night. | During day. | During day. | During day. | During day. | At night. | At night. | During day. | During day. |
| What parts of the body they indicate. | Head. | Face. | Shoulders and hands. | Breast. | Belly. | Hip. | Under the navel. | Male and female genitals. | The loins. | The knees. | The calves. | The two feet. |
| Seasons. | Vasanta. | Grishma. | Grishma. | Varsha. | Varsha. | Śarad. | Śarad. | Hemanta. | Hemanta. | Śiśira. | Śiśira. | Vasanta. |
| Their figures. | A ram. | An ox. | A man with a lyre, and a club in his hand. | Crab. | Lion. | A girl with an ear of corn in her hand. | A scale. | A scorpion. | A horse, the head and upper half of which have human shape. | A being with the face of a goat. There is much water in its figure. | A kind of boat or barge. | Two fishes. |

| | | | | | | | | | | | | |
|---|---|---|---|---|---|---|---|---|---|---|---|---|
| What kinds of beings they are. | Quadruped. | Quadruped. | Human biped. | Amphibious. | Quadruped. | Biped. | Biped. | Amphibious. | The upper half a biped, the lower half a quadruped. | The first half a biped, the latter half watery. | The first half a biped, the other half watery, or the whole a human being. | Watery. |
| The times of their strongest influence according to the different kinds. | At night. | At night. | During the day. | During the saṁdhi. | At night. | During the day. | During the day. | During the saṁdhi. | The human part during the day, the other at night. | During the saṁdhi. | The human part in daytime, the other at night. | During the saṁdhi. |

Explanation of some technical terms of astrology.

The *height* or *altitudo* of a planet is called, in the Indian language, *uccastha*, its particular degree *paramoccastha*. The *depth* or *dejectio* of a planet is called *nîcastha*, its particular degree *paramanîcastha*. *Mûlatrikoṇa* is a powerful influence, attributed to a planet, when it is in the *gaudium* in one of its two houses (cf. ii. 225).

They do not refer the *aspectus trigoni* to the elements and the elementary natures, as it is our custom to do, but refer them to the points of the compass in general, as has been specified in the table.

They call the *turning* zodiacal sign (τροπικόν) *cararâśi*, *i.e.* moving, the *fixed* one (στερεόν) *sthirarâśi*, *i.e.* the *resting* one, and the *double-bodied* one (δίσωμα) *dvisvabhâva*, *i.e.* both together.

The houses.

As we have given a table of the zodiacal signs, we next give a table of the *houses* (*domus*), showing the qualities of each of them. The one half of them above

Page 306.

the earth they call *chatra*, *i.e.* parasol, and the half under the earth they call *nau*, *i.e.* ship. Further, they call the half ascending to the midst of heaven and the other half descending to the *cardo* of the earth, *dhanu*, *i.e.* the bow. The *cardines* they call *kendra* (κέντρον), the next following houses *paṇaphara* (ἐπαναφορά), and the *inclining* houses *âpoklima* (ἀπόκλιμα):—

| The Houses. | What they indicate. | On the *aspects*, the *ascendens* being taken as basis. | Which zodiacal signs exercise the greatest influence in them. | Which planets exercise the greatest influence in them. | How much is to be subtracted from the unlucky years of the House. | How much is to be subtracted from the lucky years of the House. | How they are divided according to the horizon. | Into what classes they are divided according to the shadow of noon. |
|---|---|---|---|---|---|---|---|---|
| *Ascendens.* | Head and soul. | Basis for the calculation. | The human signs. | Mercury and Jupiter. | o | o | Ship. | Ascending bow. |
| II. | Face and property. | Two stand in aspect with the *ascendens.* | o | o | o | o | | |
| III. | The two arms and brothers. | The *ascendens* looks towards it, but it does not look towards the *ascendens.* | o | o | o | o | | |
| IV. | Heart, parents, friends, house, and joy. | Two stand in aspect with the *ascendens.* | The watery signs. | Venus and Moon. | o | o | | Descending bow. |
| V. | Belly, child, and cleverness. | Two stand in aspect with the *ascendens.* | o | o | o | o | | |
| VI. | The two sides, the enemy and riding animals. | It looks towards the *ascendens*, but the *ascendens* does not look towards it. | o | o | o | o | | |
| VII. | Under the navel and women. | Two stand in aspect with the *ascendens.* | ... | Saturn. | $\frac{1}{6}$ of them. | $\frac{1}{12}$ of them. | Parasol. | |
| VIII. | Return and death. | The *ascendens* looks towards it, but it does not look towards the *ascendens.* | ... | o | $\frac{1}{5}$ | $\frac{1}{10}$ | | |
| IX. | The two loins, journey and debt. | Two stand in aspect with the *ascendens.* | ... | o | $\frac{1}{4}$ | $\frac{1}{8}$ | | |

| The Houses. | What they indicate. | On the *aspects*, the *ascendens* being taken as basis. | Which zodiacal signs exercise the greatest influence in them. | Which planets exercise the greatest influence in them. | How much is to be subtracted from the unlucky years of the House. | How much is to be subtracted from the lucky years of the House. | How they are divided according to the horizon. | Into what classes they are divided according to the shadow of noon. |
|---|---|---|---|---|---|---|---|---|
| X. | The two knees and action. | Two stand in aspect with the *ascendens*. | The quadrupeds. | Mars. | $\frac{1}{3}$ | $\frac{1}{6}$ | Parasol. | Ascending bow. |
| XI. | The two calves and income. | It looks towards the *ascendens*, but the *ascendens* does not look towards it. | o | o | $\frac{1}{2}$ | $\frac{1}{4}$ | | |
| XII. | The two feet and expenses. | Two do not stand in aspect with the *ascendens*. | o | o | The whole. | $\frac{1}{2}$ | | |

Page 307. The hitherto mentioned details are in reality the cardinal-points of Hindu astrology, viz. the planets, zodiacal signs, and *houses*. He who knows how to find out what each of them means or portends deserves the title of a clever adept and of a master in this art.

On the division of a zodiacal sign in *nîmbahras*.

Next follows the division of the zodiacal signs in minor portions, first that in *nîmbahras*, which are called *horâ*, *i.e.* hour, because half a sign rises in about an hour's time. The first half of each *male* sign is unlucky as standing under the influence of the sun, because he produces male beings, whilst the second half is lucky as standing under the influence of the moon, because she produces female beings. On the contrary, in the *female* signs the first half is lucky, and the second unlucky.

2. In *drekkâṇas*.

Further, there are the triangles, called *drekkâṇa*. There is no use in enlarging on them, as they are simply identical with the so-called *draijânât* of our system.

3. In *nuhbahras*.

Further, the *nuhbahrât* (Persian, "*the nine parts*"),

called *navâṁśaka*. As our books of introduction to the art of astrology mention two kinds of them, we shall here explain the Hindu theory regarding them, for the information of Indophiles. You reduce the distance between 0° of the sign and that minute, the *nuhbahr* of which you want to find, to minutes, and divide the number by 200. The quotient represents complete *nuhbahras* or ninth-parts, beginning with the *turning* sign, which is in the triangle of the sign in question; you count the number off on the consecutive signs, so that one sign corresponds to one *nuhbahr*. That sign which corresponds to the last of the ninth-parts which you have is the dominant of the *nuhbahr* we want to find.

The first *nuhbahr* of each *turning* sign, the fifth of each *fixed* sign, and the ninth of each *double-bodied* sign is called *vargottama*, *i.e.* the greatest portion.

Further, the *twelfth-parts*, called *the twelve rulers*. For a certain place within a sign they are found in the following manner:—Reduce the distance between 0° of the sign and the place in question to minutes, and divide the number by 150. The quotient represents complete *twelfth-parts*, which you count off on the following signs, beginning with the sign in question, so that one twelfth-part corresponds to one sign. The dominant of the sign, to which the last twelfth-part corresponds, is at the same time the dominant of the twelfth-part of the place in question. 4. In twelfth-parts.

Further, *the degrees* called *triṁśâṁśaka*, *i.e.* the thirty degrees, which correspond to our *limits* (or ὅρια). Their order is this: The first five *degrees* of each *male* sign belong to Mars, the next following five to Saturn, the next eight to Jupiter, the next seven to Mercury, and the last five to Venus. Just the reverse order takes place in the *female* signs, viz. the first five *degrees* belong to Venus, the next seven to Mercury, the next eight to Jupiter, the next five to Saturn, and the last five to Mercury. 5. In 30 degrees or ὅρια.

These are the elements on which every astrological calculation is based.

On the different kinds of the *aspect*.

The nature of the aspect of every sign depends upon the nature of the *ascendens* which at a given moment rises above the horizon. Regarding the *aspects* they have the following rule:—

A sign does not look at, *i.e.* does not stand *in aspectu* with the two signs immediately before and after it. On the contrary, each pair of signs, the beginnings of which are distant from each other by one-fourth or one-third or one-half of the circle, stand in aspect with each other. If the distance between two signs is one-sixth of the circle, the signs forming this *aspect* are counted in their original order; but if the distance is five-twelfths of the circle, the signs forming the *aspect* are counted in the inverse order.

There are various degrees of *aspects*, viz.:—

The aspect between one sign and the fourth or eleventh following one is a *fourth-part* of an aspect;

The aspect between one sign and the fifth or ninth following one is *half* an aspect;

The aspect between a sign and the sixth or tenth following one is *three-quarters* of an aspect;

The aspect between a sign and the seventh following one is a *whole* aspect.

The Hindus do not speak of an *aspect* between two planets which stand in one and the same sign.

Friendship and enmity of certain planets in relation to each other.

With reference to the change between the friendship and enmity of single planets with regard to each other, the Hindus have the following rule:—

Page 308.

If a planet comes to stand in signs which, in relation to its rising, are the tenth, eleventh, twelfth, first, second, third, and fourth signs, its nature undergoes a change for the better. If it is most inimical, it becomes moderated; if it is moderated, it becomes friendly; if it is friendly, it becomes most friendly. If the planet comes to stand in all the other signs, its nature undergoes a change for the worse. If originally it is friendly, it becomes moderate; if it is moderate, it becomes inimical; if it is inimical, it becomes even worse. Under such circumstances, the nature of a planet is an accidental one for the time being, associating itself with its original nature.

After having explained these things, we now proceed to mention *the four forces* which are peculiar to each planet:— The four forces of each planet.

I. The habitual force, called *sthânabala*, which the planet exercises, when it stands in its *altitudo*, its *house*, or the house of its friend, or in the *nuhbahr* of its house, or its *altitudo*, or its *mûlatrikoṇa*, *i.e.* its *gaudium* in the line of the lucky planets. This force is peculiar to sun and moon when they are in the lucky signs, as it is peculiar to the other planets when they are in the unlucky signs. Especially this force is peculiar to the moon in the first third of her lunation, when it helps every planet which stands *in aspect* with her to acquire the same force. Lastly, it is peculiar to the *ascendens* if it is a sign representing a biped. Laghujâtakam, ch. ii. 8.

II. The force called *drishṭibala*, *i.e.* the lateral one, also called *drigbala*, which the planet exercises when standing in the *cardo* in which it is strong, and, according to some people, also when standing in the two houses immediately before and after the *cardo*. It is peculiar to the *ascendens* in the day, if it is a sign representing a biped, and in the night, if it is a four-footed sign, and in both the *saṁdhis* (periods of twilight at the beginning and end) of the other signs. This in particular refers to the astrology of nativities. In the other parts of astrology this force is peculiar, as they maintain, to the tenth sign if it represents a quadruped, to the seventh sign if it is Scorpio and Cancer, and to the fourth sign if it is Amphora and Cancer. Lagh. ii. 11.

III. *The conquering force*, called *ceshṭâbala*, which a planet exercises, when it is in retrograde motion, Lagh. ii. 5.

when it emerges from concealment, marching as a visible star till the end of four signs, and when in the north it meets one of the planets except Venus. For to Venus the south is the same as the north is to the other planets. If the two (——— ? illegible) stand in it (the south), it is peculiar to them that they stand in the ascending half (of the sun's annual rotation), proceeding towards the summer solstice, and that the moon in particular stands near the other planets—except the sun—which afford her something of this force.

The force is, further, peculiar to the *ascendens*, if its dominant is in it, if the two stand in aspect with Jupiter and Mercury, if the *ascendens* is free from an aspect of the unlucky planets, and none of them—except the dominant—is in the *ascendens*. For if an unlucky planet is in it, this weakens the aspect of Jupiter and Mercury, so that their dwelling in this force loses its effect.

Laghujâtakam, ii. 6. IV. The fourth force is called *kâlabala*, *i.e.* the temporal one, which the daily planets exercise in the day, the nightly planets during the night. It is peculiar to Mercury in the *saṁdhi* of its rotation, whilst others maintain that Mercury always has this force, because he stands in the same relation to both day and night.

Further, this force is peculiar to the lucky planets in the white half of the month, and to the unlucky stars in the black half. It is always peculiar to the *ascendens*.

Other astrologers also mention years, months, days, and hours among the conditions, under which the one or other of the four forces is peculiar to a planet.

These, now, are the forces which are calculated for the planets and for the *ascendens*.

If several planets own, each of them, several forces, Page 309. that one is preponderant which has the most of them. If two planets have the same number of *balas* or forces, that one has the preponderance the magnitude of which is the larger. This kind of magnitude is in the table of

ii. 215, called *naisargikabala*. This is the order of the planets in magnitude or force. Lagh. ii. 7

The years of life which the single planets bestow. Three species of these years.

The middle years which are computed for the planets are of three different species, two of which are computed according to the distance from the *altitudo*. The measures of the first and second species we exhibit in the table (ii. 215).

The *shaḍâya* and *naisargika* are reckoned as the degree of *altitudo*. The first species is computed when the above-mentioned forces of the sun are preponderating over the forces of the moon and the *ascendens* separately.

The second species is computed if the forces of the moon are preponderating over those of the sun and those of the *ascendens*.

The third species is called *aṁśâya*, and is computed if the forces of the *ascendens* are preponderating over those of sun and moon.

The first species.

The computation of the years of the first species for each planet, if it does not stand in the degree of its *altitudo*, is the following:—

Lagh. vi. 1.

You take the distance of the star from the degree of its *altitudo* if this distance is more than six signs, or the difference between this distance and twelve signs, in case it is less than six signs. This number is multiplied by the number of the years, indicated by the table on page 812. Thus the signs sum up to months, the degrees to days, the minutes to day-minutes, and these values are reduced, each sixty minutes to one day, each thirty days to one month, and each twelve months to one year.

The computation of these years for the *ascendens* is this:—

Lagh. vi. 2.

Take the distance of the degree of the star from 0° of Aries, one year for each sign, one month for each $2\frac{1}{2}$ degrees, one day for each five minutes, one day-minute for each five seconds.

The second species.

The computation of the years of the second species for the planets is the following:—

Take the distance of the star from the degree of its *altitudo* according to the just-mentioned rule (ii. 227). This number is multiplied by the corresponding number of years which is indicated by the table, and the remainder of the computation proceeds in the same way as in the case of the first species.

The computation of this species of years for the *ascendens* is this:—

Take the distance of its degree from 0° of Aries, a year for each *nuhbahr;* months and days, &c., in the same way as in the preceding computation. The number you get is divided by 12, and the remainder being less than 12, represents the number of years of the *ascendens.*

The third species.

The computation of the years of the third species is the same for the planets as for the *ascendens*, and is similar to the computation of the years of the *ascendens* of the second species. It is this:—

Take the distance of the star from 0° of Aries, one year for each *nuhbahr*, multiplying the whole distance by 108. Then the signs sum up to months, the degrees to days, the minutes to day-minutes, the smaller measure being reduced to the larger one. The years are divided by 12, and the remainder which you get by this division is the number of years which you want to find.

Laghujâtakam, ch. vi. 1.

All the years of this kind are called by the common name *âyurdâya.* Before they undergo the equation they are called *madhyamâya*, and after they have passed it they are called *sphuṭâya*, *i.e.* the *corrected* ones.

The years of life bestowed by the *ascendens.*

The years of the *ascendens* in all three species are *corrected* ones, which do not require an equation by means of two kinds of subtraction, one according to the position of the *ascendens* in the æther, and a second according to its position in relation to the horizon.

To the third kind of years is peculiar an equation by means of an addition, which always proceeds in the same manner. It is this:— Various computations for the duration of life.

If a planet stands in its largest portion or in its house, the *drekkâṇa* of its house or the *drekkâṇa* of its *altitudo*, in the *nuhbahr* of its house or the *nuhbahr* of its *altitudo*, or, at the same time, in most of these positions together, its years will be the double of the middle number of years. But if the planet is in retrograde motion or in its *altitudo*, or in both together, its years are the threefold of the middle number of years. Page 310.

Regarding the equation by means of the subtraction (*vide* ii. 228) according to the first method, we observe that the years of the planet, which is in its *dejectio*, are reduced to two-thirds of them if they are of the first or second species, and to one-half if they belong to the third species. The standing of a planet in the house of its opponent does not impair the number of its years.

The years of a planet which is concealed by the rays of the sun, and thus prevented from exercising an influence, are reduced to one-half in the case of all three species of years. Only Venus and Saturn are excepted, for the fact of their being concealed by the rays of the sun does not in any way decrease the numbers of their years.

As regards the equation by means of subtraction according to the second method, we have already stated in the table (ii. 221, 222) how much is subtracted from the unlucky and lucky stars, when they stand in the houses above the earth. If two or more planets come together in one house, you examine which of them is the larger and stronger one. The subtraction is added to the years of the stronger planet and the remainder is left as it is.

If to the years of a single planet, years of the third

species, two additions from different sides are to be made, only one addition, viz., the longer one, is taken into account. The same is the case when two subtractions are to be made. However, if an addition as well as a subtraction is to be made, you do the one first and then the other, because in this case the sequence is different.

By these methods the years become *adjusted*, and the sum of them is the duration of the life of that man who is born at the moment in question.

The single elements of the computation of the duration of life.

It now remains for us to explain the method of the Hindus regarding the *periods* (*sic*). Life is divided in the above-mentioned three species of years, and immediately after the birth, into years of sun and moon. That one is preponderating which has the most forces and *balas* (*vide* ii. 225); if they equal each other, that one is preponderating which has the greatest *portio* (*sic*) in its place, then the next one, &c. The companion of these years is either the *ascendens* or that planet which stands in the *cardines* with many forces and *portiones*. The several planets come together in the *cardines*, their influence and sequence are determined by their forces and shares. After them follow those planets which stand near the *cardines*, then those which stand in the *inclined* signs, their order being determined in the same way as in the preceding case. Thus becomes known in what part of the whole human life the years of every single planet fall.

However, the single parts of life are not computed exclusively in the years of the one planet, but according to the influences which companion-stars exercise upon it, *i.e.* the planets which stand in aspect with it. For they make it partake in their rule and make it share in their division of the years. A planet which stands in the same sign with the planet ruling over the part of life in question, shares with it one-half. That which stands in the fifth and ninth signs, shares with it one-third. That which stands in the fourth and eighth signs, shares with it one-fourth. That which stands in the seventh sign, shares with it one-seventh. If, therefore, several planets come together in one position, all of them have in common that share which is necessitated by the position in question.

The method for the computation of the years of such a companionship (if the ruling planet stands in aspect with other planets) is the following:—

How one planet is affected by the nature of another one.

Take for the master of the years (*i.e.* that planet which rules over a certain part of the life of a man) one as numerator and one as denominator, *i.e.* $\frac{1}{1}$, one whole, because it rules over the whole. Further, take for each companion (*i.e.* each planet which stands in aspect with the former) only the numerator of its denominator (not the entire fraction). You multiply each denominator by all the numerators and their sum, in which operation the original planet and its fraction are disregarded. Thereby all the fractions are reduced to one and the same denominator. The equal denominator is disregarded. Each numerator is multiplied by the sum of the year and the product divided by the sum of the numerators. The quotient represents the years *kálambúka* (*kála-bhága* ?) of a planet.

As regards the order of the planets, after the question as to the preponderance of their influence has been decided (? *text in disorder*), in so far as each of them Page 311.
exercises its individual influence. In the same way as has already been explained (*vide* ii. 230), the preponderating planets are those standing in the *cardines*, first the strongest, then the less strong, &c., then those standing near the *cardines*, and lastly those standing in the *inclined* signs.

Special methods of inquiry of the Hindu astrologers.

From the description given in the preceding pages, the reader learns how the Hindus compute the duration of human life. He learns from the positions of the planets, which they occupy on the origin (*i.e.* at the moment of birth) and at every given moment of life in what way the years of the different planets are distributed over it. To these things Hindu astrologers join certain methods of the astrology of nativities, which other nations do not take into account. They try, *e.g.*, to find out if, at the birth of a human being, its father was present, and conclude that he was absent, if the moon does not stand in aspect with the *ascendens*, or if the sign in which the moon stands is enclosed between the signs of Venus and Mercury, or if Saturn is in the *ascendens*, or if Mars stands in the seventh sign.

Laghujâtakam, ch. iii. 3.

Chap. iii. 4 (?).—Further, they try to find out if the child will attain full age by examining sun and moon. If sun and moon stand in the same sign, and with them an unlucky planet, or if the moon and Jupiter just quit the aspect with the *ascendens*, or if Jupiter just quits the aspect with the united sun and moon, the child will not live to full age.

Further, they examine the station in which the sun stands, in a certain connection with the circumstances of a lamp. If the sign is a *turning* one, the light of the lamp, when it is transferred from one place to the other, moves. If the sign is a *fixed* one, the light of the lamp is motionless; and if the sign is a *double-bodied* one, it moves one time and is motionless another.

Further, they examine in what relation the degrees of the *ascendens* stand to 30. Corresponding to it is the amount of the wick of the lamp which is consumed by burning. If the moon is full moon, the lamp is full of oil; at other times the decrease or increase of the oil corresponds to the wane and increase of the moonlight.

Chap. iv. 5.—From the strongest planet in the *cardines* they draw a conclusion relating to the door of the house, for its direction is identical with the direction of this planet or with the direction of the sign of the *ascendens*, in case there is no planet in the *cardines*.

Chap. iv. 6.—Further, they consider which is the

light-giving body, the sun or moon. If it is the sun, the house will be destroyed. The moon is beneficent, Mars burning, Mercury bow-shaped, Jupiter constant, and Saturn old.

Chap. iv. 7.—If Jupiter stands in its *altitudo* in the tenth sign, the house will consist of two wings or three. If its *indicium* is strong in Arcitenens, the house will have three wings; if it is in the other double-bodied signs, the house will have two wings.

Chap. iv. 8.—In order to find prognostics for the throne and its feet they examine the third sign, its squares and its length from the twelfth till the third signs. If there are unlucky planets in it, either the foot or the side will perish in the way that the unlucky planet prognosticates. If it is Mars, it will be turned; if it is the sun, it will be broken; and if it is Saturn, it will be destroyed by old age.

Chap. iv. 10.—The number of women who will be present in a house corresponds to the number of stars which are in the signs of the *ascendens* and of the moon. Their qualities correspond to the images of these constellations.

Those stars of these constellations which stand above the earth refer to those women who go away from the house, and those which stand under the earth prognosticate the women who will come *to* the house and enter it.

Laghujâtakam, ch. xii. 3, 4.

Further, they inquire into the coming of the spirit of life in man from the dominant of the *drekkâṇa* of the stronger planet of either sun or moon. If Jupiter is the drekkâṇa, it comes from Devaloka; if it is Venus or the moon, the spirit comes from Pitṛiloka; if it is Mars or the sun, the spirit comes from Vṛiścikaloka; and if it is Saturn or Mercury, the spirit comes from Bhṛiguloka.

Likewise they inquire into the departing of the soul after the death of the body, when it departs to that planet which is stronger than the dominant of the drekkâṇa of the sixth or eighth houses, according to a similar rule to that which has just been laid down. Page 412. However, if Jupiter stands in its *altitudo*, in the sixth house, or in the eighth, or in one of the *cardines*, or if the *ascendens* is Pisces, and Jupiter is the strongest of the planets, and if the constellation of the moment of death is the same as that of the moment of birth, in that case the spirit (or soul) is liberated and no longer wanders about.

On comets.

I mention these things in order to show the reader the difference between the astrological methods of our people and those of the Hindus. Their theories and methods regarding aerial and cosmic phenomena are very lengthy and very subtle at the same time. As we have limited ourselves to mentioning, in their astrology of nativities, only the theory of the determination of the length of life, we shall in this department of science limit ourselves to the species of the comets, according to the statements of those among them who are supposed to know the subject thoroughly. The analogy of the comets shall afterwards be extended to other more remote subjects.

The head of the Dragon is called *râhu*, the tail *ketu*. The Hindus seldom speak of the tail, they only use the head. In general, all comets which appear on heaven are also called *ketu*.

Quotations from the *Saṁhitâ* of Varâhamihira.

Varâhamihira says (chap. iii. 7–12):—

"The Head has thirty-three sons who are called *tâmasakîlaka*. They are the different kinds of the comets, there being no difference whether the head extends away from them or not. Their prognostics correspond to their shapes, colours, sizes, and positions. V. 8.—The worst are those which have the shape of a crow or the shape of a beheaded man, those which have the shape of a sword, dagger, bow and arrow. V. 9, 10.—They are always in the neighbourhood of sun and moon, exciting the waters so that they become thick, and exciting the air that it becomes glowing red. They bring the air into such an uproar that the tornadoes tear out the largest trees, that flying pebbles beat against the calves and knees of the people. They change the nature of the time, so that the seasons seem to have changed their places. When unlucky and calamitous events become numerous, such as earthquakes, land-slips, burning heat, red glow of heaven, uninterrupted howling of the wild beasts and screaming of the birds, then know that all this comes from the children of the Head. V. 11.—And if these occurrences take place together with an eclipse or the effulgence of a comet, then recognise in this what thou hast predicted, and do not try to gain prognostics from other beings but the Sons of the Head. V. 12.—In the place of the calamity, point towards their (the comets) region, to all eight sides with relation to the body of the sun."

Varâhamihira says in the *Saṁhitâ* (chap. xi. 1–7):—

"I have spoken of the comets not before having exhausted what is in the books of Garga, Parâśara, Asita and Devala, and in the other books, however numerous they may be.

"It is impossible to comprehend their computation, if the reader does not previously acquire the knowledge of their appearing and disappearing, because they are not of one kind, but of many kinds.

"Some are high and distant from the earth, appearing between the stars of the lunar stations. They are called *divya.*

"Others have a middle distance from the earth, appearing between heaven and earth. They are called *ântarikshya.*

"Others are near to the earth, falling down upon the earth, on the mountains, houses and trees.

"Sometimes you see a light falling down to the earth, which people think to be a fire. If it is not fire, it is *keturûpa*, *i.e.* having the shape of a comet.

"Those animals which, when flying in the air, look

like sparks or like fires which remain in the houses of the *piśâcas*, the devils, and of the demons, efflorescent substances and others do not belong to the genus of the comets.

"Therefore, ere you can tell the prognostics of the comets, you must know their nature, for the prognostics are in agreement with it. That category of lights which is in the air, falling on the banners, weapons, houses, trees, on horses and elephants, and that category coming from a Lord which is observed among the stars of the lunar stations—if a phenomenon does not belong to either of these two categories nor to the above-mentioned phantoms, it is a telluric *ketu*.

Page 313.

V. 5.—"Scholars differ among each other regarding the number of the comets. According to some there are 101, according to others 1000. According to Nârada, the sage, they are only one, which appears in a multitude of different forms, always divesting itself of one form and arraying itself in another.

V. 7.—"Their influence lasts for as many months as their appearance lasts days. If the appearance of a comet lasts longer than one and a half month, subtract from it forty-five days. The remainder represents the months of its influence. If the appearance lasts longer than two months, in that case state the years of its influence to be equal to the number of the months of its appearance. The number of comets does not exceed the number 1000."

We give the contents of the following table in order to facilitate the study of the subject, although we have not been able to fill out all the single fields of the diagram, because the manuscript tradition of the single paragraphs of the book either in the original or in the copy which we have at our disposal is corrupt. The author intends by his explanations to confirm the theory of the ancient scholars regarding the two numbers of comets which he mentions on their authority, and he endeavours to complete the number 1000.

Page 314

| Their names. | Their descent. | How many stars each comet has. | Sum total. | Their qualities. | From what direction they appear. | Their prognostics. |
|---|---|---|---|---|---|---|
| ... | The children of Kiraṇa. | 25 | 25 | Similar to pearls in rivulets of crystal or gold-coloured. | Only in east and west. | It bodes the fighting of the kings with each other. |
| ... | The children of the Fire (?). | 25 | 50 | Green, or of the colour of fire or of lac, or of blood, or of the blossom of the tree. | S.E. | It bodes pestilence. |
| ... | The children of Death. | 25 | 75 | With crooked tails, their colour inclining to black and dark. | S. | It bodes hunger and pestilence. |
| ... | The children of the Earth. | 22 | 97 | Round, radiant, of the colour of water or sesame oil, without tails. | N.E. | It bodes fertility and wealth. |
| ... | The children of the Moon. | 3 | 100 | Like roses, or white lotus, or silver, or polished iron or gold. It shines like the moon. | N. | It bodes evil, in consequence of which the world will be turned topsy-turvy. |
| Brahmadaṇḍa. | Son of Brahman. | 1 | 101 | Having three colours and three tails. | In all directions. | It bodes wickedness and destruction. |
| ... | The children of Venus. | 84 | 185 | White, large, brilliant. | N. and N.E. | It bodes evil and fear. |
| Kanaka. | The children of Saturn. | | ... | Radiant, as if they were horns. | In all directions. | It bodes misfortune and death. |
| Vikaca. | The children of Jupiter. | 65 | ... | Brilliant, white, without any tails. | S. | It bodes destruction and misfortune. |

| Their names. | Their descent. | How many stars each comet has. | Sum total. | Their qualities. | From what direction they appear. | Their prognostics. |
|---|---|---|---|---|---|---|
| Taskara, *i.e.* the thief. | The children of Mercury. | 51 | ... | White, thin, long. The eye is dazzled by them. | In all directions. | It bodes misfortune. |
| Kaṅkuma. | The children of Mars. | 60 | ... | It has three tails, and the colour of the flame. | N. | It bodes the extremity of evil. |
| Támasa-kílaka. | The children of the Head. | 36 | ... | Of different shapes. | About the sun and moon. | It bodes fire. |
| Viśvarûpa. | The children of the Fire. | 120 | ... | Of a blazing light like the flame. | ... | It bodes evil. |
| Aruṇa. | The children of the Wind. | 77 | ... ... | They have no body, that you could see a star in them. Only their rays are united, so that these appear as rivulets. Their colour is reddish or greenish. | ... | It bodes general destruction. |
| Gaṇaka. | The children of Prajâpati | 204 | ... | Square comets, eight in appearance, and 304 in number. | ... | It bodes much evil and destruction. |
| Kaṅka. | The children of the Water. | 32 | ... | Its (?) are united, and it is shining like the moon. | ... | It bodes much fear and evil in Puṇḍra. |
| Kabandha. | The children of the Time. | ... | ... | Like the cut-off head of a man. | | It bodes much destruction. |
| ... | ... | 9 | ... | One in appearance, nine in number. White, large. | In all directions. | It bodes pestilence. |

The author (Varâhamihira) had divided the comets into three classes: the *high* ones near the stars; the *flowing* ones near the earth; the *middle* ones in the air, and he mentions each one of the *high* and *middle* classes of them in our table separately. Page 315. Further quotations from the *Saṁhitâ* of Varâhamihira.

He further says (chap. xi. 42):—

"If the light of the middle class of comets shines on the instruments of the kings, the banners, parasols, fans, and fly-flaps, this bodes destruction to the rulers. If it shines on a house, or tree, or mountain, this bodes destruction to the empire. If it shines on the furniture of the house, its inhabitants will perish. If it shines on the sweepings of the house, its owner will perish."

Further Varâhamihira says (chap. xi. 6):—

"If a shooting-star falls down opposite to the tail of a comet, health and wellbeing cease, the rains lose their beneficial effects, and likewise the trees which are holy to Mahâdeva—there is no use in enumerating them, since their names and their essences are unknown among us Muslims—and the conditions in the realm of Cola, Sita, the Huns and Chinese are troubled."

Further he says (chap. xi. 62):—

"Examine the direction of the tail of the comet, it being indifferent whether the tail hangs down or stands erect or is inclined, and examine the lunar station, the edge of which is touched by it. In that case predict destruction to the place and that its inhabitants will be attacked by armies which will devour them as the peacock devours the snakes.

"From these comets you must except those which bode something good.

"As regards the other comets, you must investigate in what lunar stations they appear, or in what station their tails lie or to what station their tails reach. In that case you must predict destruction to the princes of those countries which are indicated by the lunar stations in question, and other events which are indicated by those stations."

The Jews hold the same opinion regarding the comets as we hold regarding the stone of the Ka'ba (viz. that they all are stones which have fallen down from heaven). According to the same book of Varâhamihira, comets are such beings as have been on account of their merits raised to heaven, whose period of dwelling in heaven has elapsed and who are then redescending to the earth.

The following two tables embody the Hindu theories of the comets :—

Page 316.

TABLE OF COMETS OF THE GREATEST HEIGHT IN THE ÆTHER.

| | | | | |
|---|---|---|---|---|
| 1 | Vasâ. | West. | It is flashing and thick, and extends itself from the north. | It bodes death and excessive wealth and fertility. |
| 2 | Asthi. | West. | Less bright than the first. | It bodes hunger and pestilence. |
| 3 | Śastra. | West. | Similar to the first. | It bodes the fighting of the kings with each other. |
| 4 | Kapâlaketu. | East. | Its tail extends till nearly the midst of heaven. It has a smoke-colour and appears on the day of new-moon. | It bodes the abundance of rain, much hunger, illness and death. |
| 5 | Raudra. | From the east in Pûrvâshâdhâ, Pûrvabhâdrapadâ, and Revatî. | With a sharp edge, surrounded by rays. Bronze-coloured. It occupies one-third of heaven. | It bodes the fighting of the kings with each other. |
| 6 | Calaketu. | West. | During the first time of its appearance it has a tail as long as a finger towards the south. Then it turns towards the north, till it becomes as long as to the south, the Great Bear and the Pole, then the Falling Eagle. Rising higher and higher it passes round to the south and disappears there. | It ruins the country from the tree Prayâga till Ujjayinî. It ruins the Middle Country, whilst the other regions fare differently. In some places there is pestilence, in others drought, in others war. It is visible between 10–12 months. |

TABLE OF COMETS OF THE GREATEST HEIGHT IN THE ÆTHER.—*Continued.*

| | | | | |
|---|---|---|---|---|
| 7 | Śvetaketu. | South. | It appears at the beginning of night and is visible during seven days. Its tail extends over one-third of heaven. It is green and passes from the right side to the left. | When these two comets shine and lighten, they bode health and wealth. If the time of their appearance exceeds seven days, two-thirds of the affairs of men and of their lives are ruined. The sword is drawn, revolutions prevail, and there will be misfortune during ten years. |
| 8 | Ka. | West. | It appears in the first half of night, its flame is like scattered peas, and remains visible during seven days. | |
| 9 | Raśmiketu(?) | The Pleiades. | It has the colour of smoke. | It ruins all human affairs and creates numerous revolutions. |
| 10 | Dhruvaketu(?) | Appears between heaven and earth wherever it likes. | It has a big body, it has many sides (?) and colours, and is bright flashing. | It bodes health and peace. |

TABLE OF COMETS OF MIDDLE HEIGHT IN THE SKY.

| Their number. | Their names. | From what direction they appear. | Description. | Their prognostics. |
|---|---|---|---|---|
| 1 | Kumuda. | West. | Namesake of the lotus, which is compared with it. It remains one night, and its tail is directed towards the south. | It bodes lasting fertility and wealth for ten years. |
| 2 | Maṇiketu. | West. | It lasts only one quarter of a night. Its tail is straight, white, similar to the milk which spurts out of the breast when it is milked. | It bodes a great number of wild animals and perpetual fertility during four and a half months. |
| 3 | Jalaketu. | West. | Flashing. Its tail has a curve from the west side. | It bodes fertility and well-being of the subjects during nine months. |
| 4 | Bhavaketu. | East. | It has a tail like that of a lion towards the south. | It is visible only one night. It bodes perpetual fertility and well-being during as many *months* as its appearance last *muhûrtas*. If its colour becomes less bright, it bodes pestilence and death. |

TABLE OF COMETS OF MIDDLE HEIGHT IN THE SKY.—*Continued.*

| Their number. | Their names. | From what direction they appear. | Description. | Their prognostics. |
|---|---|---|---|---|
| 5 | Padmaketu. | South. | It is as white as the white lotus. It lasts one night. | It bodes fertility, joy, and happiness for seven years. |
| 6 | Âvarta. | West. | It appears at midnight, bright shining and light gray. Its tail extends from the left to the right. | It bodes wealth during as many months as its appearance lasts *muhûrtas.* |
| 7 | Samvarta. | West. | With a tail with a sharp edge. It has the colour of smoke or bronze. It extends over one-third of heaven, and appears during the *saṁdhi.* | The lunar station in which it appears becomes unlucky. It ruins as well that which it bodes, as the lunar station. It bodes the unsheathing of the weapons and the destruction of the kings. Its influence lasts as many years as its appearance lasts *muhûrtas.* |

This is the doctrine of the Hindus regarding the comets and their presages. Page 312.

Only few Hindus occupy themselves in the same way as physical scholars among the ancient Greeks did, with exact scientific researches on the comets and on the nature of the other phenomena of heaven (τὰ μετέωρα), for also in these things they are not able to rid themselves of the doctrines of their theologians. Thus the Matsya-Purâṇa says:— On meteorology.

"There are four rains and four mountains, and their basis is the water. The earth is placed on four elephants, standing in the four cardinal directions, which raise the water by their trunks to make the seeds grow. They sprinkle water in summer and snow in winter. The fog is the servant of the rain, raising itself up to it, and adorning the clouds with the black colour."

With regard to these four elephants the *Book of the Medicine of Elephants* says:—

"Some male elephants excel man in cunning. Therefore it is considered a bad omen if they stand at the head of a herd of them. They are called *manguniha* (?). Some of them develop only one tooth, others three and four; those which belong to the race of the elephants bearing the earth. Men do not oppose them; and if they fall into a trap, they are left to their fate."

The Vâyu-Purâṇa says:—

"The wind and the sun's ray raise the water from the ocean to the sun. If the water were to drop down from the sun, rain would be hot. Therefore the sun hands the water over to the moon, that it should drop down from it as cold water and refresh the world."

As regards the phenomena of the sky, they say, for instance, that the thunder is the roaring of *Airâvata*, *i.e.*, the riding-elephant of Indra the ruler, when it drinks from the pond Mânasa, rutting and roaring with a hoarse voice.

The rainbow (lit. bow of Ḳuzaḥ) is the bow of Indra, as our common people consider it as the bow of Rustam.

Conclusion.

We think now that what we have related in this book will be sufficient for any one who wants to converse with the Hindus, and to discuss with them questions of religion, science, or literature, on the very basis of their own civilisation. Therefore we shall finish this treatise, which has already, both by its length and breadth, wearied the reader. We ask God to pardon us for every statement of ours which is not true. We ask Him to help us that we may adhere to that which yields Him satisfaction. We ask Him to lead us to a proper insight into the nature of that which is false and idle, that we may sift it so as to distinguish the chaff from the wheat. All good comes from Him, and it is He who is clement towards His slaves. Praise be to God, the Lord of the worlds, and His blessings be upon the prophet Muḥammad and his whole family!

# ANNOTATIONS.

VOL. I.

# ANNOTATIONS.

## VOL. I.

P. 1. *Title.*—The author proposes to investigate the *reality* (= *ḥakîka*) of Hindu modes of thought in the entire extent of the subject. He describes the religious, literary, and scientific traditions of India, not the country and its inhabitants. However, in some chapters he gives more than the title promises; *cf.* his notes on the roads and on the courses of the rivers.

The contents of the eighty chapters of the book may be arranged under the following heads:—

Chap. 1. General Introduction.

Chap. 2–11. On Religious, Philosophical, and cognate subjects.

Chap. 12–17. On Literature and Metrology, Strange Customs and Superstitions.

Chap. 18–31. On Geography, Descriptive, Mathematical, and Traditional, *i.e.* Pauranic.

Chap. 32–62. On Chronology and Astronomy, interspersed with chapters of Religious Tradition, *e.g.* on Nârâyaṇa, Vâsudeva, &c.

Chap. 63–76. On Laws, Manners and Customs, Festivals and Fast Days.

Chap. 77–80. On Astrological Subjects.

The word *maḳûla*, translated by *category*, is a technical term of Arabian philosophy. It was coined by the first Arabian translators of Aristotle for the purpose of rendering κατηγορία, and has since become current in the school language of Islam (*cf.* the Arabic title of *Aristotelis Categoriæ Græce cum versione Arabica*, &c., edid. J. Th. Zenker, Lipsiæ, 1846). The Syrian predecessors of those Arabian translators had simply transferred the Greek word just as it is into their own language; *cf. e.g.* Jacob of Edessa in G. Hoffmann's *De Hermeneuticis apud Syros Aristotelis*, Lipsiæ, 1869, p. 17.

That a Muslim author should investigate the ideas of idolaters, and not only such as Muslims may adopt, but also such as they must reject and condemn, that he quotes the Koran and the Gospel side by side (p. 4–5), is a proof of a broadness of view and liberality of mind more frequently met with in the ancient times of Islam, in the centuries before the establishment of Muhammadan orthodoxy by Alghazzâlî (died A.D. 1111), than later. There was more field for utterances of mental individuality before the ideas of all the nations of Islam were moulded into a unity which makes it difficult to recognise the individual influences of every single nation on the general development of the Muhammadan mind, before all Islam had become one huge religious community, in which local and national differences seem to have lost most of their original importance for the spiritual life of man. The work of Alberuni is unique in Muslim literature, as an earnest attempt to study an idolatrous world of thought, not proceeding from the intention of attacking and refuting it, but uniformly showing the desire to be just and impartial, even when the opponent's views are declared to be inadmissible. There can be hardly a doubt that under other circumstances, in other periods of Muslim history and other countries, the present work might have proved fatal to its author; and it shows that the religious policy of King Maḥmûd, the great destroyer of Hindu temples and idols, under whom Alberuni wrote, must have been so liberal as to be rarely met with in the annals of Islam (*cf.* pp. 268, 269).

P. 5. *The master Abû-Sahl, &c.*—Al-tiflîsî, *i.e.* a native of Tiflis in the Caucasus, is not known from other sources. I suppose he was one of the high civil functionaries of the realm or court of Maḥmûd. The name *Sahl* occurs very frequently among men of Persian descent of those times, and the title *Ustâdh* = master, is in the Ta'rîkh-i-Baihaḳî always prefixed, if not precisely as an official title, at all events as a title expressive of profound respect on the part of the speaker, to the names of the ministers and highest civil officials of Maḥmûd and Mas'ûd, such as Bû Sahl Zauzanî, Bû Sahl Ḥamdûnî, Bû Naṣr Mushkân, the minister of state, whose secretary Al-baihaḳî was, as well as to the name of Alberuni (٨٣٦, 16), but never to the names of the great military men (*cf.* on titles in the Ghaznawî empire, A. de Biberstein Kazimirski, *Menoutchehrî*, Paris, 1887, p. 308). Administrative skill was a legacy left by the organisation of the Sasanian empire to the Persians of later centuries, whilst military qualities seem entirely to have disappeared among the descendants of Rustam. For all the generals and officers of Maḥmûd and Mas'ûd were Turks, as Altuntash, Arslan Jâdhib, Arivarok, Bagtagîn, Bilkâtagin, Niyâltagin, Noshtagin, &c. The Ghazna princes spoke Persian with their civil functionaries, Turkish with their generals and soldiers (*cf.* Elliot, History of India, ii. 81, 102).

P. 5. *The Mu'tazila sect.*—The dogma, *God has no knowledge*, is part of their doctrine on the qualities of God, maintained especially by Ma'mar Ibn 'Abbâd Al-Sulamî. (*Cf.* on this and related subjects the treatise of H. Steiner, *Die Mutaziliten oder die Freidenker im Islam*, Leipzig, 1865, pp. 50, 52, 59, and Al-Shahrastânî's "Book of Religious and Philosophical Sects," edited by Cureton, London, 1846, p. 30, ll. 7–9). Proceeding from the study of Greek philosophy, the doctors of this school tried to save the free will of man as against predestination. There was once in Arabic a large literature composed by them and by their opponents, most of which is unknown, at all events not yet brought to light. Most of these books were of a polemical nature, and it is against their polemical bias that the criticism of Alberuni is directed. With regard to his own work, he expressly declares (p. 7) that it is not a polemical one. The book which Abû-Sahl had before him, and which gave rise to the discussion between him and our author, was probably one like that of Abulḥasan Al-'ash'arî (died A.D. 935), the great predecessor of Alghazzâlî, "On the Qualities of God," in which he attacks the Mu'tazila doctrine of the negation of God's omniscience. (*Cf.* W. Spitta, *Zur Geschichte Abulḥasan Al-'Ash'arî's*, Leipzig, 1876, p. 64.) The same author has also written an extensive work against the antagonists of the orthodox faith, against Brahmins, Christians, Jews, and Magians (v. ib. p. 68).

Our information regarding the ancient literature on the history of religion and philosophy (the latter proceeding from a work of the Neoplatonist Porphyrius) is very scanty, and mostly limited to titles of books. The work of Shahrastâni (died A.D. 1153) is a late compendium or مختصر (v. his pref., 1, 8). His editor, Cureton, intended to give "Observations respecting the sources from which this author has probably derived his information" (English pref., p. iv.), but, as far as I am aware, he has not carried out his intention. There is an excellent treatise on the history of religions in the *Fihrist* of Al-nadîm (composed about A.D. 987) on p. ٣١٨–٣٥١. The same author mentions, (p. ١٧٧) an older work on doctrines and religions by Alḥasan Ibn Mûsâ Alnaubakhtî (mentioned by Mas'ûdî), who also wrote against metempsychosis. Parts of a similar work of Ibn Ḥazm, an Arab of Spain (died A.D. 1064), are extant in the libraries of Vienna and Leyden. Mr. C. Schefer has recently published in his *Chrestomathie Persane*, Paris, 1883, a useful little book in Persian called كتاب بيان الاديان, composed by Abul-Ma'âli Muhammad Ibn 'Uḳail, who wrote in Ghazna, under the king Mas'ûd Ibn Ibrâhim (A.D. 1089–1099), half a century after Alberuni, whose *Indica* he quotes in his book. He calls it آراء الهند, *i.e.* "The Doctrines of the Hindus" (p. ١٣٨). Two more treatises in Persian on the history of religions are mentioned by C. Schefer, *Chrestomathie Persane*, pp. 136, 137.

An author who seems to have written on subjects connected with the history of religions is one Abû-Ya'ḳûb of Sijistân, as Alberuni (i. 64–65) quotes his theory on the metempsychosis from a book of his, called *Kitâb-kashf-almahjûb.*

Pp. 6–7. *Alêrânshahrî and Zurḳân.*—Our author has not made any use of the Muhammadan literature on the belief of the Hindus, as far as such existed before his time; evidently he did not give it the credit of a *bonâ fide* source of historical information. Throughout his book he derives his statements exclusively either from Indian books or from what he had heard himself. He makes an exception of this rule only in favour of Alêrânshahrî, the author of a general work on the history of religions. Alberuni seems to have known this book already (A.D. 1000) when he wrote his "Chronology," for there he gives two quotations, one an Eranian, and the other an Armenian tradition, on the authority of Alêrânshahrî (v. "Chronology of Ancient Nations," &c., translated by Dr. C. Edward Sachau, London, 1879, pp. 208, 211).

The word Êrânshahr was known to the Arabs as the name of the whole Sasanian empire, from the Oxus to the Euphrates. So it is used, *e.g.* by Abû-'Alî 'Ahmad Ibn 'Umar Ibn Dusta in his geographical work (British Museum, add. 23.378 on fol. 120*b*), where he describes the whole extent of it. If, however, Êrânshahr here means the place where the author Abul'abbâs was born, we must take the word in the more restricted meaning, which is mentioned by Albalâdhurî. For it is also the name of a part of the Sasanian empire, viz. one of the four provinces of Khurâsân, the country between Nîshâpur, Tûs, and Herât. Accordingly, we suppose that Alêrânshahrî means a native of this particular province. *Cf.* Almukaddasi, p. ٣١٣, Yâkût, i. ٣١٨. According to another tradition, the name Êrânshahr also applied to Nîshâpur, *i.e.* the name of the province was used to denote its capital. *Cf.* Almukaddasî, p. ٢٩٩.

Alêrânshahrî, a sort of freethinker according to Alberuni, is only once quoted (i. 326, a Buddhistic tradition on the destruction and renovation of the world). But as Alberuni praises his description of Judaism, Christianity, and Manichæism, we may suppose that the information of the *Indica* on these subjects, *e.g.* the quotation from the Gospel (p. 4–5), was taken from Êrânshahrî.

Incorporated in the work of Êrânshahrî was a treatise on Buddhism by an author, Zurkân, who is entirely unknown. Although Alberuni speaks very slightingly of this author, and although he does not mention him anywhere save in the preface, he seems to have borrowed from him those notes on Buddhistic subjects which are scattered through his work (v. *Index Rerum*, s.v. Buddhists). This sort of information is not of a very high standard, but other sources on Buddhism, literary or oral, do not seem to have been at the command of Alberuni. The Hindus with whom *he* mixed were of the Brahminical creed, not Buddhists. In the countries where he had lived, in Khwârizm, Jurjân, the country round Ghazna (Zâbulistân), and the Panjâb, there had been no opportunity for studying Buddhism; and also among the numerous soldiers, officers, artisans, and other Indians in the service of Maḥmûd in Ghazna and other places, there do not seem to have been Buddhists, or else Alberuni would have used such occasions for filling out this blank in his knowledge.

In the *Fihrist* (ed. G. Flügel, Leipzig 1871), on p. ٣٤٩–٣٥١ there is an extensive report on India and China, which is derived from the following sources:—

1. The account of Abû-Dulaf of Yanbû', who had travelled to India and China about A.D. 941.

2. That of a Christian monk from Najrân, who by order of the Nestorian Katholikos had also travelled to India and China in the years A.D. 980–987.

3. From a book dated A.D. 863, of an unknown author, a book which had passed through the hands of the famons Alkindî. Was this perhaps the work of Alêrânshahri, and the note on Buddha on p. ٣٤٧ by Zurḳân?

The origin of the chapter on Indian subjects in Shahrastâni (ed. Cureton, London, 1846), on p. ٤٤٤ *seq.* is not known. At all events, this author has not made use of Alberuni's work.

Pp. 7–8. *Greeks, Ṣûfis, Christians.*—In order to illustrate the ideas of the Hindus, and to bring them nearer to the understanding of his Muslim readers, Alberuni quotes related ideas—

1. Of the Greeks (*cf.* i. 24).
2. The Christians.
3. The Jews.
4. The Manichæans; and
5. The *Ṣûfis.*

Pantheism in Islam, the doctrine of the Ṣûfîs, is as near akin to the Neoplatonic and Neopythagorean schools of Greek philosophy as to the Vedânta school of Hindu philosophers. It was in our author's time already represented by a very large literature. He quotes some Ṣûfî sentences, *e.g.* of Abû Bakr Al-shiblî, and Abû Yazîd Albisṭâmî, who are known from other sources (i. 87, 88), and a Ṣûfî interpretation of a Koranic passage (i. 88). *Cf.* besides, the *Index Rerum* s.v. Ṣûfism. He gives i. 33, 34, several etymologies of the word Ṣûfî, which he himself identifies with *Σοφία*.

The notes relating to Mânî and the Manichæans (v. *Index Rerum*), and the quotations from their books, are probably mostly taken from Alêrânshahrî (v. p. 18). However, it must be kept in mind that, at the time of our author, the works of Mânî still existed, and he himself found the "Book of Mysteries" and others in his native country, though perhaps at a time subsequent to the date of the composition of the *Indica*. *Cf. Chronologie Orientalischer Völker*, herausgegeben von Ed. Sachau, Leipzig, 1878, Vorwort, pp. xi. and xxxvi. The following works of Mânî are quoted: "Book of Mysteries," كتاب الاسرار; *Thesaurus vivificationis* كنز الاحياء, i. 39. *Cf. Mani, seine Lehre und seine Schriften*, by G. Flügel, Leipzig, 1862.

As regards the Jews, I am not informed to what degree Jewish colonies were in those times spread over Central Asia. Alberuni derived probably his knowledge of Judaism also from Alêrânshahrî (p. 253). That in earlier years, during his stay in Jurjân, he was acquainted with a Jewish scholar is apparent from his chronological work ("Chronology of Ancient Nations," p. 269).

Alberuni's knowledge of Christianity may have been communicated by various channels besides the book of his predecessor Alêrânshahrî, as during his time it was far spread in Central Asia, and even at the court of Maḥmûd in Ghazna (*e.g. Abulkhair Alkhammâr*, p. 256), there lived Christians. It has not yet been investigated in detail how far Nestorian Christianity had been carried eastward across Central Asia towards and into China. *Cf.* Assemani's *Notitia Ecclesiarum Metropolitanarum et Episcopalium quæ sunt Patriarchæ Nestoriano Subjectæ* (*Bibliotheca Orientalis*, vol. iv. p. DCCV. *seq.*). Barhebræus speaks of Uigûri monks ܕܝܪ̈ܝܐ ܡܝܓܘܪ̈ܝܐ (ib. ii. 256), and from the same time date some of the Syriac inscriptions on Christian tombstones recently found in Russian Central Asia and published in Petersburg, 1886. Alberuni mentions Christians in his native country Khwârizm (Khiva), and in Khurâsân, and not only Nestorians, but also Melkites, whilst he expressly states that he does not know the Jacobites. *Cf.* "Chronology of Ancient Nations," pp. 283, 4; 292, 12; 295, 22; 312, 16.

Where Alberuni learned Greek philosophy, and who introduced him to the study of Plato's Dialogues and *Leges*, he does not state himself. The Arabic translations which he used, and which are tolerably correct, had passed through Syriac versions which are now no longer extant (*e.g.* those of Plato). Alberuni was personally acquainted and had literary connections with a man who was one of the first representatives of Greek learning in the Muslim world in that age, Abulkhair Alkhammâr, and it was perhaps to him that Alberuni owed part of his classical education. Abulkhair was born a Christian in Bagdad, A.H. 942. He lived some time in Khwârizm, and migrated thence, together with Alberuni and others, to Ghazna, A.D. 1017, after Maḥmûd had annexed that country to his empire. He died in Ghazna during Maḥmûd's reign, *i.e.* before A.D. 1030, and is said to have become a Muslim towards the end of his life. He was a famous physician, and wrote on medical subjects and on Greek philosophy; besides he translated the works of Greek philosophers (*e.g.* Theophrast) from Syriac into Arabic. Of his writings we may mention a "Book of Comparison of the Theory of the (Greek) Philosophers and of the Christians," "Explanation of the Theory of the Ancients (*i.e.* Greek philosophers) regarding the Creator and regarding Laws," "The Life of the Philosopher," "On the *ὕλη*," "On Meteorology," &c. His pedigree points to a Persian descent. *Cf. Chronologie Orientalischer Völker*, Einleitung, p. xxxii., *Fihrist*, p. ٢٤٥, and the work of Shahrazûri نزهة الارواح وروضة الافراح (manuscript of the Royal Library of Berlin, MSS. Orient. oct. 217, fol. 144*b*–146*a*); C. Schefer, *Chrestomathie Persane*, p. 141.

It must be observed that Alberuni, in comparing Hindu doctrines with those of Plato, follows in the wake of Megasthenes, who says: *Παραπλέκουσι δὲ καὶ μύθους, ὥσπερ καὶ Πλάτων, περί τε ἀφθαρσίας ψυχῆς καὶ τῶν καθ' ᾅδου κρίσεων καὶ ἄλλα τοιαῦτα* (Schwanbeck, Bonn, 1846, p. 138).

P. 8. *Sâṅkhya* (*or Sâṁkhyá*) and *Pâtañjala.*—The

former word is here written *sângu* سانْكُ. It may be doubtful whether the second is to be read *Pâtañjala* or *Patañjali*. Alberuni generally says كتاب باتنجل, which may be translated *the book of* (the author) *Patañjali*, or *the book* (which is called) *Patañjali* or *Pâtañjala*. Only in one place, i. 68 (٣٢, 5), he says صاحب كتاب باتنجل, *the author of the book of Patañjali*, where apparently باتنجل means the title of the book, not the name of the author. The long *a* in the Arabic writing would rather indicate the pronunciation *Pâtañjala* than *Patañjali*, but in this respect the transliteration is not always uniform, as sometimes a short Indian *a* has been rendered by a long *â* in Arabic, *e.g.* تال *tala*, براهم *brahman*, كاندهرب *gandharva*, مادلوك *madhyaloka*, سوتال *sutala*, جياننند *vijayanandin*, بار *para*, باسو *vasu*, ماهورة *mathurâ*, مهاتال *mahâtala*. Only in two places the word باتنجل evidently means the author, i. 70 (٣٣, 20), and 87 (٤٣, 3). The name of the author seems to have been current also as meaning his book. Therefore, and because in Sanskrit generally the name *Patañjali* is quoted, I have given the preference to the latter form of the name.

Alberuni has transferred large portions of his translations of the books *Sâṁkhya* and *Patañjali*, which he had published at an earlier date, into the *Indica*.

Pp. 17–19.—In a similar way to Alberuni, the poet Mîr Khusrau discourses on classical and vernacular in his *Nuh-sipihr*. He mentions the word *Sanskrit*, whilst Alberuni only speaks of *Hindî* (v. Elliot, "History of India," iii. 562, 556; also v. 570, "On the Knowledge of Sanskrit by Muhammadans").

There were Hindu dragomans in the service of Maḥmûd, both in the civil administration and in the army, large portions of which were Hindus under Hindu officers (Elliot, ii. 109; some fought in Karmân, Khwârizm, and before Merw for their Muslim master, ib. ii. 130, 131). Part of these troops were *Kannara*, *i.e.* natives of Karnâṭadeśa (here i. 173).

A specimen of these interpreters is Tilak, the son of Jai Sen (*i.e.* Tilaka the son of Jayasena). After having pursued his studies in Kashmîr, he became interpreter first to Ḳâḍî Shîrâzî Bulḥasan 'Alî, a high civil official under

Maḥmûd and Mas'ûd (Elliot, ii. 117, 123), then to Aḥmad Ibn Ḥasan of Maimand, who was grand vizîr, A.D. 1007–1025, under Maḥmûd, and a second time, 1030–1033, under Mas'ûd, and rose afterwards to be a commanding officer in the army (Elliot, ii. 125–127). This class of men spoke and wrote Hindî (of course with Arabic characters) and Persian (perhaps also Turkish, as this language prevailed in the army), and it is probably in these circles that we must look for the origin of Urdû or Hindustânî. The first author who wrote in this language, the Dante of Muhammadan India, is one Mas'ûd, who died a little more than a century after the death of King Maḥmûd (A.H. 525 = A.D. 1131). *Cf.* A. Sprenger, "Catalogue of the Arabic, Persian, and Hindustany Manuscripts of the Libraries of the King of Oudh," Calcutta, 1854, pp. 407, 485. If we had any of the Hindi writings of those times, they would probably exhibit the same kind of Indian speech as that which is found in Alberuni's book.

P. 18.—The bearing of the words وتقييدها باعراب آلخ (9, 14, 15), which I have translated "and must pronounce the case-endings either," &c., is doubtful. The word *'i'râb* means *the process or mode of Arabizing* a foreign word, and refers both to consonants and vowels. An *'i'râb mashhûr* would be *a generally known Arabic mode of pronunciation of a word of Indian origin*, an *'i'râb ma'mûl* such a pronunciation of an Indian word in Arabic as is not yet known, but invented for the purpose. *E.g.* the Sanskrit word *dvîpa* appears in two different forms, as *dîb*, ديب, which must be classed under the first head, and as *dbîp*, دبيب, which belongs to the second class. If it is this the author means, we must observe that the former class, *i.e.* the class of words which had already general currency in Arabic before he wrote his *Indica*, is insignificantly small in comparison with the large number of words which by Alberuni were for the first time presented to a reader of Arabic (v. preface of the edition of the Arabic original, p. xxvii.).

Another meaning of the word *'i'râb* is the *vowel-pronunciation at the end of the words*, chiefly the nouns; in fact, the case-endings. Accordingly, *'i'râb mashhûr* may mean *case-ending* (in German, *vocalischer Auslaut*) *as it is gene-*

*rally used* in Hindî, *e.g.* گیتا *gîtâ*, ریوتی *revatî*, and *'i'râb ma'mûl, a case-ending added to a word purposely* in order to make it amenable to the rules of Arabic declension (diptoton and triptoton), *e.g.* لنك *lanku* = Skr. *laṅkhâ*, گور *gauru* = Skr. *Gaurî*, بند *bindu* = Skr. *Vindhya*. The vocalisation of these words is liable to lead us into an error. Is بندُ an Arabic diptoton, or is its final vocal the termination of the noun in Hindî? If the former were the case, we ought also to have بندَ in genitive and accusative, and we ought to read برنٌ *a caste (varṇa)*, امليجٌ *an impure one (mleccha)*, مانٌ *a measure (mâna)*, &c. But these forms do not occur in the manuscript, and therefore I hold the termination *u* to be the Indian nominative, developed out of the *ô* of Prakrit, and still extant in Sindhî. (*Cf.* E. Trumpp, *Die Stammbildung des Sindhî*, "Journal of the German Oriental Society," xvi. p. 129; his "Grammar of the Sindhî Language," p. 32). The Arabic manuscript is not sufficiently accurate to enable us to form an opinion to what extent names in Alberuni's Hindî terminated in *u*, but we must certainly say that this is the case in the vast majority of nouns. If we are correct in this, the term *'i'râb ma'mûl* cannot mean *an artificial case-ending or one invented or added for the purpose*, because it existed already in the Indian dialect whence Alberuni took the word.

Of the words الاحتيال لضبطها بتغيير النقط والعلامات وتقييدها باعراب امّا مشهور وامّا معمول, the former half refers to the writing of the consonants (and perhaps of the *Lesezeichen*). Accordingly the latter half ought to refer to the vowels; but *'i'râb* does not mean *vowels* or *vocalisation;* it only means the vocalisation of the final consonant of the word. Therefore I am inclined to prefer the first of the two interpretations here proposed, and to translate *for in order to fix the pronunciation we must change the points* (*i.e.* the diacritical points of the consonants, ژ ز ق ڤ ف گ ک, &c.) *and the signs* (perhaps he means the Hamza, which cannot be applied to Indian sounds), *and must secure its correct pronunciation by such a process of Arabizing as is either already in general use or is carried out* (or invented) *for the purpose*. This is an example (and there are hundreds more) of the concise style of the author, so sorely fraught with ambiguity. Every single word is perfectly clear and certain, and still the sentence may be understood in entirely different ways.

P. 19, 3. *Which in our Persian grammatical system are considered as, &c.*—Literally, "Which *our companions* call having," &c. Speaking of his fellow-Muslims in opposition to the Hindus, the author always says *our companions*, *our people*, not meaning national differences, Arab, Persian, or Turk, but exclusively the difference of creed.

In Sanskrit a word (a syllable) may commence with one, two, or three consonants, *e.g. dvi*, *jyâ*, *strî*, *kshveḍa*, which is impossible in Arabic, where each syllable begins and ends with *one* consonant only. Alberuni's comparison cannot, therefore, refer to Arabic.

In Persian, the rules for the beginning and end of the syllable are different. Whilst in the ancient forms of Eranian speech a syllable could commence with two consonants, as, *e.g. fratama*, *khsapa*, Neo-Persian permits only one consonant at the beginning of a syllable, *fardum*, *shab*. However, the end of a syllable may consist of two consecutive consonants, as in *yâft* يافت, *baksh* بخش, *khushk* خشك, *mard* مرد, &c. Alberuni seems to hint at these examples, and at a doctrine of certain grammarians, who are not known, to this effect, that the first of these two consonants is to be considered as having not a complete or clear vowel, but an indistinct *hidden* one, something like a *schwa mobile* of Hebrew grammar.

There is a small number of words (or syllables) in Neo-Persian which indeed commence with the two consonants خو, as, *e.g.* خويش, خواب, استخوان, خواهر, خواستن, but they were at the author's time pronounced as a single one, if we may judge from the metrical system of the *Shâhnâma* of his contemporary Firdausi, who was only a little older than himself. (*Cf.* similar remarks of the author, i. 138, 139.)

P. 20. *Sagara.*—The story of Sagara is related in *Vishṇu-Purâṇa*, translated by Wilson-Hall, vol. iii. p. 289–295. The words وعهدى ببعضهم and فشكرت فعله آلخ might make us think that these events happened within the recollection of the author; but this is not necessarily the case. The former words may be interpreted, "*I recollect the story of a Hindu who,"* &c., *i.e.* "I recollect having heard the story," &c.; and the words with which he winds up the story may mean, "I feel thankful to my fate that it was not I and my contemporaries whom he treated thus, but former generations."

P. 21. *Shamaniyya.*—The Buddhists are in Arabic called by this name, which is derived from a Prakritic form of Sanskrit *śramaṇa* (Strabo Σαρμâναι, Hieronymus *Samanaei*), and by the word المحمرة, *i.e. the red-robed people* (= *raktapaṭa*), which refers to the red-brown (= *kâshâya*) cloaks of the Buddhist monks. *Cf.* Kern, *Der Buddhismus und seine Geschichte in Indien*, übersetzt von H. Jacobi, Leipzig, 1882, ii. 45. See another note of our author's on Buddhism in his "Chronology of Ancient Nations," pp. 188, 189. It is extremely difficult, from the utter lack of historic tradition, to check the author's statements as to the western extension of Buddhism, which certainly never reached Mosul. Before all, it will be necessary to examine how far Alberuni, when speaking of the ancient history and institutions of Eran, was under the influence of the poets of his time, Daḳîḳî, Asadî, and Firdausî, who versified Eranian folklore for the edification of the statesmen of the Samanian and Ghaznavî empires, all of them of Eranian descent. Hearing the songs of the heroic exploits of their ancestors consoled them to a certain degree for the only too palpable fact that their nation was no longer the ruling one, but subject to another; that Arabs and Turks had successively stepped into the heritage of their ancestors.

It must be observed that the negotiators of the cities of Sindh, whom they sent to the Muslim conquerors when first attacked by them, were invariably *śramaṇas* (v. Albalâdhuri), which seems to indicate that Sindh in those times, *i.e.* about A.D. 710, was Buddhistic. *Cf.* H. Kern, *Der Buddhismus und seine Geschichte in Indien*, ii. 543.

P. 21. *Muḥammad Ibn Alḳâsim.*—The brilliant career of the conqueror of Sindh falls into the years A.D. 707–714. By Albalâdhurî (p. ٤٣٦), Ibn-Al'athir, and others he is called Muḥ. Ibn Alḳâsim *Ibn Muḥammad*, not Ibn Almunabbih, as here and p. 116. When Alberuni wrote,

Islam was known in Sindh already 350 years (since A.D. 680), and was established there 320 years (since about A.D. 710). On the history of the conquest of Sindh, *cf.* Albalâdhurî's *Kitâb-alfutûh*, p. ۴۳۱, translated by Reinaud, "Fragments," p. 182; Elliot, History of India, i. 113.

Instead of Bahmanvâ read *Bamhanvâ* = *Brahmanavâṭa.*

P. 23. The words of Varâhamihira are found in his *Brihat-Saṁhitâ*, translated by Kern in the "Journal of the Royal Asiatic Society," 1870, p. 441 (ii. 15): "The Greeks, indeed, are foreigners, but with them this science is in a flourishing state. Hence they are honoured as though they were Ṛishis; how much more then a twice-born man, if he be versed in astrology."

P. 25. *Think of Socrates, &c.*—The author speaks of a *Socratic fate* or *calamity*, meaning a fate like that which befell Socrates. I do not know from what particular source Alberuni and his contemporaries derived their information about the history of Greek philosophy. There is a broad stream of literary tradition on this subject in Arabic literature, but it has not yet been investigated what was its origin, whether it proceeded from one source or from several. Those men, mostly Greek heathens from Ḥarrân or Syrian Christians, who had enjoyed the Greek education of the time, not only translated Greek literature into Syriac and Arabic for the benefit of their Arab masters, but wrote also general works on the history of Greek learning and literature, probably translating and adopting for their purpose some one of the most current school-books on this subject, used in the schools of Alexandria, Athens, Antioch, &c. Among authors who wrote such books, some being mere compilations of the famous sentences of Greek sages (doxographic), others having a more historic character, are Ḥunain Ibn 'Isḥâḳ, his son 'Isḥâḳ Ibn Ḥunain, and Ḳusṭâ Ibn Lûḳâ (*i.e.* Constans the son of Lucas). But what were the Greek works from which they took their information, and which they probably communicated to the Arabs exactly as they were? I am inclined to think that they used works of Porphyrius and Ammonius, the Greek originals of which are no longer extant.

P. 25. *Jurare in verba, &c.*—The Hindus consider, *e.g.* the sciences of astronomy and astrology as *founded upon tradition*, and their authors produce in their books side by side their own perhaps more advanced ideas and some silly notions of any predecessors of theirs, although they are fully aware that both are totally irreconcilable with each other. *Cf.* the words of Varâhamihira to this effect in *Bṛihat Saṁhitâ*, ix. 7, and the note of his commentator Utpala to v. 32. Alberuni pronounces most energetically against this kind of scientific composition when speaking of Brahmagupta in chapter lix. on eclipses.

P. 27. *Beyond all likeness and unlikeness*, an expression frequent in the description of the Deity. Literally translated: *things that are opposite to each other and things that are like each other.* Perhaps the rhyme *ḍidd* and *nidd*, *'aḍdâd* and *'andâd*, has contributed to the coining of this term. As for the idea, it may be compared with the term *dvandvâs* in Hindu philosophy = *pairs of opposites*, as pleasure and pain, health and sickness. *Bhagavad-Gîtâ*, ii. 45, vii. 27; "Yoga Aphorisms of Patañjali" (edited by Rajendralâlâ Mitra), ii. 48, p. 111.

P. 27. *Who is the worshipped one? &c.*—The greater part of this extract from Patañjali has been translated into Persian by Abulma'âli Muḥammad Ibn 'Ubaid-Allâh in his *Kitâb-bayân-al'adyân*; v. C. Schefer, *Chrestomathie Persane*, i. ۱۳۸–۱۳۹ : سوآل کدامست آن معبود که همه کان بتوفیق او راه یابند بعبادت او جوآب آنکه همه امیدها بدوست وهمه بیمها آلخ

P. 27. *Patañjali.*—The book of this name used and translated by the author had the form of a conversation between two persons, simply called "the asking one," and "the answering one," and its subject was *the search for liberation and for the union of the soul with the object of its meditation* (i. 132), *the emancipation of the soul from the fetters of the body* (i. 8). It was a popular book of theosophy, propounding in questions and answers the doctrine of the Yoga, a theistic philosophy developed by Patañjali out of the atheistic Sâṁkhya philosophy of Kapila. *Cf.* J. Davies, "Hindu Philosophy," *Sâṅkhyâ Kârikâ of Îśvara Kṛishṇa*, London, 1881, p. 116. The latter is called *nirîśvara* =

not having a lord, the former *seśvara* = having a lord. It mostly treats of *moksha* (salvation) and metempsychosis. It contained not only theory, but also tales (i. 93), Haggadic elements by way of illustration.

Alberuni's Patañjali is totally different from "The Yoga Aphorisms of Patañjali" (with the commentary of Bhoja Râjâ, and an English translation by Rajendralâlâ Mitra, Calcutta, 1883), and, as far as I may judge, the philosophic system of the former differs in many points essentially from that of the Sûtras.

Moreover, the extracts given in the *Indica* stand in no relation with the commentary of Bhoja Râjâ, although the commentator here and there mentions ideas which in a like or similar form occur in Alberuni's work, both works being intended to explain the principles of the same school of philosophy.

Besides the text of Patañjali, a commentary also is mentioned and quoted (i. 232, 234, 236, 238, 248), مفسر مفسّر باتنجل or كتاب باتنجل. It is most remarkable that the extracts from this commentary are all of them not of a philosophic, but of a plainly Paurâṇic character, treating of cosmographic subjects, the *lokas, Mount Meru*, the different spheres, &c. The name of the commentator is not mentioned. If the quotations on i. 273 *seq.* may be considered as derived from this commentary, the author was Balabhadra. V. index i. *s.v.* Patañjali.

P. 29. *Gîtâ.*—The book *Gîtâ* is, according to Alberuni, a part of the book *Bhârata* (*i.e. Mahâbhârata*, which term does not occur in the *Indica* [1]), and a conversation between Vâsudeva and Arjuna (قال باسديو لارجن). It is largely quoted in chapters relating to religion and philosophy. We have now to examine in what relation Alberuni's *Gîtâ* stands to the well-known *Bhagavad-Gîtâ* as we have it in our time. *Cf.* "Hindu Philosophy," "The Bhagavad-Gîtâ, or the Sacred Lay," translated by J. Davies, London, 1882. The latter is described as *a skilful union of the systems of Kapila and Patañjali with a large admixture of the prevailing Brahmanic doctrines.* Although the opinions regarding its origin differ widely, it can scarcely be denied that it is not free from having been influenced to a certain degree by

[1] *Cf.* Alberuni on the *Mahâbhârata*, i. 132, 133.

Christianity, and that it could not have been composed before the third Christian century. Chapter xi. gives the impression of having been modelled after a Christian apocalypsis.

The quotations from the *Gîtâ* (or *Song*) may be divided into three classes :—

(1.) Such as exhibit a close relationship with certain passages in the *Bhagavad-Gîtâ*. Parts of sentences are here and there almost identical, but nowhere whole sentences ; v. i. 40, 52, 73, 74, 86, 87, 103, 104, 218 (v. *note*), 352 ; ii. 169.

(2.) Such as show a certain similarity, more in the ideas expressed than in the wording, with passages in the *Bhagavad-Gîtâ* ; v. i. 29, 70, 71, 78, 79, 103, 104, 122.

(3.) Such as cannot be compared, either in idea or in wording, with any passage in the *Bhagavad-Gîtâ* ; v. i. 52, 53, 54, 70, 71, 73, 74, 75, 76, 78, 79, 80, 92, 122 ; ii. 137, 138.

The single texts will be discussed in the notes to the places in question.

The quotations given by Alberuni cannot have been translated from the *Bhagavad-Gîtâ* in its present form. Admitting even that the translator translated as little literally and accurately as possible (and the texts of Alberuni do *not* give this impression), there remains a great number of passages which on no account could be derived from the present Sanskrit text, simply because they do not exist there. Or has Alberuni translated a commentary of the *Bhagavad-Gîtâ* instead of the original? The text of the extracts, as given in the *Indica*, is remarkably short and precise, extremely well worded, without any repetition and verbosity, and these are qualities of style which hardly point to a commentary.

Alberuni seems to have used an edition of the *Bhagavad-Gîtâ* totally different from the one which *we* know, and which also in India seems to be the only one known. It must have been more ancient, because the notorious Yoga elements are not found in it, and these have been recognised by the modern interpreters as interpolations of a later time. Secondly, it must have been more complete, because it exhibits a number of sentences which are not found in the *Bhagavad-Gîtâ*.

Various generations of Hindu scholars have modelled and remodelled this book, one of the most precious gems of their literature, and it seems astonishing that an edition of it which existed as late as the time of Alberuni should not have reached the nineteenth century.

As regards the quotation on this page (29), it exhibits only in the substance a distant relationship with *Bhagavad-Gîtâ*, x. 3: "He who knows Me as unborn and without beginning, the mighty Lord of the world, he of mortals is free from delusion, he is free from all sin."

P. 30. *Sâṁkhya.*—The book *Sâṁkhya*, as used and translated by Alberuni, had the form of a conversation between an anchorite and a sage, and it contained a treatise on the *origines and a description of all created beings* (i. 8), a book *on divine subjects* (i. 132). It was composed by Kapila. The author quotes it largely on questions of religion and philosophy. The Sâṁkhya philosophy of Kapila is the most ancient system of thought among the Hindus, the source of the Yoga doctrine of Patañjali. *Cf.* Colebrooke, "Essays," i. 239–279; J. Davies, "Hindu Philosophy," &c., p. 101 *seq.*

The relation between Alberuni's *Sâṁkhya* and the so-called *Sâṁkhyapravacanam* ("The Sânkhya Aphorisms of Kapila," translated by Ballantyne, London, 1885) is a very distant one, and is limited to this, that there occurs a small number of passages which show a similarity of matter, not of form. The latter book (the *Sûtras*) seems to be a late secondary production; v. A. Weber, *Vorlesungen über Indische Literaturgeschichte*, p. 254, note 250. Besides, the philosophic system propounded by Alberuni under the name of *Sâṁkhya* seems in various and essential points to differ from that of the *Sûtras*; it seems altogether to have had a totally different tendency. The *Sûtras* treat of *the complete cessation of pain*; the first one runs thus: "Well, the complete cessation of pain, (which is) of three kinds, is the complete end of man;" whilst the *Sâṁkhya* of Alberuni teaches *moksha* by means of knowledge.

Next we have to compare Alberuni's *Sâṁkhya* with the *Sâṁkhya Kârikâ* of Îśvara Kṛishṇa (v. Colebrooke, "Essays," i. 272; J. Davies, "Hindu Philosophy," London,

1881). Both works teach *moksha* by means of knowledge, and contain here and there the same subject-matter. It must be observed that of those illustrative tales which Alberuni's *Sâṁkhya* gives in full length, short indications are found in the *Sâṁkhya Kârikâ.* Its author, Îśvara Krishṇa, says at the end of his book that he has written his seventy *Sûtras, excluding illustrative tales.* This is not quite correct, as sometimes, though he has not told them, he has at all events indicated them. His words show that he has copied from a book like the *Sâṁkhya* of Alberuni, in which *the tales* were not only indicated, but related at full length. *Cf.* A. Weber, *Vorlesungen über Indische Literaturgeschichte*, Berlin, 1876, p. 254, note 250. Hall considers the *S. Pravacanam* to be younger than the *S. Kârikâ.*

If, in the third place, we examine the *Bhâshya* of Gauḍapâda, we find that it is not identical with Alberuni's *Sâṁkhya*, but a near relative of it. *Cf.* the *Sâṁkhya Kârikâ*, &c., translated by Colebrooke, also the *Bhâshya* of Gauḍapâda, translated by H. H. Wilson, Oxford, 1837; Colebrooke, "Essays," i. 245. Most of the quotations given by Alberuni are found only slightly differing in Gauḍapâda, and some agree literally, as I shall point out in the notes to the single passages. Almost all the illustrative tales mentioned by Alberuni are found in Gauḍapâda, being, as a rule, more extensive in Alberuni than in Gauḍapâda. The latter seems to have taken his information from a work near akin to, or identical with, that *Sâṁkhya* book which was used by Alberuni.

According to Colebrooke (in the preface of the work just mentioned, on p. xiii.), Gauḍapâda was the teacher of Śaṁkara Âcârya, who is said to have lived in the eighth Christian century. *Cf.* also A. Weber, *Vorlesungen*, pp. 179, 254, and 260. Alberuni does not mention Gauḍapâda, as far as I can see. Or is he perhaps identical with *Gauḍa the anchorite*, whom Alberuni mentions even before Kapila? *Cf.* the passage, i. 131–132: "Besides, the Hindus have books, &c., on the process of becoming God and seeking liberation from the world, as, *e.g.* the book composed by Gauḍa the anchorite, which goes by his name."

Kapila, the father of the Sâṁkhya philosophy, is mentioned by Alberuni also as the author of a book called

*Nyâyabhâshâ*, "on the Veda and its interpretation, also showing that it has been created, and distinguishing within the Veda between such injunctions as are obligatory only in certain cases and those which are obligatory in general" (i. 132). The subject of this book is evidently not related to the Nyâya philosophy, but to the tenets of the Mîmâṁsâ philosophy, *i.e.* the Pûrvamîmâṁsâ, (Colebrooke, "Essays," i. p. 319–349; J. Davies, "Hindu Philosophy," p. 2; Thibaut, *Arthasaṁgraha*, Benares, 1882), a system of rules which are applied to the text of the Veda and its sacrificial prescriptions.

P. 31. *The anthropomorphic doctrines, the teachings of the Jabriyya sect, &c.*—The sect called Jabriyya, Jabariyya, and Mujbara teaches that the actions of man proceed from God. They are the followers of Al-najjâr. *Cf. Fihrist*, p. 179 *seq.*

The *Ahl-altashbîh*, or anthropomorphists, teach that God is similar to His creatures. *Cf. Statio Quinta et Sexta et appendix libri Mevakif*, edit. Th. Sœrensen, Leipzig, 1858, p. 362; *Kitâb-i-Yamînî* of Al-Utbi, translated by J. Reynolds, London, 1858, preface, pp. xxv. xxix.; "Book of Religious and Philosophical Sects," by Alshahrastâni, edited by Cureton, pp. 59, 61, and 75 *seq.*

I understand the passage وتحريم النظر في شيء (١٠, 11, 12) as meaning *the prohibition of the study* (not *discussion*, as I have translated, which would be المناظرة) *of a subject*, *i.e.* a question of a religious bearing; but I am not aware what particular event the author hints at by these words. At the intolerant religious policy of the Khalif Alḳâdir? King Maḥmûd was a great *Ketzerrichter*. Probably a stout adherent of the theory of the harmony of throne and altar, which his contemporaries Al-'Utbî (in his preface) and Alberuni (i. 99) call *twins*, he tried to cover the illegitimate, revolutionary origin of his dynasty, which was still fresh in the memory of the men of the time; he maintained the most loyal relations with the spiritual head of Islam, the Khalif of Bagdad, Alḳâdir (A.H. 381–422), who had clad the usurpation of his family with the mantle of legitimacy; and in order to please him, he hunted down the heretics in his realm in Khurasan as in Multân (*cf.* Reynolds, l. l., p. 438 *seq.*), impaling or stoning them. He tried to rid the Khalif of the real or suspected votaries of his opponent, the Anti-Khalif in Egypt, the famous Ḥâkim, famous by his madness and by being considered by the Druzes as the originator of their creed. The religious policy of Maḥmûd may be retraced to the following principles :—

(1.) Perfect toleration for the Hindus at his court and in his army.

(2.) Persecution of certain Muslim sectarians in the interest of the Khalif, of the Karmatians and other sects of Shiitic tendencies. (*Cf.* A. von Kremer, *Geschichte der herschenden Ideen des Islam*, Leipzig, 1868, p. 127.)

(3.) Predilection for a Muslim sectarian from Sijistân by the name of Abû-ʿAbdillâh Ibn Alkirâm, by whose influence both Sunnites and Shiites had to suffer (*cf. Alshahrastânî*, p. ٢٠). How long the influence of this man had lasted, and how far his doctrines had been carried into practice, does not appear from Alshahrastâni's account.

That, notwithstanding all this, there was a large margin for liberty of religious thought under the rule of Maḥmûd and his immediate successor, is sufficiently illustrated by the tenor of Alberuni's work. Altogether, it must be kept in mind that before Alghazzâlî the Muslim Church was not that concentrated organisation nor that all-overwhelming force which it has been ever since and keeps up in our days. To those who only know the centuries of Muslim history after the establishment of the orthodox Church, it sounds next to incredible that the military chief of a Khalif should have been an infidel (a Zoroastrian?) *Cf.* the story of Afshîn, the general of the Khalif Almuʿtasim, in *Menoutchehri, Poète Persan*, par A. de Biberstein. Kazimirski, p. 149.

P. 33. *τὸ λανθάνειν.*—The word *kumûn*, which I have thus rendered, means *to be hidden.* Not knowing to what school of Greek philosophers the author refers, I can only give the note of Reiske, "اهل الكمون, Philosophi qui omnes animas simul et semel creatas et reconditas in Adamo putant" (Freytag, *Lexicon Arabicum*, s.h.v.).

P. 33. *Pailâsôpâ, &c.*—As Syrian scholars were the author's teachers in Greek philosophy, he knows the Greek word φιλόσοφος only in its Syrian garb ܦܝܠܣܘܦܐ.

The *Ahl-aṣṣuffa* were certain persons, poor refugees and houseless men, who during the first years of Muhammad's stay in Medîna passed the night in the *ṣuffa* of the mosque of the Prophet in Medîna, which was a covered place, an appurtenance of the mosque, roofed over with palm-sticks (*Lane*).

*Abulfatḥ Albustî* was a famous poet of the time. A native of Bust in Northern Afghanistan, he was in the service of the governor, who held the place under the Sâmânî dynasty, and after the conquest of Bust by Sabuktagîn he entered the service of this prince and of his son Maḥmûd. Under Mas'ûd he lived still in Ghazna, for Baihaḳî mentions that he had fallen into disgrace and had to carry water for the royal stables. By the intervention of Baihaḳi, he was restored into the good graces of the prime minister, Aḥmad Ibn Ḥasan of Maimand. *Cf.* Elliot, "History of India, ii. 82, 84, iv. 161; Ethé, *Rûdagî's Vorläufer und Zeitgenossen*, p. 55. According to Ḥâjî Khalifa (iii. 257, iv. 533), he died A.H. 430 (A.D. 1039). For further information see Shahrazûri, *Nuzhat-al'arwâḥ*, fol. 182*b* (MS. of the Royal Library, Berlin, MSS. Orient. octav. 217); Al-Baihaḳî, *Tatimmat-ṣuwân-alḥikma*, fol. 22*b* (MS. of the same library, Petermann, ii. 737); also *Mirchondi Historia Gasnevidarum Persice*, by F. Wilken, Berlin, 1832, p. 144. Towards the end of his life he is said to have travelled with an embassy of the Khaḳân of Transoxiana to that country, and to have died there.

P. 34. *Galenus.*—The author quotes the following works of Galenus:—

(1.) λόγος προτρεπτικός.

(2.) A commentary to the aphorisms of Hippokrates, a book of which I do not know the Greek original (*cf.* i. 35, ii. 168).

(3.) كتاب الميامر (from the Syriac ܡܐܡܪ̈ܐ) = περὶ συνθέσεως φαρμάκων τῶν κατὰ τόπους.

(4.) كتاب البرهان = *the book of the proof*, of which I do not know the Greek original; *cf.* i. 97.

(5.) اخلاق النفس = *de indole animæ* (περὶ ἠθῶν ?), of which the Greek original likewise is not known to me; *cf.* i. 123, 124.

(6.) كتاب قاطاجانس = περὶ συνθέσεως φαρμάκων κατὰ γένη.

Besides, the author gives some quotations from Galenus without mentioning from what particular book they were taken; *cf.* i. 222, 320. *Cf.* on Galen's works in Arabic Dr. Klamroth, "Journal of the German Oriental Society," vol. xl. 189 *seq.*

The passage here given is found in *Προτρεπτικὸς ἐπὶ τὰς τέχνας*, ed. Abrah. Willet, Lugduni Bat., 1812, chap. ix. pp. 29, 30:—*ὡς καὶ τῶν ἀνθρώπων τοὺς ἀρίστους θείας ἀξιωθῆναι τιμῆς, οὐχ ὅτι καλῶς ἔδραμον ἐν τοῖς ἀγῶσιν ἢ δίσκον ἔῤῥιψαν ἢ διεπάλαισαν· ἀλλὰ διὰ τὴν ἀπὸ τῶν τεχνῶν ἐνεργεσίαν. Ἀσκληπιὸς γέ τοι καὶ Διόνυσος εἴτ' ἄνθρωποι πρότερον ἤστην εἴτ' ἀρχῆθεν, τιμῶν ἀξιοῦνται μεγίστων, ὁ μὲν διὰ τὴν ἰατρικὴν, ὁ δ' ὅτι τὴν περὶ τοὺς ἀμπέλους ἡμᾶς τέχνην ἐδίδαξεν.*

The two passages on p. 36 are probably taken from the *Protrepticus* too. With the former compare the words in chap. ix. (on p. 22 editio Kühn, vol. i.): *Εἰ δ' οὐκ ἐθέλεις ἐμοὶ πείθεσθαι, τόν γε θεὸν αἰδέσθητι τὸν Πύθιον.*

Shortly afterwards follows the second quotation, verses quoted by Galen from Herodotus, i. 65:

> *Ἥκεις, ὦ Λυκόεργε, ἐμὸν ποτὶ πίονα νηόν.*
> *Δίζω ἤ σε θεὸν μαντεύσομαι ἢ ἄνθρωπον,*
> *ἀλλ' ἔτι καὶ μᾶλλον θεὸν ἔλπομαι, ὦ Λυκόεργε.*

P. 35. *Plato.*—The author quotes the following works of Plato:—

(1.) *Phædo.*

(2.) *Timæus* (*cf.* also *Proclus*).

(3.) *Leges.*

Of the three quotations on this passage, the middle one is found in *Timæus*, 41A:—*Ἐπεὶ δ' οὖν πάντες κ. τ. λ., λέγει πρὸς αὐτοὺς ὁ τόδε τὸ πᾶν γεννήσας τάδε· θεοὶ θεῶν κ. τ. λ., ἀθάνατοι μὲν οὐκ ἐστὲ οὐδ' ἄλυτοι τὸ πάμπαν· οὔτι μὲν δὴ λυθήσεσθέ γε οὐδὲ τεύξεσθε θανάτου μοίρας, τῆς ἐμῆς βουλήσεως μείζονος ἔτι δεσμοῦ καὶ κυριωτέρου λαχόντες ἐκείνων οἷς ὅτ' ἐγίγνεσθε ξυνεδεῖσθε.*

The first and third quotations are not found in the Greek text, and Ed. Zeller, to whom I applied for help, thinks that both are taken from a commentary on *Timæus* by some Christian author, as *e.g.* Johannes Philoponus, the former having been derived from 40D (*περὶ δὲ τῶν ἄλλων δαιμόνων εἰπεῖν καὶ γνῶναι τὴν γένεσιν κ.τ.λ.*), the latter from passages like 32B and 92B.

The index of the works of Johannes Philoponus or Scholasticus (Steinschneider, *Al-Fârâbî*, p. 152 *seq.*) does not mention a commentary on *Timæus*, if it is not concealed under the title of one of his books, فى الكون والفساد, *i.e. on existing and perishing.* As he was a literary opponent of Nestorius, he seems to have been a strict Monophysite, which would be in keeping with the third quotation, "God is in the single number," &c. *Cf.* the note to pp. 56, 57.

P. 36. *Johannes Grammaticus* (identical with J. Philoponus and Scholasticus) is five times quoted. There are three extracts from his *Refutatio Procli*, and two more, the origin of which is not mentioned, but probably taken from the same book. The passage here mentioned is found in *Joannis Grammatici Philoponi Alexandrini contra Proclum de Mundi æternitate*, libri xviii., Venetiis, 1551, Greek and Latin, in the 18th λόγος, chap. ix. (there is no pagination; *cf.* the Latin translation, p. 95) :—

*μὴ δὲ γὰρ εἰδέναι πω ἐκείνους ἄλλό τι θεὸν πλὴν τῶν φαινομένων σωμάτων ἡλίου καὶ σελήνης καὶ τῶν λοιπῶν, ὥσπερ καὶ μέχρι νῦν τῶν βαρβάρων ὑπολαμβάνειν τοὺς πλείστους. ὕστερον δέ φησιν εἰς ἔννοιαν καὶ τῶν ἄλλων θεῶν τῶν ἀσωμάτων ἕλληνας ἐλθόντας, τῷ αὐτῷ κἀκείνους προσαγορεῦσαι ὀνόματι.*

I have not succeeded in identifying the other four quotations, i. 65. 226, 231, 284. *Cf.* on this author, *Fihrist*, p. 254, and Dr. Steinschneider, *Alfârâbi*, pp. 152, 162.

P. 37. *Baal.*—The form of the word بعلا (Syriac ܒܥܠܐ) shows that the Arabic Bible-text which Alberuni used had been translated from Syriac.

P. 39. *Mânî.*—*Vide* note to pp. 7, 8.

P. 40. *Gîtâ.*—*Cf.* with these words the *Bhagavad-Gîtâ* (of J. Davies), xv. 14, 15 :—

"Entering into the *earth*, I sustain all things by my vital force, and becoming *a savoury juice*, I nourish all herbs (v. 14).

"I become *fire*, and enter into the bodies of all that breathe, &c. And I am seated in the hearts of all : from

Me come *memory*, *knowledge*, and the power of reason," &c. (v. 15).

Davies supposes the whole of verse 15 to be an interpolation, but this remark must, as it seems, be limited to the final sentence of verse 15 only, *i.e.* to the words: "I form the Vedânta, and I am one who knows the Vedas."

P. 40. *Apollonius.*—A Greek book of Apollonius of Tyana of this title is not known to me, but it exists in Arabic, كتاب فى العلل (*Liber de Causis*), in the library of Leyden, *cf.* Wenrich, *De Auctorum Græcorum Versionibus et Commentariis Syriacis, Arabicis, &c.*, p. 239.

Pp. 40–44.—The Sâṃkhya doctrine of the twenty-five *tattvas* is found in the commentary of Gauḍapâda to the *Sâṅkhya Kârikâ* of Îśvara Kṛishṇa, where also the saying of Vyâsa (here i. 44 and 104) is found. *Cf.* the translation of H. H. Wilson, p. 79, i. 14.

P. 40. *Buddha, dharma, saṅgha.*—This note on the Buddhistic trinity probably rests on the authority of Zurḳân, as he was quoted in the book of *Erânshahrî*: *cf.* note to pp. 6, 7. It shows that Alberuni had no original information regarding Buddhism, and it justifies his harsh judgment on the worth of the tradition of Zurkân, *v.* i. 7.

The name *Buddhodana* is nothing, and by mistake derived from *Śuddhodana*, the name of Buddha's father. Perhaps Zurḳân had read not بدهودن but سودهودن, which would be *Sauddhodani*, i.e. *the son of Śuddhodana* or Buddha.

P. 41. *Vâyu Purâṇa.*—Of the Purâṇas the author had the *Âditya*, *Matsya*, and *Vâyu Purâṇas*, *i.e.* only portions of them (i. 130), and probably the whole of *Vishṇu-Purâṇa*. Most of his Pauranic quotations are taken from *Vâyu*, *Vishṇu*, and *Matsya Purâṇas*. *Cf.* on the Purâṇas, A. Weber, *Vorlesungen*, p. 206, and note 206 on p. 208.

P. 42.—The *five mothers* are a blunder of the author's instead of *the five measures*, i.e. *pañcamâtrâni* (*pañcatanmâtrâṇi*).

The combination between the senses and the elements, as it is given here and on p. 43, also occurs in the *Vaiśe-*

*shika*—philosophy of Kaṇâda: *cf.* Colebrooke, "Essays," i. 293 *seq.* Compare also *Vishṇu-Purâṇa*, i. 2, p. 35, and Hall's note 1. There are similar elements in the philosophy of the Bauddhas or Saugatas: v. Colebrooke, *l.c.* i. 416, 417.

P. 42.—The quotation from Homer is not found in the Greek text, nor do I know the Greek original of the second verse. Were they taken from some Neo-Pythagorean book?

P. 43. *Porphyry.*—This is the only quotation from Porphyry, from a book of his which is not extant in the Greek original. According to Wenrich, *l.c.* p. 287, there has once been in Syriac a translation of the fourth book of a *Liber Historiarum Philosophorum*, probably identical with the work here mentioned. The note on the Milky Way (i. 281) is perhaps taken from this same source.

P. 43. *Lacuna.*—In the Arabic text (٢١, 15) is missing the relation between the *hearing* and the *air*, the complement to the words *hearing airy* in l. 14.

P. 43. *Plato.*—As the author does not mention the source whence he took these words, I conjecture that they were derived from *Timæus*, 77, A, B, or from some commentary on this passage: *cf.* note to p. 35.

P. 45. *Matres simplices.*—*Cf.* note to p. 42. On the Sâṁkhya theory regarding the union of soul and matter, *cf. Sâṁkhya Kârikâ*, *vv.* 20, 21, 42, and Gauḍapâda's *Bhâshya*.

P. 47. *Dancing-girl.*—This example is likewise found in Gauḍapâda, p. 170 (*Bhâshya* to *v.* 59 of the *Saṁkhya Kârikâ*); that of the blind and the lame on p. 76 (to *v.* 21).

P. 48. *Mânî.*—*Vide* note to pp. 7, 8.

P. 48. *The book of Sâṁkhya, &c.*—The theory of predominance among the three primary forces (*guṇa*), *v.* in Gauḍapâda, pp. 92, 93, to *v.* 25, p. 49 to *v.* 12; the comparison of the soul with a spectator on p. 72 to v. 19 (also *Bhagavad-Gîtâ*, xiv. 23); the story of the innocent among the robbers on p. 74 to *v.* 20.

P. 49. *The soul is in matter, &c.*—The soul compared to a charioteer, v. in Gauḍapâda, p. 66 to *v.* 17.

Pp. 52–54. *Vâsudeva speaks to Arjuna, &c.*—Of these quotations from *Gîtâ*, compare the passage, "Eternity is common to both of us, &c., whilst they were concealed from you," with *Bhagavad-Gîtâ*, iv. 5: "Many have been in past time the births of me, and of thee also, Arjuna. All these I know, but thou knowest them not, O slayer of foes!"

Of the other quotations on these two pages, I do not see how they could be compared with any passage in *Bhagavad-Gîtâ*, except for the general tenor of the ideas. With the phrase, "For he loves God and God loves him," *cf. Bhagavad-Gîtâ*, xii. 14–20, "Who worships me is dear to me."

P. 54. *Vishṇu-Dharma.*—Alberuni gives large quotations from this book. He speaks of it i. 132, and translates the title as *the religion of God.*

I do not know the Sanskrit original of the book, for it is totally different from the *Vishṇu-Smṛiti*, or *Vishṇu-Sûtra*, or *Vaishṇava Dharmaśâstra*, translated by J. Jolly ("The Institutes of Vishṇu," Oxford, 1880), a law-book in a hundred chapters, similar to those of Âpastamba, Yâjnavalkya, Vasishṭha, the Gṛihyasûtras, &c. Our *Vishṇu-Dharma* is a sort of Purâṇa, full of those legends and notions characteristic of the literature of Purâṇas; but the author does not assign it to them. Most of the extracts here given are conversations between the sage Mârkaṇḍeya and Vajra, others a conversation between the king Parîksha and the sage Śatânîka. The extracts treat of mythological subjects (i. 54); the twelve suns (i. 216, 217); the pole (i. 241); the planets and fixed stars (i. 287, 288); star-legends (i. 291); the story of Hiraṇyâksha (ii. 140); the names of the Manvantaras (i. 387); the dominants of the planets (ii. 121); in particular, of chronological and astronomical subjects. The author has taken several series of names from the *Vishṇu-Dharma*. He seems to quote it sometimes without mentioning its title. So, *e.g.* I am inclined to attribute the traditions of Śaunaka (i. 113, 126) to this book. The quotation (ii. 398) on Vâsudeva, Saṁkarshaṇa, Pradyumna, and Aniruddha, as the names of Hari in the four *Yugas*, is found likewise among the doctrines of the Vaishṇava sect, the Pâñcarâtras, or Bhâgavatas: *cf.* Colebrooke, "Essays," i. 439, 440. Vishṇu is the chief god of those Hindus with whom Alberuni held relation. Were they Vaishṇava sects, and was the *Vishṇu-Dharma* a special code of theirs? On the heterodox sect of Vishṇu or Vâsudeva worshippers just mentioned, *cf.* Colebrooke, *l.c.* pp. 437–443.

Colebrooke mentions a book, *Vishṇu-Dharmottara-Purâṇa*, which is said to have comprehended the Brahmasiddhânta of Brahmagupta: *cf.* "Essays," ii. 348. This work is perhaps identical with the *Vishṇu-Dharma* used by Alberuni. As he had a copy of the *Brahmasiddhânta*, he had it perhaps as a portion of this larger work.

P. 54. *Lakshmî, who produced the Amṛita.*—For the legend of Lakshmî v. *Vishṇu-Purâṇa*, i. 9, where it is Dhanvantari who brings the Amṛita-cup, not Lakshmî. Apparently this goddess is meant here, and not Lakshmaṇa, as the manuscript has it, the brother of Râma. When Alberuni wrote this, he seems to have mistaken Lakshmî for a masculine being, or else we must write خرجه in the text ٢٧, 3, instead of خرج.

The Arabic *hanâ'a* (=*aisance, félicité*) is an attempt of Alberuni's to translate the Sanskrit *amṛita*=ambrosia, which scarcely any one of his readers will have understood. *Cf.* the Arabic text, ١٢٦, 6 (here i. 253).

P. 54. *Daksha, who was beaten by Mahâdeva.*—*Cf.* the story of the destruction of Daksha's sacrifice by order of Śiva, as communicated by Hall in his edition of Wilson's *Vishṇu-Purâṇa* as appendix to i. viii. p. 120 *seq.* (Sacrifice of Daksha, from the *Vâyu-Purâṇa*).

P. 54. *Varâhamihira.*—Of this author Alberuni quotes the following works:—

(1.) *Bṛihatsaṁhitâ.*

(2.) *Bṛihajjâtakam*, i. 158, 219, 220, ii. 118.

(3.) *Laghujâtakam*, i. 158.

(4.) *Pañcasiddhântikâ*, i. 153, ii. 7, 190.

Books of the same author, which Alberuni mentions without giving extracts from them, are *Shaṭpañcâśikâ* and هور بنج هترى (?), both with astrological contents (i. 158). Perhaps the two books called *Yogayâtrâ* and *Tikanî* (?)-*yâtrâ* (i. 158) are also to be attributed to Varâhamihira. Besides there are mentioned several commentaries, one of the *Bṛihat-Saṁhitâ* by Utpala, from Kashmîr (i. 298), and one of the *Bṛihajjâtakam* by Balabhadra.

One of the sources whence Alberuni has drawn most copiously is the *Bṛihat-Saṁhitâ*, or, as *he* calls it, the *Saṁhitâ*: *v.* the edition of the Sanskrit original by Dr. Kern, Calcutta, 1865, and his translation in the "Journal of the Royal Asiatic Society" for the years 1870, 1871, 1873, 1875. Alberuni praises Varâhamihira as an honest man of science (i. 366), and maintains that he lived 526 years before his own time, which is A.D. 1030. Accordingly, the date of Varâhamihira would be A.D. 504. *Cf.* ii. 86.

In the preface to the edition, p. 61, Kern mentions the *Shaṭpañcâśikâ* and the *Yogayâtrâ*. Both the *Bṛihat-Saṁhitâ* and *Laghujâtakam* had been translated into Arabic by Alberuni.

The passage here (p. 54) quoted is found in chap. iii. v. 13–15 ("Journal of the Royal Asiatic Society," 1870, p. 446).

P. 54. *Mânî.*—*Vide* note to pp. 7, 8.

P. 55. *Patañjali.*—*Vide* note to p. 27.

Pp. 56, 57. *Phædo.*—The two quotations from *Phædo* are the following:—

70C. παλαιὸς μὲν οὖν ἔστι λόγος, οὗ μεμνήμεθα, ὡς εἰσὶν ἐνθένδε ἀφικόμεναι ἐκεῖ, καὶ πάλιν γε δεῦρο ἀφικνοῦνται καὶ γίγνονται ἐκ τῶν τεθνεώτων, καὶ εἰ τοῦθ' οὕτως ἔχει, πάλιν γίγνεσθαι ἐκ τῶν ἀποθανόντων τοὺς ζῶντας, ἄλλο τι ἢ εἶεν ἂν αἱ ψυχαὶ ἡμῶν ἐκεῖ, κ.τ.λ.

ἆρ' οὑτωσὶ γίγνεται πάντα, οὐκ ἄλλοθεν ἢ ἐκ τῶν ἐναντίων τὰ ἐναντία, κ.τ.λ.

The sentences which in the Arabic follow after these

words ("Our souls lead an existence of their own," &c.) cannot be combined with the Greek text, and I suppose they were taken from some commentary.

The second quotation is found

72E. ὅτι ἡμῖν ἡ μάθησις οὐκ ἄλλο τι ἢ ἀνάμνησις τύγχανει οὖσα, καὶ κατὰ τοῦτοε ἀνάγκη που ἡμᾶς ἐν προτέρῳ τινὶ χρόνῳ μεμαθηκέναι ἃ νῦν ἀναμιμνησκόμθα. τοῦτο δὲ ἀδύνατον, εἰ μὴ ἦν που ἡμῶν ἡ ψυχὴ, πρὶν ἐν τῷδε τῶ ἀνθρωπίνῳ εἴδει εἶναι, κ.τ.λ.

73D. οὐκοῦν οἶσθα ὅτι οἱ ἐρασταὶ, ὅταν ἴδωσι λύραν ἢ ἱμάτιον ἢ ἄλλο τι, οἷς τὰ παιδικὰ αὐτῶν εἴωθε χρῆσθαι, πάσχουσι τοῦτο. ἔγνωσάν τε τὴν λύραν καὶ ἐν τῇ διανοίᾳ ἔλαβον τὸ εἶδος τοῦ παιδός, οὗ ἦν ἡ λύρα; τοῦτο δέ ἐστιν ἀνάμνησις.

In some sentences the Arabic and Greek texts agree literally; in others they differ to such an extent that this extract, too, does not seem to be taken from a simple translation of the text of *Phædo*, but rather from a work in which text and commentary were mixed together, and the original form of a dialogue was changed into that of a simple relation. Alberuni erroneously held this to be the original form of the book. We have arrived at a similar result in the case of Plato's *Timæus*.

Proclus has composed a commentary on the saying of Plato that the soul is immortal, in three sections: *v.* Wenrich, *De Auctorum Græcorum Versionibus*, &c., p. 288; and Zeller, *Philosophie der Griechen*, iii. 6, 780, 1. This was probably an Arabic edition of *Phædo*, and possibly that one which Alberuni used. *Cf.* note to p. 35.

The quotations from *Phædo* given farther on (pp. 65–67) agree more accurately with the Greek original, but in them, too, the dialogistic form has disappeared.

P. 57. Proclus is twice quoted, here and i. 86. Both extracts seem to be derived from some commentary on *Timæus*, which was *different* from that commentary known in our time and edited by Schneider, Breslau, 1887. The words here mentioned probably refer to *Timæus*, 44 A B C:—καὶ διὰ δὴ ταῦτα πάντα τὰ παθήματα νῦν κατ' ἀρχάς τε ἄνους ψυχὴ γίγνεται τὸ πρῶτον, ὅταν εἰς σῶμα ἐνδεθῇ θνητὸν κ.τ.λ. χωλὴν τοῦ βίου διαπορευθεὶς ζωήν, ἀτελὴς καὶ ἀνόητος εἰς Ἅιδου πάλιν ἔρχεται.

The commentary of Proclus referring to these words (pp. 842, 843, ed. Schneider) is entirely different from the Arabic words.

The other quotation (i. 86) is derived from the same book, and refers to *Timæus*, 44D:—*εἰς σφαιροειδὲς σῶμα ἐνέδησαν, τοῦτο ὃ νῦν κεφαλὴν ἐπονομάζομεν, ὃ θειότατόν τ' ἐστὶ καὶ τῶν ἐν ἡμῖν πάντων δεσποτοῦν, κ.τ.λ.*

The commentary of Proclus (ed. Schneider) breaks off a little before this passage, at the beginning of 44D.

I am inclined to believe that the work, simply introduced by "Proclus says," is identical with that one which he calls *Timæus* (*cf.* note to page 35), a work which was—

(1.) Not a simple translation of the book, but a translation and a commentary together, the one running into the other; and which

(2.) Was different from the now extant commentary of *Timæus* by Proclus. Therefore Proclus must either have made two editions of *Timæus*, or he is not really the author of the book used by Alberuni. In the one place the name is written برقلس, in the other ابرقلس.

P. 57.—The *seat* (العرش) and the *throne* (الكرسى) of God. By these two words Muḥammad calls the throne of God in the Koran. Allah's sitting on his throne, as mentioned in the Koran, has been a subject of deep speculation among Muslim theologians. *Cf. Zur Geschichte Abulḥasan Al-Aśarî's*, von W. Spitta, Leipzig, 1876, pp. 106, 107, and the note on p. 144.

P. 60. *Vishṇu-Purâṇa.*—The passage is found in Book II. chap. vi. (Wilson-Hall, ii. p. 216). The order in which the hells are enumerated and their names differ to some extent:—

| | *Alberuni.* | | *Sanskrit original.* |
|---|---|---|---|
| | Raurava. | | Raurava. |
| | Rodha. | | Rodha. |
| | Taptakumbha. | | Śûkara. |
| | Mahâjvâla. | | Tâla. |
| 5. | Śavala. | 5. | Taptakumbha. |
| | Krimîśa. | | Taptaloha. |
| | Lâlâbhaksha. | | Mahâjvâla. |
| | Viśasana. | | Lavaṇa. |
| | Adhomukha. | | Vimoha. |
| 10. | Rudhirândha. | 10. | Krimibhaksha. |

| | *Alberuni.* | | *Sanskrit original.* |
| --- | --- | --- | --- |
| | Rudhira. | | Krimîśa. |
| | Vaitaraṇî. | | Lâlâbhaksha. |
| | Krishṇa. | | Vedhaka. |
| | Asipatravana. | | Viśasana. |
| 15. | Vahnijvâla. | 15. | Adhomukha. |
| | Sandaṁśaka. | | Pûyavaha. |
| | | | Rudhirândha. |
| | | | Vaitaraṇî. |
| | | | Krishṇa. |
| | | 20. | Asipatravana. |
| | | | Vahnijvâla. |
| | | | Sandaṁśa. |
| | | | Śvabhojana. |

P. 62. *Sâṁkhya.*—I do not find anything corresponding in the *Sâṁkhya Kârikâ* nor Gauḍapâda's commentary. As for the idea, *cf.* "Sâṁkhya Aphorisms," iv. 32.

P. 63. *Âtivâhika.*—On the *âtivâhika* = that which is swifter than the wind in passing from body to body, *cf.* *Sâṁkhya Kârikâ*, ed. Colebrooke-Wilson, p. 133.

The *Barzakh* is mentioned in the Koran, 23, 102; 25, 55; 55, 20.

P. 63. *Vishṇu-Purâṇa.*—This quotation is related in substance to Book II. chap. vi. pp. 221–224: *cf.* the uninterrupted thinking (*saṁsmaraṇa*) with the *remembrance of Hari, the meditation on Vâsudeva.* Are the words of Alberuni an extract from this passage?

P. 64. *Sâṁkhya.*—The *S. Kârikâ* and Gauḍapâda do not seem to offer anything analogous to this passage.

P. 64.—*A theosoph, &c.*—The passage relating to the four degrees of metempsychosis has been translated into Persian by Abulma'âlî Muḥammad Ibn 'Ubaid-Allâh in his *Bayân al'adyân*: *v.* C. Schefer, *Chrestomathie Persane*, i. ١٣٨, l. 3–8.

*Abû-Ya'ḳûb* and his work are not known to me from other sources.

P. 65. *Johannes Grammaticus.*—*Vide* note to p. 36.

*Phædo.*—The quotations on pp. 65–67 agree pretty accurately with the Greek text.

*The body is earthy, &c.*, 81 C, D:—

Ἐμβριθὲς δέ γε, ὦ φίλε, τοῦτο οἴεσθαι χρὴ εἶναι καὶ βαρὺ καὶ γεῶδες καὶ ὁρατόν· ὃ δὴ καὶ ἔχουσα ἡ τοιαύτη ψυχὴ βαρύνεταί τε καὶ ἕλκεται πάλιν εἰς τὸν ὁρατὸν τόπον φόβῳ τοῦ ἀειδοῦς τε καὶ Ἅιδου, ὥσπερ λέγεται, περὶ τὰ μνήματά τε καὶ τοὺς τάφους κυλινδουμένη, περὶ ἃ δὴ καὶ ὤφθη ἄττα ψυχῶν σκιοειδῆ φαντάσματα, οἷα παρέχονται αἱ τοιαῦται ψυχαὶ εἴδωλα αἱ μὴ καθαρῶς ἀπολυθεῖσαι, ἀλλὰ καὶ τοῦ ὁρατοῦ μετέχουσαι, διὸ καὶ ὁρῶνται.

*It appears that these are not the souls, &c.*, 81 D–82 A:—

Εἰκὸς μέντοι, ὦ Κέβης· καὶ οὔ τί γε τὰς τῶν ἀγαθῶν ταύτας εἶναι, ἀλλὰ τὰς τῶν φαύλων, αἳ περὶ τὰ τοιαῦτα ἀναγκάζονται πλανᾶσθαι δίκην τίνουσαι τῆς προτέρας τροφῆς κακῆς οὔσης· καὶ μέχρι γε τούτου πλανῶνται, ἕως ἂν τῇ ξυνεπακολουθοῦντος τοῦ σωματοειδοῦς ἐπιθυμίᾳ πάλιν ἐνδεθῶσιν εἰς σῶμα.

Ἐνδοῦνται δὲ, ὥσπερ εἰκός, εἰς τοιαῦτα ἤθη ὁποῖ' ἄττ' ἂν καὶ μεμελετηκυῖαι τύχωσιν ἐν τῷ βίῳ. Τὰ ποῖα δὴ ταῦτα λέγεις, ὦ Σώκρατες; Οἷον τοὺς μὲν γαστριμαργίας τε καὶ ὕβρεις καὶ φιλοποσίας μεμελετηκότας καὶ μὴ διευλαβημένους εἰς τὰ τῶν ὄνων γένη καὶ τῶν τοιούτων θηρίων εἰκὸς ἐνδύεσθαι· ἢ οὐκ οἴει; πάνυ μὲν οὖν εἰκὸς λέγεις. Τοὺς δέ γε ἀδικίας τε καὶ τυραννίδας καὶ ἁρπαγὰς προτετιμηκότας εἰς τὰ τῶν λύκων τε καὶ ἱεράκων καὶ ἰκτίνων γένη.

*If I did not think that I am going, &c.*, 63 B:—

εἰ μὲν μὴ ᾤμην ἥξειν πρῶτον μὲν παρὰ θεοὺς ἄλλους σοφούς τε καὶ ἀγαθούς, ἔπειτα καὶ παρ' ἀνθρώπους τετελευτηκότας ἀμεινοὺς τῶν ἐνθάδε, ἠδίκουν ἂν οὐκ ἀγανακτῶν τῷ θανάτῳ.

P. 66. *When a man dies, a daimon, &c.*, 107 D, 108 C:—

λέγεται δὲ οὕτως, ὡς ἄρα τελευτήσαντα ἕκαστον ὁ ἑκάστου δαίμων, ὅσπερ ζῶντα εἰλήχει, οὗτος ἄγειν ἐπιχειρεῖ εἰς δή τινα τόπον, οἷ δεῖ τοὺς συλλεγέντας διαδικασαμένους εἰς Ἅιδου πορεύεσθαι μετὰ ἡγεμόνος ἐκείνου, ᾧ δὴ προστέτακται τοὺς ἐνθένδε ἐκεῖσε πορεῦσαι. τυχόντας δ' ἐκεῖ, ὧν δεῖ τυχεῖν, καὶ μείναντας ὃν χρὴ χρόνον, ἄλλος δεῦρο πάλιν ἡγεμὼν κομίζει ἐν πολλαῖς χρόνου καὶ μακραῖς περιόδοις. ἔστι δὲ ἄρα ἡ πορεία οὐχ ὡς ὁ Αἰσχύλου Τήλεφος λέγει· ἐκεῖνος μὲν γὰρ ἁπλῆν οἶμόν φησιν εἰς Ἅιδου φέρειν, ἡ δ' οὔτε ἁπλῆ οὔτε μία φαίνεταί μοι εἶναι. οὐδὲ γὰρ ἂν ἡγεμόνων ἔδει, οὐ γάρ πού τις ἂν διαμάρτοι οὐδαμόσε μιᾶς ὁδοῦ οὔσης. νῦν δὲ ἔοικε σχίσεις δὲ καὶ περιόδους πολλὰς ἔχειν· ἀπὸ τῶν ὁσίων τε καὶ νομίμων τῶν ἐνθάδε τεκμαιρόμενος λέγω. ἡ μὲν κοσμία τε καὶ φρόνιμος ψυχὴ ἕπεταί τε καὶ οὐκ ἀγνοεῖ τὰ παρόντα· ἡ δ' ἐπιθυμητικῶς τοῦ σώματος ἔχουσα, ὅπερ ἐν τῷ ἔμπροσθεν εἶπον, περὶ ἐκεῖνο πολὺν χρόνον ἐπτοημένη καὶ περὶ τὸν ὁρατὸν τόπον πολλὰ ἀντιτείνασα καὶ πολλὰ παθοῦσα βίᾳ καὶ μόγις ὑπὸ τοῦ προστεταγμένου δαίμονος οἴχεται ἀγομένη. ἀφικομένην δὲ ὅθιπερ αἱ ἄλλαι, τὴν μὲν ἀκάθαρτον καί τι πεποιηκυῖαν τοιοῦτον, ἢ φόνων ἀδίκων ἡμμένην ἢ ἄλλ' ἄττα τοιαῦτα εἰργασμένην, ἃ τούτων ἀδελφά τε καὶ ἀδελφῶν ψυχῶν ἔργα τύγχανει ὄντα, ταύτην μὲν ἅπας φεύγει τε καὶ ὑπεκτρέπεται καὶ οὔτε ξυνέμπορος οὔτε ἡγεμὼν ἐθέλει γίγνεσθαι, αὐτὴ δὲ πλανᾶται ἐν πάσῃ ἐχομένη ἀπορίᾳ, ἕως ἂν δή τινες χρόνοι γένωνται, ὧν ἐλθόντων ὑπ' ἀνάγκης φέρεται εἰς τὴν αὐτῇ πρέπουσαν οἴκησιν· ἡ δὲ καθαρῶς τε καὶ μετρίως τὸν βίον διεξελθοῦσα καὶ ξυνεμπόρων καὶ ἡγεμόνων θεῶν τυχοῦσα ᾤκησεν τὸν αὐτῇ ἑκάστη τόπον προσήκοντα.

*Those of the dead who led a middle sort of life, &c.*, and *Those who repented of their sins, &c.*, 113D–114C:—

καὶ οἳ μὲν ἂν δόξωσι μέσως βεβιωκέναι, πορευθέντες ἐπὶ τὸν Ἀχέροντα, ἀναβάντες ἃ δὴ αὐτοῖς ὀχήματά ἐστιν, ἐπὶ τούτων ἀφικνοῦνται εἰς τὴν λίμνην, καὶ ἐκεῖ οἰκοῦσί τε καὶ καθαιρόμενοι τῶν τε ἀδικημάτων διδόντες δίκας ἀπολύονται, εἴ τίς τι ἠδίκηκεν, τῶν τε εὐεργεσιῶν τιμὰς φέρονται κατὰ τὴν ἀξίαν ἕκαστος. οἳ δ' ἂν δόξωσιν ἀνιάτως ἔχειν διὰ τὰ μεγέθη τῶν ἁμαρτημάτων, ἱεροσυλίας πολλὰς καὶ μεγάλας ἢ φόνους ἀδίκους καὶ παρανόμους πολλοὺς ἐξειργασμένοι ἢ ἄλλα ὅσα τοιαῦτα τυγχάνει ὄντα, τούτους δὲ ἡ προσήκουσα μοῖρα ῥίπτει εἰς τὸν Τάρταρον, ὅθεν οὔποτε ἐκβαίνουσιν. οἳ δ' ἂν ἰάσιμα μέν, μεγάλα δὲ δόξωσιν ἡμαρτηκέναι ἁμαρτήματα, οἷον πρὸς πατέρα ἢ μητέρα ὑπ' ὀργῆς βίαιόν τι πράξαντες, καὶ μεταμέλον αὐτοῖς τὸν ἄλλον βίον βιῶσιν, ἢ ἀνδροφόνοι τοιούτῳ τινὶ ἄλλῳ τρόπῳ γένωνται, τοιούτους δὲ ἐμπεσεῖν μὲν εἰς τὸν Τάρταρον ἀνάγκη, ἐμπεσόντας δὲ αὐτοὺς καὶ ἐνιαυτὸν ἐκεῖ γενομένους ἐκβάλλει τὸ κῦμα, τοὺς μὲν ἀνδροφόνους κατὰ τὸν Κωκυτόν, τοὺς δὲ πατραλοίας καὶ μητραλοίας κατὰ τὸν Πυριφλεγέθοντα. ἐπειδὰν δὲ φερόμενοι γένωνται κατὰ τὴν λίμνην τὴν Ἀχερουσιάδα, ἐνταῦθα βοῶσί τε καὶ καλοῦσιν, οἱ μὲν οὓς ἀπέκτειναν, οἱ δὲ οὓς ὕβρισαν, καλέσαντες δ' ἱκετεύουσι καὶ δέονται ἐᾶσαι σφᾶς ἐκβῆναι εἰς τὴν λίμνην καὶ δέξασθαι, καὶ ἐὰν μὲν πείσωσιν, ἐκβαίνουσί τε καὶ λήγουσι τῶν κακῶν, εἰ δὲ μή, φέρονται αὖθις εἰς τὸν Τάρταρον καὶ ἐκεῖθεν πάλιν εἰς τοὺς ποταμούς, καὶ ταῦτα πάσχοντες οὐ πρότερον παύονται, πρὶν ἂν πείσωσιν οὓς ἠδίκησαν· αὕτη γὰρ ἡ δίκη ὑπὸ τῶν δικαστῶν αὐτοῖς ἐτάχθη· οἳ δὲ δὴ ἂν δόξωσι διαφερόντως πρὸς τὸ ὁσίως βιῶναι, οὗτοί εἰσιν οἱ τῶνδε μὲν τῶν τόπων τῶν ἐν τῇ γῇ ἐλευθερούμενοί τε καὶ ἀπαλλαττόμενοι ὥσπερ δεσμωτηρίων, ἄνω δὲ εἰς τὴν καθαρὰν οἴκησιν ἀφικνούμενοι καὶ ἐπὶ τῆς γῆς οἰκιζόμενοι.

P. 68. *Ignorance, knowledge.*—*Cf. Sâṁkhya Kârikâ, v.* 44, "By knowledge is deliverance; by the reverse, bondage."

P. 69. *These eight things, &c.*—*Cf.* the Commentary of Bhojarâjâ to "The Yoga Aphorisms of Patañjali," &c., *v.* xlv., also Gauḍapâda's *Bhâshya* to the *Sâṁkhyâ Kârikâ, v.* xxiii. (pp. 83, 84), where he quotes the work of Patañjali (*Pâtañjala*).

P. 69. *Passing through several stages.*—*Cf.* with these four stages of knowledge the "*seven kinds of enlightenment*" in "The Yoga Aphorisms," ii. *v.* xxvii., and Commentary.

The fourth stage of Alberuni's Patañjali corresponds to the seventh kind of Bhojadeva.

P. 70. *In the book Gîtâ.*—There is no passage like this in the *Bhagavad-Gîtâ*. The words, "pleasures which in reality are pains" (p. 71, 6), may be compared with *Bhagavad-Gîtâ*, v. 22: "For the pleasures that are born of (these) contacts are the wombs of pain."

A similar sentence recurs in another quotation from *Gîtâ* here on p. 78, l. pen: "Pleasures of a kind which, in reality, are disguised pains."

P. 71. *Socrates.*—The following quotation is composed of the two passages, *Phædo*, 65 B–D and 67A:—

*ὅταν μὲν γὰρ μετὰ τοῦ σώματος ἐπιχειρῇ τι σκοπεῖν, δῆλον ὅτι τότε ἐξαπατᾶται ὑπ' αὐτοῦ. Ἀληθῆ λέγεις. Ἆρ' οὖν οὐκ ἐν τῷ λογίζεσθαι, εἴπερ που ἄλλοθι, κατάδηλον αὐτῇ γίγνεταί τι τῶν ὄντων; Ναί. λογίζεται δέ γέ που τότε κάλλιστα, ὅταν μηδὲν τούτων αὐτὴν παραλυπῇ, μήτε ἀκοὴ μήτε ὄψις μήτε ἀλγηδὼν μήτε τις ἡδονή, ἀλλ' ὅ τι μάλιστα αὐτὴ καθ' αὑτὴν γίγνηται ἐῶσα χαίρειν τὸ σῶμα, καὶ καθ' ὅσον δύναται μὴ κοινωνοῦσα αὐτῷ μηδ' ἁπτομένη ὀρέγηται τοῦ ὄντος. Ἔστι ταῦτα. Οὐκοῦν καὶ ἐνταῦθα ἡ τοῦ φιλοσόφου ψυχὴ μάλιστα ἀτιμάζει τὸ σῶμα καὶ φεύγει ἀπ' αὐτοῦ, ζητεῖ δὲ αὐτὴ καθ' αὑτὴν γίγνεσθαι.*

67A.—*καὶ ἐν ᾧ ἂν ζῶμεν, οὕτως, ὡς ἔοικεν, ἐγγυτάτω ἐσόμεθα τοῦ εἰδέναι. ἐὰν ὅ τι μάλιστα μηδὲν ὁμιλῶμεν τῷ σώματι μηδὲ κοινωνῶμεν, ὅ τι μὴ πᾶσα ἀνάγκη, μηδὲ ἀναπιμπλώμεθα τῆς τούτου φύσεως, ἀλλὰ καθαρεύωμεν ἀπ' αὐτοῦ, ἕως ἂν ὁ θεὸς αὐτὸς ἀπολύσῃ ἡμᾶς. καὶ οὕτω μὲν καθαροὶ ἀπαλλαττόμενοι τῆς τοῦ σώματος ἀφροσύνης, μετὰ τοιούτων τε ἐσόμεθα καὶ γνωσόμεθα δι' ἡμῶν πᾶν τὸ εἰλικρινές· τοῦτο δ' ἐστὶν ἴσως τὸ ἀληθές.*

The words خدعت حينئذ منه (٣٥, 8) are barbaric Arabic = *τότε ἐξαπατᾶται ὑπ' αὐτοῦ*. Probably the Syriac translation had a passive word with ܡܢܗ = *ὑπ' αὐτοῦ*, and this was literally rendered in Arabic by منه. The reading of the MS. معه cannot be accounted for in any way.

P. 71. *From the book Gîtâ.*—The text is not found in the *Bhagavad-Gîtâ.*

P. 72. *Kapila, for he was born knowing.*—*Cf.* Colebrooke, "Essays," i. 242.

P. 72. *Cupidity, wrath, and ignorance.*—"The Yoga Aphorisms," ii. 3 *seq.*, mention *five afflictions:* ignorance. egoism, desire, aversion, and ardent attachment to life. Perhaps we may also compare *Sâṁkhya Kârikâ, v.* lxiii., where seven modes are enumerated by which nature binds herself: virtue, dispassionateness, power, vice, ignorance, passion, and weakness.

P. 73.—The three primary forces are *rajas, tamas, sattva.*

P. 73. *To stop all motions, and even the breathing.*—*Cf. on the stoppage of motion* and the expulsion and retention of breath, "Yoga Aphorisms of Patañjali," i. xxxiv., and the notes of Râjendralâlâ Mitra.

P. 73. *In the book Gîtâ.*—The two quotations as given here are not found in the *Bhagavad-Gîtâ.* Only the comparison with the lamp occurs in vi. 19: "As a lamp sheltered from the wind does not flicker;" this is the wonted simile of the Yogin who is subdued in thought," &c.

Also the comparison with the waters of the rivers not increasing the ocean is found ii. 70: "He attains to peace into whom all desires enter as rivers enter into the ocean, which is ever filled, and (yet) remains within its bounds," &c.

P. 74. *The following nine rules.*—Five of these commandments are mentioned in "The Yoga Aphorisms," ii. xxx., and the other four seem to be identical with the five obligations mentioned in ii. xxxii.

P. 75.—*Pythagoras.*—I do not know the Greek original of this saying. The idea of the body being a fetter to the soul is frequently met with in the book of the Neopythagorean philosophers, as Apollonius of Tyana and others;

*cf.* Zeller, *Philosophie der Griechen*, iii. 2, p. 156. For two more sentences of Pythagoras, *v.* i. p. 85, where Alberuni states that he has taken them from Ammonius, *v.* note to p. 85.

P. 75. *The book Sâṁkhya says.*—It is difficult to say whether the Arabic manuscript has يظفه or يظنه, and not knowing a Sanskrit parallel to this saying, I am thrown upon conjecture. Preferring the latter reading, I translate: "Everything which man opines (*i.e.* on which he forms an opinion) is a terminus to him, for he does not go beyond it," which may mean that as long as the thinking faculty of soul has not ceased, it is not liberated, has not attained *moksha*. Cf. *Sâṁkhya Kârikâ*, v. lxviii.: "When separation of the informed soul from its corporeal frame at length takes place, and nature in respect of it ceases, then is absolute and final deliverance accomplished."

Pp. 75, 76. *Gîtâ.*—The three quotations from this book are not found in the *Bhagavad-Gîtâ*.

P. 76. *Socrates.*—The quotations given here are found in *Phædo*, 84E–85B:—

*καὶ, ὡς ἔοικε, τῶν κύκνων δοκῶ φαυλότερος ὑμῖν εἶναι τὴν μαντικὴν, οἳ ἐπειδὰν αἴσθωνται ὅτι δεῖ αὐτοὺς ἀποθανεῖν, ᾄδοντες καὶ ἐν τῷ πρόσθεν χρόνῳ, τότε δὴ πλεῖστα καὶ μάλιστα ᾄδουσι, γεγηθότες ὅτι μέλλουσι παρὰ τὸν θεὸν ἀπιέναι οὗπερ εἰσὶ θεράποντες, κ.τ.λ. ἀλλ' ἅτε, οἶμαι, τοῦ Ἀπόλλωνος ὄντες μαντικοί τέ εἰσι καὶ προειδότες τὰ ἐν Ἅιδου ἀγαθὰ ᾄδουσι καὶ τέρπονται ἐκείνην τὴν ἡμέραν διαφερόντως ἢ ἐν τῷ ἔμπροσθεν χρόνῳ. ἐγὼ δὲ καὶ αὐτὸς ἡγοῦμαι ὁμόδουλός τε εἶναι τῶν κύκνων καὶ ἱερὸς τοῦ αὐτοῦ θεοῦ, καὶ οὐ χεῖρον ἐκείνων τὴν μαντικὴν ἔχειν παρὰ τοῦ δεσπότου, οὐδὲ δυσθυμότερον αὐτῶν τοῦ βίου ἀπαλλάττεσθαι.*

In the middle a passage has been left out by Alberuni, or by the author of that edition of *Phædo* which he used.

P. 76. *In the book of Patañjali.*—To the explanation of

the four parts of the path of liberation on pp. 76–80 I do not know a parallel from a Sanskrit source.

P. 77. *In the book Vishṇu-Dharma.—Cf.* on this the note to p. 54. The Arabic text has not Parikshit, but *Parîksha*, which name is mentioned by Hall in a note to *Vishṇu-Purâṇa*, iv., chap. xx. p. 154.

Pp. 78, 79. *The book Gîtâ.*—These three extracts are not found in the *Bhagavad-Gîtâ*. The words, "He who mortifies his lust," &c., compare with *Bhagavad-Gîtâ*, iv. 21, "Void of hope, self-restrained in thought, performing merely bodily work, he contracts no sin." Regarding the passage, "Pleasures of a kind which, in reality, are disguised pains," *v.* note to p. 70.

The expression, *the nine doors of thy body* (p. 79, 8), is also found in *Bhagavad-Gîtâ*, v. 13: "in the city of nine gates," *i.e.* in the body. *Cf.* also *Sâṁkhya Kârikâ*, *v.* xxxv.

Pp. 79, 80. *The book Gîtâ.*—These quotations cannot be compared with anything in the *Bhagavad-Gîtâ*.

P. 81. *Patañjali.*—There is a certain resemblance between these words and the last of "The Yoga Aphorisms" (iv. xxxviii.): "Isolation is the regression of the qualities devoid of the purpose of soul, or it is the abiding of the thinking power in its own nature."

Pp. 81, 82. *Sâṁkhya.*—The comparison with the wheel of the potter (not the silk-weaver) is also found in *Sâṁkhya Kârikâ*, *v.* lxvii.

P. 82. *In the book of Patañjali.*—I have not found these two passages anywhere else. As to the faculties of the perfect Yogin, *cf.* "Yoga Aphorisms," iii. 42, 44, 45.

P. 83. *The Sûfî explain the Koranic verse, &c.*—Being asked about the story of *Dhulḳarnaini* (Bicornutus, *i.e.* Alexander), Muhammad says, "*We* (*i.e.* Allah) *have made room for him on earth;*" or, as Sale translates, "*We stablished for him on earth,*" which means, *We have given him a position of well-established authority or power on earth*, and this authority or power is interpreted by Ṣûfî commentators in accordance with their tenets, perfectly harmonising with those of the Yoga philosophy.

Pp. 83, 84. *Sâṁkhya.*—With the tale of the man travelling in the night with his pupils compare a similar one in Gauḍapâda's *Bhâshya* to *Sâṁkhya Kârikâ*, v. xxx. (on p. 106).

P. 85.—*Ammonius*, a philosopher of the Neoplatonic school, v. Zeller, *Philosophie der Griechen*, iii.c. 829 *seq.* A Greek book of his which contains these extracts from Pythagoras and Empedocles is not known. He has been known to the Arabs as commentator of Aristotle: v. Wenrich, *De Auctorum Græcorum Versionibus*, p. 289; Fihrist, p. ٢٥٣.

By Heracles in the passage, "Empedocles and his successors as far as Heracles," is probably meant Heraclides Ponticus.

Pp. 85, 86. *Socrates says.*—The first extract is identical with *Phædo*, 79D, the second is composed of 80B, 80A, 81 A B, the order of the Greek text having been abandoned.

*Phædo*, 79D. Ὅταν δέ γε αὐτὴ καθ' αὑτὴν σκοπῇ, ἐκεῖσε οἴχεται εἰς τὸ καθαρόν τε καὶ ἀεὶ ὂν καὶ ἀθάνατον καὶ ὡσαύτως ἔχον, καὶ ὡς συγγενὴς οὖσα αὐτοῦ ἀεὶ μετ' ἐκείνου τε γίγνεται, ὅτανπερ αὐτὴ καθ' αὑτὴν γένηται καὶ ἐξῇ αὐτῇ, καὶ πέπαυταί τε τοῦ πλάνου καὶ περὶ ἐκεῖνα ἀεὶ κατὰ ταὐτὰ ὡσαύτως ἔχει ἅτε τοιούτων ἐφαπτομένη· καὶ τοῦτο αὐτῆς τὸ παθημα φρόνησις κέκληται.

80B. Σκόπει δή, ἔφη, ὦ Κέβης, εἰ ἐκ πάντων τῶν εἰρημένων τάδε ἡμῖν ξυμβαίνει, τῷ μὲν θείῳ καὶ ἀθανάτῳ καὶ νοητῷ καὶ μονοειδεῖ καὶ ἀδιαλύτῳ καὶ ἀεὶ ὡσαύτως καὶ κατὰ ταὐτὰ ἔχοντι ἑαυτῷ ὁμοιότατον εἶναι ψυχήν, τῷ δ' ἀνθρωπίνῳ καὶ θνητῷ καὶ ἀνοητῳ καὶ πολυειδεῖ καὶ διαλυτῷ καὶ μηδέποτε κατὰ ταὐτὰ ἔχοντι ἑαυτῷ ὁμοιότατον αὖ εἶναι σῶμα.

80A. ἐπειδὰν ἐν τῷ αὐτῷ ὦσι ψυχὴ καὶ σῶμα, τῷ μὲν δουλεύειν καὶ ἄρχεσθαι ἡ φύσις προστάττει, τῇ δὲ ἄρχειν καὶ δεσπόζειν.

81 A and B. Οὐκοῦν οὕτω μὲν ἔχουσα εἰς τὸ ὅμοιον αὐτῇ, τὸ ἀειδές, ἀπέρχεται, τὸ θεῖόν τε καὶ ἀθάνατον καὶ φρόνιμον, οἷ ἀφικομένῃ ὑπάρχει αὐτῇ εὐδαίμονι εἶναι, πλάνης καὶ ἀνοίας καὶ φόβων καὶ ἀγρίων ἐρώτων καὶ τῶν ἄλλων κακῶν τῶν ἀνθρωπείων ἀπηλλαγμένῃ, ὥσπερ δὲ λέγεται κατὰ τῶν μεμνημένων, ὡς ἀληθῶς τὸν λοιπὸν χρόνον μετὰ τῶν θεῶν διάγουσα; οὕτω φῶμεν, ὦ Κέβης, ἢ ἄλλως; οὕτω νὴ Δί', ἔφη ὁ Κέβης· Ἐὰν δέ γε, οἶμαι, μεμιασμένη καὶ ἀκάθαρτος τοῦ σώματος ἀπαλλάττηται, ἅτε τῷ σώματι ἀεὶ ξυνοῦσα καὶ τοῦτο θεραπεύουσα καὶ ἐρῶσα καὶ γεγοητευμένη ὑπ' αὐτοῦ, ὑπό τε τῶν ἐπιθυμιῶν καὶ ἡδονῶν, ὥστε μηδὲν ἄλλο δοκεῖν εἶναι ἀληθὲς ἀλλ' ἢ τὸ σωματοειδὲς οὗ τις ἂν ἅψαιτο, κ.τ.λ.

Pp. 86, 87. *Arjuna says.*—The comparison of Brahman with an *aśvattha* tree is found in *Bhagavad-Gîtâ*, xv. 1–6, and x. 26.

*The doctrine of Patañjali.*—Ideas similar to these Ṣûfî sentences are found in *Bhagavad-Gîtâ*, vi. 28–31, describing the union of the soul with Brahman.

Pp. 87, 88.—On Abû-Bakr Ash-shibli *cf.* Ibn Khallikân, translated by De Slane, i. 511–513; Abulmaḥâsin, *Annales*, ii. 313. He lived in Bagdad, was a pupil of Junaid, died A.H. 334 = A.D. 946, in Bagdad, and was buried there. On Abû-Yazîd Albisṭâmî *cf.* Ibn Khallikân, nr. 311. He died A.H. 261 = A.D. 875. Jâmi has articles on these two mystics with many quotations from them in his *Nafaḥât-al'uns* (Lee's "Persian Series," the *Nafahât-alons*, &c., or the Lives of the Soofis, by Jâmi, Calcutta, 1859, pp. 201 and 62).

P. 88. *The Sûfî explain the Koranic passage* (Sura 2, 68), *&c.*—"And when you had killed a person and were disputing among yourselves (the one throwing the blame on the other), whilst God was bringing to light what you concealed, then we spoke: Beat him (the killed person) with part of her (the killed cow mentioned in the preceding"). In that case the killed person will again become alive and tell who murdered him. "Thus God brings to life the dead ones," &c. *Cf.* A. Geiger, *Was hat Mohammed aus dem Judenthume aufgenommen?* Bonn, 1833, p. 172. Muḥammad has moulded this part of Sûra 2 from elements taken directly or indirectly from Numb. xix. 2 *seq.*, and Deut. xxi. 2 *seq.*

The Sufies try to show by this sentence that the body must be mortified before the heart can become alive by mystic knowledge.

P. 89. *Sâṁkhya.*—For the two enumerations of created beings, v. Gauḍapâda to S. Kârikâ, liii. p. 162, and xliv. p. 143.

The reading of the MS. سومين is certainly wrong. The author means *saumya* = سومى, but it would have been better to write سوم in accordance with ديت = *daitya*. As all the other words of this enumeration stand in the singular, it is not allowable to read this word in a plural form, سومين like رشين the *Ṛishis*, پترين the *Pitṛis*.

P. 90. *In the book Gîtâ.*—The first quotation on the prevalence of one of the three *guṇas, sattva, rajas, tamas*, is to be compared with *Bhagavad-Gîtâ*, xvii. 3, 4, *seq.*, and xiv. 6–8 *seq.*

The second extract, "Belief and virtue," &c. I am inclined to combine with *Bhagavad-Gîtâ*, xvi. 3, 4, *seq.*

P. 91. *People say that Zoroaster, &c.*—The author was aware of the identity of the Persian *dêv* (demon) with the Indian *deva* (god). It is in this way that he tries to account for the discrepancy of the meaning.

P. 92. *Sâṁkhya*, v. p. 89; *Vâsudeva*, v. p. 90, or *Bhagavad-Gîtâ*, xvii. 4.

P. 95. *Galenus*, περὶ συνθέσεως φαρμάκων τῶν κατὰ τόπους, ed. Kühn, vol. xiii. p. 268:—

Ξανθὴν μὲν τρίχα βάλλε μυρίπνοον ἰσοθέοιο
Οὗ λύθρος Ἑρμείας λάμπεται ἐν βοτάναις.
Κρόκου δὲ σταθμὸν φρένας ἀνέρος, οὐ γὰρ ἄδηλον,
Βάλλε δὲ καὶ δραχμὴν Ναπλίου Εὐβοέως, κ.τ.λ.
Δραχμὴν καὶ ῥίζης ψευδωνύμου, ἣν ἀνέθρεψε
Χῶρος ὁ τὸν Πίσσῃ Ζῆνα λοχευσάμενος.

The second quotation, v. on p. 271:—

ἀξιοῖ βάλλειν ἣν ψευδώνυμον εἴρηκε ῥίζαν, ἐπειδὴ στάχυς ὀνομάζεται νάρδου· βούλεται δ' αὐτὴν εἶναι Κρητικὴν, ἔνθα φησὶν, ἣν ἀνέθρεψε χῶρος ὁ τὸν Πίσσῃ Ζῆνα λοχευσάμενος, ἐπειδὴ τὸν Δία φασὶν οἱ μυθολόγοι κατὰ τὸ Δικταῖον ὄρος ἐν Κρήτῃ τραφῆναι, κρυπτόμενον ὑπὸ τῆς μητρὸς Ῥέας, ὅπως μὴ καὶ αὐτὸς ὑπὸ τοῦ πατρὸς τοῦ Κρόνου καταπόθῃ.

P. 96. *Europe, the daughter of Phœnix, &c.*—In the source whence the author drew his information about Greek legends, Greek, Hebrew, and Persian traditions seem to have been mixed together. It was synchronistic like the *Chronicon* of Eusebius, with which it is nearly related (note to p. 105), comparing the dates of Greek history with those of the Biblical and Persian history. Julius Africanus and Eusebius are the fathers of this kind of literature, but I do not know by whom the book which Alberuni used had been composed. *Cf. Eusebi chronicorum canonum quæ supersunt*, ed. A. Schœne, ii. p. 13 (Zeus), 26 (Cecrops), 32, 34 (Asterius); also the Syriac Epitome, p. 204, 206.

P. 96. *The story of Alexander* is derived from the romance of Pseudo-Kallisthenes (ed. Didot), which Eastern scholars have mistaken for a historic record.

"Man cannot oppose the gods" (p. 97, 1)=πρὸς πάντας γὰρ δυνάμεθα οἱ βασιλεῖς, πρὸς δὲ τοὺς θεοὺς οὐ δυνάμεθα (ed. Didot, i. 9).

"When then he died," &c., "from a wound in the neck," &c. (p. 97, 4)=πεσὼν δὲ Νεκτανεβὼς λαμβάνει φοβερὸν τραῦμα κατὰ τοῦ ἰσχίου αὐτοῦ (i. 14).

P. 97. *Galenus.*—*Cf.* note to p. 34.

P. 97. *Aratus.*—The author quotes the *Phænomena* and a commentary to them, which exhibits certain relations with the scholia edited by Immanuel Bekker, but is not identical with them. As I learn from my colleague, Professor C. Robert, this commentary is to be combined with the *Catasterismi* of Pseudo-Eratosthenes.

The first quotation from *Aratus* is *v.* 1 *seq.*

Ἐκ Διὸς ἀρχώμεσθα, τὸν οὐδέποτ' ἄνδρες ἐῶμεν
Ἄῤῥητον· μεσταὶ δὲ Διὸς πᾶσαι μὲν ἀγυιαί,
Πᾶσαι δ' ἀνθρώπων ἀγοραὶ, μεστὴ δὲ θάλασσα
Καὶ λιμένες· πάντη δὲ Διὸς κεχρήμεθα πάντες.
Τοῦ γὰρ καὶ γένος εἰμέν· ὁ δ' ἤπιος ἀνθρώποισιν
Δεξιὰ σημαίνει, λαοὺς δ' ἐπὶ ἔργον ἐγείρει,
Μιμνήσκων βιότοιο· λέγει δ' ὅτε βῶλος ἀρίστη
Βουσί τε καὶ μακέλῃσι· λέγει δ' ὅτε δεξιαὶ ὧραι
Καὶ φυτὰ γυρῶσαι, καὶ σπέρματα πάντα βαλέσθαι.
Αὐτὸς γὰρ τάγε σήματ' ἐν οὐρανῷ ἐστήριξεν,
Ἄστρα διακρίνας· ἐσκέψατο δ' εἰς ἐνιαυτὸν
Ἀστέρας, οἵ κε μάλιστα τετυγμένα σημαίνοιεν
Ἀνδράσιν ὡράων, ὄφρ' ἔμπεδα πάντα φύωνται.
Τῷ μιν ἀεὶ πρῶτόν τε καὶ ὕστατον ἱλάσκονται.
Χαῖρε, πάτερ, μέγα θαῦμα, μέγ' ἀνθρώποισιν ὄνειαρ,
Αὐτὸς καὶ προτέρη γενεή, χαίροιτε δὲ Μοῦσαι
Μειλίχιαι μάλα πᾶσιν, κ.τ.λ.

P. 97. *Commentary on the Phænomena of Aratus.*—The following quotation from the *Scholia Sangermanensia*, p. 55, I owe to the kindness of Professor Robert: "Crates autem Jovem dictum cœlum, invocatum vero merito aërem et ætherem, quod in his sint sidera, et Homerum Jovem dixisse in aliqua parte cœlum."

ὡς δ' ὅτι ταρφεῖαι νεφέλαι Διὸς ἐκποτίονται
—(*Ilias*, i. 3571).

The common tradition of this verse is—

ὡς δ' ὅτι ταρφεῖαι νιφάδεις Διὸς ἐκποτίονται,

and thus it has been rendered by Alberuni. *Cf.* on the *Scholia Sangermanensia*, C. Robert, *Eratosthenis Catasterismorum Reliquiæ*, Berlin, 1878, p. 21.

P. 99. *These twins, state and religion.*—*Vide* note to p. 79.

P. 100. *When Ardashîr Ibn Bâbak.*—*Cf.* with these ranks of the Persian nation under the Sasanians the "Chronology of Ancient Nations," translated by Dr. Edward Sachau, London, 1878, pp. 203 and 206; *Geschichte der Perser und Araber zur Zeit der Sasaniden*, by Th. Nöldeke, p. 437 *seq.*

P. 101. *The Vaiśya who were created from.*—In the Arabic text, ۴۹, 4, there is a lacuna, where originally stood the words "from the thigh (*ûru*) of Brahman. The Sûdra who were created from." *Cf.* Manu, *Dharmaśâstra*, i. 87, *mukha-bâhu-ûru-paj-jânâṁ.*

P. 101. *Hâdî, Ḍoma, &c.*—Of these classes of outcast people, the Badhatau are not known to me. The Caṇḍâla are well known, called *Sandâlia* by Ibn Khurdâdhbih (Elliot, "History of India," i. 16). The Hâdis and Ḍom are mentioned by Colebrooke, "Essays," ii., "Enumeration of Indian Classes," p. 169, note 3. On the latter (*cf.* Rom, the name of the gipsies), *v.* "Memoirs on the History, Folk-lore, and Distribution of the Races," &c., by Elliot, edited by Beames, London, 1869, i. p. 84. Are the Badhatau identical with the Bediyâs, mentioned in the note of Colebrooke just quoted?

P. 103. *Vâsudeva answered.*—The first quotation from *Gîtâ* is identical with *Bhagavad-Gîtâ*, xviii. 41–45; the second is similar to ii. 31–38.

P. 104.—*The saying of Vyâsa.*—*Vide* note to pp. 40–44.

P. 104. *Vâsudeva.*—This quotation from *Gîtâ* much resembles *Bhagavad-Gîtâ*, ix. 32, 33.

P. 105. *Minos.*—I cannot acquit the book on ancient history which Alberuni used of the blunder of having split the Minos of Greek traditions into two persons, a Minos and a Mianos (*sic*). *Cf.* on this source note to p. 96.

*At the time of Darius, &c.*—Except the synchronism of Persian history, the whole passage relating to Numa Pompilius may be derived from Eusebius, *Chronicon*, ii. 82:—

Νουμᾶς μετὰ Ῥωμύλον βασιλεύσας Ῥώμης πρῶτος νόμους Ῥωμαίοις εἰσήγαγεν· [ὁ αὐτὸς τὸ Καπετώλιον ἐκ θεμελίων ᾠκοδόμησεν·] ὁ αὐτὸς τῷ ἐνιαυτῷ δύο μῆνας προσέθηκε, τόν τε Ἰανουάριον καὶ τὸν Φεβρουάριον, δεκαμηναίου τοῦ ἐνιαυτοῦ πρὸ τούτου χρηματίζοντος· ὁ αὐτὸς καὶ κογγιάριον ἔδωκεν, ἀσσάρια ξύλινα καὶ σκύτινα καὶ ὀστράκινα.

P. 105. *Plato.*—These extracts from Plato's *Leges* are the remnant of an Arabic translation. We give the Greek text for the purpose of comparison:—

I. 1. Ἀθηναῖος. Θεὸς ἤ τις ἀνθρώπων ὑμῖν, ὦ ξένοι, εἴληφε τὴν αἰτίαν τῆς τῶν νόμων διαθέσεως; Κλεινίας. Θεὸς, ὦ ξένε, θεός, ὥς γε τὸ δικαιότατον εἰπεῖν, παρὰ μὲν ἡμῖν Ζεύς, παρὰ δὲ Λακεδαιμονίοις, ὅθεν ὅδ' ἐστίν, οἶμαι φάναι τούτους Ἀπόλλωνα.

I. 6. Ὥσπερ τό τε ἀληθές, οἶμαι, καὶ τὸ δίκαιον ὑπέρ γε θείας διαλεγομένους λέγειν, οὐχ ὡς πρὸς ἀρετῆς τι μόριον καὶ ταῦτα τὸ φαυλότατον ἐτίθει βλέπων, ἀλλὰ πρὸς πᾶσαν ἀρετήν, κ.τ.λ.

I. 6. οἱ Κρητῶν νόμοι οὐκ εἰσὶ μάτην διαφερόντως ἐν πᾶσιν εὐδόκιμοι τοῖς Ἕλλησιν· ἔχουσι γὰρ ὀρθῶς, τοὺς αὐτοῖς χρωμένους εὐδαίμονας ἀποτελοῦντες· ἅπαντα γὰρ τὰ ἀγαθὰ πορίζουσι.

II. 1. θεοὶ δέ, οἰκτείραντες τὸ τῶν ἀνθρώπων ἐπίπονον πεφυκὸς γένος, ἀναπαύλας τε αὐτοῖς τῶν πόνων ἐτάξαντο τὰς τῶν ἑορτῶν ἀμοιβάς, καὶ Μούσας Ἀπόλλωνά τε μουσαγέτην καὶ Διόνυσον ξυνεορταστὰς ἔδοσαν.

II. 1. ἡμῖν δὲ οὓς εἴπομεν θεοὺς ξυγχορευτὰς δεδόσθαι, τούτους εἶναι καὶ τοὺς δεδωκότας τὴν ἔνρυθμόν τε καὶ ἐναρμόνιον αἴσθησιν μεθ' ἡδονῆς, ᾗ δὴ κινεῖν τε ἡμᾶς καὶ χορηγεῖν ἡμῖν τούτους, ᾠδαῖς τε καὶ ὀρχήσεσιν ἀλλήλους ξυνείροντας, χορούς τε ὠνομακέναι τὸ παρὰ τῆς χαρᾶς ἔμφυτον ὄνομα.

P. 107. *Śântanu.*—*Cf.* *Vishṇu-Purâṇa*, iv. ch. xx. p. 158, and the notes. The story of the curse of Pându is given in the *Mahâbhârata Âdiparvan*, v. 3812 *seq.*

*Vyâsa.*—His mother is Satyavatî: *v.* *Vishṇu-Purâṇa*, l. c. The birth of Vyâsa is mentioned in *Mahâbhârata Âdiparvan*, v. 3802.

P. 108. *Pancahîr*, better *Panchîr.*—The author means the alpine countries of the Hindukush between Kashmîr and a line from Faizabad to Kabul, *i.e.* the Hazâra country, Svât, Citrâl, and Kafiristan. It is well known that polyandry exists among the Tibetan tribes in the Alps between Kashmîr and Tibet, but I am not aware whether it is also found among the inhabitants of the more western extension of the Himâlaya which he mentions, *e.g.* among the Siyâhposh. On polyandry in the Panjab *v.* Kirkpatrick in "Indian Antiquary," 1878, 86.

The Panchîr mentioned by the author is the tributary of the Kâbul-Rûd. Another Pancahir (*sic*) is mentioned by the Arab geographer Yâḳût as a city in Bactriana with rich silver mines.

*Among the heathen Arabs.*—*Cf.* here i. 185.

P. 109. *A certain Jewish marriage.*—On this custom in India and Indian tradition, *cf.* Elliot-Beames, "Memoirs," i. 274, s.v. *Karâo.*

P. 109. *Barshawâr the Girshâh.*—This seems to be a mistake, and I propose to read, as I have done in the edition of the Arabic text, پدشوارگرشاه, *i.e.*, the Shâh of Padashvârgir or Prince of Tabaristân (as *e.g.* Gîlânshâh = the Shâh of Gilân). *Cf.* P. de Lagarde, *Beiträge zur Baktrischen Lexicographie*, p. 50; Sachau, "Chronology of Ancient Nations," p. 47, 19, and note; Nöldeke, *Geschichte der Perser und Araber zur Zeit der Sasaniden*, p. 462.

P. 112.—The story of Romulus is drawn from the *Chronographia* of Joannes Malalas, book vii. (Bonn edition, p. 172).

P. 113. *Ambarîsha.*—The story of this king seems to have been taken from the *Vishṇu-Dharma*, *v.* note to p. 54. Probably Ambarisha, the son of Nabhâga, is meant, famous as a worshipper of Vishṇu. *Cf. Vishṇu-Purâṇa*, book iv. chap. ii. p. 257, note 1.

P. 116. *Nârada.*—The story of this saint, a Moses in India, is not known to me from other sources.

P. 116. *Jalam Ibn Shaibân.*—The pronunciation of the former name is conjectural, the history of this Karmatian chief unknown. The expedition of King Maḥmûd against Multân took place A.D. 1006, in the ninth year of his rule, the seventh year of his usurpation of sovereignty, in which he had left out the name of his Sâmânî liege-lord on the coins and in the public prayer, and had received the investiture, a robe and a title, from the source of all legitimacy in the Muslim world, the Khalif Alḳâdir, the great enemy and persecutor of the Karmatians. *Cf.* on this expedition Elliot, "History of India," ii. p. 441.

P. 116, l. 21.—There is an error in the calculation of the years. From the end of the Kritayuga up to the year 4132 of the Kaliyuga there have elapsed—

| | Years. |
|---|---|
| Of the Tretâyuga . . . . . . | 1,296,000 |
| Of the Dvâparayuga . . . . . . | 864,000 |
| Of the Kaliyuga . . . . . . | 4,132 |
| Sum . . . . . | 2,164,132 |

As Alberuni gives but 216,432 years, it seems he has omitted by inadvertence the cipher 1 (*Schram*).

P. 117, l. 7.—The above supposition is confirmed by this passage; it ought to be the 132 years instead of the 432 years. One can consider 132 years as a kind of arbitrary equivalent for the sum of about 100 years, but 432 years cannot be an equivalent for about 100 years (*Schram*).

P. 117, l. 10.—It must be 2,164,000 instead of 216,000 (*Schram*).

P. 117. *Varâhamihira says.*—This extract is a translation of *Bṛihat-Saṁhitâ*, chap. lviii. §§ 30–48, 56–57, on the fabrication of the idols (p. 117–120); chap. lviii. §§ 4952, on the consequences of faults in the construction of idols (p. 120); chap. lx. § 19, on the various classes of priests (p. 121); chap. lx. §§ 4, 5, on the effects of the idols (p. 121). The order of the single verses is to some extent different from that of the Sanskrit text as exhibited in the edition of Kern. In the Arabic text, p. ٥٧, ١, in the lacuna after والسهم, are required the words والسيف والترس ("the sword and shield").

P. 122. *Gîtâ.*—I do not know similar passages in *Bhagavad-Gîtâ*. The first quotation distantly reminds one of *Bhagavad-Gîtâ*, iv. 25.

P. 123. *Plato.*—This quotation shows considerable confusion in the rendering of the Greek text. *Cf. Leges*, iv. 8.

*πρῶτον μὲν, φαμέν, τιμὰς τὰς μετ' Ὀλυμπίους τε καὶ τοὺς τὴν πόλιν ἔχοντας θεοὺς τοῖς χθονίοις ἄν τις θεοῖς ἄρτια καὶ δεύτερα καὶ ἀριστερὰ νέμων ὀρθότατα τοῦ τῆς εὐσεβείας σκοποῦ τυγχάνοι, τοῖς δὲ τούτων ἄνωθεν τὰ περιττὰ καὶ ἀντίφωνα τοῖς ἔμπροσθεν ῥηθεῖσι νῦν δή· μετὰ θεοὺς δὲ τούσδε καὶ τοῖς δαίμοσιν ὅ γ' ἔμφρων ὀργιάζοιτ' ἄν, ἥρωσι δὲ μετὰ τούτους· ἐπακολουθεῖ δ' αὐτοῖς ἱδρύματα ἴδια πατρῴων θεῶν κατὰ νόμον ὀργιαζόμενα· γονέων δὲ μετὰ ταῦτα τιμαὶ ζώντων, ὡς θέμις, ὀφείλοντα ἀποτίνειν τὰ πρῶτά τε καὶ μέγιστα ὀφειλήματα, κ.τ.λ.*

The underlined words are the original of the Arabic quotation. The translator has rendered *δαίμοσιν* by آلهة (gods), *ἥρωσι* by سكينات, by which elsewhere the word *Μοῦσαι* is translated, and *ὀργιάζειν* by نَصَبَ بالسِّرّ (instead of نصب فى السِّرّ = اجتهد). He seems to have mistaken the meaning of the word *ἐπακολουθεῖ*, translating in this way: "they (the *ἱδρύματα* = اصنام) follow in rank after the *πάτρῳοι θεοί*," *i.e.* you shall not put the *πάτρῳοι θεοὶ* in the first place, but worship them *secundo loco.*

P. 123. *Galenus.*—*Vide* note to p. 34.

P. 126.—The tradition of Śaunaka from Venus (so the Arabic text), *i.e.* Śukra, is perhaps taken from the *Vishṇu-Dharma*: *v.* note to p. 54.

*Vishṇu-Purâṇa.*—Compare this quotation with book iii. chap. ii. p. 29 (ed. Wilson-Hall). The *Great Bear* is called the *Seven Ṛishis* in Sanskrit.

P. 126. *Vasukra.*—This reading does not quite accurately correspond to the Arabic signs, which must be read *Vaśukra.* I have preferred the former, because it is mentioned in the St. Petersburg Dictionary as the name of a man who occurs in the *Veda* as a poet of Vaidic hymns.

P. 127. *Galenus.*—The quotation from Galenus must be compared with the following passage in his *περὶ συνθέσεως φαρμάκων κατὰ γένη* (ed. Kühn, tom. xiii. p. 995):—

*ηὑρέθη δὲ ὑπὸ Μενεκράτους, κ.τ.λ. ἰατικὸν φάρμακον. ἐπιγέγραπται δὲ τὸ βίβλιον, κ.τ.λ. αὐτοκράτωρ ὁλογράμματος· αὐτοκράτωρ μὲν, ἐπειδὴ τούτῳ προσπεφώνηται, ὁλογράμματος δὲ διότι χωρὶς χαρακτήρων ὅλαις ταῖς συλλαβαῖς γέγραπται β′ καὶ γ′ καὶ δ′ καὶ ἑ καὶ τῶν ἄλλων ἀριθμῶν ἕκαστος, κ.τ.λ. τοῦτο δ' ἔπραξεν ὁ Μενεκράτης, ἐπειδὴ πολλάκις οὐ μόνον ἀκόντων ἁμαρτάνεσθαι συμβαίνει κατὰ τὰς γραφὰς, ἀλλὰ καὶ διὰ φθόνον ἑκόντων ἐνίων, κ.τ.λ.*

*εἰκότως οὖν ηὐδοκίμησε τὰ Δαμοκράτους βίβλια τῶν φαρμάκων εἰς μέτρα γραφέντα [καὶ εἴπερ ἅπαντα τὸν τρόπον τοῦτον ἐγέγραπτο], κάλλιστον ἂν ἦν.*

That which I have underlined forms the text as given by Alberuni.

P. 127.—*Vyâsa had four śishya.*—Cf. *Vishṇu-Purâṇa*, book iii. chap. iv.

P. 128. *A peculiar kind of recitation.*—This is a description of the four *pâṭhas, padapâṭha, kramapâṭha,* &c. *Cf.* Colebrooke, "Essays," i. 18.

P. 128. *Kâṇḍin.*—The word كانرى evidently refers to the divisions of the Yajurveda called *kaṇḍikâ.* "The text of the Yajurveda is composed of *Kânrî*, and its name (the name of Yajurveda? what name of it?) is derived from it (from *kânrî*?), *i.e.* the collection (or totality) of *kânrî.*" It does not appear which one of the names of *Yajurveda* is here meant by the author as having been derived from *kânrî.* Is there a name of Yajurveda like *kâṇḍika* or *kâṇḍin*, meaning *consisting of kaṇḍikâs?*

In *kânrî=kaṇḍikâ* the cerebral *ḍ* is rendered by an Arabic *r*, as in كرب *kuḍava*, بيارى *vyâḍi*, گرر *garuḍa*, درور *draviḍa*, نارى *nâḍî*, بنارى *vinâḍî*, بيرورج *vaiḍûrya*, &c. The termination in long *î* seems to be characteristic of the vernacular form of Indian speech, and is probably a survival of the more ancient termination *ika, ikâ*. *Cf.* R. Hörnle, "Comparative Grammar of the Gaudian Languages," § 195, 203, 205.

P. 128. *Yâjnavalkya.*—*Cf. Vishṇu-Purâṇa*, book iii. chap. v.

P. 129. *The well-known story.*—It is told by Alberuni himself, i. p. 396.

P. 131. *Vishṇu-Purâṇa.*—This index of the Purâṇas occurs in book iii. chap. vi. p. 66, 67. In the Arabic text ٦٣, 12, read گرر instead of گرد.

P. 131. *Smṛiti.*—The author erroneously calls it a book. It is the literature on law, and the twenty sons of Brahman here mentioned are authors of *Dharmaśâstras*. *Cf.* on *smṛiti* (opp. *śruti*), Colebrooke, "Essays," i. 337, 466; A. Weber, *Vorlesungen*, p. 296, note 327; *Indische Studien*, i. 232.

Alberuni sometimes quotes *the book Smṛiti*. However, he had not the book himself, but transferred those quotations from the *Brahmasiddhânta* of Brahmagupta. In reality it is the latter author who quotes it. As, according to him, the book *smṛiti* was composed by Manu (*v.* here ii. 110, 111), he means the *Dharmaśâstra* of Manu. This law code is only once clearly referred to by Alberuni (ii. 164), but in a manner which makes me think that it was not in his hands. On Manu, as the author of the great *Mânasa* (a work on astronomy and astrology?), *v.* p. 157.

P. 132. *Gauḍa.*—On the proposed identification with Gauḍapâda, *v.* note to p. 30.

*Sâṁkhya.*—*Vide* the same note.

*Patañjali.*—*Vide* note to p. 27.

*Nyâyabhâshâ.*—This my transliteration of نايبهاش will perhaps seem doubtful, as the contents of the book have no relation to the Nyâya philosophy or logical system of Gautama (*cf.* Colebrooke, "Essays," i. 280), but are clearly identical with the Mîmâṁsâ philosophy of Jaimini, who is here mentioned a few lines farther on. However, I do not know another mode of reading the word. That Kapila was the author of such a work does not seem to be known.

*Mîmâṁsâ.*—*Cf.* Colebrooke, "Essays," i. 319. In opposition to Kapila, Jaimini teaches that the Veda is primeval and superhuman. This theory and the discussions through which it has passed are also found in the history of Islam applied to the Koran. According to Islam, the Koran too is primeval and superhuman.

*Laukâyata:* read *Lôkayata.*—It is the materialistic doctrine of the Cârvâka sect that perception alone is a means of proof. *Cf.* G. A. Jacob, "Manual of Hindu Pantheism," Vedântasâra, p. 74; Colebrooke, "Essays," i. 426 *seq.*, 456 *seq.*; J. Muir, verses from the *Sarva-darśana-sangraha*, &c., illustrating the tenets of the Chârvâkas or Indian materialists, "Journal of the Royal Asiatic Society," 1861, p. 299, and "Journal of the German Oriental Society," xiv. 519.

Brihaspati is the founder of this school; his *sûtra* is quoted by Bhâskara-âcârya. The *Bârhaspatyasûtram* is mentioned by A. Weber, *Vorlesungen*, p. 263.

P. 132. *Agastya.*—His doctrine is not known to me. Is it identical with that of the Jainas? *Cf.* Colebrooke, "Essays," ii. 173.

*Vishṇu-Dharma.*—*Vide* note to p. 54.

P. 132. *Bhârata*, i.e. *Mahâbhârata*, which is repeatedly mentioned by Alberuni. *Bhagavad-Gîtâ* is a part of it (i. 132). The story of the birth of Vâsudeva and of his five brothers (i. 401–406) is taken from *Mahâbhârata.*

I am not quite certain whether Alberuni had a copy of the work. When giving quotations from the book, he does not mention it, which he probably would have done if he had had it in hand.

P. 133.—With the index of the chapters of *Mahâbhârata* *cf.* Monier Williams, "Indian Epic Poetry," p. 91 *seq.* The list of Alberuni exhibits some remarkable differences.

P. 135. *Pâṇini.*—The reading of the MS. is *pânriti*,

پانرت, which I cannot explain. If پانرن *pânrini* is the correct reading, we must remember that in the sound *ṇ* there is an admixture of the sound *r*. So Hörnle, "Comparative Grammar," p. 15, says: "The cerebral *ṇ* contains the sound of *r*, being somewhat like *rn*." In this way Alberuni has transliterated the *ṇ* in the word *baṇij*, which he writes برنج *barnij*. Accordingly we should expect to find پارنن *pârnini*, but the author seems to have written پانرن *pânrini*.

P. 135.—The word شکهت = *śishyahita*, has been deciphered by Professor Kielhorn, Göttingen.

P. 136. *Sâtavâhana.*—Other forms of the name are *Sâlavâhana*, *Sâlivâhana* (Hemacandra, i. 211); but Alberuni clearly notes the pronunciation *Samalvâhana*, which is not known to me from other sources.

P. 136.—Instead of *mâudakam* read *modakam* = *mâ udakam*.

P. 136.—*Abul'aswad*, &c., is, according to the literary tradition, the originator of their grammatical science. *Cf.* G. Flügel, *Grammatische Schulen der Araber*, p. 19 *seq.*

P. 136. *Chandas.*—In translating the chapter on metrics, I have derived much help from Colebrooke, "Essays," ii. p. 57 (on Sanskrit and Prâkrit poetry), and from Weber's edition of the Sûtras of Piṅgala (*Indische Studien*, vol. viii.). Alberuni, however, seems to have used other sources and to have followed another system, which has greatly increased the task of the translator.

P. 137. *Piṅgala.*—What are the Sanskrit forms of the names چلت *calitu*, گیست *gaisitu*, اولیاند *auliyându?*

The chapter of Brahmagupta's *Brahmasiddhânta*, of which the author here (p. 147–150) communicates a few extracts, is chap. xxi., *On the calculation of the measures of poetry and on metrics*, v. i. 155.

P. 138.—*Alkhalîl*, also mentioned i. 147, is in Arabic literature the father of the science of metrics. *Cf.* G. Flügel, *Grammatische Schulen der Araber*, p. 37.
*Sabab.*—*Cf.* Freytag, *Arabische Verskunst*, p. 64, 65.

P. 140. *Madhya.*—I do not know this term in Sanskrit, and the signs مذ admit of different transliterations. Both the terms *madhyâ* and *madhu* are used in metrical terminology, but with different meanings. *Cf.* Colebrooke, "Essays," ii. 141 (*madhu*), and ii. 136, 141 (*madhyâ*).

P. 141.—*Haribhaṭṭa?*—This name is not known to me as that of an author of a lexicographical work. The MS. clearly writes *hariuddu*, which may represent various other forms of Sanskrit names.

P. 141.—The single letters *m*, *y*, *r*, &c., denoting the single feet, are mentioned by Colebrooke, "Essays," ii. 63.

P. 142. *Place the numeral* 2, *&c.*—The rule, as explained in ll. 4, &c., differs from that one which is followed in the example (ll. 11–14), in so far as in the former place the subtraction of 1 ("*and from the product* (4) *he subtracts* 1") has been omitted. But even if we correct the text of the rule according to the exemplification, it cannot be correct, and we agree with Alberuni that something in the manuscript must have been wrong (also in the passage below, ll. 30–34). For it can be applied not to all eight feet, but only to two, viz., to

$$||< (2 \times 2 = 4 - 1 = 3 \times 2 = 6 - 1 = 5)$$

and to

$$|<| (2 \times 2 = 4 - 1 = 3 \times 2 = 6),$$

*i.e.* these two feet occupy respectively the fifth and sixth places in the arrangement on p. 141 (below).

P. 143. *The Greeks, too, &c.*—The comparison with Greek metrics is unintelligible, as something must have been dropped in the Arabic text.

P. 143. *Consonant or syllable.*—I suppose the author means syllable. The Arabic word حرف has the same inconvenience as Sanskrit *akshara* of meaning both *syllable* and *sound* (mostly *consonant*).

P. 143. *Âryâ.*—This reading is a conjecture of mine, as the MS. has *aral*, which I cannot explain. The description given by the author seems to be applicable to the

Âryâ metre, which could be known to him from his study of Brahmagupta's *Brahmasiddhânta*. *Cf.* Colebrooke, "Essays," ii. 66.

P. 144. *Skandha.*—A kind of Âryâ metre, *v.* Colebrooke, "Essays," ii. 137; or *skandhaka*, *v.* Weber, *Indische Studien*, viii. 295.

*Khafîf.*—This Arabic metre, represented in European fashion, is the following:—

– ⏑ – – | – – ⏑ – | – ⏑ – –

P. 145. *Vṛitta.*—On the metre of this name *v.* Colebrooke, "Essays," ii. 145. However the signs بْرِتُ (*b–r–t*) admit of various other ways of reading. The MS. has *britu*.

P. 147. *Śloka.*—On the rules relating to this metre *v.* Colebrooke, "Essays," ii. 107.

P. 150. *I have only seen a single leaf.*—This translation is to be replaced by, "I have only studied a single leaf."

P. 151. *Galenus.*—The quotation is found in his περὶ συνθέσεως φαρμάκων κατὰ γένη (ed. Kühn), tom. xiii. p. 996:—

ἀλλ' ἥ γε διὰ τῶν χυλῶν ὑπὸ Μενεκράτους εὑρεθεῖσα διὰ τῶνδε τῶν τριμέτρων στοιχείων ὑπὸ Δαμοκράτους γέγραπται.

P. 153. *Siddhânta.*—On the literature of the Siddhântas *v.* E. Burgess, *Sûrya Siddhânta*, p. 418–422.

*Śrîshena* is written with *kh* instead of *sh*, as *bhâshâ*=*bhâkhâ*. *Cf.* Hörnle, "Comparative Grammar of the Gaudian Languages," § 19 and 20.

*Varâhamihira.*—*Vide* note to p. 54.

Pp. 153, 154. *Brahmagupta.*—His work, the *Brahmasiddhânta*, has been very largely used by Alberuni. It exists in manuscript, but has not yet been completely edited or translated. Alberuni translated it into Arabic when he wrote the *Indica* (A.D. 1030). We do not know whether he ever finished it.

Brahmagupta was only thirty years of age when he

wrote this work. He is accused of the sin against conscience of having propagated futilities and lies in order to please the bigoted priests and the ignorant rabble of his nation, in order to avoid those dangers in which Socrates perished. *Vide* chap. lix. on eclipses, and specially ii. 111. Besides, Alberuni accuses him of undue animosity against Âryabhaṭa (i. 376).

Brahmagupta holds a remarkable place in the history of Eastern civilisation. It was he who taught the Arabs astronomy before they became acquainted with Ptolemy; for the famous *Sindhind* of Arabian literature, frequently mentioned, but not yet brought to light, is a translation of his *Brahmasiddhânta;* and the only other book on Indian astronomy, called *Alarkand*, which they knew, was a translation of his *Khaṇḍakhâdyaka*.

The latter work (here ii. 7) is also called *Karaṇakhaṇḍakhâdyaka* (i. 156). It was explained in a special commentary by Balabhadra (ii. 187).

A third composition of Brahmagupta's called *Uttarakhaṇḍakhâdyaka*, is mentioned i. 156, and quoted ii. 87, 91.

*Cf.* on Brahmagupta Colebrooke, "Essays," ii. 409 *seq.;* Dr. Bhâu Dâjî, "Brief Notes on the Age and Authenticity of the Works of Âryabhaṭa, Varâhamihira, Brahmagupta, &c.," in the "Journal of the Royal Asiatic Society," 1865, vol. i. 392 *seq.*

Notes from Varâhamihira's *Pañcasiddhântikâ* have been edited by G. Thibaut in the "Journal of the Asiatic Society of Bengal," 1884, vol. liii. p. 259.

*Sindhind* is mentioned ii. 191, as the only source of the information of Muslims on Indian astronomy and astrology. According to ii. 90, the Indian computation of the heliacal risings of the stars and the moon is identical with that given in Sindhind. It is called the *great sindhind* (*Siddhânta*) ii. 18.

Alberuni has written a treatise on it. See preface to the Arabic edition, p. xx.

P. 154. *Pulisa.*—This name and Paulisa are written Puliśa and Pauliśa in Utpala's commentary to the *Saṁhitâ* of Varâhamihira; but as Alberuni writes them constantly with a س, not ش, I am inclined to believe that he and his Pandits pronounced *Pulisa* and *Paulisa*. Alberuni has drawn from the *Pulisasiddhânta* almost as largely as from the *Brahmasiddhânta*, and was occupied with translating it (*v.* also i. 375).

The relation between Pulisa and Paulisa is this:—

*Paulisa* is the sage who communicates his wisdom in this *Siddhânta*. He was a native of Saintra, *i.e.* Alexandria.

*Pulisa* is the redactor or editor of the book. The one as well as the other is called يونانى, *Greek* (not رومى, Byzantine Greek). "Pulisa says in his *Siddhânta* that Paulisa the Greek had mentioned somewhere," &c., i. 266.

A commentator of this *Siddhânta* is mentioned i. 339 med., where I now prefer to translate: "The commentator of the *Siddhânta* of Pulisa," &c.

Pulisa quotes Parâśara (ii. 208), and is himself quoted by Âryabhaṭa jun. (i. 316).

Paulisa is quoted by Brahmagupta, i. 374 (v. note).

*Cf.* on the *Pulisasiddhânta* H. Kern, *The Bṛhat Sañhitâ*, preface, p. 48.

P. 156.—*Âryabhaṭa* senior is clearly distinguished from Âryabhaṭa junior, who is mostly called "that one from Kusumapura," *i.e.* Pâṭaliputra (Patna). Alberuni knows him only through the quotations in the works of Brahmagupta. He mentions two of his works, *Daśagîtikâ* and *Âryâshṭaśata*, which have been edited by Kern, *Ârya-bhaṭîyam*, 1874. *Cf.* Dr. Bhâu Dâjî, "Brief Notes on the Age and Authenticity of the Works of Âryabhaṭa," &c., p. 392.

P. 156. *Balabhadra.*—Of his works are mentioned:—

(1.) A *tantra.*

(2.) A *Saṁhitâ.*

(3.) A commentary of the *Bṛihajjâtakam* of Varâhamihira (p. 158).

(4.) A commentary to the *Khaṇḍakhâdyaka* of Brahmagupta.

(5.) He is supposed to be the author of the book *Khaṇḍakhâdyakaṭippâ.*

Alberuni always calls him *the commentator*, and frequently quotes him without indicating from what particular book he quotes. He gives on his authority the latitude of Kanoj and Tâneshar, and passes harsh judgment on him i. 244, 275. *Cf.* also note to p. 27.

P. 156. *Bhânurajas* (also on p. 157).—The Arabic MS. writes *Bahânarjus*, which I cannot identify. A slight alteration (of بهانرجس to بهانوجس) would give *Bhânuyaśas*, which name was suggested to me by G. Bühler.

P. 156. *Kûra-babayâ*.—As *kûra* means *rice*, ببيا, *babayâ*, must mean *mountain*. Is it a vernacular form for *parvata?*

P. 156. *Khaṇḍa-khâdyaka-tappâ*.—The MS. has *tappâ* or *tippâ* (*tuppâ*), of which I do not know the Sanskrit form. تپّا changed to تپّن would be = *ṭippanî* or commentary.

*Vijayanandin*.—Alberuni quotes from him a method for the computation of the longitude of a place (i. 313), a note on the dominants of year, month, and *horâ* (i. 343), on the circumpolar stars (ii. 90), an *ahargaṇa* rule (ii. 49, 50). An astronomer of this name is mentioned by Dr. Bhâu Dâji as anterior to Śrîsheṇa, the author of *Romakasiddhânta:* v. "The Age and Authenticity of the Works of Âryabhaṭa," &c. ("Journal of the Royal Asiatic Society," 1864), p. 408.

P. 156. *Bhadatta* (? *Mihdatta*).—The MS. reads مهدّت. Bhadatta is mentioned by Kern in the preface to his *Bṛhat Sañhitâ*, p. 29. Alberuni quotes from the work of Vitteśvara a note on the motion of the Great Bear (i. 392), on the mean places of the stars (ii. 60), on the diameters of sun and moon (ii. 79), the latitude of Kashmir (i. 317), the era used in the book (ii. 7). It must have been translated into Arabic before Alberuni wrote the *Indica*, because he complains that that part of the book which he had was badly translated (ii. 55).

P. 157. *Utpala*.—Besides these two *Karaṇas*, he has composed—

(1.) A commentary to the great *Mânasa* composed by Manu.

(2.) The *Praśnacûḍâmaṇi* (p. 158).

(3.) A commentary to the *Saṁhitâ* of Varâhamihira (p. 298).

(4.) The book *Srûdhara* (?), whence Alberuni has taken metrological and chronological notes (p. 334, 336, 361). *Cf.* on Utpala Kern's preface to his *Bṛhat Sañhitâ*, p. 61.

The book-title *râhunrâkaraṇa*, i.e. *breaking of the Karaṇas*, seems to be corrupt. One expects the word *karaṇa* in the first place, and a word for *breaking* in the second.

P. 157. On *Manu* as an authority in astronomy and astrology, v. Kern, preface to *Bṛhat Sañhitâ*, p. 42. *Cf.* note to p. 131.

P. 157. *Puñcala* (?).—The author quotes from him a statement relating to the precession of the equinoxes; he speaks highly of him, and says that a theory of his was adopted by Utpala (i. pp. 366, 367).

I do not know of such an Indian name. The nearest approach to it is *Muñjâla*, that of an astronomer quoted by Colebrooke, "Essays," ii. 330, 332.

P. 157. *Bhaḍila* (?).—The MS. has *bahattal*, and I suppose that the correct reading is *Bhaṭṭila*. The name is perhaps a derivation (diminutive ?) from *bhaṭṭa*, as *kumârila* from *kumâra*, *pushaṇḍhila* from *shaṇḍha*. Alberuni quotes him, ii. 208, in the chapter on the *yogas*.

On Parâśara and Garga *cf.* Kern, *Bṛhat Sañhitâ*, preface, pp. 31, 33; on Satya, Jivaśarman, p. 51; on Maṇittha, p. 52. Mau is probably identical with Maya: v. Weber, *Vorlesungen*, p. 270.

P. 158. *Of Varâhamihira, &c.*—This author has composed not only the *Shaṭpañcâśikâ* and *Horâpañcahotriya* (?), but also the *Yogayâtrâ*, *Tikanîyâtrâ* (?), and *Vivâhapaṭala*: v. Kern, *Bṛhat Sañhitâ*, preface, pp. 25, 26; his translation of the *Yogayâtrâ* in Weber's *Indische Studien*, x. 161.

The name of the author of the book on architecture is missing in the Arabic text. If it was not likewise a work of Varâhamihira's, it may have been composed by Nagnajit or Viśvakarman: v. Kern, *l. c.* p. 51.

P. 158. *Srûdhava.*—I do not know the corresponding Sanskrit form. It seems to be some relative of *śruti*. If *śrutayas* had currency in the meaning of *traditions*, I should identify it with *srûdhava*. Is it = *śrotavya*?

The word is the title of two different books, one by Utpala from Kashmîr (v. note to p. 157), and the one here mentioned, on *omina* and *portenta*, lucky and unlucky days, &c. It probably contained the names of the twenty-four *horâ* (i. 344); it mentioned the names of the third parts of the day (ii. 120), the names of the *vishṭi* (ii. 201), the unlucky days of the year (ii. 192), the name of Vikramâditya (ii. 6, *vide* note to the place).

The reading of the word بنگال as *Bangâla* is probably not correct. Is it = *puṇyakâla ?*

P. 158. *Gudhâmana* (?), in the Arabic *jûrâman.*—As the word is translated by *unknown*, one thinks of a derivation of the word *guh* = to conceal (v. *gûḍha*). The Arabic characters may also be read *cûḍâmaṇi.* If *praśna jûrâman* (?) really meant what Alberuni says, one would expect *gûḍhapraśna.*

P. 158. *Sangahila, Piruvâna.*—I do not know the Sanskrit equivalents of these two names. The former might be a word like *śṛiṅkhala* or *śṛiṅgalâ* (*Syncellus ?*). Pṛithûdaka is the author of a commentary on the *Brahmasiddhânta :* v. Colebrooke, "Essays," ii. 411.

P. 159. *Caraka.*—The ancient Arabic translation of his medical work is sometimes quoted by Alberuni, and to judge from these quotations the translation was not free from blunders nor the manuscript-tradition free from the effects of carelessness : *v.* a quotation on weights, i. 162, 163 ; one on the origin of medicine, i. 382. *Cf.* Weber, *Vorlesungen*, pp. 284, 289.

P. 159. *Pañcatantra.*—*Cf.* on this book and on Ibn Almuḳaffa's share in its translation, Benfey's introduction to his translation of the *Pancatantra* (Leipzig, 1859). On the translations of the book and on the influence which King Maḥmûd of Ghazna has had on its fate, *cf.* Colebrooke, "Essays," ii. 148. The work of Ibn Almuḳaffa' is that one edited by S. de Sacy, 1816.

P. 160. *Chapter XV.*—For the translation of this chapter on metrology, I have derived much help from Colebrooke, "On Indian Weights and Measures" ("Essays," i. 528 *seq.*), and Marsden's *Numismata Orientalia*, new edition, Part I., "Ancient Indian Weights," by E. Thomas, London,

1874; A. Weber, *Ueber ein Fragment der Bhagavati*, II. Theil, p. 265 note.

The weight of one dirham = one-seventh *mithkâl*, dates from the time of the Khalif Omar.

The weight of one dirham = seven *dânak*, is peculiar to India in the author's time, for in general one dirham = six *dânak*. *Cf.* Sauvaire, *Matériaux pour servir à l'Histoire de la Numismatique et de la Métrologie Musulmanes*, Paris, 1882, pp. 43, 81, 98; on the *mithkâl*, p. 35; on the *fuls*, p. 108. On the ancient denars of Sindh *cf.* Elliot, "History of India," i. 11 (Abû Zaid), 24 (Mas'ûdi), 35 (Ibn Haukal).

P. 162. *Varâhamihira.*—This passage is *Brihat Samhitâ*, chap. lviii. v. 1. The following quotation on *yava, andî, mâsha*, and *suvarna*, I do not find in his *Samhitâ*.

P. 162. *Caraka.*—The Arabic translation of this book is not extant. The Indian words which occur in the extracts from this book are not so accurately written as those in Alberuni's own work, and offer more difficulties in the way of identification: *v.* note to p. 159.

P. 162. *Jîvaśarman.*—The words "As I have been told (by him)," may better be translated "As I have heard it from him." Alberuni does not quote from a book of his, but only says "he *has told, mentioned*," "I have heard from him." Accordingly, he seems to have been a contemporary and personal acquaintance of Alberuni's, in the same way as Śrîpâla. Alberuni relates on his authority details regarding a festival in Kashmîr and Svât, ii. 181, 182. Besides, a Jîvaśarman is mentioned as the author of a *Jâtakam*, i. 157, who seems to have been a different person altogether, and lived before the time of Varâhamihira: *v.* Kern's Preface to *Brhat Sañhitâ*, p. 29.

P. 164. *Varâhamihira.*—This quotation seems to correspond to *Brihat Samhitâ*, chap. xxiii. v. 2. At all events, it is the passage to which Śrîpâla refers.

*Śrîpâla.*—Alberuni quotes him a second time, i. 240, where he speaks of a star, *śûla*, as observed in Multân, which people considered as unlucky, and ii. 209, he copies from him the names of the twenty-seven yogas. Perhaps Śrîpâla was a scholar living at Multân in the time of the author. Alberuni does not mention a book of his.

P. 165. *Śiśupâla.*—The story of Krishṇa's killing Śiśupâla (*Śiśupâlabadha*) is told in the *Mahâbhârata*, Sabhâ-Parvan, v. 1336 *seq.*

P. 165. *Alfazârî* is one of the fathers of Arabian literature, the first propagator of Indian astronomy among the Arabs. His works are, as far as I am aware, not extant. Probably this Muḥammad Ibn Ibrâhîm Alfazârî was the son of Ibrâhîm Ibn Ḥabib Alfazârî, the first constructor of astrolabes among the Arabs, who as a surveyor partook in the foundation of Bagdad. *Cf. Fihrist*, p. ٢٧٣. Gildemeister, in his *Scriptorum Arabum de rebus Indicis loci*, p. 101, gives the translation of an article of Alḳifṭi on our Fazârî.

According to the quotations of Alberuni (*v.* index *s. v.* Alfazârî), this scholar used the word *pala* in the meaning of day-minute; he reckoned the circumference of the earth in اجوان, *i.e. yojanas*; he (together with Ya'ḳûb Ibn Ṭâriḳ) mentions a town, *Târa*, in a sea in Yamakoṭi; he gives a method for the computation of the longitude of a place from two latitudes; his book contained the cycles of the planets as derived from Hindu scholars, the members of an embassy from some part of Sindh, who called on the Khalif Almanṣûr, A.H. 154 (= A.D. 771). Alberuni charges him with having misunderstood the meaning of the word Âryabhaṭa, which he is said to have used as meaning $\frac{1}{1000}$ of the measures of the great Siddhânta, *i.e.* the *Brahmasiddhânta* of Brahmagupta. Lastly, Alfazârî (together with Ya'ḳûb) has used the word بذماسه (*padamâsa?*) in the sense of *adhimâsa* (leap-month). On the whole, Alberuni finds that the tradition of Indian astronomy by Alfazârî is not very trustworthy, and that in it the names or *termini technici* are often corrupt and badly written.

As Alfazârî and Ya'ḳûb Ibn Ṭâriḳ are sometimes mentioned in the same context, there must have been a close relation between these two authors, the nature of which I have no means for examining. Have both learned from the same Hindu scholar, and have they independently of each other committed their information to writing? Or has the one made a new edition or a commentary of the work of the other? *Vide* note to p. 169 (Ya'ḳûb).

P. 165. *Sibi.*—The word occurs thrice, and is written سيى (*siyî?*); only in one place it seemed to be سبى, but on repeated comparison of the MS. I find that originally here, too, was written سبى. I do not know a measure of such a name. Perhaps it is the *bisi*, of which 16 = 1 *panti* (p. 166, l. 2 in Somanâth). *Cf.* Colebrooke, "Essays," i. 536; sixteen *bisis* = one *panti*.

P. 166. *Khwârizmian.*—The comparison of the measures of this country, the modern Khiva, will remind the reader that it was the native country of the author.

P. 166. *Varâhamihira.*—I have not succeeded in finding this quotation in his *Saṁhitâ*.

P. 167. *Varâhamihira.*—The passage here quoted is *Saṁhitâ*, chap. xviii. v. 26–28.

P. 167. *'Ajrân.*—Alberuni only mentions the plural form, not the singular, which would be *jûn* or *jaun*, *jôn*. I take the word to be the Arabized form of *yojana*. The change from *yojana* to *jôn* was perhaps facilitated by a Prakritic pronunciation on the part of the Hindu teachers of Alfazârî, according to which a *j* between two vowels may be dropped. *Cf.* *gao* = *gaja*, *raadam*, *rajata* (Vararuci, ii. 2).

P. 168.—*Archimedes* fixed $\pi$ as a measure between $3\frac{1}{7}$ and $3\frac{10}{71}$. *Cf.* J. Gow, "Short History of Greek Mathematics," Cambridge, 1884, p. 235.

P. 169.—*Ya'ḳûb Ibn Târiḳ* seems to have been the most prominent predecessor of Alberuni in the field of astronomy, chronology, and mathematical geography on an Indian basis. He is frequently quoted in the *Indica*, much more than Alfazârî.

Here he gives the measures of the circumference and the diameter of the zodiacal sphere in *yojanas*, in which Alberuni recognises the system of Pulisa. He speaks of a city, Târa, within a sea in Yamakoṭi (i. 303). He gives the measures of the radius, diameter, and circumference of the earth in *yojanas* (i. 312), a statement on the latitude of Ujain, and a quotation from the book *Arkand* on the same subject (i. 316). He mentions the four *mânas* or measures of time, *sauramâna*, *cândramâna*, &c. (i. 353). His work contained tables of the revolutions of the planets, borrowed from a Hindu who had come in an embassy from Sindh to the court of the Khalif Almanṣûr, A.H. 154 (=A.D. 771), but Alberuni finds in these tables considerable deviations from those of the Hindus (ii. 15). He is accused of having misunderstood the word Âryabhaṭa, so as to take it not for the name of an author, but for a technical term meaning $\frac{1}{1000}$ of the measures employed in the great Siddhânta (that of Brahmagupta), on ii. 18, 19. He called the leap-month پذماسه (*padamâsa?*) instead of *adhimâsa* (ii. 23). He gives an incorrect method for the computation of the solar days in the *ahargaṇa* and for the reduction of years into days (by the side of a correct one) on ii. 26, 34, 38. He gives further details of the *ahargaṇa* computation (ii. 44, 45), and a table indicating the distances of the planets from the earth, borrowed from a Hindu, A.H. 161 (=A.D. 777-778), on ii. 67, 68.

Accordingly the work of Ya'ḳûb seems to have been a complete system of astronomy, chronology, and mathematical geography. It is called *Compositio Sphærarum* and also الزيج, *i.e. Canon*.

Alberuni sometimes criticises Ya'ḳûb, and maintains that he had committed errors, that he mis-spelled the Indian words, and that he simply borrowed the tables from his Hindu authority without examining them by calculation.

On his relation to Alfazârî, *v.* note to p. 165.

When Alberuni wrote his Chronology, he did not possess the work of Ya'ḳûb, fort here he gives a note on the four *mânas* and on the word پذماسه (*padamâsa?*) on the authority of Ya'ḳûb, but taken from the work of another author. *Vide* my translation, p. 15.

As Ya'ḳûb studied in the years A.H. 154 and 161 (A.D. 771, 778), he must have lived in the second half of the eighth Christian century (probably in Babylonia). This is nearly all we know of him. *Cf.* Reinaud, *Mémoire sur l'Inde*, p. 313; Steinschneider, *Zeitschrift der Deutschen Morgenländischen Gesellschaft*, 24, 332, 354.

The *Fihrist*, p. ٢٧٨, has a note on him in which there

is some confusion. The work *Compositio Sphærarum* is erroneously mentioned among the works of 'Uṭârid Ibn Muḥammad, whilst it is apparently identical with the work here called *Canon*. It consisted of two parts, one on the sphere and one on the periods (the *yugas?*). According to Fihrist, he had written two more books, one on the division of the sine in *kardajât*, and another on *what is derived from the arc of the meridian*.

Regarding the embassy from Sindh, from which the Arabs are said to have got the first information on Indian astronomy, in fact, the two works of Brahmagupta, the *Brahmasiddhânta* (*Sindhind*) and the *Khaṇḍakhâdyaka* (called *Arkand*), I cannot find any historical account in the Arabic annals. We do not learn anything from Ibn Wâḍiḥ or Ṭabarî of the presence of a Sindhî embassy in Babylonia in the year 154 (A.D. 771), as Alberuni has it, nor in the year 156 (A.D. 773), as Alḥusain Ibn Muḥammad Ibn Alâdamî maintains (Gildemeister, *Scriptorum Arabum de rebus Indicis loci*, p. 101), nor of the presence of Hindu scholars in Babylonia in the year 161 (A.D. 777). This only is related by Ibn Wâḍiḥ, that when Abulabbâs Saffâḥ, the first Abbaside Khalif, was dying in Anbâr, there arrived at his court an embassy from Sindh, A.H. 136 (A.D. 753). At all events, at the time of the Khalif Almanṣûr, Sindh obeyed this prince, and Islam had spread not only in Sindh, but far beyond it into the adjacent countries, both by war and by commerce. There must have been many occasions for petty Hindu princes in Sindh to send special missions to the political centre of the Muslim realm.

When Ya'ḳûb wrote, the *Arkand* (*Khaṇḍakhâdyaka*) had already been translated into Arabic. By whom? By Alfazârî?

In the first fifty years of Abbaside rule there were two periods in which the Arabs learned from India, first under Manṣûr (A.D. 753–774), chiefly astronomy, and secondly under Hârûn (786–808), by the special influence of the ministerial family Barmak, who till 803 ruled the Muslim world, specially medicine and astrology.

P. 170. *Socrates.*—I do not know the Greek form of this *dictum*. It must be observed that according to the common tradition hides of animals were first prepared for vellum at Pergamum long after Socrates.

P. 171. On the fabrication of papyrus, *cf.* Wilkinson, "Manners and Customs of the Ancient Egyptians," ii. p. 180.

P. 172. *As for the Greek alphabet, &c.*—The source of this tradition on the origin of the Greek alphabet seems to be certain scholia to the *Ars Grammatica* of Dionysius Thrax: *v.* Immanuel Bekker, *Anecdota Græca*, Berlin, 1816, vol. ii. p. 780 *seq.* The synchronistic notes point more to Joannes Malalas; perhaps these things were originally mentioned in the lacuna O 129.

*Asidhas* seems to be a mistake for Palamedes, *Agenon* for Agenor.

P. 173. *Bahmanwâ.*—Read *Bamhanwâ.* Other forms of the name are *Bâmirân* and *Bâînvâh*: *v.* Elliot, "History of India," i. 34, 189, 369, and the papers of Haig in the "Journal of the Royal Asiatic Society, 1884, p. 281, and of Bellasis in the "Journal" of the Bombay branch, vol. v., 1857, p. 413, 467.

For Kannara, *v.* note to pp. 17–19. Andhradeśa identified by Cunningham with Telingâna, *v.* his "Ancient Geography of India," p. 527.

*Bhaikshukî.*—Alberuni writes *Baikshuka*, probably *that of the bhikshu* or beggar-monks, *i.e.* the *śramaṇa* or Buddhistic monks. Is the *Audunpûr* mentioned by Alberuni, identical with the famous Buddhistic monastery *Udaṇḍapuri* in Magadha (?). *Cf.* H. Kern, *Der Buddhismus und seine Geschichte in Indien*, German by H. Jacobi, Leipzig, 1882, vol. ii. p. 545.

What Malvashau is I do not know (Malla-vishaya ?).

P. 175. To the orders of numbers, *cf.* Weber, *Vedische Angaben über Zeittheilung und hohe Zahlen*, in *Zeitschrift der Deutschen Morg. Gesellschaft*, xv. 132.

Pp. 178, 179. This table has already been published by F. Wöpcke, *Mémoire sur la Propagation des Chiffres Indiens*, p. 103 *seq*; A. C. Burnell, "Elements of South Indian Palæography," ii. ed., p. 77. Compare also E. Jaquet, *Mode d'Expression Symbolique des Nombres Em-*

*ployé par les Indiens, les Tibétains et les Javanais*, (*Extrait du Journal Asiatique*); Brown, "Sanskrit Prosody and Numerical Symbols," London, 1869, p. 49 *seq.*

P. 181. *Pushaṇḍhila.*—The eunuch is called *shaṇḍha*. This seems to be a diminutive form compounded with the word *puṁs* (G. Bühler).

P. 182. *They magnify the nouns of their language, &c.*—This somewhat enigmatic sentence seems to have the following meaning:—An Arabic word, *e.g.* *ḳarsh* (a sea-animal), is magnified, *i.e.* receives a larger form, by being changed into the diminutive form, *i.e.* *ḳuraish* (a small sea-animal, as a proper noun, the name of the tribe to which Muḥammad belonged). The diminutive form serves the purpose of magnifying the form of the word: *cf.* Kashshâf to Koran, 106, 2, والتصغير للتعظيم (not للتفخيم). If the Hindus magnify their nouns by giving them the feminine gender, this must be referred to some of the pleonastic suffixes, *e.g.* *â*, *î*, which are added to Indian nouns without altering their meaning. In appearance they are the terminations of the feminine gender, in reality euphonic changes of the more ancient suffixes *aka* and *ika*, *e.g.* *paṭâ*, board, by the side of *paṭ*. *Cf.* Hörnle, "Comparative Grammar of the Gauḍian Languages," § 194 *seq.*

P. 183.—An explanation of the Indian chess has been published by A. Van der Linde, *Geschichte und Litteratur des Shachspiels.*

P. 189. *Nâgârjuna.*—*Cf.* on him A. Weber, *Vorlesungen*, pp. 306, 307; H. Kern, *Der Buddhismus und seine Geschichte in Indien*, ii. 501; Beal, "Indian Antiquary," 1886, 353.

P. 189. *Vyâḍi.*—A lexicographer of this name is mentioned in a certain connection with Vikramâditya by Colebroke, "Essays," ii. 19.

P. 190. *Raktâmala* = *rakta* = red, and *amala* = *emblica officinalis.* I do not see how the word could be understood to mean *oil* and *human blood.*

P. 191. *Bhojadeva.*—*Cf.* on this king of Mâlava, Lassen, *Indische Alterthumskunde*, iii. p. 845 *seq.*

P. 192. *Vallabhî.*—On the end of this city, *cf.* Lassen, *Indische Alterthumskunde*, iii. 532 *seq.*, and also Nicholson and Forbes on the ruins of the place, in "Journal of the Royal Asiatic Society," vol. xiii. (1852), p. 146, and vol. xvii. (1860), p. 267.

P. 196. *For it is not navigable.*—This passage agrees almost literally with Plato's *Timæus*, 25D:—

*διὸ καὶ νῦν ἄπορον καὶ ἀδιερεύνητον γέγονε τὸ ἐκεῖ πέλαγος, πηλοῦ κάρτα βραχέος ἐμποδὼν ὄντος ὃν ἡ νῆσος ἱζομένη παρέσχετο.*

P. 197. *The various tribes of the Zanj.*—The traditions of the Arabs regarding Eastern Africa have been collected by Marcel Devic in his *Le Pays des Zendjs*, Paris, 1883.

P. 197. The configuration of the northern coast of the Indian Ocean seems to have been a favourite subject of Alberuni, for he mentions it again on p. 270.

P. 199. *Mâhûra*, so written by Alberuni, is written مهره, *Mahura*, by his elder contemporary Al-'utbi, more in keeping with the Sanskrit vowels (*Mathurâ*).

Alberuni reckons the distances in *farsakh*, regarding the measure of which he unfortunately does not give accurate information. According to i. 167, 1 yojana = 32,000 yards = 8 miles; 1 mile = 4000 yards; and according to i. 200, 1 farsakh = 4 miles = 1 kuroh; 1 farsakh = 16,000 yards. *Cf.* also Aloys Sprenger, *Die Post- und Reiserouten des Orients*, Vorrede, p. xxvi., who proves that one Arabian mile = *præter propter* 2000 metres = 2186 yards, whilst the English geographical mile = 2025 yards. If we, therefore, want to compare Alberuni's distances with English miles, we must reckon—

1 English mile = $1\frac{161}{2025}$ Arabian mile.
1 Arabian mile = $\frac{2025}{2186}$ English mile.
1 *farsakh* = 4 Arabian miles = $3\frac{771}{1093}$ English miles.

P. 200. Alberuni gives sixteen itineraries which seem to have been communicated to him by the military and civil officers of King Maḥmûd (on some of these roads he had marched with large armies, *e.g.* to Kanoj and to Somanâtha), from merchants and sailors, from Hindu and Muslim travellers. The starting-points of these itineraries are Kanoj, Mâhûra (now Muttra), Anhilvâra (now Pattan), Dhâr in Mâlavâ, and two less known places, Bâri, the temporary capital of the realm of Kanoj, after the old capital had been taken by the Muslims, and a place called Bazâna.

These itineraries are—1. From Kanoj to Allahabad, and thence towards the eastern coast of India as far as Kâñcî (Conjeveram), and farther south. 2. From Kanoj (or Bâri) to Benares, and thence to the mouth of the Ganges. 3. From Kanoj eastward as far as Kamroop, and northward to Nepal and the Tibeṭan frontier. 4. From Kanoj southward as far as Banavâsi on the southern coast. 5. From Kanoj to Bazâna or Nârâyan, the then capital of Guzarât. 6. From Muttra to Dhâr, the capital of Mâlavâ. 7. From Bazâna to Dhâr and Ujain. 8. From Dhâr in Mâlavâ towards the Godâvari. 9. From Dhâr to Tâna, on the coast of the Indian Ocean. 10. From Bazâna to Somanâtha, on the south coast of Kathiavar. 11. From Anhilvâra to Tâna, on the west coast, north of Bombay. 12. From Bazâna *viâ* Bhâtî to Loharânî, at the mouth of the Sindh river. 13. From Kanoj to Kashmîr. 14. From Kanoj to Pânipat, Attok, Kâbul, Ghazna. 15. From Babrahân to Addishtân, the capital of Kashmîr. 16. From Tîz, in Makrân, along the coast as far as Setubandha, opposite Ceylon.

*Cf.* the following latitudes and longitudes, taken from the *Canon Masudicus* :—

Tree of Prayâga, 25° 0′ lat., 106° 20′ long. ; Kuraha, 26° 1′ lat., 106° 40′ long. ; Tiauri, 23° 0′ lat., 106° 30′ long. ; Kajûrâha, 24° 4′ lat., 106° 50′ long. ; Bazâna (?) or Nârâyan, 24° 35′ lat., 106° 10′ long. ; the country Kannakara, 22° 20′ lat., 107° 0′ long. ; Sharvâr, 24° 15′ lat., 107° 50′ long. ; Pâṭaliputra, 22° 30′ lat., 108° 20′ long. ; Mungiri, 22° 0′ lat., 109° 10′ long. ; Dûgum, 22° 40′ lat., 110° 50′ long. ; Bâri, 26° 30′ lat., 105° 50′ long. ; Dûdahî, 25° 40′ lat., 102° 10′ long. ; Dahmâla, 31° 10′ lat., 100° 55′ long. ; Shirshârala, 38° 50′ lat., 102° 10′ long. ; Bhillamâla, 23° 50′ lat., 87° 45′ long. ; Bamhanvâ, 26° 40′ lat., 85° 0′ long. ; Loharânî, 24° 40′ lat., 84° 25′ long. ; Daibal, 24° 10′ lat., 82° 30′ long. ; Bhâtiya, 28° 40′ lat., 96° 0′ long. ; Ujain, 24° 0′ lat., 100° 50′ long. ; Tîz, 26° 15′ lat., 83° 0′ long. ; Kandi, 33° 40′ lat., 95° 50′ long. ; Dunpûr, 33° 45′ lat., 96° 25′ long. ; Tanjore (?), 15° 0′ lat., 115° 0′ long. ; Rameshar, 13° 0′ lat., 118° 0′ long. ; Jahrâvar, 39° 50′ lat., 96° 15′ long. ; كدرد 31° 1′ lat., 95° 55′ long. Longitude is reckoned from the coast of the Atlantic ; that of Bagdad is 70°.

P. 200. *Barhamshil* = *Brâhmanaśaila* = Brahmin's rock (?).

*Tree of Prayâga*=Allahabad, at the confluence of Ganges and Jumna.

In line 20 after 12 *farsakh* (in the Arabic only 12 without *farsakh*) there is apparently a lacuna.

*Uwaryahâr.*—One expects an indication of Orissa (Ûriyâdeśa). The word might also be read *Ûrîyahâr*. Is *Urîyadhârâ* meant? *Ûrdabîshau* perhaps = *ûrdhva-vishaya*.

*Jaur's possessions, i.e.* the Cola empire; *v.* also here, i. 209, and Lassen, *Indische Alterthumskunde*, ii. 435, iv. 230 *seq*.

P. 200. *Bârî.*—Regarding the situation of this place the following statements must be taken into account:—It was situated ten farsakh or three to four days' march distant from Kanoj towards the east, east of the Ganges, in the neighbourhood of the confluence of the rivers رهب and كوينى and Sarayu. It was twenty-five farsakh distant from Oudh. The name *Bârî* occurs also in Elliot-Beames, "Memoirs," ii. 83, as that of a subdivision of the district Agra.

P. 201. *Kâmrû* is apparently *Kâmarûpa* and Tilvat = Tirhoot. The latter is by mistake also written *Tanvat*. Are we to read *Tirût?* The word is perhaps composed of *Tarû*, the name of the nation who lived there, and a word like *bhukti*.

*The empire of Shilahat.*—Is this to be identified with Sylhet, the province of Assam?

*Bhoteshar* seems to be *bhauṭṭa-iśvara*, lord of the *bhauṭṭas*, or Tibetans.

P. 202. *Kajûrâha* is = *kharjûra-bhâga*.

*Tiaurî.*—According to a well-known rule of Prakrit (Vararuci, ii. 2), the name *Τιάτουρα* (Ptolemy, vii. i. 63) would become something like Tiaurî. As there is a lacuna in the Arabic manuscript, the situation of this place cannot be accurately defined.

*Kannakara.*—This is probably identical with *Kamkar*, the realm of the Balharâ, according to Mas'ûdi: *v.* Elliot, "History of India," i. 25.

P. 202. *Bazâna.*—The reading is conjectural. For an identification v. Archæological Survey of India, ii. 242. For *Sahanyâ* (*Suhaniyâ*) v. *ibid.* ii. 399.

On Guzarât, the empire of the Gurjjara kings, not identical with modern Guzerat, *cf.* Cunningham, "Ancient Geography of India," p. 312 *seq.*; Elliot, *l. c.* p. 358.

*Jadûra.*—This reading is uncertain. Perhaps all the signs of the Arabic text (احرجدوره) are the name of a place.

P. 202. *Bâmahûr* is perhaps identical with Ptolemy's *Βαμμόγουρα* (Pt. vii. i. § 63), as in some cases an *h* represents an elder *g*; *e.g.* چندراهه Candarâha = *Candrabhâgâ*, ديوهر *devahar*=*devagriha*, *kulahara* (Prakrit) = *kulagriha*.

P. 203. *Namâvur, Alîspûr.*—Are these names to be identified with *Nimâr* and *Ellichpur* in Central India? *Cf.* G. Smith, "Geography of British India," pp. 339, 347.

P. 203. *Śarabha.*—This digression of the author's is repeated by Muḥammad 'Aufî in his story-book: *v.* Elliot, "History of India," ii. 202.

P. 205. *Anhilvâra* = Analavâṭa = modern Pattan in Northern Baroda: *v.* G. Smith, *l. l.* p. 297; Elliot, "History of India," i. 363.

*Lârdesh* = *Λαρική* of Ptolemy, vii. i. 4.

*Bihroj* = Broach = *Βαρύγαζα*, G. Smith, p. 263.

*Rihanjûr* is probably identical with *'Αγρινάγαρα* (Ptolemy, vii. i. § 63). Two consonants frequently undergo a metathesis, if one of them is a *liquid*. *Agrinagara* has become Arginagara, and the *g* is here represented by an *h*, as in *Candarâha* = *Candrabhâgâ*.

*Loharânî* seems to be identical with *Λωνίβαρε* of Ptolemy, vii. i. § 2. A metathesis of the middle consonants has taken place, and *b* has become *h*. It is also called *Lohâniyye* (i. 316).

P. 205.—*Jâlandhar* is the *Κυλινδρινή* of Ptolemy, vii. i. § 42, G. Smith, p. 207.

*Ballârar* = *Vallâpura*, v. Cunningham, *l. c.* pp. 135, 133. Is it identical with modern Phillaur? G. Smith, p. 208.

P. 206.—*Karîtal* = *Kapisthala* = Καμβίσθολοι (Megasthenes), now *Kapoorthala*, G. Smith, p. 208. *Vide* also *Kaithal* in Elliot's "History of India," ii. 337, 353.

*Mandahûkûr*. *Cf.* Elliot, *l. c.* i. 530.

P. 206. *Kusnarî*.—I am inclined to identify this river with the *Kunhar* (G. Smith, p. 231). Is the Mahvî = Kishen-Ganga?

P. 207.—*Ûshkârâ* is explained by Cunningham, *l. c.* p. 99, as Hushkapura, Huvishkapura and Barâmûla as *Varâhamûla*.

P. 208.—*Tâkeshar* is perhaps to be explained as *Takkaiśvara*, like Bhoteshar = Bhauṭṭa-îśvara. *Cf.* on *Ṭakka*, Cunningham, *l. c.* p. 749.

*Râjavarî* seems to be identical with Rajaori (G. Smith, p. 228).

P. 208. *The coast of India begins with Tîz*.—*Cf.* with this route along the coast that one given by Ibn Khurdâdbih in Elliot, "History of India," i. 15, 16; A. Sprenger, *Die Post- und Reiserouten des Orients*, pp. 80–82.

*Munha* = Skr. *mukha*, Prakrit *muhaṁ*, Hindî *muṅh*: *v.* Hörnle, "Comparative Grammar," § 116.

*Daibal*.—On the identification with Karâci v. Elliot, "History of India," i. 375. Daibal-Sindh is the *Diulcindi* of Duarte Borbosa, translated by Stanley, p. 49 (Hakluyt Society).

Pp. 208, 209.—*Baroî* = Baroda, *Kanbâyat* = Kambay, *Bihroj* = Broach. *Sûbâra* is identical with Skr. *Śûrpâraka*, Ptolemy's Σούπαρα, and the *Sufâla* of the Arabs. *Tâna* = Skr. *sthâna*, and *Sandân* is perhaps = *saṁdhâna*. To Sûbâra, *cf.* Bhagvánlál Indraji, "Antiquarian Remains of Sopara," &c., "Journal" of the Bombay branch, 1881, 1882, vol. xv. p. 273.

P. 209.—*Panjayâvar* seems to be a mistake for some older form of the name *Tanjore*.

*Râmsher* = *Râmeśvara*?—On Râma and the monkeys of the Kishkindha mountains *cf.* the fourth book of the *Râmâyaṇa*.

P. 210.—The theory of the rising and disappearing of the Dîva islands seems to have been a favourite one of the author's, for he explains it in three different places; *v.* p. 233, and ii. 106.

P. 211.—*Shauḥaṭ* is explained by Johnson as a tree whence bows are made, and *mulamma'* means *having different colours.* What particular sort of wood this means I do not know.

P. 211.—*Indravedi* must be changed into *Antarvedi*, "the old name of the Lower Doáb, extending from about Etawah to Allahabad." Elliot-Beames, "Memoirs," ii. 10; Elliot, "History of India," ii. 124.

Is *Bhâtal* identical with Ptolemy's *Παταληνή*?

P. 213. *We have already mentioned*, viz. on p. 17.

P. 214. *ὧραι καιρικαί, i.e.* the ancient division of day and night, each in twelve equal parts, of whatsoever length day and night happened to be. These hours were different in the different seasons of the year. On the contrary, the *ὧραι ἰσημεριναί*, probably of scientific origin, are the twenty-fourth part of a nychthemeron, always equal throughout the course of the whole year. *Cf.* Ideler, *Handbuch der Chronologie*, i. 86.

P. 214. *Horâ.*—The Persian *nîmbahra* means *half part*, and in astrology one-half or fifteen degrees of a sign of the zodiac; *v.* ii. 222.

P. 214, l. 30.—The distance between the sun and the degree of the ascendens divided by fifteen gives in hours the time which has passed since sunrise; the dominus of the day being at once the dominus of the first hour, the rule here given is evidently correct (*Schram*).

P. 215.—For names of planets *v.* E. Burgess, *Sûrya Siddhânta*, pp. 422, 423, and A. Weber, *Indische Studien*, ii. 261.

Instead of آنثير read آفنير, *âvaneya.* The word *bibatâ* is probably some form of *vivasvant.*

The reader will notice the Greek names *heli* ἥλιος, *ârâ*

*Ἄρης*, *hemna* *Ἑρμῆς*, *jîva* *Ζεύς*, *âsphujit* *Ἀφροδίτη*, *koṇa* *Κρόνος*.

Pp. 216, 217, 218. *Vishṇudharma*.—*Vide* note to p. 54.

P. 217. *Table*.—I shall here give the names of the months as the author probably pronounced them, but cannot be held responsible for the details of the vowel-pronunciation: *cetr*, *béshâk*, *jert*, *âshâr*, *shrâban*, *bhadro*, *âshûj*, *kârtik*, *manghir*, *posh*, *mâg*, *pâgun*. Perhaps most of these names terminated in short *u*, as *manghiru*. *Cf.* the Hindustani names in Dowson's "Grammar of the Urdû," 1887, p. 259.

The *vernacular* names of the suns are perhaps to be pronounced: *rabi*, *bishnu*, *dhâta*, *bidhâta*, *arjamu*, *bhagu*, *sabita*, *pûsha*, *trashta*, *arku*, *dibâkaru*, *anshu*.

The difference between vernacular and classical speech is repeatedly referred to. *Vide* i. 18 (*v.* note), 218.

P. 218. *With the tradition of the Vishṇudharma*.—After these words must be added the following, which I have overlooked in translating: "And further he (*i.e.* Vâsudeva) has spoken in the *Gîtâ*, '*I am like the vasanta, i.e.* the equinox, *among the six parts of the year*.' This too proves that the tradition as given in the first table is correct." Cf. *Bhagavad-Gîtâ*, x. 35.

P. 218.—Compare the table of the *nakshatras* with E. Burgess, *Sûrya Siddhânta*, p. 468.

P. 219.—*Varâhamihira*.—*Vide* note to p. 54.

P. 220.—The Greek names *kriya* κριός, *tâmbiru* ταῦρος, *jituma* δίδυμοι, *pârtîna* παρθένος, &c., are declared to be not generally known. *Cf.* A. Weber, *Indische Studien*, ii. 259. Instead of *jitu* read *cetthu*.

P. 222. *Galenus*.—I have not been able to verify this quotation about Asclepius in the Greek works of Galenus.

P. 223. *From the belief of the nations who lived in ancient times in and round Babel, &c.*—That information to which the author here refers was probably derived from the books of the Manichæans.

P. 223. *Plato.*—This quotation is not identical with *Timæus* 36 B–D, but apparently derived therefrom. It runs :—

*ταύτην οὖν τὴν ξύστασιν πᾶσαν διπλῆν κατὰ μῆκος σχίσας μέσην πρὸς μέσην, κ.τ.λ. τὴν δ' ἐντὸς σχίσας ἑξαχῇ ἑπτὰ κύκλους ἀνίσους, κ.τ.λ.*

*Cf.* note to p. 35.

Pp. 223, 224.—On *Brahmagupta* and *Pulisa*, *v.* notes to pp. 153, 154.

P. 225. *Vasishṭha, Âryabhaṭa.*—The author does not take the theories of these men from their own works ; he only knew them by the quotations in the works of Brahmagupta. He himself states so expressly with regard to Âryabhaṭa. *Cf.* note to p. 156, and the author, i. 370.

P. 225, 227. *Balabhadra.*—*Vide* note to p. 156.

P. 226. *Aristotle.* *Cf.* his *Phys.* vii. 1, and *Metaph.* xii. 8, 24.

P. 226. *Ptolemy.*—*Cf.* the edition of Halma, Paris, 1813, tome i. p. 2 :

*τὸ μὲν τῆς τῶν ὅλων πρώτης κινήσεως πρῶτον αἴτιον, εἴ τις κατὰ τὸ ἁπλοῦν ἐκλαμβάνοι, θεὸν ἀόρατον καὶ ἀκίνητον ἂν ἡγήσαιτο, καὶ τὸ τούτου ζητητέον εἶδος θεολογικὸν, ἄνω που περὶ τὰ μετεωρότατα τοῦ κόσμου τῆς τοιαύτης ἐνεργείας νοηθείσης ἂν μόνον, καὶ καθάπαξ κεχωρισμένης τῶν αἰσθητῶν οὐσίων.*

P. 226. *Johannes Grammaticus.*—*Vide* note to p. 36. I have not been able to find this quotation in the Greek text.

Pp. 228, 229.—The author repeatedly complains of the great verbosity of the Sanskrit caused by the necessities of the authors, who will only write in metre, and require a great number of synonyms, in order that one word may fit into the metre if others will not. *Cf.* i. 213, 217, 299.

P. 229. *For those men who, &c.*—This is the only passage in which Alberuni clearly speaks of his Pandits. Apparently he tried hard to learn Sanskrit, but could not succeed on account of the difficulties of which he himself complains, and he studied Indian literature in the same manner as the first English scholars in Bengal, by the help of native Pandits.

P. 230. Table.—*Cf. Vishṇu-Purâṇa*, ii. 209, where the fifth and seventh earths are called *mahâtala* and *pâtâla*.

Also the *Vâyu-Purâṇa* (ed. Rajendralâlâ Mitra, Calcutta, 1880) offers somewhat different names, viz. *atalam*, *sutalam*, *vitalam*, *gabhastalam*, *mahâtalam*, *śrîtalam*, *pâtâlam*, and *kṛishṇa-bhaumam*, *pâṇḍu*, *raktam*, *pîta*, *śarkara*, *śilâmayam*, *sauvarṇa* (vol. i. p. 391, v. 11–14).

P. 231. *The spiritual beings, &c.*—This list of names is literally taken from *Vâyu-Purâṇa*, vol. i. p. 391, v. 15–394, v. 43 (*Adhyâya*, 50).

P. 231. *Johannes Grammaticus.*—I have not been able to find this quotation in the Greek text, nor the verse of Homer. *Vide* note to p. 36.

P. 231. *Plato.*—Cf. *Timæus*, 41A:—

Θεοὶ θεῶν ὧν ἐγὼ δημιουργὸς πατήρ τε ἔργων, ἃ δι' ἐμοῦ γενόμενα ἄλυτα ἐμοῦ γ' ἐθέλοντος· τὸ μὲν οὖν δὴ δεθὲν πᾶν λυτόν, τό γε μὴν καλῶς ἁρμοσθὲν καὶ ἔχον εὖ λύειν ἐθέλειν κακοῦ.

P. 232. *Vishṇu-Purâṇa.*—The seven lokas. *Vide* ii. 226, 227.

P. 232. *The commentator of the book of Patañjali.*—*Cf.* note to p. 27.

P. 233. *Dibajât.*—This remark was already made on p. 210.

P. 235. *Vishṇu-Purâṇa.*—*Vide* the *dvîpas* and seas, *Vishṇu-Purâṇa*, ii. 109.

P. 236. *Lokâloka*, which means a *not-gathering place*. Apparently the author had not quite understood the nature of the compound *loka-aloka*, i.e. *world and not-world*.

P. 237. *Vishṇu-Purâṇa.*—The first quotation seems to correspond to ii. 211–213, the second to ii. 204, and the third (on p. 238) to ii. 225–227.

*Śeshâkhya* is apparently a mistake for *Śesha-âkhya*, i.e. *having the name of Śesha*.

P. 240.—The story of Viśvâmitra's attempt at creating a second world is taken from *Râmâyaṇa*, i. chaps. lvii.–lx.; but here the king is called *Triśaṅku*.

P. 240.—On *Śrîpâla*, *v.* note to p. 164. The city of Multân is in various places mentioned by the author in such a remarkable manner as makes me think that he knew it, and that he had lived there for some time. When King Maḥmûd, A.H. 408 (A.D. 1017), had returned from Khwârizm-Khîva after the conquest of the country, and had carried along with him the princes of the conquered house of Ma'mûn, many scholars (among them Alberuni), officers, and soldiers, did he send some of these (among them Alberuni) as state prisoners to Multân, which he had conquered years before? In this way, nineteen years later (A.H. 427), the princes of the family of Altuntash, who had ruled Khwârizm after the Ma'mûnis, were treated by Maḥmûd's grandson, Majdûd, who sent them as state prisoners to Lahore. At all events, it is perfectly certain that Alberuni cannot have been in favour with King Maḥmûd, or he would have dedicated one of his books to him. *Cf.* Sachau, *Zur ältesten Geschichte und Chronologie von Khwârizm*, i. pp. 16, 28.

P. 240.—*Aljaihânî* is one of the fathers of Muslim literature on geography and travels in the eastern part of the Khaliphate, minister of one of the Sâmânî kings of Central Asia towards the end of the ninth Christian century. His work is most extensively quoted, but has not yet come to light. *Cf.* Aloys Sprenger, *Die Post- und Reiserouten des Orients*, Vorrede, p. xvii.

P. 241. *When Brahman wanted*, &c.—On the division of Brahman, on Dhruva, &c., *cf.* *Vishṇu-Purâṇa*, i. pp. 104, 161 *seq.*

P. 242. 1020 *to* 1030 *stars.*—This is the number of stars enumerated in the star-catalogue of 'Abdurraḥmân Ṣûfî (*cf.* Schjellerup, *Description des Étoiles fixes par Alṣûfî*, St. Petersburg, 1874), which Alberuni has transferred into his *Canon Masudicus.*

*Should those men breathe and receive*, &c.—I am not quite certain whether I have found out the right meaning of these words or not.

P. 243. *The commentator Balabhadra*, &c.—*Vide* note to p. 156.

P. 245, l. 10.—The values here given correspond to the greatest declination of 24°. So AT = 1397′ is the sine of 24°, BT = 298′ the versed sine of 24°, and TH the difference between this latter and the radius 3438′ (*Schram*).

P. 245, l. 12. *Kardajât.*—The word *kardaja* seems to be derived from the Persian *karda* = *cut*, meaning a *segment.* The radius is equal to 3438 minutes of the periphery, which are called *kardajât.* *Cf.* i. 275, and ii. 205.

P. 246, 1.—Read 24° instead of 23°.

P. 246. *Âryabhaṭa of Kusumapura* is repeatedly quoted by Alberuni. He mentions the orders of the numbers from *ayutam* to *parapadma*, i. 176. Here he speaks of the height of Mount Meru, on the longitude of Kurukshetra, i. 316 (where he quotes Pulisa and Pṛithusvâmin), on the day of the Devas and that of the Pitaras, i. 330. He calls the *cashaka vinâḍî*, i. 335. From a book of his it is quoted that 1008 *caturyugas* are one day of Brahman; half of it is *utsarpiṇî*, the other half *avasarpiṇî* (Jaina terms), i. 371. Unfortunately I cannot read the title of this book; the signs may be الننف, and it must remain uncertain whether it is an Arabic word with the article or an Indian one.

Alberuni warns the reader not to confound this Âryabhaṭa with the elder scholar of this name, to whose followers he belongs. In this place (i. 246) Alberuni does not seem to have used a work of Âryabhaṭa *junior* himself, but to have taken these words of his from a commentary of Balabhadra. We learn here that the book had been translated into Arabic, but do not learn which particular work of Balabhadra's. Was it his commentary on the *Khaṇḍakhâdyaka* of Brahmagupta? *Vide* note to p. 156. That Alberuni had made a new edition of the Arabic version of the *Khaṇḍakhâdyaka* is known (*v.* edition of the Arabic original, pref. p. xx.); perhaps he had also procured himself an Arabic translation of Balabhadra's commentary. *Cf.* on this younger Âryabhaṭa, Kern, *Bṛhat Sañhitâ*, preface, pp. 59, 60, and Dr. Bhâu Dâjî, "Brief Notes on the Age and Authenticity of the Works of Âryabhaṭa, Varâhamihira," &c., p. 392. Alberuni always calls him Âryabhaṭa of Kusumapura (Patna), to distinguish him from his elder namesake.

P. 247. *Śuktibâm.*—This seems to be some vernacular form for *Śuktimat. Vishṇu-Purâṇa*, ii. 127. Rikshabâm =*Ṛiksharat* (?).

P. 248. *The Vishṇu-Purâṇa says.*—I do not find this quotation in the *Vishṇu-Purâṇa. Cf. V. P.* ii. 117.

P. 248. *The commentator of the book of Patañjali.*—*Vide* note to p. 27.

P. 249. *Alerânshahrî.*—*Vide* note to pp. 6, 7.

P. 249. *Ardiyâ* and Girnagar (?) are apparently the same mountains which the Avesta calls *hara berezaiti* and *taera*.

P. 254. *Vishṇu-Purâṇa.*—The quotations from the *V. P.* given in this chapter are found in ii. p. 191 *seq.*

P. 254.—*Jaunu*, as here the river Yamunâ is called, corresponds to the Prakrit form prescribed by Vararuci ii. 3, viz. *Jauṇâ*.

P. 257. *Vâyu-Purâṇa.*—The names of the rivers are

found in the 45th *Adhyâya*, vol. i. pp. 349–350. The order of enumeration of the mountains in the Sanskrit text is this: Pâriyâtra, Ṛiksha, Vindhya, Sahya, Malaya, Mahendra, Śukti.

V. 97.

vedasmṛitir vedavatî vṛitradhnî sindhur eva ca
varṇâśâ candanâ caiva satîrâ mahatî tathâ.

V. 98.

parâ carmmaṇvatî caiva vidiśâ vetravaty api
śiprâ hy avantî ca tathâ pâriyâtrâsrayâḥ smṛitâḥ.

V. 99.

śoṇo mahânadaś caiva narmmadâ sumahâdrumâ
mandâkinî daśârṇâ ca citrakûṭâ tathaiva ca.

V. 100.

tamasâ pipyalâ śroṇî karatoyâ piśâcikâ
nîlotpalâ vipâśâ ca bañjulâ bâluvâhinî.

V. 101.

siterajâ śuktimatî makruṇâ tridivâ kramât
ṛikshapâdât prasûtâs tâ nadyo maṇinibhodakâḥ.

V. 102.

tâpî payoshṇî nirbbandhyâ madrâ ca nishadhâ nadî
venvâ vaitaraṇî caiva śitivâhuḥ kumudvatî.

V. 103.

toyâ caiva mahâgaurî durgâ câ 'ntaḥśilâ tathâ
vindhyapâdapraśûtâś ca nadyaḥ puṇyajalâḥ śubhâḥ.

V. 104.

godâvarî bhîmarathî kṛishṇâ vaiṇy atha vañjulâ
tuṅgabhadrâ suprayogâ kâuverî ca tathâ, pagâ
dakshiṇâpathanadyas tu sahyapâdâd viniḥsṛitâḥ.

V. 105.

kṛitamâlâ tâmravarṇâ pushpajâty utpalâvatî
malayâbhijâtâs tâ nadyaḥ sarvâḥ śitajalâḥ śubhâḥ.

V. 106.

trisâmâ ṛitukûlyâ ca ikshulâ tridivâ ca yâ
lâṅgûlinî vaṁśadharâ mahendratanayâḥ smṛitâḥ.

V. 107.

ṛishikâ sukumârî ca mandagâ mandavâhinî
kûpâ palâśinî caiva śuktimatprabhavâḥ smṛitâḥ.

P. 259.—Very similar to this enumeration of rivers is that in the *Vâyu-Purâṇa*, adhyâya 45, vv. 94–108:—

V. 94.

pîyante yair imâ nadyo gaṅgâ sindhusarasvatî
śatadruś candrabhâgâ ca yamunâ sarayûs tathâ.

V. 95.

irâvati vitastâ ca vipâśâ devikâ kuhûḥ
gomatî dhutapâpâ ca bâhudâ ca dṛishadvatî.

V. 96.

kauśikî ca tṛitîyâ tu niścirâ gaṇḍakî tathâ
ikshu lohita ityetâ himavatpâdaniḥsṛitâḥ.

The following verse, already given in the note to p. 273, mentions the rivers flowing from the Pâriyâtra.

P. 259. *Vedasinî.*—Write *Vidâsinî.*

P. 259. *Kâyabish.*—The realm of Kâyabish is here identified with Kâbul. The signs may be read *Kâyabish* or *Kâyabshi*; only the consonants are certain. This reminds one forcibly of the name of the Indo-Scythian king *Kadaphes.* A dental sound between two vowels may in later forms be represented by a *y*, as *e.g.* in *Biyattu* = *Vitastâ.* Or is the word to be combined with Panini's *Kâpishî* (*Capissene* in Pliny)? *Cf.* Paṇini and the geography of Afghanistan and the Panjâb in "Indian Antiquary," 1872, p. 21.

P. 259. *Ghûzak.*—This pass (*'aḳaba* in Arabic) is also mentioned in Elliot, "History of India," ii. 20, 449 (Ghûrak).

P. 259. *Below the town of Parvân.*—It is mentioned in the maps at about the distance of eight miles, as the crow flies, north of Tschârikar. The road from Anderâb to Parvân has been sketched by Sprenger, *Post- und Reiserouten*, map nr. 5.

P. 259. *The rivers Nûr and Ḳirâ.*—Read *Ḳirâṭ* instead of Ḳirâ. *Cf.* Elliot, *l. c.* ii. 465.

P. 260.—*Bhâtul* seems to mean a sub-Himalayan country between the Beas and the Satlej. It occurs only here and p. 211 (together with Antarvedi). Masudi (Elliot, "History of India," i. 22) mentions it as the name of one of the five rivers of Panjab.

*The union of the seven rivers.*—This tradition apparently refers to the *hapta hendu* of the Avastâ, Vendidad i. 73.

P. 261. *Matsya-Purâṇa.*—Not having this book at hand, I give the corresponding passage from the *Vâyu-Purâṇa*, adhyâya 47, vv. 38–58:—

V. 38.

nadyâḥ śrotas tu gaṅgâyâḥ pratyapadyata saptadhâ
nalinî hrâdinî caiva pâvanî caiva prâggatâ.

V. 39.

sitâ cakshuś ca sindhuś ca pratîcîṁ diśam âśritâḥ
saptamî tv anugâ tâsâṁ dakshiṇena bhagîrathî, &c.

V. 42.

upagacchanti tâḥ sarvâ yato varshati vâsavaḥ
sirindhrân kuntalâṇs cînân varvarân yavasân druhân.

V. 43.

rushâṇâṁś ca kuṇindâṁsca aṅgalokavarâṁś ca ye
kṛitvâ dvidhâ sindhumaruṁ sitâ 'gât paścimodadhiṁ.

V. 44.

atha cînamarûṁś caiva naṅgaṇân sarvamûlikân
sâdhrâṁs tushârâṁs tampâkân pahlavân daradân śakân
etân janapadân cakshuḥ srâvayanti gato 'dadhiṁ.

V. 45.

daradâṁś ca sakâśmirân gândhârân varapân hradân
śivapaurân indrahâsân vadâtiṁś ca visarjayân.

V. 46.

saindhavân randhrakarakân bhramarâbhirarohakân
śunâmukhâṁs cordhvamanûn siddhacâraṇasevitân.

V. 47.

gandharvân kinnarân yakshân rakshovidyâdharoragân
kalâpagrâmakâṁś caiva pâradân sîgaṇân khasân.

V. 48.

kirâtâṁś ca pulindâṁś ca kurûn sabharatân api
pañcâlakâśimâtsyâṁś ca magadhâṅgâṁs tathaiva ca.

V. 49.

brahmottarâṁś ca vaṅgâṁśca tâmaliptâṁs tathaiva ca
etân janapadân âryyân gaṅgâ bhâvayate śubhân.

V. 50.

tataḥ pratihatâ vindhye pravishṭâ dakshiṇodadhim
tataś câ 'hlâdinî puṇyâ prâcinâbhimukhî yayau.

V. 51.

plâvayanty upabhogâṁś ca nishâdânâñ ca jâtayaḥ
ghivarân ṛishakâṁś caiva tathâ nilamukhân api.

V. 52.

keralân ushṭrakarṇâṁś ca kirâtân api caiva hi
kâlodarân vivarṇâṁś ca kumârân svarṇabhûshitân.

V. 53.

sâ maṇḍale samudrasya tirobhûtâ 'nupûrvataḥ
tatas tu pâvanî caiva prâcim eva diśaṅ gatâ.

V. 54.

apathân bhâvayantî 'ha indradyumnasaro pi ca
tathâ kharapathâṁś caiva indraśaṅkupathân api.

V. 55.

madhyen 'dyânamaskarân kuthaprâvaraṇân yayau
indradvîpasamudre tu pravishṭâ lavaṇodadhiṁ.

V. 56.

tataś ca nalinî câ 'gât prâcimâśâṁ javena tu
tomarân bhâvayanti ha haṁsamârgân sahûhukân.

V. 57.

pûrvân deśâṁs ca sevanti bhittvâ sâ bahudhâ girîn
karṇaprâvaraṇâṁś caiva prâpya câ 'śvamukhân api.

V. 58.

sikatâparvatamarûn gatvâ vidyâdharân yayau
nemimaṇḍalakoshṭhe tu pravishṭâ sâ mahodadhiṁ.

P. 262. *Vishṇu-Purâṇa.*—This quotation occurs *V. P.* ii. 192. Instead of Anutapata, Shikhi, and Karma, read *Anutaptâ, Śikhi,* and *Kramu.*

P. 263. *Created.*—This word seems to prove that Alberuni already adhered to the dogma of orthodox Islam, that the Koran had been created by God from all eternity, and had been preserved on a table in heaven before God revealed it to mankind by the mouth of his prophet, Muḥammad.

P. 264. *Ibn Almuḳaffa'* ('Abdallâh) and *'Abdalkarîm* are also mentioned in the author's "Chronology of Ancient Nations," pp. 80 and 108.

P. 265. *For this the astronomers requite them, &c.*—When writing these criticisms, the author probably thought of Brahmagupta. *Cf.* the chapter on eclipses, ii. 110 *seq.*

P. 267. *Yamakoṭi, Laṅkâ, &c.*—*Cf.* the same names in *Sûrya-Siddhânta,* xii. 38–40.

P. 268. *Âryabhaṭa, Vasishṭha, Lâṭa.*—All the astronomers quoted in this context were not known to the author from their own works, but only through quotations in the works of Brahmagupta. Also the words of Varâhamihira (here and p. 272) seem to be quotations of Brahmagupta (evidently p. 276), although they possibly might have been taken from Varâhamihira's *Pañcasiddhântikâ*. Pulisa, of course, must be excepted, as his *Siddhânta* was in the hands of Alberuni, and in course of being translated by him.

P. 271. *Amarâvatî, Vaivasvata, &c.*—*Cf.* on these four cities *Vishṇu-Purâṇa*, ii. 240.

P. 273. *Âpta-purâṇa-kâra.*—I do not see how the Arabic signs must be read. The translation of the term means *the true ones who follow the Purâṇa.*

P. 274, l. 37.—TA being the sine of $3\frac{3}{4}°$ is equal to 225′, its square to 50,625; TB the versed sine of $3\frac{3}{4}°$ is 7′, and HT = radius — TB = 3438′ — 7 = 3431 (*Schram*).

P. 275, l. 3.—The following calculation seems to have been made very negligently, for there are several faults in it. The radius 795° 27′ 16″ is correctly determined, for employing the ratio 7 : 22 between diameter and circumference, we are indeed led to this number. But already in the determination of BC there is a fault. Alberuni seems to have converted 0° 7′ 42″ into yojanas, instead of converting 0° 7′ 45″; for 360° being equivalent to 5000 yojanas, we get for 1° 13 yojana, 7 krośa, $444\frac{4}{9}$ yards, for 1′ 1 krośa, $3407\frac{11}{27}$ yards, and for 1″ $123\frac{37}{81}$ yards, and reckoning with those numbers we get 0° 7′ 42″, and not 0° 7′ 45″, which corresponds to 57,035 yards. Further, the rule he makes use of is completely erroneous; it is not true that the relation between the height of two observers is the same as the relation between the sines of their respective fields of vision. If this were the case, we should have $\sec \alpha - 1 : \sin \alpha = \sec \beta - 1 : \sin \beta$, or the quotient $\frac{\sec \alpha - 1}{\sin \alpha}$ would be a constant for every value of $\alpha$, which, of course, is not the case. But even with his incorrect rule we cannot find the numbers he has found. This rule is 4 yards : sine of field of vision = 57,035 yards : 225′, so one would have sine of field of vision $= \frac{4 \times 225'}{57035}$; but he finds the sine of the field of vision equal to 0° 0′ 1″ 3‴, which corresponds to $\frac{1000'}{57035}$, and not to $\frac{900'}{57035}$. Therefore Alberuni seems to have reckoned $4 \times 225 = 1000$ instead of 900. Also the length of each degree is not quite correct; it is not 13 yojana, 7 krośa, $333\frac{1}{3}$ yards, but, as above stated, 13 yojana, 7 krośa, $444\frac{4}{9}$ yards. Lastly, if we convert by means of this *number* 0° 0′ 1″ 3‴ into yards, we find $129\frac{5}{9}$ yards, so that the $291\frac{5}{9}$ yards he speaks of seem to have been arrived at by an erroneous metathesis of the original ciphers (*Schram*).

P. 277. *Prâṇa.*—*Cf.* on this measure of time here i. 334, 335.

P. 278. *The inhabitants of Mount Meru, &c.*, till *as a westward motion*, almost identical with *Sûrya-Siddhânta*, xii. 55.

P. 281. *There is a story of an ancient Greek, &c.*—Probably taken from Porphyry's book on the opinions of the most prominent philosophers about the nature of the sphere. *Vide* note to p. 43.

P. 289. *The Greeks determined, &c.*—The author has given a description of the winds, according to the Arabian and Persian views, in his "Chronology of Ancient Nations," pp. 340, 341.

P. 291. *Atri, Daksha, &c.*—The legends here referred to are found in *Vishṇu-Purâṇa*, i. 153, ii. 21 *seq.*

P. 294.—*The Ṛishi Bhuvana-kośa* (*i.e.* globe) is only mentioned in this place, and not known to me from other sources. His work, the title of which is not given, seems to have treated of geography.

P. 295. *Samnâra* (?).—Thus the manuscript seems to have it. The signs may also be read *Samnâd.*

P. 297. *Kûrmacakra.*—*Vide* on this term a note of H. Kern, *Bṛihat Saṁhitâ*, translation, to the title (*kûrmavibhâga*) of chap. xiv.

P. 298. *Utpala, a native of Kashmîr.*—*Vide* note to p. 157.

P. 298.—*Stone-tower, i.e.* the *Λίθινος πύργος* of Ptolemy, vi. 13, 2.

P. 299.—Bûshang, a place near Herat, to the west. Sakilkand, also Iskilkand, is identified with *Alexandria* by Elliot, "History of India," i. 366, note 1. Perhaps it is identical with Σιγὰλ πόλις of Stephanus. *Cf.* Droysen, *Geschichte des Hellenismus*, iii. 2, 217.

P. 299.—This extract from *Vâyu-Purâṇa* is found in *adhyâya* 45, vol. i. pp. 350–353, vv. 109–136. Alberuni gives the directions in the following order: east, south, west, north; whilst the Sanskrit text has this order: north, east, south, west. In comparing the following text with Alberuni, the *varietas lectionis* given in the footnotes of the Calcutta edition can sometimes be used with advantage.

V. 109.

kurupâñcalâḥ śâlvâś caiva sajâṅgalâḥ

V. 110.

śûrasenâ bhadrakârâ bodhâḥ śatapatheśvaraiḥ
vatsâḥ kisashṭâ kulyâś ca kuntalâḥ kâśikośalâḥ.

V. 111.

atha pârśvê tilaṅgâś ca magadhâś ca vṛikaiḥ saha.

V. 115.—North.

vâhlîkâ vâḍhadhânâś ca âbhîrâḥ kâlatoyakâḥ
aparîtâś ca śûdrâś ca pahlavâś carmakhaṇḍikâḥ.

V. 116.

gândhârâ yavanâś caiva sindhusauvîrabhadrakâḥ
śakâ hradâḥ kulindâś ca paritâ hârapûrikâḥ.

V. 117.

ramaṭâ raddhakaṭakâḥ kekayâ daśamânikâḥ
kshatriyopaniveśâś ca vaiśyaśûdrakulâni ca.

V. 118.

kâmbojâ daradâś caiva varvarâḥ priyalaukikâḥ
pînâś caiva tushârâś ca pahlavâ vâhyatodarâḥ.

V. 119.

âtreyâś ca bharadvâjâḥ prasthalâś ca kaserukâḥ
lampâkâ stanapâś caiva pîḍikâ juhuḍaiḥ saha.

V. 120.

apagâś câ 'limadrâś ca kirâtânâñ ca jâtayaḥ
tomârâ haṁsamârgâśca kâśmîrâs taṅgaṇâs tathâ.

V. 121.

cûlikâś câ hukâś caiva pûrṇadarvâs tathaiva ca

V. 122.—East.

andhravâkâḥ sujarakâ antargiri vahirgirâḥ
tathâ pravaṅgavaṅgeyâ mâladâ mâlavarttinaḥ.

V. 123.

brahmottarâḥ pravijayâ bhârgavâ geyamarthakâḥ
prâgjyotishâś ca muṇḍâś ca videhâs tâmaliptakâḥ
mâlâ magadhagovindâḥ.

V. 124B.—South.

pâṇḍyâś ca keralâś caiva caulyâḥ kulyâs tathaiva ca
setukâ mûshikâś caiva kumanâ vanavâsikâḥ
mahârâshṭrâ mâhishakâḥ kaliṅgâś ca.

V. 126.

abhîrâḥ saha cai 'shîkâ âṭavyâś ca varâś ca ye
pulindrâ vindhyamûlikâ vaidarbhâ daṇḍakaiḥ saha.

V. 127.

pinikâ maunikâś caiva asmakâ bhogavarddhanâḥ
nairṇikâḥ kuntalâ andhrâ udbhidâ nalakâlikâḥ.

V. 128.

dâkshiṇâtyâś ca vaideśâ aparâṅs tân nibhodhata
śûrpâkârâḥ kolavanâ durgâḥ kalîtakaiḥ saha.

V. 129.

puleyâś ca surâlâś ca rûpasâs tâpasaiḥ saha
tathâ turasitâś caiva sarvê caiva parâksharâḥ.

V. 130.

nâsikyâ 'dyâś ca ye cânye ye caivâ 'ntaranarmadâḥ
bhânukacchrâḥ samâheyâḥ sahasâ śâśvatair api.

V. 131.

kacchîyâś ca surâshṭrâs, ca anarttâś câ 'rvudaiḥ saha.

V. 132.—West.

mâlavâś ca karûshâś ca mekalâśco 'tkalaiḥ saha
uttamarṇâ daśârṇâś ca bhojâḥ kishkindhakaiḥ saha.

V. 133.

tosalâḥ kosalâś caiva traipurâ vaidikâs tathâ
tumurâs tumburâś caiva shaṭsurâ nishadhaiḥ saha.

V. 134.

anupâs tuṇḍikerâś ca vitihotrâ hy avantayaḥ.

V. 135.

nigarharâ haṁsamârgâḥ kshupaṇâs taṅgaṇâḥ khasâḥ.

V. 136.

kuśaprâvaraṇâś caiva hûṇâ darvâḥ sahûdakâḥ
trigarttâ mâlavâś caiva kirâtâs tâmasaiḥ saha.

Pp. 300–303.—This extract from Varâhamihira's *Samhitâ* is taken from chap. xiv. *Cf.* the text in Kern's edition, p. 87, the *varietas lectionis*, pp. 12–14, and his translation in "Journal of the Asiatic Society," 1870, p. 81–86. The number of discrepancies between these two traditions is very considerable. In many places Alberuni and his Pandit may not have read their manuscript with sufficient accuracy; in others, the Sanskrit manuscript-tradition may exhibit blunders arising from a not uncommon confusion of characters that are much like each other. The Arabic manuscript-tradition is on the whole correct, but the copyist of the Arabic text, too, may have contributed in some case to increase the number of errors. To some Indian names he has added explanatory glosses, *e.g. Saurîra, i.e.* Mûltân and Jahrâvâr. It is a pity he has done this so sparingly.

P. 303.—*Ya'kûb and Alfazârî.*—*Vide* notes to pp. 169 and 165.

P. 304.—*Abû-Ma'shar*, author of many books, chiefly on astrology, died A.H. 272 = A.D. 885. He is known to the Middle Ages in Europe as Albumaser.

P. 306. *Cupola of the earth.*—If this expression has not been derived from the Indian, the question arises, Who introduced it among the Arabs? Was it Alfazârî?

P. 306. *Râvaṇa the demon.*—The author refers to the fifth and sixth books of the *Râmâyaṇa*, which he apparently did not know, or he would not have called it, as he constantly does, *the story of Râma and Râmâyaṇa*; *v.* pp. 307, 310, and ii. 3. I have not succeeded in deciphering the name of the fortress; the Arabic signs cannot be combined with the name Trikûṭa.

P. 308.—*A straight line from Laṅkâ to Meru* is also mentioned on p. 316. The first degree of longitude, according to the Indian system, is also described in *Sûrya-Siddhânta*, i. 62. Instead of Kurukshetra the author seems to have pronounced *Kurukketra.* At all events, he did not write a *sh*. Therefore the compound *ksh* must have undergone the Prakritic change into *kkh*, as in *pokkharo*=*pushkara* (Vararuci, iii. 29).

P. 309.—*These wares are deposited, &c.*—This kind of commerce with savage nations is the same as that carried on by Carthage with tribes on the west coast of Africa; *v.* Herodotus, iv. 196; C. Müller, *Geographi Græci Minores*, i. p. xxvii., and Meltzer, *Geschichte der Karthager*, p. 232 and 506.

P. 310.—*Langabâlûs* is identified with the Nicobar

Islands by A. Sprenger, *Post- und Reiserouten des Orients*, p. 88.

P. 312. *Deśântara.*—*Vide* the rule for its computation in *Sûrya-Siddhânta*, i. 60, 61.

*Alarkand, Ibn Ṭârik.*—*Cf.* note to p. 169.

P. 312.—*Al-arkand* is identified by Alberuni with the *Khaṇḍakhâdyaka* of Brahmagupta (ii. 7). In another place (ii. 48) the author identifies the word *arkand* with *ahargaṇa*. Both of these identifications can hardly be justified phonetically, and therefore I prefer to suppose as the Sanskrit original of *Arkand* a word like *Âryakhaṇḍa*, whilst apparently the word *harkan* (title of an Arabic calendar, ii. 52) is identical with *ahargaṇa*.

The author complains of the Arabic translation of *Al-arkand* being a bad one, and at some time of his life (probably after the composition of the *Indica*) he has published a new and amended edition of this translation. *Cf.* preface to the Arabic edition, p. xx. The Arabic *Arkand* has not yet been discovered in the libraries of Europe. The author has borrowed from this book the following notes:—(1) 1050 yojanas are the diameter of the earth (i. 312, 316). (2) The latitude of Ujain is 22° 29′, and that of Almanṣûra 24° 1′ (i. 316). Here the author states that also Ya'ḳûb Ibn Ṭârik had quoted the book, but erroneously. (3) The straight shadow in Loharânii is $5\frac{3}{5}$ digits (i. 316). (4) Alberuni quotes from *Alarkand* a method for the computation of the era *Shakh*, by which the Gupta era is meant (ii. 48, 49).

P. 312.—On the relation between yojana and mile, *v.* note to p. 199.

P. 312, l. 22.—Using the ratio of 7 : 22 between diameter and circumference, we find 3300 yojanas as the circumference corresponding to a diameter of 1050 yojanas. So 3300 yojanas is the circumference of the earth given in the handbook *Al-arkand*. This agrees with the last lines of p. 315, where it is said that 3200 yojanas are 100 yojanas less than the value given by *Al-arkand* (*Schram*).

P. 313. *The author of Karaṇatilaka, i.e. Vijayanandin.* —*Vide* note to p. 156.

P. 313.—*Vyastatrairâśika* is a technical term for a certain algebraic calculation. *Cf.* Colebrooke, "Algebra," p. 34, § 76.

P. 314.—*Alfazârî in his canon,* which was a translation of the *Brahmasiddhânta* of Brahmagupta; *v.* note to pp. 153, 165.

P. 314, l. 11.—The calculation of the *deśântara* is, as Alberuni remarks, quite erroneous, as the difference of longitude is not taken into account (*Schram*).

P. 315, l. 25.—The number in the lacuna must be 80, for Alberuni says at the bottom of the page, "If we invert the calculation and reduce the parts of the great circle to yojanas, according to this method we get the number 3200." But to get 3200 we must multiply $\frac{360}{9}$ by 80. The rule, "Multiply the yojanas of the distance between two places by 9 and divide the product by 80," serves to convert this distance given in yojanas into degrees. This distance, then, is considered as the hypothenuse of a right-angled triangle, one of the sides of which is the difference of the latitudes, the other the unknown difference of the longitudes; this latter is found by taking the root of the difference of the squares of hypothenuse and known side. This difference of longitude is then expressed in degrees; to get it expressed in day-minutes we must further divide by 6, as there are 360° in a circle, but only 60 day-minutes in a day (*Schram*).

P. 316.—*The line connecting Laṅkâ with Meru,* already mentioned on p. 308.

P. 316. *Ya'ḳûb Ibn Ṭâriḳ, Alarkand.*—*Vide* note to p. 169, 312.

P. 317. *Catlaghtagîn.*—Not knowing the etymology of this Turkish name, I am also ignorant of its pronunciation. The second part of the compound seems to be *tagîn* =

*valorous*, as in Toghrultagin, *i.e. valorous like a falcon.* As جيلغن, *jîlghan*, means a large spear, one might think of reading *Jîlghattagîn*, i.e. *valorous with the spear*, but this is very uncertain. Another name of a similar formation is *kutlughtagîn, katlagh*, but probably entirely different. *Vide* Biberstein-Kazimirski, *Menoutschehri* preface, p. 136; Elliot, "History of India," ii. 352, iii. 253.

P. 317.—*Karaṇasâra* by Vitteśvara; *v.* note to p. 156.

P. 317.—The fortress *Lauhûr*, also mentioned p. 208 as Lahûr, must not be confounded with Lauhâvar or Lahore. Situation unknown. According to the author's *Canon Masudicus*, it has latitude 33° 40′, longitude 98° 20′. Comparing these latitudes with those given in Hunter's Gazetteer, we do not find that they much differ:—

| | Hunter. | Alberuni. |
|---|---|---|
| Ghazna . . . . . | 33° 34′ | 33° 35′ |
| Kâbul . . . . . | 34° 30′ | 33° 47′ |
| Peshavar . . . . . | 34° 1′ 45″ | 34° 44′ |
| Jailam . . . . . | 32° 55′ 26″ | 33° 20′ |
| Siyalkote . . . . . | 32° 31′ | 32° 58′ |
| Multân . . . . . | 30° 12′ | 29° 40′ |

On the identity of Waihand and Attok, *cf.* Cunningham, "Ancient Geography of India," p. 54.

Mandakkakor (the name is differently written) was the fortress of Lahore, according to the author's statement in his *Canon Masudicus*.

Nandna is explained by Elliot ("History of India," ii. 450, 451) as a fort on the mountain Bâlnâth, a conspicuous mountain overhanging the Jailam, and now generally called Tilla. *Cf.* also Elliot, *l. c.* ii. 346, note 347, 366.

The places Dunpûr (pronunciation perfectly uncertain) and *Kandî* (also read Kirî), *the station of the Amîr*, seem to have been on the road from Ghazna to Peshavar. Near the latter place was fought the decisive battle between King Mas'ûd and his blinded brother Muḥammad, A.D. 1040, and there the former was murdered by the relatives of those who ten years earlier had thought to win his favour by betraying his brother, and were killed or maltreated in reward. *Cf.* Elliot, *l. c.* iv. 199, note 1, 138, ii. 150, 112 (Persian text, p. 274), 273, note 3.

I conjecture Dunpûr to have been identical with Jalalabad or some place near it. Latitude of Jalalabad, 34° 24′; that of Dunpûr, 34° 20′.

*Kandî*, more southern than Dunpûr and nearer to Kâbul, must have been a place like Gandamak or near it. If it is called *the station (post-relai) of the Amîr*. We may understand by this Amîr the father of King Maḥmûd, the Amîr Sabuktagîn, who first constructed the roads leading to the Indian frontier, as Alberuni informs us on p. 22.

On the identification of Bamhanwâ or Almansûra in Sindh, *v.* Cunningham, *l. l.* p. 271 *seq.*

The statements of Alberuni regarding the Kabul valley and environs have been laid down in a sketch-map of Aloys Sprenger, *Post- und Reiserouten des Orients*, No. 12; the Punjâb and the approaches of Kashmîr, ibid. No. 13.

P. 319.—*Muḥammad Ibn*, &c., is the famous *Razes* of the Middle Ages, who died probably A.D. 932. The author has written a catalogue of his works which exists in Leyden; *v. Chronologie Orientalischer Völker von Alberuni*, Einleitung, p. xi.; Wüstenfeld, *Geschichte der Arabischen Aerzte*, No. 98.

P. 320.—*Alexander of Aphrodisias* is the famous commentator of Aristotle, who lived in Athens about 200 after Christ. *Cf.* Fihrist, p. 252, and Zeller, *Geschichte der Griechischen Philosophie*, 3, 419. The quotation is found in Aristotle, *Phys.* vii. 1.

P. 320. *Varâhamihira.*—This quotation corresponds to *Saṁhitâ*, i. v. 6, 7. Instead of Kumbhaka the Sanskrit text has Kaṇâda.

P. 322. *Timæus.*—This quotation seems to be derived from 42 D E:—

τὸ δὲ μετὰ τὸν σπόρον τοῖς νέοις παρέδωκε θεοῖς σώματα πλάττειν θνητά, κ.τ.λ. καὶ λαβόντες ἀθάνατον ἀρχὴν θνητοῦ ζώου, κ.τ.λ.

In the Arabic text, p. ١٦٣, 17, read ماتنة instead of مانّية, and ماتنا instead of مانّيا.

P. 324. *That being who is above him, i.e.* a being of the next higher order.—The opposite of the term لمن يعلوه is لمن دونه (for the being of the next lower order) on p. ١٧٧, 20 (translation i. 351).

P. 325. *Vishṇu-Purâṇa.*—The first words, *Maharloká lies, &c., there is one kalpa,* are found in ii. chap. vii. p. 226. The sons of Brahman are mentioned in *Vishṇu-Purâṇa,* ii. 200, note. The name Sanandanâda (Sananda-nâtha?) is perhaps a mistake for Sanâtana. *Cf. Sâṁkhya Kârikâ* with the commentary of Gauḍapâda by Colebrooke-Wilson, p. 1.

P. 325. *Abû-Ma'shar.*—*Vide* note to p. 304.

P. 325. *Alerânshahrî.*—*Vide* note to pp. 6, 7.

P. 327. *The country without latitude, i.e. niraksha* in Sanskrit.—*Vide* p. 267, and *Sûrya-Siddhânta,* xii. 44, note.

P. 330. *Âryabhaṭa of Kusumapura, i.e.* junior.—*Cf.* note to p. 246.

P. 333.—The terms *parârdha* and *kha* have been explained, pp. 175, 178.

P. 334. *The book Srûdhava by Utpala.*—*Vide* notes to pp. 157, 158.

A system of the measures of time has also been given by Colebrooke, "Essays," i. 540 *seq.*

P. 336. *Ś-M-Y.*—This name is so written here and p. 337. The Arabic signs are to be read *Shammî* or *Shamiyyu.* I do not know a Sanskrit name of this form. Is it = *Samaya?*

The same name seems to occur a third time, ii. 188, but is there written *S-M-Y.* Alberuni says that S-M-Y had *dictated* a method for the computation of the *saṁkrânti;*

he therefore, perhaps, was a scholar of the time and a personal acquaintance (teacher ?) of Alberuni's. The title of a book of his is not mentioned.

P. 338.—*The spêd muhra* or *white shell*, an Indian blowing instrument, is also mentioned by Elliot, "History of India," ii. 215, note.

Purshûr (پرشور), as the manuscript has, is probably a mistake for پرشاور, *Purushâvar*, *i.e.* Peshavar.

P. 338. *Horæ æquinoctiales* and *temporales*.—*Vide* note to p. 214.

P. 339. *The commentator of the Siddhânta, Pulisa*.—Read instead of this, "The commentator of the Siddhânta of Pulisa," and compare note to pp. 153, 154. Who this commentator was is not mentioned.

P. 340.—*Abhijit* means the 8th *muhûrta* of the day. The Arabic form ابجتی corresponds perhaps to Sanskrit *abhijiti*.

P. 340. *Vyâsa*.—This statement points to Mahâbhârata, the Âdi-parvan, v. 4506; but the chronological detail is not found there.

P. 340. *Śiśupâla*.—*Vide* note to p. 165.

P. 342.—The names of the dominants of the *muhûrtas* are also mentioned in the following four lines taken from Aufrecht's Catalogue of the Sanskrit manuscripts of the Bodleian Library, p. 332*a* :—

rudrâhimitrapitaro vasuvârivisve vedhâ vidhiḥ śatamakhaḥ puruhûtavahnî.

naktaṁcaraś ca varuṇâryamayonayaś ca proktâ dinê daśa ca paṁca tathâ muhûrtâḥ

niśâmuhûrtâ giriśâjapâdâhirbudhnyapûshâśviyamâgnayaśca.

vidhâtṛicaṁdrâditi jîvavishṇutigmadyutitvâshṭrasamiraṇâś ca.

P. 343. *Except the astrologers.*—*Cf.* the meaning of *horâ* in astrology, ii. 222.

P. 343. *Vijayanandin.*—*Vide* note to p. 156. The title of his book would be in Arabic غرة الزيجات (*Ghurrat-alzîjât*).

P. 344. *Names of the horâs.*—I have not found these names in Sanskrit. Perhaps they are mentioned in some commentary to *Sûrya Siddhânta*, xii. 79.

On *Srûdhava*, *v.* note to p. 158.

P. 347. *Physical scholars know, &c.*—There is a similar passage on the physical effects of moonlight in the author's "Chronology of Ancient Nations," p. 163. I am afraid I have not caught the sense of the sentence, "and that she affects (?) linen clothes," &c.

P. 348. *Atuh* (?).—The MS. seems to read *âtvahhu*.

The word برية, BRBA, is perhaps a mistake for برته, *barkhu*, which, according to the table, ii. 197 (*cf.* Trumpp, "Grammar of the Sindhi Language," p. 158), is the name of the first day of a *paksha*.

P. 348. *Veda.*—The author gives six quotations from the *Veda:* one taken from *Patañjali* (i. 29), one from *Sâṁkhya* (i. 31), two from the *Brahmasiddhânta* of Brahmagupta (ii. 110, 111), and two quotations which were probably communicated to him by his Pandits, as he does not mention a particular source whence he took them (i. 348 and ii. 348).

P. 352. *Vâsudeva.*—The quotation corresponds to *Bhagavad-Gîtâ*, viii. 17.

*The book Smṛiti.*—*Vide* note to p. 131. This quotation seems to have been taken from Manu, *Dharmaśâstra*, i. 72.

P. 353.—The information on the four *mânas* (*cf. Sûrya-Siddhânta*, chap. xiv.), as given by Ya'ḳûb, was the only one at the disposal of Alberuni at the time when he wrote his "Chronology" (*v.* English edition, p. 15). It was communicated to him by the *Kitâb-alghurra* of Abû Muḥammad Alnâ'ib Alâmulî. The *four different kinds of spaces of time* mentioned there are the four *mânas, saura, sâvana, candra* and *nakshatra*.

P. 353.—*Bhukti*, in Arabic *buht*, is the daily motion of a planet; *cf. Sûrya-Siddhânta*, i. 27, note, and here, ii. 195. The Arabic form does not seem to have passed through an intermediate stage of a Prakritic nature, for in Prakrit it would have been *bhuttî* (Vararuci, iii. 1).

P. 355. *The sâvana-mâna is used, &c.*—*Cf.* the similar rules in *Sûrya-Siddhânta*, xiv. 3, 13, 15, 18, 19.

P. 356. *Uttarâyaṇa.*—On the two *ayanas cf. Sûrya-Siddhânta*, xiv. 9.

P. 357. *Ṛitu.*—*Vide* the description of the six seasons in *Sûrya-Siddhânta*, xiv. 10, 16.

P. 358. *Dominants of the halves of the months.*—I do not know a Sanskrit list of these names. The *Âśana* (*Âshunu*) perhaps means *Aśvin* or *Aśvinî*.

P. 359.—*Dimas* (probably pronounced *dimasu*) = Sanskrit *divasa*, is the shibboleth of the Indian vernacular dialect spoken round Alberuni, and probably by himself. I do not know which dialect this was, nor whether there are any traces of it in our days. The change between *v* and *m* is also observed in the following examples:—چرمنمت *carmanmat* = *carmaṇvatî* (Chambal), هممنت *himamant* = *himavant*, جاكملك *jâgamalku* = *yâjnavalkya*, مچى *maccî* = *vatsya*, سكريم *sugrîmu* = *sugrîva*. Some examples of the change of *v* to *m* are also given by Hörnle, "Comparative Grammar," § 134.

P. 359. *The three sounds h, kh, and sh, &c.*—On the pronunciation of *sh* as *kh*, *cf.* Hörnle, *l. c.* § 19, and on the further change of *kh* to *h*, ibid. § 19. Examples of the former change are numerous in the *Indica*; of examples of the latter, *cf.* منهه *munha* = *mukha*, ببرهان *babrahân* = *raprakhâna* (?), and also آهاری *âhârî*, *cf.* *âshâḍha*, کهکند *kihkind* = *kishkindha*. In Prakrit *muham* = *mukha* (Vararuci, ii. 27).

P. 361. *Srûdhava by Utpala.*—*Vide* note to p. 157.

P. 362. 1 *ghaṭî* = 16 *kalâ.*—*Cf.* with these measures of time the statements on pp. 336, 337.

P. 364, *Chapter XL.*—It has also been translated by Reinaud, *Fragments Arabes et Persans*, pp. 155–160.

P. 364. *Saṁdhi udaya* and *saṁdhi astamana.*—One would expect *saṁdhyudaya* and *saṁdhyastamana*, but there is no trace of a *y*. The forms have a vernacular character, and must be explained according to the analogy of دُتِ *duti* = *dyuti*, and انتز *antazu* = *antyaja*.

*Hiraṇyakaśipu.*—The story of this king and his son Prahlâda is told by the *Vishṇu-Purâna*, ii. 34 *seq.*

P. 366. *Saṁdhi.*—The way it is used in astrology is shown by the table, ii. 219.

P. 366. *Puñjala.*—*Vide* note to p. 157. The tradition here given is very similar to that mentioned by Colebrooke, "Essays," ii. 332, 333.

P. 366, l. 35.—We find that the beginning of the Hindu solar year 854 Sakakala takes place A.D. 932, March 22, 6 *ghaṭî* 40′ 15″, which corresponds to March 22, 7 h. 40 m. civil Greenwich time, whilst the real instant of the solstice is March 15, 12 h. 15 m. civil Greenwich time, so that the solstice precedes the calculation by 6 days and 19 hours, which agrees very well with the 6° 50′ which Puñjala mentions (*Schram*).

P. 368. *Ahargaṇa = ahar + gaṇa.*—The author's erroneous explanation is repeated ii. 26.

*Sind-hind = siddhânta.*—It may be questioned whether the inorganic *n* has been introduced into the word by the Arabs, or whether it existed already in the pronunciation of the Hindus from whom they learned the word. I do not know of a rule to this effect in Prakrit or vernacular, but there are certain Indian words which apparently show a similar phonetic process. *Cf. e.g.* Prakrit *uṭṭô* (Sanskrit, *ushṭra*), which in Eastern Hindhî has become *ũṭ* or *uñṭ*. Hörnle, "Comparative Grammar of the Gauḍian Languages," § 149.

P. 370. *Âryabhaṭa, sen.*—*Vide* note to p. 156.

Âryabhaṭa of Kusumapura. *Vide* note to p. 246.

The word I cannot decipher may be read السهـ, *i.e.* the article and three consonants with three dots above them, something like الشفف.

P. 371. *Utsarpiṇî, avarsarpiṇî,* are terms employed in the Jaina system. *Cf.* Colebrooke, "Essays," ii. 186, 194.

P. 372. *The book Smṛiti mentions.*—This is Manu, *Dharmaśâstra*, i. 80.

P. 375. *A translation of his whole work, &c.*—*Cf.* note to pp. 153, 154. Alberuni was translating the *Pulisa-Siddhânta*, which until that time had not yet been translated into Arabic by Muslim scholars, because they did not like its theological tendency.

P. 376. *Brahmagupta.*—*Vide* note to pp. 153, 154.

P. 378. In writing the introductory sentences of chap. xliii., the author seems to have had in mind Plato's *Timæus*, 22C: πολλαὶ καὶ κατὰ πολλὰ φθοραὶ γεγόνασιν ἀνθρώπων καὶ ἔσονται, κ.τ.λ.

P. 379. *The pedigree of Hippocrates* is known from Tzetzes, chil. vii. host. 115. *Cf.* "The Genuine Works of Hippocrates," translated by Fr. Adams, London, 1849, vol.

i. p. 23. The name انلوسوس seems to be a repetition of the name Hippolochos, ابولوخس. If it is dropped from the list, we have the fourteen generations which the author counts between Hippocrates and Zeus.

The Arabic ماخلون seems to be a mistake for ماخاون, *Machaon*.

P. 380. *Paraśurâma.—Vide* this legend in *Vishṇu-Purâṇa*, iv. 19 (here added from the *Mahâbhârata*).

P. 380. *Buddhodana.—Vide* my conjecture as to the origin of this name in note to p. 40.

The *Muḥammira*.—This term has been explained in note to p. 21.

P. 382. *Garga, the son of.*—The name of his father is written *Jashû* or *Jashô* (here and p. 397). Could this be Yaśodâ?

P. 382.—*'Alî Ibn Zain* was a Christian physician in Merw; *cf.* Shahrazûrî, MS. of the Royal Library, Berlin, MS. Or., octav. 217, fol. 144*b*; the same in Baihaḳî, ibid. No. 737, fol. 6*a*. According to this tradition, his son was the author of the famous medical book *Firdaus-alḥikma*. *Cf.* also Fihrist, p. 296 and notes; Wüstenfeld, *Geschichte der Arabischen Aerzte*, No. 55.

*The book Caraka.—Vide* note to p. 159.

P. 383. *Kriśa, the son of Âtreya.*—If this is what the author means, the Arabic signs مرس must be altered to برس. *Cf.* A. Weber, *Vorlesungen*, p. 284, note 309.

P. 383.—The quotation from Aratus is *Phænomena*, vv. 96–134. I give the text from Imm. Bekker, *Aratus cum Scholiis*, Berlin, 1828:—

Ἀμφοτέροισι δὲ ποσσὶν ὑποσκέπτειο Βοώτεω
Παρθένον, ἥ ῥ᾽ ἐν χερσὶ φέρει Στάχυν αἰγλήεντα.
εἴτ᾽ οὖν Ἀστραίου κείνη γένος, ὅν ῥά τέ φασιν
ἄστρων ἀρχαῖον πατέρ᾽ ἔμμεναι, εἴτε τευ ἄλλου,
εὔκηλος φορέοιτο· λόγος γε μὲν ἐντρέχει ἄλλος

ἀνθρώποις, ὡς δῆθεν ἐπιχθονίη πάρος ἦεν,
ἤρχετο δ' ἀνθρώπων κατεναντίη, οὐδέ ποτ' ἀνδρῶν
οὐδέ ποτ' ἀρχαίων ἠνήνατο φῦλα γυναικῶν,
ἀλλ' ἀναμὶξ ἐκάθητο καὶ ἀθανάτη περ ἐοῦσα.
καί ἑ Δίκην καλέεσκον· ἀγειρομένη δὲ γέροντας
ἠέ που εἰν ἀγορῇ ἢ εὐρυχόρῳ ἐν ἀγυιῇ,
δημοτέρας ἤειδεν ἐπισπέρχουσα θέμιστας.
οὔπω λευγαλέου τότε νείκεος ἠπίσταντο,
οὐδὲ διακρίσιος περιμεμφέος οὐδὲ κυδοιμοῦ·
αὔτως δ' ἔζωον. χαλεπὴ δ' ἀπέκειτο θάλασσα,
καὶ βίον οὔπω νῆες ἀπόπροθεν ἠγίνεσκον·
ἀλλὰ βόες καὶ ἄροτρα καὶ αὐτὴ πότνια λαῶν
μυρία πάντα παρεῖχε Δίκη, δώτειρα δικαίων.
τόφρ' ἦν ὄφρ' ἔτι γαῖα γένος χρύσειον ἔφερβεν.
ἀργυρέῳ δ' ὀλίγη τε καὶ οὐκέτι πάμπαν ὁμοίη
ὡμίλει, ποθέουσα παλαιῶν ἤθεα λαῶν.
ἀλλ' ἔμπης ἔτι κεῖνο κατ' ἀργύρεον γένος ἦεν.
ἤρχετο δ' ἐξ ὀρέων ὑποδείελος ἠχηέντων
μουνάξ· οὐδέ τεῳ ἐπεμίσγετο μειλιχίοισιν·
ἀλλ' ὁπότ' ἀνθρώπων μεγάλας πλήσαιτο κολώνας,
ἠπείλει δὴ ἔπειτα καθαπτομένη κακότητος,
οὐδ' ἔτ' ἔφη εἰσωπὸς ἐλεύσεσθαι καλέουσιν.
οἵην χρύσειοι πατέρες γενεὴν ἐλίποντο
χειροτέρην· ὑμεῖς δὲ κακώτερα τεξείεσθε.
καὶ δή που πόλεμοι, καὶ δὴ καὶ ἀνάρσιον αἷμα
ἔσσεται ἀνθρώποισι, κακοῖς δ' ἐπικείσεται ἄλγος.
ὣς εἰποῦσ' ὀρέων ἐπεμαίετο, τοὺς δ' ἄρα λαοὺς
εἰς αὐτὴν ἔτι πάντας ἐλίμπανε παπταίνοντας.
ἀλλ' ὅτε δὴ κἀκεῖνοι ἐτέθνασαν, οἱ δ' ἐγένοντο,
χαλκείη γενεὴ, προτέρων ὀλοώτεροι ἄνδρες,
οἳ πρῶτοι κακοεργὸν ἐχαλκεύσαντο μάχαιραν
εἰνοδίην, πρῶτοι δὲ βοῶν ἐπάσαντ' ἀροτήρων,
καὶ τότε μισήσασα Δίκη κείνων γένος ἀνδρῶν
ἔπταθ' ὑπουρανίη.

P. 384. *The commentator of the book of Aratus.*—This

commentary is not identical with the scholia edited by Bekker. *Cf. Eratosthenis Catasterismorum Reliquiæ*, rec. C. Robert, pp. 82–84.

P. 385. *Plato.*—This quotation is from *Leges*, iii. 677; but the phrases forming the conversation have been omitted.

ΑΘΗΝ. Τὸ πολλὰς ἀνθρώπων φθορὰς γεγονέναι κατακλυσμοῖς τε καὶ νόσοις καὶ ἄλλοις πολλοῖς, ἐν οἷς βραχύ τι τὸ τῶν ἀνθρώπων λείπεσθαι γένος, κ.τ.λ. ὡς οἱ τότε περιφυγόντες τὴν φθορὰν σχεδὸν ὄρειοί τινες ἂν εἶεν νομεῖς ἐν κορυφαῖς που, σμικρὰ ζώπυρα τοῦ τῶν ἀνθρώπων γένους διασεσωσμένα, κ.τ.λ. καὶ δὴ τοὺς τοιούτους γε ἀνάγκη που τῶν ἄλλων ἀπείρους εἶναι τεχνῶν καὶ τῶν ἐν τοῖς ἄστεσι πρὸς ἀλλήλους μηχανῶν εἴς τε πλεονεξίας καὶ φιλονεικίας καὶ ὁπόσ' ἄλλα κακουργήματα πρὸς ἀλλήλους ἐπινοοῦσιν.

P. 387.—*Cf.* with this table *Vishṇu-Purâṇa*, book iii. chap. i. and ii., and the Bombay edition, 1886.

*Stâmasa* seems to be a mistake for *Tâmasa*.

*Caitraka* instead of *caitra* seems to have been derived from an erroneous reading of the beginning of the Sanskrit *caitrakiṁpurushâdyâśca*.

*Sudirya* seems to have risen from a wrong division of the words *Paraśu* (other readings *Parabhu, Parama*) *Divya*. The Bombay edition reads *prajâḥparamadivyâdyâstasya*.

*Antata*, the name of Indra in the fifth Manvantara, can hardly be combined with the *Vibhu* of Sanskrit tradition.

*Sindhu, Reva.*—These words, whatever their proper pronunciation may be, are not found in the Sanskrit text.

*Puru Muru* is Sanskrit *Uru Puru*, but *Pramukha* is a gross mistake, for the text has *urupuruśatadyumnapramukhâḥ*, *i.e.* Uru, Puru, Śatadyumna, and others.

*Nabasa* and *Dhrishṇa* are mistakes for *Nabhaga* and *Dhrishṭa*.

*Virajas, Aścarvarî, Nirmogha.*—The Sanskrit text runs *viracâścorvarîvâṁścanirmohâdyâs*, which Alberuni has divided into *viraja-aścorvarîvâṁśca-nirmoha.* Cf. *Scor-*

*varî Vâṁśca* on p. 394. Wilson reads the second name *Arvarîvat*.

*Mahâvîrya*, name of Indra in the ninth Manvantara, instead of *Adbhuta*, rests on a misinterpretation of these words: *teshâm indrô mahâvîryô bhavishyatyadbhutô dvija*.

*Sudharmâtman*.—The Sanskrit text has *Sarvadharmâ*.

*Devata Vânupadevâśca*, instead of *Devavat* and *Upadeva*, rests on a wrong division of the words *devavânupadevaśca*.

*Vicitra-adyâ*, a mistake for *vicitrâdyâ*, *i.e. Vicitra and others*.

*Urur*, *Gabhî* (*sic* MS.), *Budhnya-adyâ*, a mistake for *urugabhîrabudhnyâdyâ*, *i.e. Uru*, *Gabhîra*, *Budhnya*, *and others*.

P. 388. *The same book relates*, viz., *Vishṇu-Purâṇa*, iii. p. 20.

On *Priyavrata*, *v.* ibid. ii. p. 101.

P. 389. *A pious woman*, viz., Arundhatî, v. p. 390.

P. 390. On the Seven Ṛishis, or Ursa Major, *cf.* Colebrooke, "Essays," ii. 310.

P. 391. The almanac or calendar from Kashmîr for the Śaka-year 951 (A.D. 1029) is quoted in two other places, ii. 5 and ii. 8.

P. 391. On the ancient astronomer Garga, *cf.* Kern, *Bṛhat Saṅhitâ*, preface, p. 33 *seq.*

P. 392. *Only by* 525 *years*.—*Cf.* on *Varâhamihira* note to p. 54.

P. 392. *Karaṇasâra* by Vitteśvara.—*Vide* note to p. 156.

P. 394.—This table is taken from *Vishṇu-Purâṇa*, book iii. chaps. i. and ii.

2. *Manvantara: Dattu Nirishabha*.—A mistake for *Dattoni Ṛishabha*.

*Niśvara*.—Alberuni read *Nirśava*.

*Ścorvarî Vâṁśca*.—The author has wrongly divided the

word *śeorvarîvâṁśca* (ed. Bombay *śeorvarîvâṁśca*). *Cf.* note to p. 387.

4. *Manvantara: Jyoti* (read *Jyotis*) *Dhâman.*—Mistake for *Jyotirdhâman.*

*Caitrogni*, as the author has, is a mistake for *Caitrâgnî.*

*Varaka.*—Ed. Bombay, *Vamaka; Wilson-Hall, Vanaka.*

5. *Manvantara: Rurdhrabâhu* has risen through the wrong division of the two words *vedaśrîrûrdhrabâhu.*

*Apara* has by mistake been taken for a proper noun in the following words:—*ûrdhrabâhustathâparaḥ.*

*Subâhu* (*Srabâhu?*).—The Sanskrit text has *sradhâman.*

6. *Manvantara: Atinâman.*—The Arabic text has *atimânu.* Or are we to read اتنام instead of اتمان?

*Carshayaḥ* (= *and the Ṛishis*) by mistake derived from the following passage:—*saptâsanniticarshayaḥ.*

9. *Manvantara: Harya*, in the Sanskrit tradition *Bharya.* Perhaps we must read بهب instead of هب.

*Medhâdhṛiti* (Wilson-Hall), *medhâmṛiti* (ed. Bombay). Alberuni seems to have read *Vedhâdhṛiti*, if we are not to read ميذهادت instead of بيذهادت.

10. *Manvantara: Satya* (Wilson-Hall).—The Arabic has something like *Sattayô.*

*Sukshetra.*—The Arabic has *Sushera* instead of *Satyaketu.* Perhaps the author has overlooked this word and copied the following one, viz., *Sukshetra.*

11. *Manvantara: Niścara*, in the Arabic *viścara.*

*Agnîdhra* = *Agnitejas.* The Arabic has *agnîtru* اكنيتر, which is perhaps to be changed to اكنتجز (*agnitejas*).

*Nagha.*—Wilson-Hall, *Anagha.*

12. *Manvantara: Sutaya*, in the Sanskrit text *sutapâśca.* Perhaps the author has read *sutayâśca.*

*Dyuti* and *Iścânyas* have by mistake been derived from the following verse—

*tapodhṛitirdyutiścânyaḥsaptamastutapodhanaḥ.*

13. *Manvantara: Tatvadarśica*, mistake for *Tatvadarśin*, for the Sanskrit text has *tatvadarśica.*

*Vyaya*, mistake for *Aryaya.* The author seems to have read *dhṛitimân vyayaśca* instead of *dhṛitimânaryayaśca.*

14. *Manvantara: Agniba* instead of *Agnibâhuḥ.*

*Gnîdhra.*—The ed. Bombay reads *mâgadhognîdhranvaca.* Other readings, *Grîdhra, Agnîdhra.*

*Yuktasa* and *Jita* are taken from the following verse—

*yuktas-tathâ-jitaś-cânyo-manuputrân ataḥ śṛiṇu.*

P. 395.—*Vâlakhilyas* are known as pigmy sages from the *Vishṇu-Purâṇa*, but I do not find there this story of them and Śatakratu.

P. 396. *Bali, the son of Virocana*, and his Vazîr *Venus, i.e.* Śukra.—*Vide Vishṇu-Purâṇa*, iii. p. 19, note. There is a Hindu festival called after him *Balirâjya*; *v.* ii. 182.

P. 397. *Vishṇu-Purâṇa.*—This quotation is found III. ii. p. 31.

P. 398.—The second quotation from *Vishṇu-Purâṇa* is III. iii. p. 33.

*Kali, the son of Jashô* (?).—*Vide* note to p. 382.

P. 398.—The names of the Vyâsas of the twenty-nine Dvâpara-yugas have been taken from *Vishṇu-Purâṇa*, III. iii. pp. 34–37. The author's tradition differs a little from the Sanskrit text, in so far as he does not always combine the same Vyâsa with the same Dvâpara, particularly towards the end of the list. The names agree in both traditions, except *Trivrishan*, for which the Arabic has something like *Trivarta* or *Trivṛitta*. Besides, in the word Riṇajyeshṭha (in Arabic *Rinajertu*) the author has made a mistake. The Sanskrit verse runs thus—

*kṛitaṁjayaḥ saptadaśe riṇajyoshṭâdaśe smṛitaḥ.*

Alberuni has read *riṇajyeshṭoshṭâdaśe* instead of *riṇajyeshṭâdaśe*, and has wrongly divided these words into *riṇajyeshṭo-ashṭâdaśe* instead of *riṇajyo ashṭâdaśe*. Further, he has been guided by the analogy of *jyaishṭha* (the name of the month), which in vernacular was pronounced *jertu*, in changing *riṇajyeshṭa* into *rinajertu*.

P. 398. *Vishṇu-Dharma.*—In mentioning Vâsudeva, Saṁkarshaṇa, &c., as the names of Vishṇu in the yugas, this source agrees with the teaching of the sect of the Bhâgavatas or Pâñcarâtras.—*Vide* Colebrooke, "Essays," i. 439, 440.

P. 401.—The story of the birth of Vâsudeva, *i.e.* Kṛishṇa, is related in the *Vishṇu-Purâṇa*, book v. chap. iii.

P. 403. *The children of Kaurava, &c.*—The following traditions are taken from the *Mahâbhârata:* the dice-playing from book ii., or *sabhâparvan;* the preparing for battle from book v., or *udyogaparvan;* the destruction of the five brothers by the curse of the Brahmin from book xvi., or *mausalaparvan;* their going to heaven from book xvii., or *mahâprasthânikaparvan.*

The introductory sentence of this relation, وكان اولاد كورو على بنى العمومة, literally, "The children of Kaurava were over their cousins," is odd, and perhaps not free from a lacuna. Pâṇḍu had died, and his children grow up in Hastinapura, at the court of Kaurava, *i.e.* Dhṛitarâshṭra, their uncle, the brother of Pâṇḍu. One expects a sentence like "The children of Kaurava cherished enmity against their cousins," but as the Arabic words run, one could scarcely translate them otherwise than I have done. The children of Kaurava had "the charge of their cousins," &c.

P. 407. On the *akshauhiṇî cf.* H. H. Wilson, "Works," 2d edit., iv. p. 290 (on the art of war as known to the Hindus).

*Mankalus* seems to be a mistake for *Myrtilus. Cf. Eratosthenis Catasterismorum Reliquiæ*, rec. C. Robert, p. 104. The source of Alberuni seems to have been a book like the chronicle of *Johannes Malalas.*

The second tradition, taken from a commentary on Aratus' *Phænomena* (*vide* note to p. 97), is found in the same book, *Eratosthenis, &c.*, p. 100, 98. For this information I am indebted to my colleague, Professor C. Robert.

P. 408.—The number 284,323 of people who ride on chariots and elephants is a mistake for 284,310. I do not see what is the origin of this surplus of 13 men. However, the wrong number must be kept as it is, since the author reckons with it in the following computation.

# ANNOTATIONS.

## VOL. II.

P. 1.—The famous chronological chapter xlix. consists of two parts of very different value. Part i., on p. 2–5, an explanation of the mythical eras of the Hindus, is taken from the *Vishṇu-Dharma*, on which work *cf.* note to i. p. 54.

Part ii., on p. 5–14, containing information of a historical character, has not been drawn from a literary source. If the author had learned these things from any particular book or author, he would have said so. His information is partly what educated people among Hindus believed to be historic and had told him, partly what he had himself observed during his stay among Hindus and elsewhere. That their historic tradition does not deserve much credit is matter of complaint on the part of the author (on pp. 10, 11), and that altogether the description of historic chronology, as far as he was able to give it, is by no means in all points satisfactory, is frankly admitted by the author himself (on p. 9). Whatever blame or praise, therefore, attaches to this chapter must in the first instance be laid to the charge, not of Alberuni, but of his informants. What he tells us is to be considered as the *vulgata* among educated Hindus in the north-west of India in his time.

Although the tales which had been told Alberuni may not have been of a high standard, still it is much to be regretted that he has not chosen to incorporate them into his *Indica* (*cf.* p. 11, 1–6).

Whether his hope (expressed on p. 8), that he might some day learn something more of this subject, was realised or not, I cannot make out. However, the stray notes on Indian chronology scattered through his *Canon Masudicus*, which he wrote some years after the *Indica*, do not seem to betray that his Indian studies had made much progress.

In all researches on Indian chronology, Alberuni's statements play an eminent part, specially those relating to the epochs of the Śaka and Gupta eras. *Cf.* among others the following publications:—

Fergusson, "On Indian Chronology," "Journal of the Royal Asiatic Society," vol. iv. (1870), p. 81; and "On the Saka, Samvat, and Gupta Eras," vol. xii. (1880), p. 259.

E. Thomas, "The Epoch of the Guptas," ibid. vol. xiii. (1881), p. 524.

Oldenberg, "On the Dates of Ancient Indian Inscriptions and Coins," "Indian Antiquary," 1881, p. 213.

Fleet, "The Epoch of the Gupta Era," ibid., 1886, p. 189.

Drouin, "Chronologie et Numismatique des Rois Indo-Scythes," in "Revue Numismatique," 1888, premier trimestre, pp. 8 *seq.*

M. Müller, "India, What can it teach us?" pp. 281, 286, 291.

P. 2.—As the author had to compare a number of different eras with each other, he stood in need of a common standard to which to reduce all of them, and for this purpose he chose the New-Year's Day or first Caitra of the year 953 of the Śaka era, which corresponds to—

(1.) A.D. 1031, 25th February, a Thursday.
(2.) A. Hijrae 422, 28th Safar.
(3.) A. Persarum 399, 19th Ispandârmadh-Mâh.

The Naurôz or New-Year's Day of the Persian year 400 fell on 9th March 1031 A.D., which is the day 2,097,686 of the Julian period (*Schram*).

P. 2, l. 30.—This refers to the year of the kaliyuga 3600, as there have elapsed 10 divya years or 3600 years of the present yuga. On the next page Alberuni makes the calculation for the gauge-year, or the year 4132 of the kaliyuga. A kalpa being a day of Brahman, 8 years, 5 months, 4 days correspond to $8 \times 720 + 5 \times 60 + 4 \times 2$, or 6068 kalpas, or 26,213,760,000,000 years. Of the present kalpa there have elapsed six manvantaras or 1,840,320,000 years, seven samdhis or 12,096,000 years, twenty-seven caturyugas or 116,640,000 years, the kritayuga or 1,728,000 years, the tretayuga or 1,296,000 years, the dvaparayuga or 864,000 years, and of the kaliyuga 4132 years; so altogether of the seventh manvantara 120,532,132 years, of the kalpa 1,972,948,132 years, and of Brahman's life 26,215,732,948,132 years, as stated p. 3, ll. 6–9 (*Schram*).

P. 3. *It was I who told it to Yudhishṭhira, &c.*—The author of *Vishṇu-Dharma* refers in these words to the third *parvan* (*vanaparvan*) of the *Mahâbhârata*.

P. 4, l. 29.—From the beginning of Brahman's life to that of the present kalpa there have elapsed 6068 kalpas or 6068 × 1008 × 4,320,000 or 26,423,470,080,000 years. Six manvantaras = 6 × 72 × 4,320,000 or 1,866,240,000 years; twenty-seven cataryugas = 27 × 4,320,000 or 116,640,000 years; three yugas + 4132 years = 3 × 1,080,000 + 4132 or 3,244,132 years. The latter number represents the years elapsed of the caturyuga; adding to it successively the other numbers of years, we find the numbers given ll. 29–31 of this page. The Arabic manuscript has 26,425,456,200,000 instead of 26,425,456,204,132 (*Schram*).

P. 6, l. 3.—In the book *Srûdhava, &c.*, *cf.* note to i. p. 158.

*Candrabîja.*—I first took the reading of the manuscript to be جندربير, but now I believe I can see a pale dot above the last consonant, so that we may read جندربيز.

On the *shashṭyabda*, or sixty-years cycle, *cf.* chap. lxii. p. 123.

P. 6. *The epoch of the era of Śaka, &c.*—Alberuni speaks of this era in his *Canon Masudicus* (composed during the reign of Mas'ûd) in the following terms: الوقت بلغة الهند هو كال واشهر التواريخ عندهم وخاصّة عند منجّميهم شككال اى وقت سق ويحسب من سنة هلاكه لانّه كان متغلّبا عليه والرسم فيه وفى غيره ان تذكر سنيه التامّة دون الناقصة. (Beginning of the sixth chapter, book i., copied from the Codex Elliot, now in the British Museum.)

Translation: "*Time* is called *Kâla* in the language of the Hindus. The era most famous among them, and in particular among their astronomers, is the *Śakakâla*, i.e. *the time of Śaka.* This era is reckoned from the year of his destruction, because he was ruling (rather, tyrannising) over it (*i.e.* over that time). In this as well as in other eras it is the custom to reckon only with complete, not with incomplete or current years."

Then the author goes on to give rules for the comparison of the Śaka era with the Greek, Persian, and Muslim eras.

A later author, 'Abû-Sa'îd 'Abd-alḥayy Ibn Alḍaḥḥâk Ibn Maḥmûd Gardêzî (Gardez, a town east of Ghazna), has reproduced the information of Alberuni on the Śaka era in Persian. Not having the original (MS. Ouseley 240, Bodleian Library, Oxford) at my disposal, I give a translation made years ago:—

"The Hindu era is called شكال, because كال (*kâla*) means *time*, and شك (*Śaka*) is the name of a king whose death was made an era; he did the Hindus a great deal of harm, so they made the date of his death a festival" (Oxford manuscript, p. 352).

The place *Karûr* is also mentioned in the *Chachnâma*. *Vide* Elliot, "History of India," i. 139, 143, 207.

P. 7. *Al-arkand.*—*Cf.* note to i. 312. The book does not seem to exist in the collections of Arabic manuscripts in Europe.

P. 8.—The pronunciation of the names Kanîr, Bardarî, Mârîgala, and Nirahara (Nira-gṛiha?) is more or less conjectural.

Alberuni identifies *Mârîgala* with *Takshaśila* (vol. ii. 302), *i.e.* the Taxila of the ancients. The name *Mârîgala* seems to be preserved in that of a *range of hills lying only two miles to the south of Shahdhesi* (Cunningham, "Ancient Geography of India," p. 111). The place is also mentioned in the *Ṭâbaḳâti-Nâṣirî*. *Vide* Elliot, "History of India," ii. 271, 273.

P. 9.—*Durlabha*, a native of Multân, is only twice mentioned. Here the author quotes from him a method for the computation of the Śaka era, and p. 54 a method for the computation of *ahargaṇa*. According to him, the Indian year commenced with the month Mârgaśîrsha, but the astronomers of Multân commenced it with Caitra (p. 10).

P. 10. *Barhatakîn.*—The name occurs only in this one

place. If it were an Indian name, I should think of something like *Vṛihatkína* (or *Vṛihatketu* برهتكيت). If it is Turkish, it is a compound, the second part of which is *tagín* (as in *Toghrultagín* and similar names). As the author declares the dynasty to be of Tibetan origin, the question is whether the name may be explained as Tibetan.

P. 10. *Var.*—As the Arabic verb may be connected either with the preposition *bi* or with the accusative, we may read either *bvr* or *vr*.

P. 10, l. 25. *He began to creep out.*—In the Arabic text, p. ٢٠٧, 8, read اخذ يخرج instead of احد يخرج.

P. 11. *Kanik.*—Only the three consonants *KNK* are certain. We may read them *Kanik* or *Kanikku*, which would be a Middle-Indian *Kanikkhu* for Sanskritic *Kanishka*. Thus the name Turk was pronounced by the Middle-Indian tongue as *Turukkhu*, and Sanscritisized as *Turushka*.

This Zopyrus-story was reproduced by Muḥammad 'Aufî. *Cf.* Elliot, "History of India," ii. 170.

P. 13. *Lagatúrmán.*—The uncouth formation of this name seems to point to a Non-Indian (Tibetan ?) origin. I at first thought to combine it with the name of the Tibetan king, *Langtarma*, who abolished Buddhism, A.D. 899 (*v.* Prinsep, "Useful Tables," ii. 289), as our Lagatûrmân was the last of a series of Buddhistic kings, and as the names resemble each other to some extent. However, this combination seems delusive.

The name Kallar is written *Kallr* كلر. Could this name be combined with *Kulusha* (Kalusha ?), which *e.g.* occurs as the name of the Brahmin minister of the Mahratta Râja Sambaji ?

P. 13, l. 17. *The Brahman kings.*—The word *sâmanta* means *vassal*.

*Kamalû* was a contemporary of the prince 'Amr Ibn Laith, who died A.D. 911. *Cf.* Elliot, "History of India," ii. 172. Is the name a hypokoristikon of one like *Kamalavardhana ?*

*Ânandapâla*, *Bhîmapâla*, and *Trilocanapâla* mean *having Śiva as protector.* If, therefore, these princes, like the Indo-Scythian kings (*cf.* Drouin, *Revue Numismatique*, 1888, 48), were Śiva-worshippers, we must explain the name *Jaipâl* perhaps as *Jayâpâla*, i.e. *having Durgâ* (the wife of Śiva) *as protector.* *Cf.* the Hindu kings of Kabul in Elliot, "History of India," ii. 403 *seq.* (in many points antiquated).

The name *Trilocanapâla* (here *Tarûcanpâl*) has been much disfigured in the Arabic writing. *Vide* the Puru Jaipal in Elliot, *l.c.*, ii. 47, 463, 464.

P. 13, l. 14. *The latter was killed.*—The Arabic manuscript has قىل, which may be read قيل (*narratum est*) or قتل (*interfectus est*). I have not been able to ascertain whether the year in question was that of the enthronisation of Trilocanapâla, or that of his death. I prefer, however (with Reinaud), to read قتل, "*he was killed*," because evidently the author stood so near to the events in question that he could have ample and trustworthy information, and that, in fact, an *on dit* (قيل) seems here entirely out of place.

P. 13, l. 22. *The slightest remnant*, literally *one blowing fire*, a well-known simile for *nobody*. *Cf. e.g.* Hasan Nizâmî in Elliot's "History of India," ii. 235, l. 13.

P. 15.—For Alfazârî and Ya'ḳûb Ibn Ṭariḳ, *cf.* note to i. 165, 169.

*Muḥammad Ibn Isḥâḳ of Sarakhs* is mentioned only here and in the tables on pp. 16 and 18, besides in Alberuni's "Chronology" (English edition, p. 29).

P. 16, l. 6 of the table.—It is not clearly said in the text that the anomalistic revolution is meant, but the numbers which Alberuni quotes leave no doubt on the subject. The days of a kalpa are 1,577,916,450,000, which being divided by the number 57,265,194,142, give for one revolution $27\frac{31756208166}{57265194142}$ days, or 27 days 13 h. 18 min. 33 sec., whilst the anomalistic revolution of the moon is equivalent to 27 days 13 h. 18 min. 37 sec., an agreement so very close, that every doubt that there could be meant anything but the anomalistic revolution is completely excluded. Moreover, the number of the revolutions of the apsis, 488,105,858, being augmented by 57,265,194,142, is equal to 57,753,300,000, the number of sidereal revolutions; and, indeed, the revolutions of the apsis, *plus* the anomalistic revolutions, must be equal to the siuereal revolutions (*Schram*).

P. 16.—The note in the table "The anomalistic revolution of the moon is here treated," &c., is not quite clear, and probably materially incorrect. That the term حامة القمر means the anomaly (ἀνωμαλία in Greek, *kendra* (κέντρον) in Sanskrit), was first pointed out to me by my friend and colleague, Prof. Förster; but this note, which seems to be intended as a sort of explanation of the term, does not exactly render what astronomers understand by *anomaly*. Literally translated it runs thus: "The *Ḥâṣṣat-alḳamar* stands in the place of the *apsis*, because the result is its (whose? the apsis'?) share, since it (the *ḥâṣṣat-alḳamar*) is the difference between the two motions" (لانّ ما يخرج يكون حصّته الى (not او) هى فضل ما بين الحركتين). Accordingly, we must translate the term as "falling to the moon as her lot or share," viz., movement, in Arabic الحركة الحاصّة القمر. Therefore, in the Arabic text, pp. ٢٠٩ and ٢١٠, 8 write حاصّة intead of حامّة.

P. 19.—Abû-alḥasan of Ahwâz is mentioned only in this place. He seems to have been a contemporary of Alfazârî and Ya'ḳûb Ibn Ṭâriḳ.

P. 20.—*Annus procrastinationis.*—*Vide* the author's "Chronology" (English edition), p. 73. *Malamâsa*, in Hindustani *malmâs*. *Vide* Dowson, "Hindustani Grammar," p. 258.

P. 21, l. 24.—A caturyuga or 4,320,000 solar years consists of 53,433,300 lunar months or 1,602,999,000 lunar days; so one solar year has $371\frac{31}{480}$ lunar days, and the difference between the solar and lunar days of a year is $11\frac{31}{480}$. The proportion 360 lunar days : $11\frac{31}{480}$ days $= x$ lunar days : 30 days gives for $x$ the number of

$976\frac{464}{5311}$, which is equivalent to $976\frac{4176}{47799}$. *Vide* p. 24, l. 23 (*Schram*).

P. 22, l. 17.—Read $22^{\text{iii}}$ instead of $23^{\text{iii}}$ (*Schram*).

P. 23. *Padamâsa.*—This seems to be an old mistake which has crept into the Arabic manuscripts of the works of Alfazârî and Ya'ḳûb. *Cf.* the author's "Chronology" (English edition), p. 15.

P. 27.—The rule given in the first fifteen lines of this page is completely erroneous, and consequently the example calculated after this rule is so too. The right method would be the following:—"The complete years are multiplied by 12; to the product are added the months which have elapsed of the current year. The sum represents the partial solar months. You write down the number in two places; in the one place you multiply it by 5311, *i.e.* the number which represents the universal adhimâsa months. The product you divide by 172,800, *i.e.* the number which represents the universal solar months. The quotient you get, *as far as it contains complete months*, is added to the number in the second place, and the sum so obtained is multiplied by 30; to the product are added the days which have elapsed of the current month. The sum represents the candrâhargaṇa, *i.e.* the sum of the partial lunar days." These two proceedings would be identical, if we were not to omit fractions; but as an adhimâsa month is only intercalated when it is complete, we must first determine the number of adhimâsa months, and, *omitting the fractions*, change them to days; whilst when we multiply beforehand by 30, the fractions of the adhimâsa months are also multiplied, which is not correct. This is at once seen in the example which he works out after this rule, and we wonder that Alberuni himself did not see it. He is calculating the ahargaṇas for the beginning of a year, consequently also for the beginning of a month, and, notwithstanding, he is not at all surprised to find (p. 30) 28 days and 51 minutes of the month already passed.

The adhimâsa days are nothing else than adhimâsa months converted into days. As the number of the adhimâsa months must be a whole, so the number of the adhimâsa days must be divisible by 30. Accordingly, the number quoted, p. 29, l. 30, not being divisible by 30, is at once recognised as erroneous, and it is astonishing when he says in the following lines, "If, in multiplying and dividing, we had used the months, we should have found the adhimâsa months and multiplied by 30, they would be equal to the here-mentioned number of adhimâsa days." In this case certainly the number ought to be divisible by 30. Perhaps he would have found the fault, if not, by a strange coincidence, the difference between the true value and the false one had been exactly 28 days or four complete weeks, so that though the number considered is an erroneous one, yet he finds, p. 30, l. 9, the right week-day.

Alberuni finds, p. 29, l. 2, as the sum of days from the beginning of the kalpa to the seventh manvantara 676,610,573,760. Further, he finds, l. 7, that from the beginning of the seventh manvantara till the beginning of the present caturyuga there have elapsed 42,603,744,150 days, and, l. 12, that till the beginning of the kaliyuga there have elapsed 1,420,124,805 days of the present caturyuga. Adding these numbers, we find that the sum of days elapsed from the beginning of the kalpa to that of the caturyuga is 720,634,442,715; but as he finds, p. 30, l. 5, that from the same epoch to the gauge-date there have elapsed 720,635,951,963 days, so the gauge-date would be 1,509,248 days after the beginning of the kaliyuga. Now we know that the gauge-date is 25th February 1031 (see p. 2, l. 17, and note), or the day 2,097,686 of the Julian period, whilst the first day of the kaliyuga, as is generally known, coincides with the 18th February 3102 before Christ or with the day 588,466 of the Julian period, so that the difference of the two dates is 1,509,220, and not 1,509,248 days.

To this result we shall also come when working out Alberuni's example after the method stated in the beginning of this note. Instead of p. 29, l. 16, we should then have: the years which have elapsed of the kalpa up to that year are 1,972,948,132. Multiplying them by 12, we get as the number of their months 23,675,377,584. In the date which we have adopted as gauge-year there is no month, but only complete years; therefore we have nothing to add to this number. It represents the partial solar months. We multiply it by 5311 and divide the product by 172,800; the quotient $727,661.633\frac{3463}{3600}$ represents the adhimâsa months. Omitting the fractions, we add 727,661,633 to the partial solar months 23,675,377,584, and get 24,403,039,217 as the partial lunar months. By multiplying this number by 30 we get days, viz., 732,091,176,510. As there are no days in the normal date, we have no days to add to this number. Multiplying it by 55,739 and dividing the product by 3,562,220, we get the partial ûnarâtra days, viz., $11,455,224,575\frac{123439}{356222}$. This sum of days without the fraction is subtracted from the partial lunar days, and the remainder, 720,635,951,935, represents the number of the civil days of our gauge-date. Dividing it by 7, we get as remainder 4, which means that the last of these days is a Wednesday. Therefore the Indian year commences with a Thursday. The difference between 720,635,951,935 and the beginning of the kaliyuga 720,634,442,715 is, as it ought to be, 1,509,220 days (*Schram*).

In the beginning of chap. lii., in the Arabic text, ٢١٦, 8, it seems necessary to write شهور and الشهور instead of ايّام and الايّام.

P. 29, l. 10. *Thursday.*—The Arabic manuscript has *Tuesday.*

P. 30, l. 10–17.—This ought to run as follows:—We have found above $727,661,633\frac{3463}{3600}$ for the adhimâsa months; the wholes represent the number of the adhimâsas which have elapsed, viz., 727,661,633, whilst the fraction is the time which has already elapsed of the current adhimâsa month. By multiplying this fraction by 30 we get it expressed in days, viz., $\frac{3463}{120}$ days, or 28 days 51 minutes 30 seconds, so that the current adhimâsa month wants only 1 day 8 minutes 30 seconds more to become a complete month (*Schram*).

P. 31, l. 19.—The number 1,203,783,270 is found by adding the $30 \times 1,196,525$ or 35,895,750 adhimâsa days to the 1,167,887,520 solar days (*Schram*).

P. 31, l. 24.—The number of days from the beginning of the caturyuga to the gauge-date is here found by Pulisa's method to be 1,184,947,570, whilst p. 33, l. 16, the number of days from the beginning of the caturyuga to that of the kaliyuga is found to be 1,183,438,350. The difference between both numbers is (as it ought to be) 1,509,220 days (*Schram*).

P. 33, l. 24.—The method of Âryabhaṭa is the same as that given before, only the numbers by which we are to multiply and to divide, are different according to his system, which supposes a different number of revolutions in a kalpa. According to Âryabhaṭa the elder, a caturyuga has 1,577,917,500 days (see vol. i. p. 370, l. 28). As to the revolutions of sun and moon, they seem to be the same as given by Pulisa. The tables, pages 16 and 17, are not quite correct in this, as they give, for instance, for the revolutions of the moon's node and apsis the 1000th part of their revolutions in a kalpa, whilst in vol. i. p. 370, l. 16, it is said that, according to Pulisa and Âryabhaṭa, the kalpa has 1008 caturyugas. But p. 19, l. 15, the numbers 4,320,000 for the sun and 57,753,336 for the moon are given as possibly belonging to the theory of Âryabhaṭa. The same numbers are cited by Bentley in his "Historical View of the Hindu Astronomy," London, 1825, p. 179, as belonging to the system of the so-called spurious Ârya Siddhanta. It is doubtless the same system, for if we compare the number of days between the beginning of the kalpa and that of the kaliyuga, which Bentley states in the above-cited book, p. 181, to be 725,447,570,625, with the same sum quoted by Alberuni, p. 33, l. 29, there can scarcely be a doubt as to the identity of both systems, especially as this number 725,447,570,625 is a curious one, giving Thursday for the first day of the kalpa, whilst the other systems give Sunday for this date. Of this book Bentley says, p. 183: "It would be needless to waste any more time in going over its contents; what has been shown must be perfectly sufficient to convince any man of common sense of its being a downright modern forgery;" and p. 190, "The spurious Brahma Siddhanta, together with the spurious Ârya Siddhanta, are doubtless the productions of the last century at farthest." Perhaps he would have chosen more reserved expressions, if he had known that this "production of the last century" was already cited by Alberuni.

When we adopt these numbers for a caturyuga, *i.e.* 1,577,917,500 civil days, 4,320,000 revolutions of the sun and 57,753,336 revolutions of the moon, and consequently 53,433,336 lunar months, we find the numbers belonging to a yuga by dividing the above numbers by four, as in this system the four yugas are of equal length. Thus we get for a yuga 394,479,375 civil days, 1,080,000 solar years, and consequently 12,960,000 solar months, and 388,800,000 solar days, 13,358,334 lunar months, 400,750,020 lunar days, 398,334 adhimâsa months, and 6,270,645 ûnarâtra days. To find the number 725,449,079,845 mentioned, p. 33, l. 31, as the sum of days between the beginning of the kalpa and the gauge-date, we are to proceed as follows:—From the beginning of the kaliyuga to our gauge-date there have elapsed 4132 years, which multiplied by 12 give 49,584 as the partial solar months. This number multiplied by the universal adhimâsa months 398,334, and divided by the universal solar months 12,960,000, gives $1523\frac{44837}{45000}$ as the number of adhimâsa months. This number, without the fraction added to the solar months 49,584, gives 51,107 as the number of the partial lunar months, which multiplied by 30 gives 1,533,210 as the number of the partial lunar days. This number multiplied by the universal ûnarâtra days 6,270,645 and divided by the universal lunar days 400,750,020 gives $23{,}990\frac{2473785}{4452778}$ as the sum of the partial ûnarâtra days; and 23,990 subtracted from the partial lunar days 1,533,210 gives 1,509,220 as the civil days elapsed of the kaliyuga till the gauge-date, identical with the number found in note to p. 27. These 1,509,220 days added to the 725,447,570,625 days which separate the beginning of the kalpa and the kaliyuga, give the number of 725,449,079,845 days cited p. 33, l. 31. Finally, the number of days elapsed of Brahman's life before the present kalpa, is got by multiplying the number of days in a kalpa, *i.e.* 1,590,540,840,000 (see page 370, vol. i.) by 6068, the number of the kalpas elapsed before the present one (*Schram*).

P. 34, l. 32.—There is here the same fault as that which

led Alberuni to a false result, p. 27. The multiplication by 30 must be made after dropping the fraction of the adhimâsa months, not before (*Schram*).

P. 36, l. 1.—The lacuna must have contained a phrase like this:—"In three different places; they multiply the number in the lowest place by 77, and divide the product by 69,120." This follows clearly from the explanation which he gives in the following page (*Schram*).

P. 36, l. 9.—Read *lunar* instead of *solar*, in the Arabic (٢٢٣, 7, last word), القمريّة instead of الشمسيّة.

P. 36, l. 10.—The expression is a very concise one, so that it is not quite clear what is meant (l. 14) by the "middle number."—It is to be understood in the following manner: "This number of the partial lunar days is written down in two different places, one under the other. The one of these is "in the uppermost place" (l. 17); they multiply the lower number by 11, and write the product under *it*. Then they divide it, *i.e.* the product, by 403,963, and add the quotient to the middle number, *i.e.* to the product of eleven times the partial lunar days (*Schram*).

P. 36, l. 26.—A certain number of months $A$ is to be divided by $65\frac{1155}{15933}$. If we wish to get the same result by dividing only by 65, we must subtract from $A$ a certain number $X$ which is to be determined by the equation $\frac{A}{65\frac{1155}{15933}}=\frac{A-X}{65}$. This equation gives for $X$ the value $X = A\left(\frac{\frac{1155}{15933}}{65\frac{1155}{15933}}\right)$, or, reduced, $X=A(\frac{1155}{1036800})$, or at last $X=A(\frac{77}{69120})$. The equation $X=A\left(\frac{\frac{1155}{15933}}{65\frac{1155}{15933}}\right)$ can also be written in the form $65\frac{1155}{15933} : \frac{1155}{15933} = A : X$, that is, as Alberuni states it (l. 30), "the whole divisor stands in the same relation to its fractions as the divided number to the subtracted portion" (*Schram*).

P. 36, l. 33.—Alberuni has not made the calculation given

above in a general way, but he has made it only for a special case, for the gauge-date. He finds the fraction $\frac{77}{69120}$, which he would find for every other date, as this fraction is independent of the number $A$ (*Schram*).

P. 37, l. 26.—Here again a certain number of ûnarâtra days $A$ is to be divided by $63\frac{50663}{55739}$. If we wish to get the same result by dividing only by $63\frac{10}{11}$, or, which is the same, by $\frac{703}{11}$, we must add to $A$ a certain number $X$, which is determined by the equation

$$\frac{A+X}{\frac{703}{11}} = \frac{A}{63\frac{50663}{55739}} \text{ or } A+X = A\left(\frac{703}{11\times 63\frac{50663}{55739}}\right) \text{ or } X = A\left(\frac{703 - 11\times 63\frac{50663}{55739}}{11\times 63\frac{50663}{55739}}\right)$$

$$= A\left(\frac{703 - 702\frac{55642}{55739}}{702\frac{55642}{55739}}\right) \text{ or } X = A\left(\frac{\frac{97}{55739}}{\frac{39184420}{55739}}\right) = A\left(\frac{97}{39184420}\right)$$

or at last, dividing numerator and denominator by 97, we find $X = \frac{A}{403963\frac{9}{97}}$. The $\frac{9}{97}$ are neglected (see p. 38, l. 9) (*Schram*).

P. 38, l. 25.—The Arabic manuscript has 77,139, instead of 7739, as Dr. Schram demands; *v.* p. 39, l. 7, and p. 40, l. 8.

P. 39, l. 20.—Here he grants that the 28 days which we get over 727,661,633 months are to be reckoned after the beginning of the month Caitra, so that the result found, p. 29, l. 30, agrees with the 28th, not with the first Caitra (*Schram*).

P. 39, l. 24.—The middle number was multiplied by $\frac{2481}{9600}$; a solar year has $365\frac{2481}{9600}$ days (l. 36), or 52 weeks 1 day and $\frac{2481}{9600}$ of a day. By adding the product of the number of years multiplied by $\frac{2481}{9600}$ to this number itself, we get the sum of days by which these years exceed whole weeks. The rest of the calculation is sufficiently explained by Alberuni himself (*Schram*).

P. 41, l. 19.—This is the same case as p. 36, only the numbers are a little different. If $A$ is the number of months to be divided by $32\frac{35552}{66389}$, and we wish to subtract a number from $A$ so as to get the same result by dividing the difference by 32 only, we have the equation

$$\frac{A}{32\frac{35552}{66389}} = \frac{A - X}{32}$$

which gives for $X$ the value

$$A\left(\frac{\frac{35552}{66389}}{32\frac{35552}{66389}}\right) \text{ or } X = A\left(\frac{35552}{2160000}\right) \text{ or } X = A\left(\frac{1111}{67500}\right).$$

Alberuni has again made the calculation for a special case, the gauge-date, and found the same fraction (*Schram*).

P. 41, l. 20.—"This number of days," viz., the number of solar days corresponding to the given date (*Schram*).

P. 41, l. 33.—The MS. has 974 instead of 976.

P. 42, l. 3.—The number of solar days, 1,555,222,000, is here taken as divisor instead of the number of adhimâsa months, 1,593,336. The fraction ought to be $976\frac{104064}{1593336}$ $= 976\frac{4336}{66389}$, the common divisor 24 (*Schram*).

P. 42, l. 6.—Alberuni does not seem to have understood Pulisa's calculation which is correct, although there seems to be a lacuna in its explanation. According to Pulisa's theory, there are in a caturyuga 1,555,200,000 solar days and 1,593,336 adhimâsa months. Dividing the first number by the second, we get as the time within which an adhimâsa month sums up $976\frac{104064}{1593336}$ days. So one would get the number of adhimâsa months by dividing the given number of solar days by the number $976\frac{104064}{1593336}$; but Pulisa prefers not to reckon with the fraction, so he diminishes the number of given days by a certain amount and divides only by 976. The number which is to be subtracted from the given days is easily found by the following equation:—

Let $D$ be the number of given solar days; we then have

$$\frac{D}{976\frac{104064}{1593336}} = \frac{D - X}{976} \text{ or } X = D\left(\frac{\frac{104064}{1593336}}{976\frac{104064}{1593336}}\right) \text{ or } X = D\left(\frac{\frac{104064}{1593336}}{\frac{1555200000}{1593336}}\right)$$

$$\text{or } X = D\left(\frac{104064}{1555200000}\right).$$

Now 384 is a common divisor to 104,064 and the divisor 1,555,200,000. So we get $X = D\frac{271}{4050000}$, just as Pulisa finds it (*Schram*).

P. 42, l. 22.—Not only is it not "quite impossible that this number should, in this part of the calculation, be used as a divisor," but it needs must be used as a divisor. This we see at once when, instead of working out the calculation with special numbers, we make it algebraically. Let $S$ be the number of solar days in a caturyuga, and $A$ the number of adhimâsa months in a caturyuga. Then the number of days within which one adhimâsa month sums up, will be found by dividing $S$ by $A$. By this division we shall get wholes and a fraction; let the wholes be represented by $Q$ and the numerator of the fraction by $R$. We then have $\frac{S}{A} = Q + \frac{R}{A}$ or $S = AQ + R$. Now if, the given number of solar days being $D$, we have to divide $D$ by $Q + \frac{R}{A}$ to get the number of adhimâsa months, but as we wish to divide by $Q$ alone, we must subtract from $D$ a number $X$, which will be found by the equation

$$\frac{D}{Q+\frac{R}{A}} = \frac{D-X}{Q} \text{ or } X = D\left(\frac{\frac{R}{A}}{Q+\frac{R}{A}}\right) \text{ or } X = D\left(\frac{R}{AQ+R}\right)$$

As $AQ + R$ is equal to $S$, we have $X = D\frac{R}{S}$, where $S$ is the number of solar days in a caturyuga, which must necessarily be a divisor in this part of the calculation (*Schram*).

P. 42, l. 31.—As one ûnarâtra day sums up in $63\frac{50663}{55739}$ lunar days (see p. 37, l. 17), we have again the equation

$$\frac{L}{63\frac{50663}{55739}} = \frac{L-X}{63} \text{ or } X = L\left(\frac{\frac{50663}{55739}}{63\frac{50663}{55739}}\right) \text{ or } X = L\left(\frac{50663}{3562220}\right)$$

where $L$ represents the number of the given lunar days.

P. 44, l. 1.—The number 720,635,951,963 is not correct, as we have seen in note to p. 27. It is too great by 28 days. But the number of adhimâsa days, 21,829,849,018 (l. 10), is also 28 days too great. So the difference is again correct. There is the same fault as at p. 27. The calculation ought to run as follows:—The partial civil days which have elapsed up to our gauge-date are 720,635,951,935. This number is given, and what we want to find is how many Indian years and months are equal to this sum of days. First we multiply the number by 55,739 and divide the product by 3,506,481; the quotient is $11,455,224,575\frac{1934309}{3506481}$ ûnarâtra days. We add 11,455,224,575 to the civil days; the sum is 732,091,176,510 lunar days. Dividing this number by 30, we get as quotient 24,403,039,217 lunar months (and no fraction; so we see that the date in question consists of a number of months only, or, what is the same, that the date corresponds to the beginning of a month). Multiplying the lunar months by 5311 and dividing the product by 178,111, we get $727,661,633\frac{166224}{178111}$ adhimâsa months'; 727,661,633 adhimâsa months subtracted from the 24,403,039,217 lunar months give 23,675,377,584 solar months, which divided by 12 give 1,972,948,132 years and no fraction. So we find the given date corresponding not only to the beginning of a month, but also to that of a year. We find the same number of years of which the gauge-date consists (see p. 29, l. 17) (*Schram*).

P. 45, l. 12.—This rule must indeed be based on some complete misunderstanding, for it is absolutely erroneous, as Alberuni rightly remarks (*Schram*).

P. 46, l. 1.—If we calculate from the beginning of the kalpa or the caturyuga, there are in the epoch neither fractions of the adhimâsa months nor of ûnarâtra days; but as the great number of days embraced by such long periods makes the calculation wearisome, the methods set forth in this chapter start neither from the beginning of the kalpa nor from that of the caturyuga, but from dates chosen arbitrarily and nearer to the time for which they are to be employed. As such epochs are not free from fractions of the adhimâsa months and ûnarâtra days, these fractions must be taken into account (*Schram*).

P. 46, l. 27.—The numbers employed here do not belong to Brahmagupta's, but to Pulisa's system. The year taken as epoch is the year 587 Śakakâla. As we have seen, p. 31, ll. 8–10, that in the moment of the beginning of our gauge-date or of the year Śakakâla 953, there have elapsed 3,244,132 years of the caturyuga, there must have elapsed

3,243,766 years of the caturyuga till the beginning of the year 587 Śakakâla. We must now first calculate the adhimâsa months and ûnarâtra days for this epoch. After Pulisa's method (p. 41, l. 29), we have: 3,243,766 years are equal to 38,925,192 solar months or 1,167,755,760 solar days. This number multiplied by 271 and divided by 4,050,000 gives $78,138\frac{4043}{5625}$. As here the nearest number is to be taken, we get 78,139, which, subtracted from 1,167,755,760, gives 1,167,677,621. This latter number divided by 976 gives as the number of adhimâsa months $1,196,391\frac{5}{976}$. Now 1,196,391 adhimâsa months are equal to 35,891,730 adhimâsa days, which, added to 1,167,755,760 solar days, give 1,203,647,490 lunar days. According to Pulisa's theory (see p. 26, l. 9), there are in a caturyuga 1,603,000,080 lunar and 25,082,280 ûnarâtra days; so one ûnarâtra day sums up in $63\frac{63379}{89673}$ lunar days. Therefore we should have to divide the given number of lunar days $L$ by $63\frac{63379}{89673}$, but we prefer to subtract from $L$ a certain number $X$, and to divide the rest by $63\frac{10}{11}$ or $\frac{703}{11}$. The number $X$ will be given by the equation $\frac{L}{63\frac{63379}{89673}} = \frac{L-X}{\frac{703}{11}} = \frac{11\ L - 11\ X}{703}$. This equation gives for $X$ the value $X = \left(\frac{\frac{439}{89673}}{703\frac{439}{89673}}\right) L$ or $X = \left(\frac{439}{48980558}\right) L$ or $X = \left(\frac{1}{111573\frac{11}{439}}\right) L$, or nearly $11\ X = \frac{11\ L}{111573}$.

Now $L$ being equal to 1,203,647,490 lunar days, $11\ L$ will be equal to 13,240,122,390 lunar days; this number divided by 111,573 gives $118,667\frac{89109}{111573}$. Taking the nearest number, we subtract 118,668 from 13,240,122,390 and get 13,240,003,722, which divided by 703 gives $18,833,575\frac{497}{703}$ as the number of ûnarâtra days. This added to the 1,203,647,490 lunar days gives for the date of our epoch the number of civil days 1,184,813,915.

This number divided by 7 gives 5 as remainder. Now the last day before the present caturyuga was a Monday (see p. 33, l. 11), therefore the last day before our epoch is a Saturday, and any number of days clapsed since that epoch if divided by 7 will indicate by the remainder, the week-day counted from Sunday as 1, as it is said, p. 47, l. 19. Now the whole method is easily recognised as thoroughly correct. Instead of multiplying the partial solar days by $\frac{271}{4050000}$, we multiply them by $\frac{1}{14945}$, which is sufficiently correct, as $\frac{271}{4050000}$ is equal to $\frac{1}{14944\frac{176}{271}}$. As besides the whole adhimâsa months there is yet a fraction of $\frac{5}{976}$ adhimâsa months in our epoch, we add 5 before dividing by 976. The calculation of the ûnarâtra days has already been explained; but as in our epoch besides the whole ûnarâtra days there is still a fraction of $\frac{497}{703}$ ûnarâtra days, we must add 497 before dividing by 703. The whole proceeding is thus explained (*Schram*).

P. 48, l. 11.—The calculation has been made for the complete years elapsed *before* our gauge-date. So we get the week-day of the last day *before* the first Caitra of the gauge-date, and if this is a Wednesday, the first Caitra itself is a Thursday; *cf.* p. 30, l. 9.

The first day of this epoch corresponds to the day 1,964,031 of the Julian period. Adding 133,655 to 1,964,031, we have for the first Caitra 953 the day 2,097,686 of the Julian period, as it ought to be (*Schram*).

P. 48, l. 21.—The 18th Isfandârmadh of Yazdajird 399 corresponds in fact to Wednesday, 24th February 1031, the day before the first Caitra 953 Śakakâla (see note to p. 2, l. 17) (*Schram*).

P. 49, l. 22. *By six years.*—The Arabic manuscript has *seven* instead of *six*.

P. 50, l. 1.—The method here employed is based on Pulisa's theory. According to this theory, the solar days must be divided by $976\frac{4336}{66389}$ to get the adhimâsa months. Now $976\frac{4336}{66389}$ with sufficient accuracy is equal to $976\frac{2}{30}$ or $\frac{29282}{30}$.

If $S$ represents the number of solar months, the solar days or $30\,S$ are to be divided by $\frac{29282}{30}$, or, what is the same, $900\,S$ must be divided by 29282.

To get the ûnarâtra days, the lunar days must be divided by $63\frac{63379}{69673}$ (see note to p. 46, l. 27). Now $63\frac{63379}{69673}$ is equal to $\frac{703\frac{439}{69673}}{11}$, or with sufficient accuracy $\frac{703\frac{2}{317}}{11}$, or at least equal to $\frac{210902}{3300}$. So the multiplications and divisions of this method are explained.

The constant numbers which are to be added, are inherent to the epoch. The year 888 Śakakâla corresponds to the year 3,244,067 of the caturyuga; 3,244,067 years are equal to 38,928,804 solar months, or 1,167,864,120 solar days. These solar months multiplied by 66,389 and divided by 2,160,000 give $1,196,502\frac{4063}{180000}$ adhimâsa months, or 35,895,060 adhimâsa days. This added to the 1,167,864,120 solar days gives 1,203,759,180 lunar days. Eleven times this number is equal to 13,241,350,980; this latter number divided by 111,573 gives $118678\frac{90486}{111573}$, or the nearest number 118,679. Subtracting this from 13,241,350,980, the remainder is 13,241,232,301, which being divided by 703, gives $18,835,323\frac{232}{703}$ ûnarâtra days; these days subtracted from the lunar days give for the number of civil days 1,184,923,857. Dividing this last number by 7, we get the remainder 5; and as the last day before the present caturyuga was a Monday (see p. 33, l. 11), the last day before the epoch here adopted is a Saturday, so that any number of days elapsed since that epoch, if divided by 7, will indicate by the remainder the week-day counted from Sunday as 1. The first day of this epoch corresponds to the day 2,073,973 of the Julian period. We have found in our epoch the fraction of adhimâsa month $\frac{4063}{180000}$, which is equal to $\frac{660\frac{178766}{180000}}{29282}$ or very nearly $\frac{661}{29282}$ adhimâsa month, so we must add 661 before dividing by 29282.

The fraction of ûnarâtra days $\frac{232}{703}$ is equal to $\frac{69,600\frac{461}{703}}{210902}$ or nearly to $\frac{69601}{210902}$. Therefore we must add 69,601 before dividing by 210,902. Alberuni has, instead of this number 69,601, the number 64,106, 4 instead of 9, and the last three numbers reversed (*Schram*).

P. 50, l. 35.—We had 780 months; adding thereto the 23 adhimâsa months, we have 803 months, which being multiplied by 30 give 24090, and not 24060 days. All the following faults are the consequences of this one (*Schram*).

P. 51, l. 2.—It ought to be "adding thereto 69,601, we

get the sum 79,566,601. By dividing it by 210,902, we get the quotient 377, *i.e.* ûnarâtra days, and a remainder of $\frac{56547}{210902}$, *i.e.* the *avamas.*" (In the Arabic text, p. ٣٣٧, 17, the reading of the MS. ought not to have been altered.) The correct result is 23,713 civil days. If we divide this number by 7, we find the remainder 4, which shows again that the last day before our gauge-date is a Wednesday. By adding 23,713 to 2,073,973, we get for the first Caitra 953 the day 2,097,686 of the Julian period, as it ought to be (*Schram*).

P. 51, l. 4.—Read 377, instead of 307.

P. 51, l. 9.—This method works with numbers much less accurate than the preceding ones. It is assumed that one adhimâsa month sums up in $32\frac{4}{7}$ solar months. So the solar months are divided by $32\frac{4}{7}$ or by $\frac{228}{7}$, or, what is the same, they are multiplied by $\frac{7}{228}$. For the time within which an ûnarâtra day sums up, there is simply taken $63\frac{10}{11}$, and the lunar days are divided by $63\frac{10}{11}$ or $\frac{703}{11}$, or, what is the same, multiplied by $\frac{11}{703}$. The epoch corresponds to the year 427 Śakakâla, or the year 3,243,606 of the caturyuga. This number of years is equal to 38,923,272 solar months, which, multiplied by 66,389 and divided by 2,160,000, give $1,196,331\frac{29789}{30000}$ adhimâsa months. The author has taken 1,196,332 adhimâsa months and neglected the little fraction $\frac{211}{30000}$, so that he has no fractions of adhimâsa months. These 1,196,332 adhimâsa months added to the 38,923,272 solar months give 40,119,604 lunar months or 1,203,588,120 lunar days. Multiplying by 11, we have 13,239,469,320, which divided by 111,573 gives $118,661\frac{105567}{111573}$ or 118,662. Subtracting this from 13,239,469,320, we have 13,239,350,658, which divided by 703 gives $18,832,646\frac{520}{703}$ for the number of ûnarâtra days. So the fraction of ûnarâtra days is $\frac{520}{703}$, very near to that adopted by the author of the method, viz., $\frac{514}{703}$. By subtracting the ûnarâtra days from the lunar days we get as the number of civil days 1,184,755,474, which is divisible by 7. So, as the last day before the caturyuga was Monday, the last day before this epoch is also Monday, and the number of days elapsed since this epoch if divided by 7, will give a remainder which indicates the week-day, counting Tuesday as 1. The first day of this epoch corresponds to the day 1,905,590 of the Julian period (*Schram*).

P. 51, l. 24.—It is easily understood why this method is called that of the Siddhânta of the Greeks. It is assumed that an adhimâsa month sums up in $32\frac{4}{7}$ or $\frac{228}{7}$ solar months. Now $\frac{228}{7}$ solar months are equal to $\frac{19}{7}$ solar years. Therefore this method is apparently an application of the cycle of nineteen years of the Greeks (*Schram*).

P. 52, l. 2.—32 months 17 days 8 ghaṭî and 34 cashaka are only another expression for $32\frac{4}{7}$ months (*Schram*).

P. 52, l. 10.—The number of civil days is 192096; dividing by 7, we have as remainder 2. As in this method (see note to p. 51, l. 9) Tuesday is to be reckoned as 1, this gives for the last day before our gauge-date Wednesday. Adding 192,096 to 1,905,590, we get as the first Caitra 953 the day 2,097,686 of the Julian period, as it ought to be (*Schram*).

P. 52, l. 20. *Al-harḳan.*—This book is mentioned only in this passage. The author calls it a *canon*, زيج, *i.e.* a collection of astronomical, chronological, and astrological tables and calculations. Whether it was an original composition in Arabic or translated from Sanskrit, and from what original, we do not learn from him. The word seems to be an Arabic rendering of *ahargaṇa*. Alberuni quotes from this book the computation of an era the epoch of which falls 40,081 days later than that of the Persian era, and compares it with the gauge-date (p. 53).

P. 52, l. 22.—If the epoch should fall 40,081 days after that of the era Yazdajird, it would fall on the first Caitra of the year 664 Śakakâla; but this is not the case. The first of Sha'bân of the year 197 coincides with the beginning of Vaiśâkha 735. As there are 72 years to be subtracted, we should come to Vaiśâkha 663, and to begin with the beginning of a year, the epoch must be postponed to Caitra 664. But this is of no importance, as we shall see that Alberuni altogether misunderstood the method here given (*Schram*).

P. 52, l. 24.—These two dates do not agree to a day. The first Ferwerdinmâh Yazdajird coincides with 16th June 632; 40,081 days later was Monday, 12th March 742, whilst the 21st Daimâh of the year 110 of Yazdajird corresponds to Sunday, 11th March 742. But as the date itself is erroneous, this is of no importance (*Schram*).

P. 52, l. 27.—As the numbers which form multiplications and divisions in this method are identical with those of the Pañca Siddhântikâ (p. 51), we can reckon the constants by the directions there given. The epoch of the method of Al-harkan is the beginning of Sha'bân of the year 197. But this date corresponds to the beginning of Vaiśakha 735 Śakakâla. So we should have for this date the following calculation:—Subtracting 427 from 735 years and 1 month, we get 308 years 1 month, or 3697 months; 3697 multiplied by 7 and divided by 228 gives for the number of adhimâsa months $113\frac{115}{228}$; the 113 adhimâsa months added to the 3697 solar months give 3810 lunar months or 114,300 lunar days. This number multiplied by 11 is 1,257,300; we add 514, which gives us 1,257,814; this divided by 703 gives for the number of ûnarâtra days $1789\frac{147}{703}$. So we should have all the numbers wanted for our epoch if, in fact, this epoch were the true epoch. But we have to add 864 months to the interval. Therefore these 864 months, which must always be added, must first be subtracted from the epoch, so that this latter is thrown back by 72 years. Now 72 years or 864 solar months multiplied by 7 and divided by 228 give the number of $26\frac{120}{228}$ adhimâsa months. These together with the 864 solar months are 890 lunar months or 26,700 lunar days, which multiplied by 11 and divided by 703 give $417\frac{549}{703}$ ûnarâtra days. So we have to subtract from the numbers first found $26\frac{120}{228}$ adhimâsa months and $417\frac{549}{703}$ ûnarâtra days. The number of adhimâsa months inherent to our true epoch will then be $113\frac{115}{228} - 26\frac{120}{228} = 86\frac{223}{228}$, or with sufficient accuracy 87 without a fraction, and the number of ûnarâtra days $1789\frac{147}{703} - 417\frac{549}{703} = 1371\frac{301}{703}$. Therefore no fraction is to be added to the adhimâsa months, whilst to the ûnarâtra days there must be added $\frac{301}{703}$, or nearly $\frac{11 \times 28}{703}$. Therefore we must add 28 (not 38) before multiplying by $\frac{11}{703}$. The 114,300 lunar days of the first epoch diminished by the 26,700 lunar days of the 72 years, give 87,600 lunar days. Subtracting therefrom 1371 ûnarâtra days, we have 86,229 civil days, which being divided by 7 give as remainder 3. So the last day before this epoch is Thursday, and the number of days elapsed since the epoch of this method, if divided by 7, will give a remainder indicating the week-day, counting Friday as 1. The first day of this epoch corresponds to the day 1,991,819 of the Julian period (*Schram*).

P. 53, l. 1.—It must be 28, not 38 (see preceding note) (*Schram*).

P. 53, l. 6.—We must add 1, if we wish to have the week-day of the date itself, not that of the last day before it.

P. 53, l. 8.—Here Friday is considered as the first day of the week, not, as in the Indian books, Sunday. This ought to have been remarked (*Schram*).

P. 53, l. 9.—Alberuni's notes to this method of Alharḳan are perhaps the weakest part of his work. His very first remark shows a complete misunderstanding of the whole calculation. The method is correct, for the months of the seventy-two years with which it begins are solar. If, as Alberuni would have them, they were lunar, and the rest of the months, as he understands it, were lunar too, then the calculation would simply be nonsense; for finding adhimâsa months is nothing else than finding the number which we must add to convert solar months into lunar ones. But when the months are already lunar, how can one add anything to them to make them once more lunar? (*Schram*).

P. 53, l. 15.—The example he works out is as erroneous as the remarks on the method itself. It must be clear to anybody who examines the method given on p. 52, that by the words (l. 29), "Add thereto the months which have elapsed between the first of Sha'bân of the year 197 and the first of the month in which you happen to be," there can only be meant solar months. The author fixed the initial epoch in his calendar by saying "1 Sha'bân 197," instead of fixing it in the Indian calendar by saying "first Vaiśakha 735." This accidental circumstance, which is of no consequence, induced Alberuni to think that he was to take the interval in lunar months, as the Arabic calendar has only lunar months, and he did not notice that lunar months in this part of the calculation would be absolutely impossible. He takes, in fact, in the example, the interval in lunar months, for there are 2695 lunar months between the first Sha'bân 197 and first Rabi' I. 422, and to these 2695 lunar months he adds the 864 months which he knows to be solar. Then he changes all these mingled months, of which the greatest part are already lunar, to lunar ones, as if they all were solar, and at last he wonders that the result is nonsense, and tries to amend the method. The only fault in the matter is that he did not understand the method.

If we wish to exemplify the method of the canon *Alharkan* in the case of our gauge-date, *i.e.* the first Caitra 953 Śakakâla, we must proceed as follows:—Subtracting from 953 years 735 years 1 month, we get as interval 217 years 11 months or 2615 solar months; adding thereto 864 solar months, we have 3479 solar months. This multiplied by 7 and divided by 228 gives for the number of adhimâsa months $106\frac{185}{228}$; adding the 106 adhimâsa months to the 3479 solar months, we get 3585 lunar months, or 107,550 lunar days. We add 28, and multiplying 107,578 by 11, we have 1,183,358, which number divided by 703 gives the number $1683\frac{209}{703}$ for the ûnarâtra days. Subtracting the 1683 ûnarâtra days from the 107,550 lunar days, we have 105,867 civil days. We add 1 in order to get the week-day of the first Caitra 953, and dividing by 7, we get as remainder 7. And as here Friday is considered as 1, so 7 corresponds to Thursday, and the first Caitra 953 is found to be Thursday. By adding 105,867 to 1,991,819 we have for the first Caitra of the year 953 the day 2,097,686 of the Julian period, as it ought to be (*Schram*).

P. 53, l. 33.—The emendation is as erroneous as the example was. The 25,958 days are counted from the epoch falling 40,081 days after that of Yazdajird to the first Sha'bân 197. But 25,958 days are equal to 879 Arabic months, or 73 years and 3 months. Further, he takes again the interval in lunar months, so that now in the amended method he has nothing but lunar months, which he changes to lunar months as if they were solar. So he gets a number which is, of course, absolutely erroneous, but he thinks it to be correct, for in the last instance he commits a new fault by *subtracting* 1 instead of adding it. And so by an accidental combination of different faults he finds by chance a week-day which agrees with that of the day before our gauge-date (*Schram*).

P. 54, l. 12.—As the multiplications and divisions of this method have already been explained in the note to pp. 36 and 37, we have here to account for the constant numbers only which are inherent to the epoch. The epoch is 854 Śakakâla, which corresponds to the year 1,972,948,033 of the kalpa. Multiplying 1,972,948,033 by 12, we find 23,675,376,396 solar months, which multiplied by 1,593,300,000, the adhimâsa months of a kalpa, and divided by 51,840,000,000, the solar months of a kalpa, give the quotient $727,661,597\frac{6463}{14400}$ as the number of adhimâsa months. Adding the 727,661,597 adhimâsa months to the 23,675,376,396 solar months, we have 24,403,037,993 lunar months or 732,091,139,790 lunar days. This latter number multiplied by 25,082,550,000, the ûnarâtra days of a kalpa, and divided by 1,602,999,000,000, the lunar days of a kalpa, gives for the number of ûnarâtra days $11,455,224,000\frac{347481}{356222}$. Subtracting the 11,455,224,000 ûnarâtra days from the 732,091,139,790 lunar days, we find as the number of civil days elapsed from the beginning of the kalpa to this epoch 720,635,915,790, a number which divided by 7 gives as remainder 0. So, as the last day preceding the kalpa was a Saturday (see p. 28, l. 31), the last day before this epoch is also a Saturday, and any number of days elapsed since this epoch, if divided by 7, shows by its remainder the week-day counted from Sunday as 1. The fraction of the adhimâsa months inherent to the epoch has been found to be $\frac{6463}{14400}$. Now $\frac{6463}{14400}$ is equal to $\frac{29\frac{2459}{14400}}{65}$, or very nearly $\frac{29}{65}$; so we add 29 before dividing by 65. The fraction of the ûnarâtra days is $\frac{347481}{356222}$. Now again $\frac{347481}{356222}$ is equal to $\frac{685\frac{267073}{356222}}{703}$, or nearly $\frac{686}{703}$; so we add 686 before dividing by 703.

The first day of this epoch coincides with the day 2,061,541 of the Julian period (*Schram*).

P. 55, l. 5.—This method consists in finding first the difference of the mean longitude of sun and moon. The numbers are Pulisa's. There are in a caturyuga 4,320,000 revolutions of the sun, and 57,753,336 revolutions of the moon. The difference, 53,433,336, is the number of lunar months. In every lunar month the moon gains one revolution or 360 degrees over the sun. Dividing 53,433,336 by the solar years 4,320,000, we find as the number of lunar months belonging to one solar year $12\frac{132778}{360000}$. So in every solar year the moon gains over the sun $12\frac{132778}{360000}$ revolutions.

Omitting the whole revolutions which have no interest, the moon gains over the sun $\frac{132778}{360000}$ revolutions, or, what is the same, $132\frac{778}{1000}$ degrees. Now $\frac{778}{1000}$ degrees are equal to $46\frac{68}{100}$ or to $46\frac{34}{50}$ minutes. So the moon gains over the sun in every solar year 132 degrees $46\frac{34}{50}$ minutes. By multiplying the number of years by 132 degrees $46\frac{34}{50}$ minutes, we find the number of degrees which the moon has gained in the given interval over the sun. Now if in the beginning of this epoch sun and moon had been together, this would be the difference of the mean longitude of sun and moon. But as this was only in the beginning of the caturyuga, but not at the moment of our epoch, there is an initial difference between the longitudes of sun and moon which must be added. Our epoch, or the year 821 Śakakâla, corresponds to the year 3,244,000 of the caturyuga. Multiplying 3,244,000 by the number of lunar months 53,433,336, and dividing by the number of solar years 4,320,000, we find that in these 3,244,000 years the moon gained over the sun $40,124,477\frac{112}{360}$ revolutions. Dropping again the whole revolutions, we see that the moon was in advance of the sun at the moment of our epoch by $\frac{112}{360}$ revolutions, or 112 degrees. Therefore these 112 degrees must be added, and all the numbers of this method find in this their explanation. The result for our gauge-date, 358° 41′ 46″, is the number of degrees, minutes, and seconds by which the moon is in advance of the sun at the moment of the beginning of the *solar* year 821, that is, in the moment when the sun enters Aries. As in the beginning of the luni-solar year sun and moon must have been in conjunction, the beginning of the luni-solar year has preceded that of the solar year by an interval which was just sufficient for the moon to make 358° 41′ 46″ in advance of the sun. Now as the moon gains 360 degrees in a lunar month or 30 lunar days, so she gains 12° in every lunar day. Therefore dividing 358° 41′ 46″ by 12, we get the number of lunar days and fractions by which the luni-solar year's beginning preceded that of the solar year. The fractions of the lunar days are changed to ghaṭis and cashakas. Thereby we get 29 days 53 ghaṭis 29 cashakas as the time by which the beginning of the luni-solar year preceded the sun's entering Aries, in agreement with the fraction of the adhimâsa month found on p. 31, l. 17. For $\frac{44837}{45000}$ adhimâsa months are also equal to 29 days 53 ghaṭis 29 cashakas. The number 27 days 23 ghaṭis 29 cashakas which he gives, p. 55, l. 25, is obtained by dividing 328° 41′ 46″, and not 358° 41′ 46″, by 12 (*Schram*).

P. 55, l. 17.—The Arabic manuscript has 328 instead of 358.

P. 55, l. 33.—The number is 132° $46\frac{34}{50}$, and not 132° 46′ 34″ (as the Arabic manuscript has). Therefore the *portio anni* is not 11° 3′ 52″ 50‴, but 11 days 3 ghaṭis 53 cashakas 24″; and the *portio mensis* not 0° 55′ 19″ 24‴ 10$^{iv}$, but 0 days 55 ghaṭis 19 cashakas 27‴.

The reason of this calculation is the following:—In a year or 12 solar months the moon gains over the sun 132° $46\frac{34}{50}$. As she gains 12 degrees in every lunar day, the twelfth part of these degrees will represent the sum of lunar days and their fractions which the solar year contains over 360, that is to say, the sum of adhimâsa days and their fractions. One solar month containing 0 adhimâsa days 55 ghaṭis 19 cashakas 27‴, the number of solar months within which one adhimâsa month or 30 lunar days sum up, will be found by dividing 30 days by 0 days 55 ghaṭis 19 cashakas 27″. This gives 2 years 8 months 16 days 3 ghaṭi 55 cashaka.

P. 56, l. 1.—There must be a great lacuna, for the first

lines of this page are absolutely without meaning. I am inclined to attribute this lacuna to the source whence the author drew this information, *i.e.* the Arabic translation of Karaṇasâra.

P. 59, l. 23.—The calculation should be made in the following manner:—The sum of days of the kaliyuga is multiplied by the star-cycles of a kalpa and divided by the civil days of a kalpa, viz., 1,577,916,450,000. So we get the revolutions and part of a revolution which the planet has made during the time elapsed since the beginning of the kaliyuga. But in the beginning of the kaliyuga all planets have not been in conjunction; this was only the case in the beginning of the kalpa. Therefore to the fractions of revolutions which the planet made since the beginning of the kaliyuga, we must add its place at this beginning itself, *i.e.* the fraction of a revolution which every planet had at the beginning of the kaliyuga, the whole revolutions being of no interest. But Brahmagupta adds these numbers before dividing by the civil days of the kalpa, and this is quite natural, both fractions having by this proceeding the same divisor. Therefore what he calls the *basis*, ought to be the fraction of every planet at the beginning of the kaliyuga multiplied by the civil days of the kalpa; but he has made a great mistake. Instead of multiplying the fractions by the civil *days* of a kalpa, viz., 1,577,916,450,000, he has multiplied them by the years of a kalpa, viz., 4,320,000,000. Therefore all numbers given on p. 60 as the *bases* are entirely erroneous. To find the fractions for each planet and the *bases* we have the following calculation:—From the beginning of the kalpa to that of the kaliyuga there have elapsed 1,972,944,000 years; so to get the places of the planets at the beginning of the kaliyuga we ought to multiply the revolutions of each planet by 1,972,944,000, and to divide them by the years of a kalpa, 4,320,000,000. As these two numbers have the common divisor 432,000, we multiply the revolutions of each planet by 4567 and divide them by 10,000. This will give us the place of the planet at the beginning of the kaliyuga. We have thus for the single planets:—

For Mars, 2,296,828,522 revolutions multiplied by 4567

and divided by 10,000 give $1,048,961,585\frac{9974}{10000}$ revolutions; so the place of Mars at the beginning of the kaliyuga is $\frac{9974}{10000}$ of a revolution.

For Mercury, 17,936,998,984 revolutions multiplied by 4567 and divided by 10,000 give $8,191,827,435\frac{9928}{10000}$ revolutions; so the place of Mercury is $\frac{9928}{10000}$ revolutions.

For Jupiter, 364,226,455 revolutions multiplied by 4567 and divided by 10,000 give $166,342,221\frac{9985}{10000}$ revolutions; so his place is $\frac{9985}{10000}$ revolutions.

For Venus, 7,022,389,492 revolutions multiplied by 4567 and divided by 10,000 give $3,207,125,280\frac{9964}{10000}$; so her place is $\frac{9964}{10000}$ revolutions.

For Saturn, 146,567,298 revolutions multiplied by 4567 and divided by 10,000 give $66,937,284\frac{9966}{10000}$ revolutions; and his place is $\frac{9966}{10000}$ revolutions.

For the sun's apsis, 480 revolutions multiplied by 4567 and divided by 10,000 give $219\frac{2160}{10000}$ revolutions; and its place is $\frac{2160}{10000}$ revolutions.

For the moon's apsis, 488,105,858 revolutions multiplied by 4567 and divided by 10,000 give $222,917,945\frac{3486}{10000}$ revolutions; and its place is $\frac{3486}{10000}$ revolutions.

For the moon's node, 232,311,168 revolutions multiplied by 4567 and divided by 10,000 give $106,096,510\frac{4256}{10000}$ revolutions; and its place is $\frac{4256}{10000}$ revolutions.

Multiplying now the place of every planet by 1,577,916,450,000, we get the following *bases* for the single planets:—

For Mars, 1,573,813.867,230.
" Mercury, 1,566,555,451,560.
" Jupiter, 1,575.549.575.325.
" Venus, 1,572,235,950,780.
" Saturn, 1,572,551.534,070.
" the sun's apsis, 340,829.953.200.
" the moon's apsis, 550.061.674,470.
" the ascending node, 671,561,241,120 (*Schram*).

P. 67, l. 14. A.H. 161.—According to p. 15, the year was A.H. 154. *Cf.* note to i. 169.

P. 71.—With the orbits of the planets *cf. Sûrya-Siddhânta*, xii. 90, note.

Pp. 74 *seq.*—As for the Arabic terminology of these pages, it deserves to be noticed that—

(1.) القطر المعدّل means *the true distance* = Sanskrit *mandakarṇa.*

(2.) That القطر المقوّم means *the true distance of the shadow's end*; and

(3.) *Sinus totus*, جيب الكلّ = Sanskrit *trijîvâ* or *trijyâ*, means *the sinus of three zodiacal signs or 90 degrees, i.e.* the radius.

P. 74, ll. 17, 18.—Instead of TC = طح the Arabic manuscript has KC = كح, which has been corrected by Dr. Schram.

P. 75, l. 34.—The lacuna must be something like the following:—"For *KC* must be divided by the divisor kept in memory" (*Schram*).

P. 78, l. 27.—This and the two following passages are not clear. Alberuni does not seem to have understood the subject, for the shadow is neither the greatest nor the mean, but the true shadow; and the shadow from which one is to subtract, *i.e.* 1581, is nothing else than the earth's diameter, which also is neither the mean nor the greatest, but always the same (*Schram*).

P. 79.—*Alkhwârizmî* is mentioned here and ii. 114 (on the various colours of eclipses). According to *Fihrist*, p. ٢٧٤, he composed an epitome of the Sindhind (*Brahma-Siddhânta*). He is famous as the author of a work on algebra, edited by Rosen, London, 1831. *Cf.* also. L. Rodet, *L'Algèbre d'Alkhwârizmî et les Methodes Indienne et Grecque* ("Journal Asiatique," 101 (1878), pp. 5 *seq.*).

P. 82. *Two suns, two moons, &c.*—This theory, as well as the expression *fish* (a name for the polar star?), seem to be of Jaina origin. *Cf.* Colebrooke, "Essays," ii. 201.

P. 84.—*Cf.* with this table of the *Nakshatras* a paper of Thibaut, "The Number of the Stars constituting the several Nakshatras according to Brahmagupta, &c.," the "Indian Antiquary," 1885, p. 43; also Colebrooke, "Essays," ii. 284, and *Sûrya-Siddhânta*, p. 321.

P. 89, l. 32.—In the Arabic text, p. ٣٤٦, 15, read الف instead of الفين. The number of years is 1800, not 2800.

P. 90. *Kâlâṁśaka.*—This term (also *kâlâṁśa*) is explained in *Sûrya-Siddhânta*, note to ix. 5.

The work *Ghurrat-alzîjât*, only once mentioned, is perhaps identical with the *Kitâb-alghurra*, which Alberuni quotes in his "Chronology" (my translation, p. 15 *et passim*). Its author was Abû-Muḥammad Alnâ'ib Alâmuli, who has used the work of Ya'ḳûb Ibn Ṭârik. *Cf.* note to i. 169.

P. 90, l. 21.—Emendation of the *khaṇḍakhâdyaka* (also on p. 91), *i.e.* Uttarakhaṇḍakhâdyaka.

On Vijayanandin (l. 26), the author of *Karaṇatilaka*, *cf.* note to i. p. 156.

P. 101.—The enumeration of mountains, here taken from the *Matsya-Purâṇa*, may be checked by the help of *Vishṇu-Purâṇa*, ii. 141, note 2, and ii. 191 *seq.* The last name is written *bahâshîr* in the Arabic, which I cannot identify with an Indian name. Perhaps it is a blunder for *mahâshîr*, which might represent *mahâśaila*. *Vide* *Vishṇu-Purâṇa*, II. iv. p. 197.

P. 101.—On the *Aurva* legend, *cf.* *Vishṇu-Purâṇa*, III. viii. p. 81, note.

P. 102.—The story of Soma, the husband of the daughters of Prajâpati (the lunar stations), occurs in its elements already in the Vedic period. *Cf.* H. Zimmer, *Altindisches Leben*, pp. 355, 375.

P. 104.—On the Hindu theory of ebb and flow, *cf.* *Vishṇu-Purâṇa*, ii. 203, 204. The two names, of which I have not found the Indian equivalents, are written *baharn* and *vuhar* in the Arabic.

P. 105. *The Vishṇu-Purâṇa says.*—The author seems to refer to *Vishṇu-Purâṇa*, II. iv. p. 204: "The rise and fall of the waters of the different seas is five hundred and ten (not 1500) inches" (or finger-breadths).

P. 106.—The author's theory of the origin of the Dibajât has already been mentioned, vol. i. 233.

P. 110.—As to the strictures of the author on the sincerity of Brahmagupta, *cf.* note to p. 25 (here ii. p. 263). The passages which excited the indignation of Alberuni do not express the view of Brahmagupta, but were simply taken by him from older books—in fact, written *pûrva-śâstrânusârena.* *Cf.* Kern, translation of *Bṛihat-Saṁhitâ*, note to chap. iii. v. 4 (p. 445).

P. 114, l. 12. *Kinds of eclipses.*—Read instead of this, *colours of the eclipses.* On Alkhwârizmî, *cf.* note to ii. 79.
What the author here mentions as a view of the Hindus, agrees literally with *Sûrya-Siddhânta*, vi. 23.

P. 116.—On the *Khaṇḍakhâdyaka*, the Sanskrit original of the Arabic *Sindhind*, *cf.* note to i. 153, 154.

P. 118.—On the *Bṛihajjâtakam* of Varâhamihira, *cf.* note to i. 219.

P. 119.—Rules for finding the dominants or regents of the day, month, and year are given in the *Sûrya-Siddhânta*, i. 51, 52; xii. 78, 79.

P. 120.—On the *srûdhava* (?) of Mahâdeva, not to be confounded with the book of the same title by Utpala, *cf.* note to i. 157.

P. 120. *Table of the serpents.*—The names of this table must be compared with the names in *Vishṇu-Purâṇa*, ii. 74, 285. The words *Suku* and *Cabrahasta* seem to be mistakes of the Arabic copyist for *Vâsuki* and *Cakrahasta.*

P. 121.—The names of the dominants of the planets are not known to me from a Sanskrit source. Therefore the pronunciation of some of them remains uncertain.

Pp. 121, 122.—The names of the dominants of the Nakshatras are given by A. Weber, *Ueber den Vedakalender Namens Jyotisham*, p. 94. *Cf.* also *Sûrya-Siddhânta*,

viii. 9, pp. 327 *seq.*, and *Vishṇu-Purâṇa*, II. viii., notes on pp. 276, 277.

Instead of *Mitra*, the deity presiding over Anurâdhâ, it would perhaps be better to write *Maitra*, and in the Arabic میتر (*Vishṇu-Purâṇa*, ii. p. 277).

The latter part of this list in the Arabic text is not free from confusion.

The regent of Uttarabhâdrapadâ is placed side by side with Pûrvabhâdrapadâ, whilst the latter station is left without its regent, which is *aja ekapât* (*Sûrya-Siddhânta*, p. 343). A part of this word seems to be extant in the square for *aśvinî*, which has اشو كبار. Perhaps this is to be read *aśvin ajaikapâd*, اشو اجيكباد, in which case the Arabic copyist has made two blunders, dropping part of the word *ajaikapâd* and placing it in the wrong square.

P. 123.—On the sixty-years cycle *cf.* *Sûrya-Siddhânta*, i. 55, and xiv. 17; Varâhamihira, *Bṛihat-Saṁhitâ*, viii. 20–53.

P. 125.—For the names Samvatsara, Parivatsara, &c., *cf.* *Bṛihat-Saṁhitâ*, viii. 24; *Sûrya-Siddhânta*, xiv. 17, note; Weber, *Ueber den Vedakalender genannt Jyotisham*, p. 34–36.

Pp. 127, 128.—The dominants of the single *lustra* are given in *Bṛihat-Saṁhitâ*, chap. viii. 23.

The names of the single years exhibit some differences from the Sanskrit text (*Bṛihat-Saṁhitâ*, viii. 27–52).

No. 8, بهابس instead of *bhâva*, has risen from a wrong division of the words of the text—

*śrîmukhabhâvasâhvau*,

i.e. *śrîmukha-bhâva-sâhvau*.

No. 9, جى instead of جو = *yuvan*, is perhaps a mistake of the copyist of the Arabic text.

No. 15, بش, *visha* (in Kern's edition *vṛisha*), is not a mistake, but a different reading. The word in brackets (*Vṛishabha*) is to be cancelled.

No. 18, نَتَ, *natu*, cannot be combined with *pârthiva*. It corresponds to *nataṁ*. *Cf.* Kern's various readings to chap. viii. 35.

No. 30, جتر. The name of the thirtieth year is *durmukha.* Perhaps the reading جتر has risen from a wrong division of these words (viii. 38)—

*manmatho 'sya parataśca durmukhaḥ*,

so as to represent the elements *-ca dur-*.

No. 34, سرب (*śarva*), seems to be a mistake for *śarvari* or *sarvarin.*

No. 40, *parâvasu* is the reading of some manuscripts for *parabhâva.* *Cf.* Kern, various readings to viii. 41.

No. 48. This year is called *ânanda* by Kern, but the reading of Alberuni, *vikrama*, occurs also in Sanskrit manuscripts. *Cf.* various readings to viii. 45.

No. 56. The ندبه of the text seems to be a blunder of the copyist for *dundubhi* (viii. 50).

No. 57, *aṁgâra* or *aṁgâri*, the reading of certain manuscripts instead of *udgâri* (viii. 50).

No. 58 and 60. The words كتاكر (instead of ركتاكر) and كرو = *raktâksha* and *kshaya*, seem to be examples of a phonetic change between *sh* and *r*.

The same list of names is given in *Sûrya-Siddhânta*, i. 55, note.

P. 130.—With this chapter on the four parts of the life of a Brahman *cf.* *Vishṇu-Purâṇa*, book III. chap. ix.

P. 131.—The complete verse of Bashshâr is this—

> "The earth is dark, but the fire is bright,
> And the fire is worshipped, since there is fire."

This is the saying of a man whose parents had come as prisoners of war from Tukhâristân on the Upper Oxus, but he was born in Baṣra, and lived in Bagdad under the Khalif Almahdî. As he stood under the accusation of being a heretic (Zoroastrian or Manichæan), or, according to another version, because he had composed satirical verses on the Khalif, he was, notwithstanding his great age, sentenced to be beaten, and died in consequence, A.H. 167 = A.D. 784. *Cf.* Ibn Khallikân, *Vita*, No. 112.

P. 134, l. 1.—The south, as the direction foreboding evil, has already once been mentioned in connection with the islands Laṅkâ and Vaḍavâmukha, *vide* i. 307, 308.

Pp. 134, 135.—With this description of Âryâvarta *cf.* Manu, ii. 17 *seq.*; Vâsishṭha, i. 12; and Baudhâyana, i. 1, 9–12 ("Sacred Laws of the Âryas," translated by G. Bühler, Oxford, 1879–82).

P. 135.—On the vegetables which must not be eaten, *cf.* Manu, v. 5, and Vâsishṭha, xiv. 33. *Nâlî* seems to be = Sanskrit *nâlikâ.*

P. 136.—The contents of this chapter are nearly related to *Vishṇu-Purâṇa*, book III. chap. viii.

P. 137.—The story of King Râma, the Brahmin, and the *Caṇḍâla*, taken from the *Râmâyaṇa*, *vide* in Wilkins' "Hindu Mythology" (Calcutta, 1882), p. 319.

Pp. 137, 138.—The two quotations of Alberuni from the *Bhagavadgîtâ* can hardly be compared with any passage in the book in its present form. *Cf.* note to i. 29.

P. 139.—On the *aśvamedha* or horse-sacrifice, *cf.* Colebrooke, "Essays," i. 55, 56.

Pp. 140, 141.—This legend, as given on the authority of the *Vishṇu-Dharma*, is not known to me from a Sanskrit source.

P. 142.—As the original of this quotation from the *Purâṇas* is not known to me, the pronunciation of some of the proper nouns remains uncertain.

P. 143.—The story of Sagara, Bhagîratha, and the Ganges, is related by H. H. Wilson, "Works," vol. ii. p. 168. *Cf.* also Wilkins' "Hindu Mythology," p. 385. The source of this legend is the first book of *Râmâyaṇa.*

P. 145.—I do not know the original of this quotation from Varâhamihira's *Saṁhitâ.*

Pp. 145, 146.—The words here attributed to Śaunaka are probably taken from the *Vishṇu-Dharma. Cf.* note to i. 54.

P. 147.—The story of the head of Brahman is part of the legend of Śiva's fight with the Asura Jalandhara. *Cf.* Kennedy's "Researches," p. 456.

P. 149.—This and the following chapters treat of subjects which are discussed more or less in every Indian law-book, as in those of Manu, Ápastamba, Gautama, and others. Alberuni, however, does not seem to have drawn directly from any of these books, but rather from his own experience, from what his Pandits had told him, and what he himself had observed during his stay in India.

P. 153.—Alḥajjâj was governor of Babylonia during twenty years under the Omayyade Kalif 'Abdulmalik (684–704) and his son Alwalîd (704–714).

P. 153. *That a Brahmin and a Caṇḍâla are equal to him.*—*Cf.* the saying of Vyâsa, the son of Parâśara, here vol. i. p. 44.

P. 155.—On the forbidden degrees of marriage, *cf.* Manu, iii. 5.

P. 156.—On *garbâdhâna*, *sîmaṁtonnayanam*, &c., *cf.* the *Dharmaśâstra* of Gautama, viii. 14; also the *Gṛihyasûtras* of Aśvalâyana, i. 13, 14.

P. 157. *Thus, when Kâbul was conquered, &c.*—The sentence added in brackets to indicate the meaning of the author's words, as I understand them, ought to run thus: "(which proves that he abhorred the eating of cows' meat and sodomy, but that he did not consider harlotry as anything baneful or unlawful)."

The detail in the history of Kâbul here alluded to is not known from other sources, *e.g. Balâdhurî.* During the Omayya Kaliphate of Damascus, both Kâbul and Sijistan bravely fought against the Muslims. During certain years they were subdued and had to pay tribute, but Kâbul always remained under the sway of its Hindu (Brahmin) kings of the Pâla dynasty. It was incorporated into the Khalif's empire under the Abbaside Ma'mûn; it had to receive a Muslim governor, but retained at his side the Hindu Shâh. The same double rule existed in Khwârizm.

About A.D. 950–975 the city of Kâbul was already Muslim, whilst the suburb was inhabited by the Hindus (and by Jews). Kâbul was the coronation-city for the Pâla dynasty, as Königsberg in Prussia for the Hohenzollerns. Even when they ceased to reside in Kâbul, they had to be crowned there.

By the Ispahbad, mentioned by Alberuni, I understand the Hindu governor who ruled over the city for the Pâla king. Our author applies a title of the Sasanian empire to the official of a Hindu empire.

In what year the negotiation referred to by Alberuni took place is not known. Perhaps under Ma'mûn, when the city was definitely ceded to the Muslim conquerors.

It seems to have been the public opinion among Muslims that Hindus considered fornication as lawful, as Ibn Khurdâdhbih expresses it (Elliot, "History of India," i. 13), whilst, according to Alberuni, they considered it indeed as unlawful, but were lax in punishing it.

P. 157.—The Buyide prince 'Aḍud-aldaula, who held Persia under his sway, died A.H. 372=A.D. 982. Not long before Alberuni wrote, the last of their dominions had been annexed to the empire of Mahmûd of Ghazna.

P. 158.—'Iyâs Ibn Mu'âwiya was judge in Baṣra under the Omayya Khalif Omar Ibn 'Abdala'zîz, and died there, A.H. 122=A.D. 740.

P. 159—With the author's description of the ordeals, *cf.* Manu, viii. 114 *seq.*, and a translation of the chapter on ordeals from the *Vyâvahâra Mayûkha* by G. Bühler, in "Journal of the Asiatic Society of Bengal," 1867, vol. xxxv. pp. 14 *seq.*; Stenzler, *Die Indischen Gottesurtheile*, in *Zeitschrift der Deutschen Morgenländischen Gesellschaft*, ix. p. 661. The last-mentioned kind of ordeal (p. 160) is also described in Elliot's "History of India," i. 329 (the Sindian ordeal of fire).

P. 164. *According to a passage in the book Manu.*—*Cf.* Manu, ix. 118.

P. 166.—For the first quotation from *Phædo*, 81D, *cf.* note to i. p. 65. The second quotation can hardly be identified with any passage in *Phædo.* Perhaps it is derived from a commentary on the following words, 81C:—

ἀλλὰ διειλημμένην γε, οἶμαι, ὑπὸ τοῦ σωματοειδοῦς, ὃ αὐτῇ ἡ ὁμιλία τε καὶ συνουσία τοῦ σώματος διὰ τὸ ἀεὶ ξυνεῖναι καὶ διὰ τὴν πολλὴν μελέτην ἐνεποίησε ξύμφυτον.

P. 167.—The quotation from *Phædo* is found 115C–116A:—

Θάπτωμεν δέ σε τίνα τρόπον; ὅπως ἄν, ἔφη, βούλησθε, ἐάνπερ γε λάβητέ με καὶ μὴ ἐκφύγω ὑμᾶς, κ.τ.λ.

ἐγγυήσασθε οὖν με πρὸς Κρίτωνα, ἔφη, τὴν ἐναντίαν ἐγγύην ἢ ἣν οὗτος πρὸς δικαστὰς ἠγγυᾶτο, οὗτος μὲν γὰρ ἦ μὴν παραμενεῖν. ὑμεῖς δὲ ἦ μὴν μὴ παραμενεῖν ἐγγυήσασθε, ἐπειδὰν ἀποθάνω, ἀλλὰ οἰχήσεσθαι ἀπιόντα, ἵνα Κρίτων ῥᾷον φέρῃ, καὶ μὴ ὁρῶν μου τὸ σῶμα ἢ καιόμενον ἢ κατορυττόμενον ἀγανακτῇ ὑπὲρ ἐμοῦ ὡς δεινὰ πάσχοντος μηδὲ λέγῃ ἐν τῇ ταφῇ, ὡς ἢ προτίθεται Σωκράτη ἢ ἐκφέρει ἢ κατορύττει, κ.τ.λ.

ἀλλὰ θαρρεῖν τε χρὴ καὶ φάναι τοὐμὸν σῶμα θάπτειν καὶ θάπτειν οὕτως, ὅπως ἄν σοι φίλον ᾖ καὶ μάλιστα ἡγῇ νόμιμον εἶναι.

P. 168. *Galenus, &c.*—I do not know the Greek original of this quotation. *Cf.* note to i. p. 35.

P. 69.—The words of Vâsudeva are a quotation from *Bhagavad-Gîtâ*, viii. 24.

P. 171. *Johannes Grammaticus.*—*Cf.* note to i. 36.

P. 171.—The two quotations from *Phædo* are found in 62C:—

ἴσως τοίνυν ταύτῃ οὐκ ἄλογον μὴ πρότερον αὑτὸν ἀποκτιννύναι δεῖν, πρὶν ἀνάγκην τινὰ θεὸς ἐπιπέμψῃ, ὥσπερ καὶ τὴν νῦν ἡμῖν παροῦσαν.

And 62B:—

ὡς ἔν τινι φρουρᾷ ἐσμεν οἱ ἄνθρωποι καὶ οὐ δεῖ δὴ

ἑαυτὸν ἐκ ταύτης λύειν οὐδ' ἀποδιδράσκειν, κ.τ.λ. τὸ θεοὺς εἶναι ἡμῶν τοὺς ἐπιμελουμένους καὶ ἡμᾶς τοὺς ἀνθρώπους ἓν τῶν κτημάτων τοῖς θεοῖς εἶναι.

P. 174.—For the *Vishṇu-Purâṇa*, *vide* note to i. 54. The reading *Dure* is not certain, as the Arabic text has only دوری.

The names *Dilîpa*, *Dushyanta*, and *Yayâti* have been verified by means of the index to *Vishṇu-Purâṇa*.

P. 175, last line.—On the festival of the birth of Vâsudeva-Kṛishṇa (*Kṛishṇajanmâshṭamî*), *cf.* Weber, "Indian Antiquary," 1874, p. 21; 1877, p. 161; *Zeitschrift der Deutschen Morgenländischen Gesellschaft*, vi. p. 92.

P. 176, l. 11.—The Arabic manuscript has آتج, *i.e. âtaj*. For the word *aṭṭâṭaja*, *cf.* H. H. Wilson, "Essays and Lectures," ii. 232.

P. 176, l. 19. *Devasînî*.—The latter half of this word is apparently a derivation from the root *svap* = to sleep. In Prakrit *sleep* = *siviṇo* (Sanskrit *svapna*). *Vide Vararuci*, i. 3.

P. 177, l. 20.—*Deotthînî*, also called *deotthân* and *diṭṭhwan*. *Cf.* H. H. Wilson, "Glossary of Technical Terms," pp. 133, 134, 143, and "Memoirs on the History, Folklore, and Distribution of the Races of the North-Western Provinces of India," by H. Elliot, edited by J. Beames, i. 245.

P. 177.—The here-mentioned *bhîshma-pañca-râtri* seems to be identical with the *bhîshma-pañcakam* mentioned by Wilson, "Essays and Lectures," ii. 203.

P. 177.—The name *Gaur-t-r*, گورتر, occurs also ii. 179, and is apparently a vernacular form for *gaurî-tṛitîyâ*. *Cf.* Wilson, *l. l.* p. 185.

P. 178.—With this calendar of festivals are to be compared the treatise of H. H. Wilson, "The Religious Festivals of the Hindus," in his "Essays and Lectures," ii. p. 151 *seq.*, and Garcin de Tassy, *Notice sur les fêtes popu-*

*laires des Hindous*, Paris, 1834. This chapter, as well as the preceding one, would perhaps receive much light from the *Jyotirvidhâbharaṇam*, chap. xxi. *Cf.* Weber, "Journal of the German Oriental Society," vol. xxii. p. 719, and xxiv. p. 399.

This chapter has been translated into Persian by Abû-Sa'îd Gardezî (manuscript of the Bodleian Library in Oxford, Ouseley 240). *Cf.* note to ii. 6.

P. 178. *Agdûs.*—The Arabic has only اكدوس, which might be something like *ajya-divasa.*

*Muttai.*—This pronunciation is given by the manuscript. The name, not to be confounded with the Arabic name *Mattâ* (Matthæus), is perhaps identical with the name of a prince of Siwistan mentioned by Elliot, "History of India," i. 145–153.

*Hindolî-caitra.*—*Cf. Dola-yâtrâ* or *Holî* of Wilson, p. 223.

*Bahand.*—*Vide* Wilson, *l. c.*, and *vasanta*, here ii. 179.

P. 179. *Gaur-t-r.*—*Cf.* note to ii. 177.

P. 180. *Gâihat* (?), &c.—In the Arabic text the word ما must be added before يطعم.

In the following line there is a lacuna, which in my translation I have filled up by the help of the Persian translation of Gardêzî which runs thus:— كاهت بود (sic) واين روز هشم بود كه اندر اين روز زندانيان را طعام دهند. In another place Gardêzî writes كاهت.

P. 181.—On *Jîvaśarman*, *cf.* note to i. 164.

P. 182. *Kîrî* (?).—This is perhaps only a misspelling of the Arabic copyist for كندى, *Kandî* (*Gandî Ribâṭ-ala'mîr*). *Cf.* note to i. 317, and Elliot, "History of India," ii. 112, 150; iv. 138; *Baihaḳî*, ed. Morley, p. 274. It is the place where King Mas'ûd was murdered.

Pp. 182. *Dîbâlî*=*dîpâvali* (row of lamps).—*Cf.* Wilson, "Glossary of Technical Terms," p. 114. Gardezî has ديوالى, *dîvâlî.*

P. 183. *Sâgârtam = śâkâshṭamî.—Cf.* Wilson, "Essays," ii. 208.

P. 183.—*Câmâha* seems to be = *caturdaśî mâgha, mânsartagu = mânsâshṭaka, pûrârtaku = pûrâshṭaka,* and *mâhâtan = mâghâshṭamî. Cf.* Wilson, "Essays," ii. 183, 184, 181.

P. 183.—The festival *dhola* seems to be identical with *holi, holikâ* or *dol-jâtrâ. Cf.* Wilson, p. 147, 210. Instead of *dhola* the Persian translation of Gardêzî has هولى, *hôlî.*

P. 184. *Śivarâtri.—Cf.* Wilson, p. 210.

P. 184.—*Pûyattanu* is perhaps = *pûpâshṭamî.* Cf. *pûpâshṭakâ.*

P. 186.—On the 15th Mâgha, as the beginning of kaliyuga, *cf.* Wilson, "Essays and Lectures," ii. p. 208. Alberuni seems to have taken his information regarding the *yugâdyâ* or beginning of a *yuga* from *Vishṇu-Purâṇa,* III. chap. xiv. p. 168.

P. 187, l. 5.—The number of lunar days, 1,603,000,010 (*sic* MS.), must, according to Dr. Schram, be altered to 1,603,000,080.

P. 188. *Vishuva.*—On the use of this term in astronomy, *cf. Sûrya-Siddhânta,* iii. 6, note.

P. 188.—On *Sumaya* (?), *cf.* note to i. 336.

P. 189, l. 17, after the table.—The solar year is 365 days $15^{i}\ 30^{ii}\ 22^{iii}\ 30^{iv}$, not 365 days $30^{i}\ 22^{ii}\ 30^{iii}\ 0^{iv}$. Accordingly the last line must run thus: "(*i.e.* 1 day $15^{i}\ 30^{ii}\ 22^{iii}\ 30^{iv}$ are equal to $\frac{4027}{3200}$)" (*Schram*).

P. 190, l. 7.—The *bhâgahâra* is not 572, as the manuscript has, but 576, and the fraction $\frac{725}{576}$ (*Schram*).

P. 190.—*Auliatta* (?). The name is written اولت بن سهاوى. A more literal rendering is this: "And that which A. the son of S. has dictated of the same (subject), is based on the theory of Pulisa." This author seems to have been contemporaneous with Alberuni, as also Samaya (ii. 188).

P. 190. *Varâhamihira.*—*Cf.* note to i. 54.
The term *shaḍaśîtimukha* is explained in *Sûrya-Siddhânta*, xiv. 6, note.

P. 191.—On the *Parvan*, *cf.* chap. lx.

P. 192. *Saṁhitâ.*—The author quotes here the *Bṛihat-Saṁhitâ*, chap. xxxii. 24-26.

P. 192.—On the book *Srûdhava*, *cf.* note to i. 157 and ii. 120. Is the word = *sarvadhara?*

P. 194.—With the theory of the *karaṇas*, cf. *Sûrya-Siddhânta*, ii. 67–69.

P. 195.—For an explanation of the term *bhukti*, *cf.* *Sûrya-Siddhânta*, i. 27, note.

P. 197.—The names of the *common karaṇas* are found in *Sûrya-Siddhânta*, ii. 69, note.
The other names are Indian numerals of a vernacular stamp. The corresponding Sindhî forms are *barkhu* (?), *biô*, *ṭriô*, *cothō*, *panjō*, *chahô*, *satō*, *athō*, *nāō*, *ḍahō*, *yârhō*, *bârhō*, *têrhō*, *coḍhō*. *Cf.* Trumpp, "Sindhi Grammar," pp. 158, 174. The form *pancâhî* (=the 15th) has, as far as I can see, no analogy in the vernacular dialects.

P. 199.—*Saṁkrânti* means the sun's entrance into a sign of the zodiac. *Cf.* *Sûrya-Siddhânta*, xiv. 10, note.

P. 200. *Alkindî.*—The way in which this scholar has transformed the Hindu theory of the *karaṇas* is instructive, as showing how Indian subjects were handled by the Arabs before Alberuni, even by the most learned and enlightened among them. The first knowledge of these things was probably communicated to the Arabs by the translation of the *Brahma-Siddhânta* (*Sindhind*) and *Khaṇḍakhâdyaka* (*Arkand*) of Brahmagupta. On Alkindi, *cf.*

G. Flügel, *Alkindî, genannt der Philosoph der Araber*, Leipzig, 1857 (in vol. i. of the *Abhandlungen für die Kunde des Morgenlandes*).

P. 201.—The names of the *vishṭis*, as taken from the *Srûdhava* (of Mahâdeva?—*cf.* note to ii. 120), are not known to me from a Sanskrit source. However, *vaḍavâmukha*, *ghora*, and *kâlarâtri* seem to be certain. The words بلو and جوال might be *plava* and *jvâla*, but كرّال ?

The other series of names of the *vishṭis*, according to Alkindî, which by a mistake have been omitted in the Arabic text, may be transliterated in this way:—

(1.) Shûlpî (*śûlapadî ?*).
(2.) Jamadûd (*yâmyodadhi ?*).
(3.) Ghora.
(4.) Nastarînish.
(5.) Dârunî (*dhâriṇî ?*).
(6.) Kayâlî.
(7.) Bahayâmani.
(8.) Bikata (*vyakta ?*).

P. 204. *On the yogas.*—The contents of this chapter are near akin to those of chap. xi. of the *Sûrya-Siddhânta*. Compare also in the same book ii. 65, 66. The technical term *pâta*, which literally means *fall* (for its astrological meaning, *cf. l. c.* xi. 5, note), has in Arabic been rendered by the word سقوط, *i.e. falling* (page ٣٠, 11, 24), here ii. 207, 208, 209. In the Arabic text on p. ٢٩٩, 7, read بدّل instead of بدلّة, and to the word بيدرت, l. 16, it must be added that the manuscript has بيدران.

P. 205.—On the *Karaṇatilaka* of Vijayanandin, *cf.* note to i. 156.

P. 207.—The *bhuktyantara* has been explained, ii. 195.

P. 208.—*Syâvabala* (?) seems to have been a Hindu from Kashmîr who had become a Muslim, and wanted, by means of an *Arabic* book, to be informed on certain chapters of *Hindu* astrology. The pronunciation *Syâvabala* is not certain. The Arabic manuscript has *siyâwpal*.

P. 208.—On the Brahmin *Bhaṭṭila*, *cf.* note to i. 157. The names of the yogas which he mentions are not known to me from other sources. The names *gaṇḍânta*, *kâla-daṇḍa*, and *vaidhṛita* are certain, and *barh* is probably *varsha*.

P. 209.—On Śripâla, *cf.* note to i. 164.

P. 210.—With the names of this table *cf. Súrya-Siddhânta*, ii. 65, note (also p. 432). The جفكر of the Arabic seems to be a mistake for جفكم, *vishkambha*; No. 15, كتند, a mistake for كند, *gaṇḍa*.

Instead of *âyushmant* (name of the third yoga), the Arabic has رازكم (*rájakama?*); instead of *vyatipâta* it has كنبات (*gatipâta?*).

P. 211.—The contents of this astrological chapter are principally taken from the *Laghujâtakam* (*i.e.* the smaller book of nativity) by Varâhamihira, of which the chapters i. ii. have been translated by A. Weber (*Indische Studien*, 2, 277 *seq.*), whilst the remainder has been translated by H. Jacobi (*De Astrologiæ Indicæ* horâ *appellatæ originibus. Accedunt Laghujâtaki capita inedita* iii.–xii., Bonn, 1872). Alberuni does not always adhere to the order of the paragraphs which we have in the Sanskrit text, and for certain parts he seems to have drawn from some commentary.

The exact meaning of the term *seconds of the stars* (the same page, ll. 23, 24), ثواني النجوم, is not known to me.

Pp. 213–215.—The *table of planets* is taken from chapters ii. iii. iv. of the *Laghujâtakam*.

For the reading of the terms *naisargika*, *vimiśra*, and *shaḍâya* (p. 215), I am indebted to Prof. H. Jacobi, Kiel.

The number 25, كه, in the column with the heading *The scale of their magnitude*, seems to be a mistake for 3, ج.

Pp. 217–219.—This table of the zodiacal signs has been taken from *Laghujâtakam*, chap. i.

Pp. 221, 222.—This table of the *Houses* has been taken from *Laghujâtakam*, chap. i. 15.

P. 234.—The notes on comets and other meteorological subjects, with which the author concludes his book, have been taken from the *Bṛihat-Saṁhitâ* of Varâhamihira.

Pp. 237–238.—This table of comets is taken from *Bṛihat-Saṁhitâ*, chap. xi. 10–28.

The *children of the fire* are called *hutâśasutâḥ* in Sanskrit, in Arabic اولاد الشان, which I cannot explain.

Pp. 241–244.—This table of comets is taken from *Bṛihat-Saṁhitâ*, chap. xi. 29–51.

The reading بنمكيت, instead of *padmaketu*, seems to be a mistake of the copyist for بذمكيت.

P. 245. *Book of the medicine of elephants.*—On this and similar literature, *cf.* A. Weber, *Vorlesungen über Indische Literaturgeschichte*, p. 289.

# INDEX I.


â = âditya, i. 215
abda, ii. 118
abdhi, i. 178
Abhâpûrî, i. 200
âbhâstala, i. 230
Abhi, i. 303
abhijit, i. 340, 341, 342; ii. 66, 85, 87, 122
Abhîra, i. 300, 301, 302
abhra, i. 178
Âbika (?), i. 299
âcârya, i. 155
Âcûd (?), ii. 143
Âdarśa, i. 302
âḍhaka, i. 162, 163, 164
adhas, i. 290
adhimâsa, ii. 20 *seq.*, 23; universal or partial, ii. 23
Adhishṭhâna, i. 207; ii. 181
adhomukha, i. 61
âdi, i. 178; ii. 23
âdi-purâṇa, i. 130
Aditi, ii. 121
Âdittahaur, i. 206
âditya, i. 116, 179, 215, 216, 291
âdityavâra, i. 213
âditya-purâṇa, i. 130, 168, 217, 229, 230, 232, 248, 368
âdityaputra, i. 215
adri, i. 178
aga, i. 178
agastya, i. 132; ii. 66, 91, 92, 94
Agastyamata, i. 132
Agdûs (?), ii. 178
âgneya, i. 290, 297, 301; ii. 203
Âgneya, i. 358
Agni, i. 131, 178, 242, 342, 357, 358, 394; ii. 121, 125
Agnika (!), i. 394
Agnîdhra, i. 394
agnihotrin, i. 102
Agnijihva, i. 231
Agnimukha, i. 231
Agnîtya, i. 302
Agniveśa, i. 159
agokîru, i. 220
ahan, i. 368; ii. 26
ahaṅkâra, i. 41
ahargaṇa, i. 355, 368; ii. 26, 27 *seq.*, 34, 46 *seq.*, 48, 60, 116, 184
Ahâri, ii. 179
Ahirbudhnya, i. 342; ii. 66, 122
âhoî, ii. 180
ahorâtra, i. 359
aindra, i. 135
Airâvata, ii. 245
aiśâna, i. 290, 297; ii. 202
aiśânya, i. 303
Aja, i. 342, 358.
Aja ekapâd, ii. 122
Ajodaha (Ayodhyâ), i. 200
Âkara, i. 301
âkâśa, i. 178
akshara, i. 172
akshauhiṇî, i. 179, 403, 407, 408
akshi, i. 178
Alika, i. 300
Alîspûr, i. 203
Amarâvatî, i. 271
Amarâvatîpura, i. 271
amâvâsya, i. 348; ii. 185, 197
ambara, i. 178, 303
ambaratala, i. 230
Ambarîsha, i. 113
Ambashṭha, i. 301
amṛita, i. 54, 253, 262, 344; ii. 107
aṁśaka, i. 140, 144
aṁśâya, ii. 227
aṁśu, i. 217, 230
aṁśumant, i. 217
anala, ii. 128
Ânandapâla, i. 135; ii. 13

Ananta, i. 237, 247, 298
Ânâr, i. 205
Ânartta, i. 300, 302
Andhra, i. 299, 300, 301
Andhradeśa, i. 173
Andhrî, i. 173
andî, i. 161, 162, 163
aṅga, i. 178, 301
aṅgâra, ii. 128
Aṅgiras, i. 131, 215, 291, 390; ii. 127
aṅgula, i. 166
Anhilvâra, i. 153, 205; ii. 6, 7
anîkinî, i. 407
Anila, i. 342
Ânila, i. 248
Aniruddha, i. 398
Añjana, i. 300
aṅka, i. 174
anta, i. 220
Antaka, i. 342
antara, i. 178; ii. 195
Antardvîpa, i. 302
Antariksha, i. 398
ântarikshya, ii. 235
Antarvedi, i. 211 (notes).
Antaḥśilâ, i. 257
antya, i. 175
antyaja, i. 101
aṇu, i. 337
Anuhlâda, i. 231
anurâdhâ, i. 218, 391, 393; ii. 85, 86, 122, 176
Anûru, i. 253
Anutaptâ, i. 262
anuvatsara, ii. 125
Anuviśva, i. 303
âpaddharma, i. 133
Apâṁmûrti, i. 394
apâna, i. 339
Apara (?), i. 394
Aparânta (?), i. 300
Aparântaka, i. 302
Âpas, i. 342; ii. 122
Âpastamba, i. 131
apratidhṛishya, i. 372
apsaras, i. 247, 248
Apsûr, i. 202
âpta-purâṇa-kâra, i. 237
âra, i. 215
araṇya, i. 133
Âravâmbashṭha, i. 302
arbuda, i. 176
arbudam, i. 177
ardhanâgarî, i. 173
Ardîn, i. 202
ârdrâ, i. 218; ii. 66, 84, 86, 121
argha, ii. 95
Arhant, i. 119, 121
Arhata (?), ii. 142
Ari, i. 300
Arjuna, i. 29, 52, 352, 403; ii. 138
Ârjunâyana, i. 302
arka, i. 179, 215, 217; ii. 125
ârki, i. 215
Arkutîrtha, i. 200
Aror, i. 205, 260
artha, i. 178
Arthayâshava (?), i. 299
Aruṇâ, i. 259
Aruṇa, i. 255; ii. 143, 238
Arundhatî, i. 390
Âruṇi, i. 394
Arvasudhana (?), i. 303
âryâ, i. 143
Âryabhaṭa, i. 156, 168, 225, 227, 244, 246, 266, 267, 268, 275, 277, 280, 370, 373, 376, 377, 386; ii. 16, 17, 18, 19, 33, 111, 190
Âryabhata (of Kusumapura), i. 176, 246, 316, 330, 335, 370
Âryaka, i. 254
Aryaman, i. 217, 242, 342; ii. 121, 199
âryâshṭaśata, i. 157, 386
âryâvarta, i. 173; ii. 6
âśâ, i. 179
âśâla (?), i. 230
Âśana (?), i. 358
Asâvil, i. 209
âsbati (?), i. 215
Aśćârvarî, i. 387
âshâḍha, i. 211, 217, 218, 357, 358, 403; ii. 96, 99, 100, 173, 176, 179, 193
ashṭa, i. 178
ashṭaka, ii. 183
ashṭi, i. 179
Âsî, i. 202
asipattravana, i. 61
asita, i. 215; ii. 235
âślesha, i. 218, 291; ii. 84, 121
Asmaka, i. 300, 302
âsphujit, i. 215
âśramavâsa, i. 133
aśoka, ii. 180
Astagiri, i. 302
asthi, ii. 241
asura, i. 90, 247, 325, 331
aśvamedha, i. 133; ii. 2, 139
Aśvavadana, i. 301
Aśvamukha, i. 262

Aśvatara, i. 231, 247
aśvattha, i. 86 ; ii. 140, 141
Aśvatthâman, i. 133, 394, 398, 405, 406
âśvayuja, i. 217, 218, 358, 403 ; ii. 98, 173, 177, 179, 186, 193
aśvin, i. 159, 178 ; ii. 122, 128
aśvinî, i. 218, 242, 369 ; ii. 84, 86, 122, 128
atala, i. 230
Âṭavya, i. 300
âtharvaṇaveda, i. 127, 129
atidhṛiti, i. 179
atin, ii. 197
Atinâman, i. 394
ativâhika, i. 63
âtman, i. 351
âtmapurusha, i. 321
Âtreya, i. 163, 300, 383
Atri, i. 131, 291, 301, 390, 394
attâtaja, ii. 176
atvh (?), i. 348
atyashṭi, i. 179
Audumbara, i. 300
Auliatta (?), ii. 190
Aurva, ii. 101
Autata (?), i. 387
auttami, i. 387
avama ii. 38, 43, 47, 48, 50, 51, 53, 54
âvaueya, i. 215
Avanti, i. 298, 301
Âvarta, ii. 244
avasarpiṇî, i. 371
avaśvâsa, i. 339
avyakta, i. 40
ayana, i. 356, 366 ; ii. 118
Âyanâ (?), i. 257
âyurdâya, ii. 228
ayuta, i. 175
ayutam, i. 176, 177

b = Budha, i. 215
Babrahân, i. 206
Bâdara, i. 302
badhatau (?), i. 101, 102
Baga, i. 208
Baha, i. 261
bahand, ii. 178
Bahîmarvara, i. 261
Bahrój (v. Bihroj), i. 205, 261
Bâhudâsa (?), i. 259
bahudhânya, ii. 127
bakshûta (?), ii. 208
bala, ii. 226, 230
Balabandhu, i. 387
Balabhadra, i. 156, 157, 158, 225, 227, 236, 238, 248 (?), 241, 243, 244, 246, 273, 274, 275, 279, 281, 282, 317, 401, 403 ; ii. 70, 75, 187
Balabhid, ii. 127
Baladeva, i. 118
Baladevapattana, i. 301
bâlâgra, i. 162
Balâhaka, ii. 101
bâlava, ii. 197, 199
Bali, i. 117, 129, 231 387, 396 ; ii. 3, 11, 145, 182
Balirâjya, ii. 182
Ballâvar, i. 205
Bâlûka (!), i. 257
Bâluvâhiṇî, i. 257
Bâmahûr, i. 202
Bamhanvâ (not Bahmanvâ), i. 21, 173, 205, 316
Banârasî (Benares), i. 200
Banavâs, i. 202
Baṅgâla, i. 158
baṇij, ii. 197, 199
Bañjulâ, i. 257
bâra, i. 213
Baramûlâ, i. 207
Barbara, i. 261 302 ; ii. 129
Bardarî, ii. 8
bardî (?), i. 405
barh, i. 359
Barhamśil, i. 200
Bârî, i. 200, 201, 261
barkhu, i. 359, 348 (?) ; ii. 197
Barodâ, i. 403
Barûî, i. 208 ; ii. 105
barsh, i. 359
Barshâvar (Peshavar), i. 211
Bârvancat, i. 261
Baśârṇa (!), i. 300
bava, ii. 197, 199
Bavârîj, i. 208
Bazâna (?), i. 202, 205, 300
Benares, i. 22, 156, 173 ; ii. 146, 147
Bhadatta (?), i. 156
Bhadila (?), i. 157
Bhadrakâra (!), i. 299
Bhadra, i. 300, 301
bhâdrapada, i. 217, 218, 340, 358, 403 ; ii. 8, 98, 173, 175, 177, 180, 193
Bhadrâśva, i. 249
Bhaga, i. 217, 358 ; ii. 121, 128
bhâgahâra, ii. 30, 189, 190
Bhagavat, i. 255
Bhâgavata, i. 121, 131

Bhagavatî, i. 118, 120 ; ii. 177, 179, 180
Bhâgeya (?), i. 342
Bhagîratha, ii. 143, 144
Bhâilsân, i. 202
bhaikshukî, i. 173
Bhalla, i. 303
Bhânurajas (?), i. 156
bhânu, i. 178, 215, 217
Bhânuyaśas (?), (cf. Bhânurajas), i. 157
Bhânukacchra (?), i. 300
bhâra, i. 165
bhara, i. 130
Bharadva, i. 300
Bharadvâja, i. 394, 398
bharaṇî, i. 218 ; ii. 84, 122
Bharata, i. 262, 294
Bhârata, i. 29, 117, 132, 134 ; ii. 1, 147, 152
Bhâratavarsha, i. 249, 294, 295, 296, 297
Bhârgava, i. 132, 215, 372, 398
Bharma (?), ii. 120
bharna (?), ii. 104
Bharukaccha, i. 301
Bhâtal, i. 211
Bhâti, i. 205
Bhâtiya, i. 173
Bhaṭṭila, ii. 208
Bhâtul, i. 260
bhaumya, i. 215
bhautya, i. 387
bhâva, ii. 127
bhavaketu, ii. 243
Bhâvin (?), i. 254
Bhavishya, i. 131
bhavishya-purâṇa, i. 130
Bhillamâla, i. 153, 267
Bhîma, ii. 13
Bhîmapâla, ii. 13
Bhîmarathî, i. 257
Bhîmasena, i. 403
Bhishma, i. 133
bhîshmapañcarâtrî, ii. 177
Bhogaprastha, i. 302
Bhogavardhana, i. 300
Bhoja, i. 300
Bhoteshar, i. 201, 206
bhramara, ii. 92
Bhṛigu, i. 77, 215, 291
bhṛiguputra, i. 215
bhṛiguloka, ii. 233
Bhujaga, i. 342
bhukti, i. 353 ; ii. 80, 83, 195, 200, 205, 206, 207
bhuktyantara, ii. 195
bhûmi (?), i. 387
Bhûmihara, i. 203
bhûpa, i. 179
bhûri, i. 175
Bhûrishena, i. 387
bhûrja, i. 171
bhûrloka, i. 45, 232, 233, 238
bhûta, i. 90, 92, 93, 178
Bhûtapura, i. 303
Bhuvanakośa, i. 294
bhuvarloka, i. 45, 232, 238
bibatâ (?), i. 215
Bihat, i. 201
Bihrôj, i. 209
bist (?), i. 165, 166
Bîtra, i. 262
Bitûr, i. 259
biya, ii. 197
Biyâha, i. 259, 260
Biyatta, i. 206, 259, 260
Blv (? plava), ii. 202
Bodha, i. 299
bodhana, i. 215
Brahmadaṇḍa, ii. 237
brahmâdi (?), ii. 116
Brahmagupta, i. 147, 150, 153, 154, 156, 168, 223, 224, 241, 243, 267, 272, 276, 277, 279, 280, 282, 283, 312, 314, 335, 368, 369, 370, 372, 373, 374, 376, 377, 386 ; ii. 4, 7, 15, 16, 17, 18, 19, 24, 28, 31, 46, 59, 71, 73, 74, 75, 76, 77, 78, 82, 90, 110, 111, 112, 186, 189, 192
brahmâhorâtra, i. 331
brahmaloka, i. 233
brahman, i. 28, 54, 72, 77, 89, 92, 94, 100, 116, 118, 125, 129 ; his sons, i. 131, 134, 153, 155, 157, 159, 176, 241, 256, 266, 321, 322 seq., 331, 332, 342, 350, 352, 360, 361, 363, 369, 380, 386 ; ii. 2 ; life of, ii. 28, 63, 99, 115, 116, 118, 120, 145, 147, 199, 237
Brahman, era of, ii. 1
brâhmaṇa, i. 100, 102, 104, 121
brahmaṇa (?), ii. 159
brahmâṇḍa, i. 131, 221 seq., 237
brahmâṇḍa-purâṇa, i. 130
Brahmâṇî, i. 119
Brahmapura, i. 303
brahma-purâṇa, i. 130
Brahmaputra, i. 387
brahmarshi, i. 93, 247
Brahmarûpa, i. 256
Brahmasâvarṇi, i. 387

brahmasiddhânta, i. 138, 153; table of contents, i. 154, 223, 224, 267, 276, 352; ii. 110, 112
Brahmavaivarta, i. 131
Brahmin, ii. 95, 96, 98, 100, 109, 110, 111, 136 *seq.*, 149, 151, 153, 179, 180, 181, 183, 185, 191
Brahmottara, i. 262
Bṛihaspati, i. 132, 393
bṛihaspativâra, i. 213
budha, i. 215
budhavâra, i. 213
Buddha, i. 40, 119, 121, 158, 243; ii. 169
Buddhodana, i. 40, 380
Budhnya, i. 387
burlû (?), i. 204

c=candra, i. 215
Cabrahasta (?), ii. 120
cadur (!), ii. 127
caitra, i. 212, 217, 218, 358, 369, 394, 403; ii. 8, 10, 39, 48, 123, 173, 176; festivals, ii. 178, 186, 187, 193
caitra-cashati (?), ii. 179
Caitraka (?), i. 387
cakhaka, i. 334
cakra, i. 114, 117, 118, 341; ii. 101, 107
cakrasvâmin, i. 117; ii. 103
Cakshabhadra (?), ii. 120
Cakshu, i. 261
câkshukha, i. 387
Cakshus, i. 261
câkshusha, i. 387
calaketu, ii. 241
Calitu (?), i. 137
câmâha, ii. 183, 184
câmara, i. 140
Câmuṇḍâ, i. 120
camû, i. 407
caṇa (?), i. 163
Cañcûka, i. 302
caṇḍâla, i. 101, 239, 344, 381; ii. 137, 138, 153
Candanâ, i. 259
Candarâha, i. 260
candra, i. 178, 215, 216; ii. 21, 101
câ ndra, i. 135, 215
Candrabhâgâ, i. 259
Candrabîja (?), ii. 6
Candrâha, i. 206, 259
candrâbargaṇa, ii. 27
candramâna, i. 353, 354
candraparvata, ii. 143
Candrapura, i. 300
candrâyaṇa, ii. 173
cântima (?), i. 344
Caraka, i. 159, 162, 382
Carmadvîpa, i. 301
Carmakhaṇḍila, i. 300
Carmaṇvatî, i. 257, 259; ii. 134
Carmaraṅga, i. 302
Carshayaḥ (!), i. 394
cashaka, i. 334 *seq.*, 337; ii. 52, 56, 189
caturyuga, i. 325, 354, 359, 368 *seq.*, 372 *seq.*, 386, 398; ii. 1, 2, 17, 18, 28, 57 *seq.*, 186, 189
catushpada, ii. 197, 198, 200
Caulya, i. 299
caudahî, ii. 197
caut, ii. 197
ceshṭâbala, ii. 225
chaudas, i. 136
chidra, i. 178
cikitsâ, i. 355
Cîna, i. 261, 303; ii. 239
Cipitanâsika, i. 302
Cîranivasana, i. 303
citrâ, i. 218, 342; ii. 85, 121, 127
citrabhânu, ii. 127
Citrakûṭa, i. 301
Citrâṅgada, ii. 120
Citrapala, i. 257
Citrakûtâ, i. 257
Citraśâlâ, i. 255
Citrasena, i. 387
C-n-d-sara (?), ii. 143
Cola, i. 301; ii. 239
Colika (?), i. 301
Cyavana, i. 231

DADHI, i. 178, 235
dadhimaṇḍa, i. 235
dadhisâgara, i. 156, 235
Dahâla, i. 202
dahana, i. 178
dâhariya (?), i. 344
dahin, ii. 197
Dahmâla, i. 205
Daibal, i. 208
Daihak, i. 189
daitya, i. 91, 231, 237, 247, 248, 267, 272, 279, 280, 364; ii. 140
daityântara, i. 266
Daksha, i. 54, 131, 291, 387
dakshakula, i. 357
dakshaputra, i. 387
dakshiṇa, i. 290
Dâkshiṇâtya, i. 300

dakshiṇâyara, i. 356, 357
Dâmara, i. 303
damariyâ (?), i. 344
Damin, i. 254
Dâmodara, i. 403
dânadharma, i. 133
Dânak, i. 203
dânava, i. 91, 231, 237, 248, 256, 272, 330, 331
dânavaguru, i. 215
Daṇḍa, i. 303; ii. 97
Dandahamâr (?), ii. 176
Daṇḍaka, i. 300
Daṇḍakâvana, i. 301
dantin, i. 178
Dantura, i. 301
Darada, i. 261
Daraur, i. 200
darbha, ii. 130, 131
Dardura, i. 301
Dârva, i. 303
Darvad, i. 209
daśagîtikâ, i. 157, 386
daśalaksha, i. 176
daśam, i. 175
Dâsameya, i. 303
Darva, i. 300
Daśapura, i. 301
Daśaratha, i. 117, 306, 372
Dâsârṇa, i. 301
Daśârṇâ, i. 257
daśasahasra, i. 176
Dâsera (!), i. 302
Daseruka (!), i. 300
dasra, i. 178, 342
dasta, i. 166
Datta, i. 394
deotthinî, ii. 177
deśântara, i. 312, 314, 315
deva, i. 90, 91, 92, 95, 159, 176, 247, 248, 252, 256, 266, 272, 330, 331; ii. 63, 66, 96, 99, 139, 140, 141, 177, 279, 280, 357
devagriha, ii. 178
devaka, i. 330, 352, 369, 372
Devakirti, i. 158
Devala, i. 132; ii. 235
devaloka, ii. 233
devamantrin, i. 215
Devâṅiga, i. 387
devapitâ, i. 215
devapurohita, i. 215
devasinî, ii. 176
Devaśreshta, i. 387
Devata (?), i. 387
devejya, i. 215
Devikâ, i. 259
Dhâman, i. 394
Dhanañjaya, i. 231, 398
dhanishtha, i. 218, 291; ii. 85
dhanishṭhâ, ii. 122, 124
dhanu, i. 166, 220
Dhanushman (!), i. 302
Dhanya, i. 254
Dhâr, i. 202, 203
Dhâra, i. 191
dharaṇî, i. 178
dharma, i. 40, 132, 242, 291
Dharmâraṇya, i. 300
dharmasâvarṇi, i. 387
Dhâtṛi, i. 217, 238, 342; ii. 127
dhî, i. 178
Dhivara, i. 262
dhôla, ii. 183
Dhṛishṇa, i. 387
Dhṛitaketu, i. 387
Dhṛitarâshṭra, i. 108, 403
dhṛiti, i. 179
Dhṛitimat, i. 394
dhruva, i. 239, 241
dhruvagṛiha (?), ii. 180
Dhûlika (?), i. 261
dhruvaketu (?), ii. 242
dhurâ (?), ii. 21
dhurâshâḍha, ii. 21
Dhutapâpâ, i. 259
dhyânagrahâdhyâya, i. 155
dibâlî, ii. 182
dikshita, i. 102
Dilipa, ii. 174
dimasu, i. 359
Dipâpâ, i. 262
Diptimat, i. 394
Dirghagriva, i. 302
Dirghakeśa, i. 302
Dirghamukha, i. 302
Dirvari (Drâviḍî), i. 173
Dirvarideśa, i. 173
diś, i. 178, 179
Divakaubâr, i. 210
Divâkara, i. 158, 215, 217
Diva-kûdha, i. 210
divasa, i. 359
Divârśa (!), i. 301
Divaspati, i. 387
divya, i. 42, 374; ii. 235
divyâhorâtra, i. 329
Divyatattva, i. 157
divyavarsha, i. 359, 368; ii. 2
Diyâman, i. 205
Dkish (?), ii. 140
ḍomba, i. 101, 102

Dramiḍa, i. 302
draṅkshana, i. 161
Draviḍadeśa, i. 173
Draviṇa, ii. 101
drekkâṇa, ii. 229, 233
dṛigbala, ii. 225
Drihâla (?), i. 300
Dṛishadvatî, i. 259
dṛishṭibala, ii. 225
Droṇa, i. 133, 162, 163, 164, 254, 394, 398, 405, 406; ii. 101
Drûta, i. 259
Dûdahi, i. 202
Dûgum, i. 201
Dûgumpûr, i. 200
dundubhi, ii. 128
Dunpûr, i. 206, 211, 317
Durga, i. 300
Durgâ, i. 257
Durgavivṛitti, i. 135
Durlabha, ii. 9, 10, 54
durmati, ii. 128
durtama (?), i. 371
Durvâsas, i. 404
Duryodhana, i. 133
Dushyanta, ii. 174
duvâhi, ii. 197
duvê, ii. 174
Dvaipâyana, i. 398
dvâpara, i. 372, 397, 398
dvâpara-yuga, i. 126, 373; description, i. 380; ii. 5; its beginning, ii. 186
Dvâr, i. 207
dvijeśvara, i. 216
dvîpa, i. 168, 233, 234, 235, 236, 243, 251 *seq.*, 265, 295, 301, 388; ii. 144
dvisvabhâva, ii. 220
Dyuti, i. 394
Dyutimat, i. 394

Ekacaraṇa, i. 303
ekam, i. 175
ekanakta, ii. 172
Ekapada, i. 301
Ekavilocana, i. 302
Elâpatra, ii. 120

ga, i. 140
gabhastala, i. 230
Gabhastimat, i. 230, 296
Gabhîra, i. 387
gadâ, i. 133
gagana, i. 178
gâihat (?), ii. 180
Gaisitu (?), i. 137
gaja, i. 178, 300
Gajakarṇa, i. 231
Gâlava, i. 394
gaṇa, i. 407
gana (?), ii. 181
Gaṇaka, ii. 238
Gaṇapati (?), ii. 121
Gaṇarâjya, i. 301
gaṇḍa, i. 203
Gaṇḍakî, i. 259
gaṇḍânta, ii. 208
gandha, i. 42
Gandhamâdana, i. 248, 249
Gandhâra, i. 21, 259, 261, 300, 303
gandharva, i. 89, 91, 238, 247, 262, 303
gândharva, i. 296
Gandharvî, ii. 142
Gaṅgâ, i. 200 *seq.*, 203, 253, 254, 259, 261; ii. 144
Gaṅgâdvâra, i. 199
Gaṅgâsâgara, i. 261
Gangâsâyara, i. 201
Gangeya, i. 202
gara, ii. 197, 199
Garbha, i. 236
garbhâdhâna, ii. 156
Garga, i. 157, 342, 382, 390, 391; ii. 96, 110, 235
garuḍa, i. 114, 130 131, 193, 194, 231, 253, 344
Gauḍa, the anchorite, i. 132
Gauḍaka, i. 301
gaura, i. 161
Gaura (?), ii. 143
Gauragrîva, i. 300
Gaurî (Gandi), i. 173
Gaurî, i. 119; ii. 121, 179, 182, 183
Gaur-t-r (gaurî-tṛitîyâ), ii. 177, 179
Gautama, i. 131, 394, 398
gâyatrî, i. 147
ghana, i. 140, 144, 146
ghaṭî, i. 334 *seq.*, 337, 338, 349, 362, 366; ii. 48, 52, 56, 189, 190, 195, 200
ghaṭikâ, i. 279, 282, 286
Ghora, ii. 202
Ghorwand, i. 259
Ghosha, i. 300, 303
ghṛitamaṇḍa, i. 235
Ghûzak, i. 259
Giri, i. 302
Girnagara, i. 301
gîtâ, quoted, i. 29, 30, 40, 52–54, 70–72, 73–74, 75, 76, 78, 79, 80, 86, 90, 103–104, 122

Gnidhra (!), i. 394
go, i. 178
Godâvar, i. 203
Godâvari, i. 257
gokarṇa, i. 167
Gomati, i. 259
gomeda, i. 235
gomedadvîpa, i. 235, 255
Gomukha, i. 231
Gonarda, i. 301
Govinda, i. 299, 403
graha, i. 140
grâha, i. 204
grishma, i. 357
Guḍa, i. 300
gûḍhâmana (?), i. 158
gûhaniya, i. 344
gulma, i. 407
guṇakâra, ii. 30, 189, 190
gûnâlabid (?), ii. 181
Gupta, ii. 5, 7, 49
Guptakâla, ii. 7, 9, 49
guru, i. 138, 140, 145, 146, 215, 342; ii. 121
Guruhâ, i. 302
guvâna-bâtrij, ii. 182
Guzarât, i. 202
Gvalior, i. 202

HÂDÎ (?), i. 101, 102
Hâhu (!), i. 257
Haihaya, i. 302
Haṁsamârga, i. 262
Haṁsapura, i. 298
Hârahaura, i. 298
Haramakôṭ, i. 207
harbâli (?), ii. 180
Hari, i. 254, 342, 362, 393
Haribhaṭṭa (?), i. 141
Haripurusha, i. 252
Hârita, i. 131
harivaṁśa-parvan, i. 133
Harivarsha, i. 249
Harsha, ii. 5, 7
Haryâtman, i. 398
hasta, i. 218; ii. 85, 121
hastin, i. 140, 141, 146
hattha, i. 166
haubava (?), i. 408
Havishmat, i. 394
Havya, i. 394
Hayagrîva, i. 231
heli, i. 215
Hemagiri, i. 302
hemalamba, ii. 128
hemakûṭa, i. 247, 249
Hemakûṭya, i. 301
hemanta, i. 357
Hematâla, i. 302
hemna, i. 215
Himagiri, i. 249
himagu, i. 215
himamayûkha, i. 215
himaraśmi, i. 215
Himavân, i. 302
Himavant, i. 119, 246, 247, 248, 258, 261, 294, 295, 308; ii. 179
Hindhu, ii. 129
hindolî-caitra, ii. 178
Hiraṇmaya, i. 249
Hiraṇyakaśipu, i. 364
Hiraṇyâksha, i. 231; ii. 140
Hiraṇyaroman, i. 394
homa, i. 128; ii. 96, 133
horâ, i. 343; their names, 344
horâ-pañca-hotṛiya (?), i. 158
horâdipati, i. 343
Hrâdinî, i. 261, 262
Hṛishîkeśa, i. 403
Hudvuda (?), i. 300
Hûhaka (!), i. 300
Hûna, i. 300, 302
Hutâśa, ii. 127
hutâśana, i. 178

IDÂVATSARA, ii. 125
ikshu, i. 235
Ikshulâ, i. 257
ikshurasoda, i. 235
ikhûnu (?), i. 178
Ikshvâku, i. 387
ilâ (?), i. 230
Ilâvṛita, i. 248
Indra, i. 89, 92, 93, 113, 119, 159, 217, 231, 252, 271, 292, 342, 357, 361, 386, 387, 393, 396, 398; ii. 101, 102, 115, 127, 128, 175, 246
Indradvîpa, i. 262
Indradyumna, i. 262
Indradyumnasaras, i. 262
Indrâgni, i. 342, 358; ii. 121
Indramaru, i. 261
Indrâṇî, i. 120
Indravêdi (v. Antarvedi), i. 211
indriya, i. 178
indriyâṇi, i. 43
Indu, i. 153, 178, 215; ii. 121
Irâva, i. 206, 260
Irâvati, i. 259
Iścânyas (!), i. 394
Ishîka, i. 300
ishṭin, i. 102

ishu, i. 178
îśvara, i. 31, 179, 361, 362, 363; ii. 127

JADÛRA (?), i. 202
Jâgara, i. 230, 300
Jahrâvar, i. 260, 300, 302
Jailam, i. 206, 207, 259, 317
Jaimini, i. 127, 132
Jájâboti, i. 202
Jajjamau, i. 200
Jajjanir, i. 206
jalaketu, ii. 243
Jâlandhar, i. 205
jalapradânika, i. 133
jalâśaya, i. 178
jalatantu, i. 204
Jamadagni, i. 394
jambu, i. 235; ii. 129
jambudvîpa, i. 235, 243, 251, 258
janâ (?), i. 163
janaloka, i. 232
Janârdana, i. 254
Janarta (?), i. 231
Jandrâ, i. 202
Jaṅgala, i. 299
Jâṅgala, i. 300
Janpa, i. 200
Jânujaṅgha, i. 387
Jarmapattana (?), i. 301
Jaśu (?), i. 382, 397
jâtaka, i. 100, 157
jâtakarman, ii. 156
Jaṭâsura, i. 303
Jaṭâdhara, i. 301
Jaṭhara, i. 301
Jatt, i. 401
Jattaraur, i. 202
Jaun (Yamunâ), i. 199, 200 *seq.*, 206, 254, 259, 261
Jaur, Hindu king, i. 200, 209
jaya, ii. 127
Jayanta (?), i. 231
Jayantî, ii. 175
Jayapâla, i. 135; ii. 13
Jimûr, i. 209
Jîmûta, ii. 101
Jina, i. 119, 243
jinaloka, i. 238
Jishṇu, i. 153
Jita, i. 394
jitu, i. 220 (? cettham)
jituma, i. 220
jîva, i. 215, 358
jîvaharaṇî, i. 344
Jîvaśarman, i. 157, 164; ii. 181, 182
jña, i. 215
Jriṅga, i. 302
jûga, i. 220
Jûdarî, i. 211
Jvâla (?), ii. 202
jvalana, i. 140, 141, 143, 145, 146, 178
jyaishṭha, i. 217, 218, 340, 358, 403; ii. 173; festivals, ii. 179, 193
jyeshṭhâ, i. 218; ii. 85, 86, 122
Jyotis, i. 394
Jyotisha, i. 300
Jyotishmat, i. 394

KA, ii. 242
Kabandha (?), i. 231; ii. 238
Kâbul, i. 206, 259, 317; ii. 157
Kâca (?), i. 261
Kacch, i. 208, 260
Kacchâra, i. 303
Kacchîya, i. 300
kadamba, i. 272
Kadara, ii. 129
Kadrû, i. 252
Kaikaya, i. 302
Kailâsa, i. 248, 302; ii. 142, 143
Kailâvata, i. 302
Kaj, i. 260
Kajûrâha, i. 202
Kakutstha, ii. 176
kalâ, i. 160, 335, 337, 362
kâlabala, ii. 226
kâlabhâga (?), ii. 231
Kâlâjina, i. 301
Kâlaka, i. 302
kâlâṁśaka, ii. 90
Kâlanemi, i. 231
Kâlanjar, i. 202
Kalâpagrama, i. 262
kâlarâtri, i. 344; ii. 203
kalasi, i. 166
Kâlatoyaka, i. 300
Kâlavṛiuta, ii. 129
Kâlayavana, ii. 5
kâlayukta, ii. 128
kali, i. 140, 382, 397; ii. 1, 198
Kalîdara, i. 262
Kâlika (?), i. 261
kalikâla, ii. 1, 5
Kaliṅga, i. 231, 298, 299, 301
Kâliya, i. 231
kaliyuga, i. 325, 373; description, i. 380, 397, 399; ii. 1, 4, 17, 18, 28, 59, 60; its beginning, ii. 186
Kâlkoṭi, i. 300

Kallar, ii. 13
Kalmâsha (?), ii. 121
kalpa, i. 54, 175, 279, 325, 332, 350, 352, 354, 360, 362, 368 *seq.*, 386; ii. 1, 15 *seq.*, 17, 18, 23, 28, 57 *seq.*, 118
kalpâhargaṇa, i. 368; ii. 116
kalpana, i. 368
Kalyâṇavarman, i. 158
Kamalû, ii. 13
kâma, i. 140, 141, 145, 146
kamaṇḍalu, i. 118
Kambala, i. 231, 247
Kâmboja, i. 302
Kâmrû, i. 201
Kaṁsa, i. 340, 401, 403; ii. 180
Kâmyakavana, ii. 3
Kanaka, i. 302; ii. 237
Kanashṭharâjya (?), i. 303
Kanbâyat, i. 208
Kâñcî, i. 301
Kand, i. 203
Kaṇḍakasthala, i. 301
Kandhâr (Gandhâra), i. 206
Kandî, i. 317; ii. 182.
kâṇḍin, ii. 128
Kanik, ii. 11 *seq.*
Kanik-caitya, ii. 11
Kanîr, ii. 8
Kânjî, i. 200, 209
Kaṅka, ii. 101, 238
Kankaṭa, i. 301
Kannakara, i. 202
Kannara, i. 173
Kanoj, i. 21, 165, 173, 198, 199, 200 *seq.*, 261, 317; ii. 5, 8, 11, 129
Kaṇṭhadhâna, i. 302
kanyâ, i. 219, 220
kapâlaketu, ii. 241
Kapila, i. 72, 132, 255, 302, 321, 325, 397
Kapishṭhala, i. 300
karabha, i. 167
karâla, i. 344
Karamoda (?), i. 257
karaṇa, i. 155, 156, 157, 354; ii. 194 *seq.*, 197, 198, 200
karaṇacûḍâmaṇi, i. 157
karaṇakhaṇḍakhâdyaka, i. 156
karaṇaparatilaka, i. 157
karaṇapâta, i. 157
karaṇasâra, i. 156, 317, 392; ii. 7, 54, 60, 79, 80
karaṇatilaka, i. 156, 313, 343; ii. 7, 50, 60, 80, 205, 206
karâra (?), ii. 181
Karaskara, i. 300
Karatoyâ, i. 259
kark (=khaḍga), i. 204
karkâdi, i. 356
karkadannu (khaḍgadanta !), i. 204
karkaṭa, i. 220
Karkota, ii. 120
Karkoṭaka, i. 247; ii. 120
Karlî, town, i. 317
Karma, i. 262, v. *Kramu*
karman, i. 321
Kârmaṇeyaka, i. 301
Karmâra, i. 231
karmendriyâṇi, i. 44
Karṇa, i. 133
Karṇaprâvaraṇa, i. 262, 300, 302
Karnâṭa, i. 173, 301; ii. 135
Karnâṭadeśa, i. 173
karsha, i. 163
kârttika, i. 217, 218, 358, 403; ii. 98, 173, 177; festival, ii. 182, 186, 193
Kârttikeya, i. 54
Karûr, ii. 6
Karûsha, i. 300
Karvaṭa, i. 300
Kaśerumat, i. 296
Kashmir, i. 21, 22, 108, 126, 135, 173, 174, 205, 206 *seq.*, 211, 258, 303, 317, 391, 393; ii. 8, 9, 104, 148, 178, 181
kâshṭhâ, i. 336 *seq.*, 362
Kâśi, i. 299, 300
Kaśyapa, i. 216, 242, 252, 291, 394; ii. 96, 100
Kâśyapapura, i. 298
Kâtantra, i. 135
Kâtyâyana, i. 131
katt, i. 206
kaulava, ii. 197, 199
Kaumârî, i. 120
Kaunindâ, i. 303
Kauṅkuma, ii. 238
Kaurava, i. 403
kaurba, i. 220
Kausalaka, i. 301
Kaushaka (?), i. 262
Kauśikî, i. 259
Kaustuba, i. 261
Kauverya, i. 301
Kâvanâ, i. 259
Kavara, i. 261
Kavâṭadhâna (?), i. 302
Kâverî, i. 257
Kavinî, i. 261

Kavital, i. 206
Kâvya, i. 394
Kâyabish, i. 259
Kerala, i. 299
Keralaka, i. 301
Keśadhara, i. 302
Kesari i. 231
Keśava, i. 218, 361, 362, 403
Keśvara, i. 342 ; ii 121
ketu, ii. 234, 236
Ketumâla, i. 249
keturûpa, ii. 235
kha, i. 178 333, 350
Khajara, i. 302
khadira, ii. 99
khaṇḍa, i. 156, 295, 302
khaṇḍakhâdyaka, i. 156, 312 ; ii. 7. 46, 49, 60, 79, 83, 86, 87, 90, 91, 116, 119, 184, 187
khaṇḍakhâdyakatippâ (?), i. 156
khara, ii. 127
Kharapatha, i. 262
khârî, i. 164
kharva, i. 175, 176, 177
Khasa (?), i. 262
Khasha, i. 301, 303
Khastha, i. 302
khendu, i. 179
Kumbhakarṇa, ii. 3
Khyâti, i. 387
Kihkind, i. 209
Kîkara, i. 262
kîlaka, ii. 128
Kiṁnara, i. 262
Kiṁpurusha, i. 249, 251, 262 ; ii. 142
kinnara, i. 91
kinstughna, ii. 197, 198
Kirâ, i. 259
Kira, i. 303
Kiraṇa, ii. 237
Kirâta, i. 262, 300, 302, 303
Kiri (v. Kandi), ii. 182
Kirpa (?), i. 257
Kirva (?), i. 257
Kisadya, i. 299
Kishkindha, i. 300, 301
kishku, i. 167
Kodara (?), i. 300
Kokala, i. 303
Kolavana, i. 300
Kollagiri, i. 301
Koṅkaṇa, i. 301
koṇa, i. 215
Kopa, i. 300
Kosala, i. 299, 300, 301
koṭi, i. 92, 175, 176, 177, 236, 248, 284, 303, 304
koṭipadma, i. 176
Krâla (?), i. 300 ; ii. 202
Kramu, ii. 262 (v. notes)
Krathanaka, i. 231
Kratu, i. 390
krauñca, i. 235, 302
Kravya, i. 302
kṛicchra, ii. 172
kṛimiśa, i. 60
Kṛipa, i. 394
Krira-samudra, i. 301
kṛishṇa, i. 61, 231, 255, 257, 398
kṛishṇabhûmi, i. 230
kṛishṇapaksha, i. 359
Krishṇavaiḍûrya, i. 301
kṛita, i. 178, 372
Kṛitamâlâ, i. 257
Kṛitaṁjaya, i. 398
Krauñcadvîpa, i. 235, 254, 301
kṛitayuga, i. 116, 373 ; description, i. 379 ; ii. 182 ; its beginning, i. 396, 397, 398 ; ii. 186
kṛiti, i. 179 ; ii. 129
kṛittikâ, i. 140–145, 218, 291, 344 ; ii. 84, 121
Kṛiśa (?), i. 383
kriya, i. 220
kroḍa, i. 344
krodha, ii. 128
krodhin, ii. 128
krośa, i. 166, 167, 275
Krûra (?), i. 261
krûrâkshi (?), i. 215
kshatriya, i. 101, 104, 125, 247. 388 ; ii. 95, 98, 136, 155, 157, 161, 162, 170, 191
kshaya, ii. 128
Kshemadhûrta (?), i. 303
Kshetrapâla, i. 120
kshîra, i. 235, 284
kshirodaka, i. 235
Kshudramîna, i. 302
kshairitâ (?), ii. 186
kshaṇa, i. 335, 337
kshâra, i. 235
Kubata, i. 261
Kubera, i. 119 ; ii. 115
Kucika, i. 303
Kûdaishahr (?), ii. 181
kuḍava, i. 162, 163, 164, 165
Kuhû, i. 259
kuja, i. 215
Kukura, i. 300
kûla, i. 356

Kulârjak, i. 207
Kulata, i. 261
Kulika, i. 344, 345
Kuliuda, i. 298, 300
kulira, i. 220
Kulûta, i. 303
Kulûtalahada, i. 302
Kulya, i. 299
Kumârî, i. 257
kumbha, i. 220
kumbhakarṇa, ii. 3
Kumbhaka, i. 321
Kumuda, i. 255 ; ii. 243
Kumudvatî, i. 257
Kunatha, i. 303
Kuñjáradarî, i. 301
Kûnk, i. 200
Kunkan (Konkan), i. 203
Kuntala, i. 299, 300
Kupatha (?), i. 262
kûra-babayâ (?), i. 156
Kuraha, i. 200
Kurava, i. 302
kûrma, i. 131
kûrmacakra, i. 297
kûrma-purâṇa, i. 130
kuroh, ii. 66
Kuru, i. 132, 249, 262, 292, 299, 380
Kurukshetra, i. 308, 316 ; ii. 147
Kurura, i. 254
kuśa, i. 235, 397
kuśadvîpa, i. 235, 254, 325
Kushikâna, i. 262
Kuśaprâvaraṇa, i. 262
Kusnâri, i. 206
kusuma, i. 140, 146
kusumakâra, i. 357
Kusumanaga, i. 301
Kusumapura, i. 316, 330, 335, 370
kuṭâra, i. 120
kuṭhâra, i. 181
Kuṭi, i. 205
kuṭṭaka, i. 155

LA, i. 140
Ladda (?), i. 205
laghu, i. 138
Lagatûrmân, ii. 13
laghu, i. 145, 146
Lahore, i. 259
Lahûr, i. 208
laksha, i. 175, 236, 284
Lakshmî, i. 54 ; ii. 182
lâlâbhaksha, i. 61
Lamghân, i. 259, 317 ; ii. 8
Lampâka, i. 300
Lanbagâ, i. 259 ; ii. 8
Lâṅgûlinî, i. 257
Laṅkâ, i. 209, 267, 268, 301, 303, 306 *seq.*, 316, 370
Lârân, i. 209
Lârdesh, i. 205
Lârî, i. 173
Lâta, i. 153, 268, 269, 280
Lâṭadeśa, i. 173
Lauhâvur (Lahore), i. 206, 208
Lauhûr, castle, i. 317
Laukâyata, i. 132
laukikakâla, ii. 9, 54
lava, i. 336, 337, 362
lavaṇa, i. 235
lavaṇamushṭi, i. 156
lavaṇasamudra, i. 235
Likhita, i. 131
likhyâ, i. 162
liṅga, i. 117, 131, 181 ; ii. 102, 103
Litta (?), i. 300
liyaya, i. 220
locana, i. 178
Lohâvar, ii. 8
lokakâla, ii. 8
lokânanda, i. 157
Lônî, ii. 6
Loharânî, i. 205, 208, 260, 316
Lohitâ, i. 259
Lohita, i. 231 ; ii. 143
Lohitanadî, ii. 143
Lohitya, i. 301
loka, i. 59, 232, 238
lokâloka, i. 236, 237, 249, 284, 286
lokapâla, i. 247
Lûpa (?), i. 257

MADDHYANDÂ (?), ii. 142
Mâdhava, i. 403
Madhra (?), i. 300
Madhu, i. 394
Madhusûdana, i. 403
madhya (?), i. 140, 141, 143, 144, 145, 146, 175
madhyadeśa, i. 173, 198, 251, 290
madhyaloka, i. 59
madhyama, ii. 195
madhyamâya, ii. 228
Madra, i. 302
Madraka, i. 303
madri (?), i. 161
Madura, i. 298
madya (?), i. 252
Maga, i. 21, 121
Magadha, i. 299
Magadha, i. 262, 298, 301

Mâgadha, i. 255, 394
mâgha, i. 211, 217, 218, 403; ii. 177; festivals, 183, 186
maghâ, i. 218, 390, 391; ii. 84, 121, 124, 180
mahâbhûta, i. 41, 42, 321, 382
Mahâcin, i. 207
Mahâdeva, i. 54, 92, 93, 94, 117, 118, 119, 120, 121, 130, 131, 136, 158, 176, 179 181, 292, 342, 361, 362; ii. 6, 102, 103, 120, 125, 140, 143, 144, 147, 179, 180, 181, 182, 184, 192, 239
Mahâgauri, i. 257
Mahâgriva, i. 301
Mahâjambha, i. 231
mahâjvâla, i. 60
Mahâkâla, i. 202
mahâkalpa, i. 332
mahâkhya (?), i. 230
Mahâmegha, i. 231
Mahânada, i. 257
Mahanâra, i. 259
mahânavami, ii. 179
mahâpadma, i. 175, 176, 247; ii. 120
Mahârâshtra, i. 299
maharloka, i. 232, 238, 325
Mahârṇava, i. 302
Mahâśaila, ii. 101
mahâśaṅku, i. 176
mahâtala, i. 230
mâhâtan, ii. 183
Mahâṭavi, i. 301
mahâtrij, ii. 183
Mahâvikâ (?), i. 257
Mahâvirya, i. 386
Mahendra, i. 242, 247, 257, 301
mâheya, i. 215, 300
mahidhara, i. 178
Mahisha, i. 254, 299, 325
Mahoshṇisha, i. 231
Mahrattadeshu, i. 203
Mâhûra, i. 199, 202; ii. 147, 175
Mahvi, i. 206
Mainâka, ii. 101
maitra, i. 358
Maitreya, i. 63, 388, 397
Maitreyi, ii. 174
Maivâr, i. 202
makara, i. 204, 219, 220; ii. 93
makarâdi, i. 356
mala, ii. 20
Mâla, i. 299
Malada (?), i. 300
malamâsa, ii. 20
Mâlava, i. 173, 191, 202, 219, 299 300, 303, 308
Mâlavartika, i. 299
Malaya, i. 200, 247, 257, 301
Malayaparvata, i. 248
Mâlindya, i. 301
Malla, i. 300
Malvâri, i. 173
Malvashau, i. 173
Mâlyavant, i. 248
mâna, i. 166, 353, 355
Mânahala, i. 303
manas, i. 44
mânasa, i. 157, 247, 255, 256, 366; ii. 143, 245
Mânasottama, i. 256
manda, i. 215; ii. 142
Mandaga, i. 255
Mandagir, i. 203
Mandahûkûr, i. 206
Mandâkini, i. 257; ii. 142
Mandakkakor, i. 317
Mandavâhini, i. 257
Mâṇḍavya, i. 157, 300, 302, 303
Mandeha, i. 254
maṅgala, i. 178, 215, 261
maṅgalabâra, i. 213
manguniha (?), ii. 245
maṇiketu, ii. 243
Maṇimân, i. 302
Maṇittha, i. 157
manmatha, ii. 127
Manojava, i. 387
mânsartagu, ii. 183
Manu, i. 131, 132, 157, 179, 241, 386; his children, 387, 393; ii. 110, 111, 118, 127, 162
manushyâhorâtra, i. 328
manushyaloka, i. 59
manvantara, i. 179, 241, 291, 359, 361, 367, 369, 372 *seq.*, 386 *seq.*; their names, 387, 393, 398; ii. 1, 2, 17, 118, 119
Mara, i. 261
Mâraka, i. 302
mârgaṇa, i. 178
mârgaśirsha, i. 217, 218, 358, 402, 403; ii. 10, 174; festivals, 182, 193
marici, i. 163, 242, 390
Mârikala, i. 302
Mârigala, ii. 8
Mârkaṇḍeya, i. 54, 131, 241, 321, 340, 360, 372, 386; ii. 2, 3, 64, 66
mârkaṇḍeya-purâṇa, i. 130
Maru, i. 261, 300

Marucîpaṭṭana, i. 301
Marukuccâ, i. 302
Marut, ii. 199
mâsa, i. 179, 359
mâsârdham, i. 178
mâsha, i. 160, 161, 162, 163 164 ; ii. 206
Mashaka (!), i. 299
mâsopavâsa, ii. 173
Maṭhara, i. 302
Mathurâ, i. 300, 308, 401, 403 ; ii. 5
mâtrâ, i. 139, 140
matsya, i. 131, 300
Mâtsya, i. 262
matsya-purâṇa, i. 130, 168, 235, 236, 247, 248, 251, 252, 254, 255, 258, 261, 271, 284, 285, 286, 325 ; ii. 62, 65, 101, 102, 142, 245
Mau, i. 157
mausala, i. 133
mâyâ, i. 344
Meda, i. 300
Medhâdhṛiti, i. 394
Megha, i. 231
Meghavân, i. 302
Mekala, i. 300, 301
Meru, i. 243 *seq.*, 257, 265, 271, 274, 302, 303, 308, 316 ; according to the Buddhists 326, 327, 329 ; ii. 82, 96, 129, 142
mesha, i. 220
meshâdi, i. 357
Mihrân, i. 260
mimâṁsâ, i. 132
mîna, i. 220
Mithilâ, i. 301
mithuna, i. 219, 220
Mirat (Meerut), i. 205
Mitra, i. 217, 242, 342 ; ii. 122, 199
Mitrâkhya, ii. 115
mleccha, i. 19, 302 ; ii. 137
modaka, i. 136
moksha, i. 70, 80 ; ii. 133
mokshadharma, i. 133
mora, i. 166
Mrâvarta, i. 249
Mṛiga, i. 255
mṛigalâñchana, i. 137 ; ii. 102
mṛigaśiras, ii. 86
mṛigaśirsha, i. 218, 342 ; ii. 84, 121
mṛigavyâdha, ii. 91
mṛitasaṁjîvan, i. 254
mṛittâla, i. 230
mṛityasâra, i. 344
Mṛityu, i. 398
Mrûna, i. 261
Mucukunda, i. 231
Mudrakaraka (?), i. 299
Muhrân (Sindh), i. 204
muhûrta, i. 239, 287, 337, 338 *seq.*, 341 ; their names, 342, 366 ; ii. 118, 119, 243, 244
Mukta, i. 301
mûla, i. 218, 298 ; ii. 85, 122, 179
Mûlasthâna, i. 298
mûlatrikoṇa, ii. 225
Mûlika (!), i. 300
Mûltân (mûlastâna), i. 21, 116, 153, 205, 211, 240, 260, 300, 302, 308, 317 ; ii. 6, 8, 9, 54, 145, 148, 184
Mundla (!), i. 299
Mungiri, i. 200
Munha, i. 208
muni, i. 93, 178, 238
Muñja, i. 231
Muru, i. 387
Mûshika, i. 299
Muttai, ii. 178

NABASA (?), i. 387
Nâbhâga, i. 394
nâḍi, i. 335
naga, i. 178
nâga, i. 91, 178, 247, 267, 344 ; ii. 120, 197, 198
Nâgadvîpa, i. 296
nâgaloka, i. 59
nâgara, i. 173
Nâgarapura, i. 156
Nagarasamvṛitta, i. 257, 296
Nâgârjuna, i. 189
Nagarkoṭ, i. 260 ; ii. 11
Nagha, i. 394
nagna, i. 121
Nagnaparṇa, i. 301
Nahusha, i. 93
Naipâl, i. 201
nairṛita, i. 290, 297, 301
nairṛiti, ii. 203
naisargika, ii. 215, 227
naisargikabala, ii. 227
Naitika (?), i. 300
nakha, i. 179
nakshatra, ii. 64
nakshatramâna, i. 353, 354
nakshatranâtha, i. 216
Nakula, i. 403
Nalaka, i. 300
nâli, ii. 135
Nâlikera, i. 301
Nalinî, i. 261, 262
nalva, i. 166

nâmakarman, ii. 156
Namâvur, i. 203
Namiyya, i. 203
Namuci, i. 231
nanda, i. 178, 231, 401; ii. 120
nandagola, i. 401 ; ii. 148
Nandanâ, i. 257
nandana, ii. 127
Nandanavana, i. 244 ; ii. 96
nanda-purâṇa, i. 130
Nandavishṭha, i. 303
Nandikeśvara, i. 93
Nandna, i. 317
Nara, i. 387
Nârada, i. 116, 131, 237, 357 ; ii. 96, 101, 236
Naraka, i. 236
naraloka, i. 59
Narasiṁha, i. 365, 366
narasiṁha-purâṇa, i. 130
Nârâyaṇa, i. 94, 106, 118, 129, 132, 176, 193, 202, 216, 241, 242, 342, 363, 395 *seq.*, 398, 403 ; ii. 127, 145, 167
Nârimukha, i. 302
Narmadâ, i. 257, 259
Nâsikya, i. 300, 301
nâtha, ii. 103
Naumand (?), ii. 129
navakaṇḍa, i. 297
navakhaṇḍaprathama, i. 294, 296
navan, i. 178
navin, ii. 197
netra, i. 178
niḥâgha, i. 357
niḥśvâsa, i. 339
nikharva, i. 175, 176
Nila, i. 231, 247, 249 ; ii. 142
Nilamukha, i. 262
nimesha, i. 335 *seq.*, 337, 362
Nirahara, ii. 8
niraksha, i. 267
Nirâmaya, i. 387
Nirbindhyâ, i. 257
Nirishabha (!), i. 394
Nirmogha, i. 387
Nirmoha, i. 394
nirṛiti, i. 358 ; ii. 122
Nirutsuka, i. 394
Niśâkara, i. 342
Niśacara, i. 394
Niścirâ, i. 259
niśeśa, i. 216
Nishaba (?), i. 262
Nishadha, i. 247, 248, 249, 257, 301 ; ii. 142
nishkubâda (?), i. 231
Nishprakampa, i. 394
Niśvara, i. 394
nitala, i. 230
nivra, i. 140
niyutam, i. 176, 177
nṛipa, i. 179
Nṛisiṁhavana, i. 302
Nûr, i. 259
nyagrodha, i. 256
nyarbuda, i. 175, 176
nyâyabhâshâ, i. 132

OM, i. 173
odâd (?), ii. 183
Oḍra, i. 301

PADA, ii. 23
pâda, i. 143, 144, 145, 147, 148, 150, 160
padamâsa, ii. 23
Padha, i. 300
padma, i. 114, 131, 175, 176 ; ii. 120
padmaketu, ii. 244
Padmanâbhi, i. 403
Padma-Tulya (?), i. 300
Padnâr, i. 209
Pahlava, i. 300
Paila, i. 127
paitâmaha, i. 153
Pâjaya (?), i. 257
paksha, i. 140, 143, 145, 146, 178, 359 ; ii. 118
pala, i. 162, 163, 164, 165
palâśa, ii. 131
Palâśini, i. 257
Palhava, i. 261
pâli, i. 161
Palola, i. 303
Pañcahasta, i. 387
pancâhi, ii. 197
Pâñcâla, i. 133, 262, 298, 299
pañca mâtaras, i. 42
Pañcanada, i. 260, 302
pañca-siddhântikâ, i. 153 ; ii. 7, 51 190
Pañcaśikha, i. 325
pañcatantra, i. 159
Panchir, i. 108, 259
panci, ii. 197
Pâṇḍava, i. 178
Pâṇḍava-kâla, ii. 1, 5
Pâṇḍu, i. 107, 132, 133, 199, 300, 380, 403
Pâṇḍya, i. 299
Pâṇini, i. 135

Pânipat, i. 205
pânîya, i. 235
Panjayâvar (?), i. 209
panti, i. 166
pâpagraha, i. 216
Parâ, i. 257, 259
parâka, ii. 173
paramapada, ii. 2
parapadma, i. 176
parârdha, i. 174, 175, 333
parârdhakalpa, i. 333
Parâśara, i. 44, 63, 107, 131, 157, 369, 388, 394, 397; ii. 96, 208, 235
Pârasava, i. 302
Paraśurâma, i. 380
paraśvadha, ii. 203
Pârata, i. 302
parâvasu, ii. 128
Pareśvara, i. 158
paridhâvin, ii. 128
Pariksha, i. 77, 113
parivatsara, ii. 125
Pâriyâtra, i. 247, 257, 259, 300
Parjanya, i. 217, 394
Parnâśâ, i. 257, 259
pârthiva, i. 42; ii. 127
pârtîna, i. 220
parvan, i. 132; ii. 115 *seq.*, 119, 191
Parvân, i. 259
parvata, i. 140, 141, 143, 145, 146, 178; ii. 101, 199
Parvatamaru, i. 262
parvati (?), ii. 181
paścima, i. 290
pâshâṇabhûmi, i. 230
Paśupâla, i. 303
pâta, ii. 207
pâtâla, i. 59, 230, 397; ii. 140
Pâṭaliputra, i. 200
pâtañjala, i. 8
Patañjali, i. 27, 55-56, 68-70, 76, 80, 81, 82, 87, 93, 132, 189, 232, 234, 235, 236, 238, 248
Patheśvara, i. 299
patti, i. 407
pattṛin, i. 178
Paulisa, i. 153, 266
Pauṇḍra, i. 301
Paurava, i. 303
pausha, i. 217, 218, 358, 403; ii. 174, 177; festivals, 183, 193
pâvaka, i. 178
pavana, i. 178
Pâvanî, i. 261, 262
pavitra, ii. 130
Payoshṇî, i. 257
Phalgulu, i. 302
phâlguna, i. 217, 218, 358, 403; ii. 174; festivals, 183, 193
Phaṇikâra, i. 301
Pheṇagiri, i. 302
pilumant (?), ii. 129
piṇḍa, ii. 104
Piṇḍâraka, ii. 120
Piṅgala, i. 137; ii. 128
Piṅgalaka, i. 303
Pinjaur, i. 205
Pipyala, i. 257
Piruvâna (?), i. 158
Piśâbika (?), i. 257
piśâca, i. 89, 90, 92, 247; ii. 236
Pita, i. 255
pîtabhûmi, i. 230
pitâmaha, i. 178, 361
pitanda (?), ii. 142
pitaras, i. 89, 93, 232, 248, 330, 357; ii. 121, 128, 133
pitṛi, i. 342
pitṛiloka, i. 233, 236, 238; ii. 233
pitṛînâmahorâtra, i. 328
pitṛipaksha, ii. 180
pitrya, i. 358
Pivara, i. 394
plaksha, i. 235
plava, ii. 128
plavaṅga, ii. 128
Pojjihana (!), i. 300
prabhava, ii. 127
Pradyumna, i. 118, 158, 398
Prâgjyotisha, i. 299, 301
prahara, i. 337
Prahlâda, i. 365
prajâpati, i. 89, 92, 94, 159, 291, 357, 398; ii. 102, 121, 125, 127, 238
prakṛiti, i. 41
pramâṇa, i. 353
pramâdin, ii. 128
pramâthin, ii. 127
pramoda, ii. 127
Pramukha (?), i. 387
prâṇa, i. 277, 334 *seq.*, 337, 339, 361, 394
Praśastâdri, i. 302
praśna-gûḍhâmana (?), i. 158
prastha, i. 162, 163, 164, 165
prasthâna, i. 133
prathama, i. 295
Prathanga (?), i. 299
Pratimaujas, i. 394
Prâtragira (?), i. 299
Prayâga, i. 200; ii. 170 241

práyaścitta, i. 355
prayuta, i. 175, 176, 177
preta, i. 90
Prishaka, i. 262
pṛitaná, i. 407
pṛithivî, i. 238
Pṛithu, i. 292, 394
Prithûdakasvâmin, i. 158
Pṛithusvâmin, i. 316
Priyavrata, i. 241, 387
Proshṭhapada, ii. 127
puhâi (?), ii. 180
pûhaval (?), ii. 183
Puhliṅga (!), i. 299
Pulaha, i. 390
Pulastya, i. 390
Pulindra, i. 300
Pulisa, i. 153, 154, 168, 169, 224, 266, 275, 276, 278, 312, 313, 316, 335, 339, 370, 374, 375, 376, 377; ii. 4, 18, 19, 24, 31, 41. 42, 58, 67, 69, 70, 72, 74, 91, 187, 190, 192, 208
Pulisa-siddhânta, i. 153, 177, 275, 333; ii. 31
Pûkala, i. 302
Pûkara, ii. 147
Puleya, i. 300
Pulinda, i. 262
punarvasu, i. 218; ii. 66, 84, 121, 176, 180
Puñcala (?), i. 157, 366, 367
Puñjâdri, i. 303
puṇyakâla, ii. 187, 191, 192
purâṇas, i. 92; ii. 136
purâṇa, i. 130, 233, 238, 264, 273, 283; ii. 110, 113
Purandara, i. 387, 397
pûrârtaku, ii. 183
Purika, i. 301
Pûrṇa, i. 262
pûrṇimá, i. 348; ii. 185, 197
purohita, ii. 132
Purshâvar (Peshavar), i. 206, 259, 317
Purshûr (Peshavar?), i. 338
Puru, i. 387
purusha, i. 31, 40, 321
purusha, i. 324, 332, 333, 350, 351, 360, 386; ii. 118
Purushâda, i. 300
purushâhorâtra, i. 332
Purushaparvata, i. 248
Purushâvar (v. Purshâvar), ii. 11
pûrva, i. 290
pûrvabhâdrapadâ, i. 218, 240; ii. 85, 122
Pûrvadeśa, i. 173
pûrvaphalguni, i. 218, 291; ii. 85, 121, 128
pûrvâshaḍhá, i. 218, 291; ii. 85, 122.
pûshan, i. 217, 342, 358; ii. 122
pushaṇḍila (?), i. 181
Pushkala, i. 254
Pushkalâvati, i. 302
pushkara, i. 235, 254, 261; ii. 120
pushkaradvîpa, i. 235, 255, 256, 284, 286
Pushpajâti, i. 257
pushya, i. 218, 291; ii. 66, 84, 121
pûthi, i. 171
pûyattanu (?) ii. 184

Rada (?), i. 231
Rahab, i. 261
râhu, i. 293; ii. 234
râhucakra, i. 292
râhunrâkaraṇa (?), i. 157
râi, ii. 11
raibhya (?). i. 387
raivata, i. 387
Raivataka, i. 302
raja, i. 162
râjadharma, i. 133
Râjagiri, i. 205, 208
Râjanya, i. 302
râjarshi, i. 93
rajas, i. 40, 399
Râjauri, i. 202
Râjâvari, i. 208
râkshasa, i. 89, 90, 91, 92, 231, 247, 248, 262, ; ii. 3, 128
rakta, i. 215
raktabhûmi, i. 230
raktâksha (?), ii. 128
raktâmala, i. 190
Râma, i. 117, 121, 166, 209, 258, 306. 307, 310, 372, 380, 397; ii. 3, 137
Râmadî (?), i. 257
Râmâyaṇa, i. 307, 310; ii. 3
Rameshar (?), i. 209
Râmsher (?), i. 209
Ramyaka, i. 249
randhra, i. 178
Raṅka, i. 192
rasa, i, 42, 178, 188
rasâtala, i. 230
rasâyana, i. 80, 188, 191, 193
rasâyana-tantra, i. 156
Râshṭra, i. 301, 303
raśmi, i. 178

raśmiketu (?), ii. 242
ratha, i. 407, 408
râtri, i. 359
raucya, i. 387
raudra, i. 344, 358 ; ii. 128, 241
raurava, i. 60
Râvaṇa, i. 306, 307, 380 ; ii. 3
Râvaṇaśiras, i. 179
ravi, i. 215, 216, 217, 342
ravicandra, i. 178
Rebha (?), i. 387
reṇu, i. 162
Revanta, i. 119
revatî, i. 218, 291, 342, 369 ; ii. 66, 85, 86, 122, 177, 180
ṛic, i. 128
Ṛigveda, i. 127, 128
Rihanjûr, i. 205
Ṛiksha, i. 257
Ṛiṇajyeshṭha (?), i. 398
Ṛishabha, i. 301 ; ii. 101
ṛishi, i. 93, 106, 130, 237, 239, 241, 404 ; ii. 96, 103
Ṛishika, i. 257
Ṛishika, i. 301
Ṛishyamûka, i. 301
Ṛishyaśriṅga, i. 394
Ṛitadhâman, i. 387
ṛitu (?), i. 178, 357, 359 ; ii. 118
Ṛitukûlyâ, i. 257
rodha, i. 60
rodhakṛit, ii. 128
rodhinî, i. 218
rohiṇî, i 218 344, 401 ; ii. 66, 84, 96, 97, 99, 100, 102, 121, 175, 176, 177
Rohîtaka, i. 308, 316
Romaka, i. 267, 303
Romaka-siddhânta, i. 153
rudhira, i. 61
rudhirândha, i. 61
Rudra, i. 94, 179, 342, 362, 363 ; ii. 120, 121, 140
rudraputra, i. 387
rukmâksha (?), ii. 129
Rûm, i. 268, 272
Rumana (?), i. 299
Rûmîmaṇḍala, i. 262
rûpa, i. 42, 140, 178
rûpa-pañca (?), ii. 179
Rûpaka, i. 300
Rûrasa (?), i. 261
Rûrdhwabâhu (!), i. 394
ruvu, i. 161, 162

Sabâtî (?), i. 261
śabda, i. 42
sabhâ-parvan, i. 133
Sadâśiva, i. 361, 362, 363
Saddânâ (?), i. 257
sâdhâraṇa, ii. 128
sâgara, i. 178
Sagara, i. 20 ; ii. 143, 176, 169
sâgârtam, ii. 183
sahadeva, i. 403
Sahanyâ, i. 202
sahasram, i. 175, 177
sahasrâṁśu, i. 179
Sahâwî (?), ii. 190
Sahishṇu, i. 394
Sahya, i. 247, 257
śailasutâpati, ii. 125
Śailodâ, ii. 143
saindhava, i. 173, 261
Saintra, i. 153
Sairîkîrṇa (?), i. 301
Sairindha, i. 303
Śaka, i. 300, 302 ; ii. 5, 6, 8
śâka, i. 235
śâkadvîpa, i. 235, 252, 253
śakakâla, i. 366, 390, 391, 392 ; ii. 6, 7, 9, 28, 123, 129, 188, 190
śâkaṭa, i. 135
śâkaṭâyana, i. 135[1]
śakra, i. 358 ; ii. 122
Śakrânala, ii. 128
śakti, i. 118, 119, 363
śakuni, ii. 197, 198, 200
śakvara, i. 241
śalâka, i. 239
Salila, i. 261
Sâlkot, i. 317
śâlmali, i. 235
śâlmalidvîpa, i. 235, 254
Sâlva, i. 299
Sâlvanî (!), i. 300
Śalya, i. 133
sama, i. 371
Samalvâhana, i. 136
sâman, i. 129
Sâmanta, ii. 13
Samatata, i. 301
sâmaveda, i. 127, 129, 396
Samaya (?), i. 336, 337 ; ii. 188
Sâmba, i. 118
sâmba-purâṇa, i. 130
Sâmbhapura, i. 298
Sâmbhapurayâtrâ, ii. 184
saṁdhi, i. 128, 364, 366, 369, 372 ; ii. 2, 17, 110, 133, 225, 226, 244
saṁdhi-astamana, i. 364
saṁdhi udaya, i. 364
saṁdhyâṁśa, i. 372, 373

saṁhitâ, i. 157, 167, 298, 299, 320, 389, 391; ii. 66, 86, 88, 92, 107, 110, 111, 115, 123, 126, 145, 192, 235
śamî, ii. 141
Śaṁkara, ii. 147
Saṁkarshaṇa, i. 398
Sâṁkhya, i. 8; quoted, i. 30, 48, 62, 64, 75, 81, 83, 89, 92, 132
saṁkrânti, i. 344; ii. 188, 189, 190, 199
samnâra (?), i. 205
samudra, i. 175, 178
Samûhuka, i. 262
Saṁvarta, i. 131; ii. 244
saṁvartaka, ii. 101
Saṁvatsara, i. 242; ii. 8, 9, 123, 125, 129
Saṁyamaṇipura, i. 271
śanaiścara, i. 215
śanaiścarabâra, i. 213
Sanaka, i. 325
Sananda, i. 325
Sanandanâtha, i. 325
sandaṁśaka, i. 61
Sandân, i. 209
Sâṇḍî (?), ii. 142
Saṅgabila (śṛinkhala ?), i. 158
Saṅgavanta (?), i. 261
saṅgha, i. 40
Śankara, i. 94
śaṅkha, i. 114, 131, 301, 338; ii. 120
Śaṅkhâksha, i. 231
śaṅku, i. 166, 175, 176
Śaṅkukarṇa, i. 231
Śaṅkupatha, i. 262
śânta (?), ii. 188
Śântahaya, i. 387
Sântanu, i. 107
śânti, i. 133, 387
Śântika, i. 302
sânta, i. 358
saptan, i. 178
saptarshayas, i. 389
śara, i. 178
sâra, i. 113
śarabha, i. 203
Śarad, i. 357; ii. 93
śârada, i. 117, 303
Śaradhâna, i. 302
śarâśitimukha, ii. 190
Sârasvata, i. 158, 300, 398
Sarasvatî, ii. 99, 142
śârâvali, i. 158
Sarayu, i. 259; ii. 143
Sarayuśati (?), ii. 143
śarkara, i. 230
sarpa, ii. 129
sârpa, i. 358
Sarpâs, ii. 121
sarpis, i. 235
Sarsuti, i. 257, 261, 405; ii. 105, 142
Sarva, i. 259, 261
sarvadhârin, ii. 127
sarvajit, ii. 127
śarvari (?), ii. 128
Sarvatraga, i. 387
Śaryâti, i. 387
śaśalakshaṇa, ii. 102
Śaśideva, i. 135
śaśidevavṛitti, i. 135
śaśin, i. 178; ii. 115
śastra, ii. 241
sat, ii. 197
śatabhishaj, i. 218; ii. 85, 122
śatadyumna, i. 387
Śâtaka, i. 303
Śatakratu, i. 396
śatam, i. 175
Śatânîka, i. 77
Śatarudra, i. 259
Śataśîrsha, i. 231
Śatâtapa, i. 131
Śâtavâhana, i. 136
satin, ii. 197
sattra, i. 344
satva, i. 40
Satya, i. 157, 394, 399
Satyaka, i. 385
satyaloka, i. 232, 233, 238
Saulika, i. 301
Saumya, i. 89, 215, 296, 344, 358; ii. 128
Śaunaka, i. 77, 113, 126, 380; ii. 145
sauptika, i. 133
saura, i. 215
saurâhargaṇa, ii. 27
sauramâna, i. 353, 354
Sauvira, i. 298, 300, 302
Sâva, i. 259
śavala, i. 60
Savana, i. 394
sâvana, i. 328; ii. 21
sâvanâhargaṇa, ii. 27
sâvanamâna, i. 353
Savañjulâ, i. 257
Śavara (?), i. 300, 301
sâvarṇi, i. 387
savitâ, ii. 121
savitṛi, i. 216, 217, 398; ii. 121

sâyaka, i. 178
Ścorvarî (!), i. 394
senâmukha, i. 407
Śesha, i. 231
Śeshâkhya, i. 237
Setubandha, i. 209, 307
Setuka, i. 299
shaḍâya, ii. 215, 227
Shakruṇâ (?), i. 257
Shamilân, i. 206
Sharvâr, i. 200
Sharvat, i. 259
shashṭyabda, ii. 5, 6, 123, 124, 129
shaṭ, i. 178 ; ii. 177
Shataldar (Satlej), i. 259, 260
shatpañcâśikâ, i. 158
Shattumâna (?), i. 300
shidda (?), ii. 39
Shilahat, i. 201
Shirshâraha, i. 205
Shmâhina (?), i. 259
sibi (?), i. 165
Śibika, i. 301
Śibirâ, i. 301
siddha, i. 93, 192, 238, 247
siddhamâtṛikâ, i. 173
siddhânta, i. 153, 155 ; of Pulisa, 224, 266, 339, 374 ; ii. 18
Siddhapura, i. 267, 268, 303, 304
siddhârtha, ii. 128
Śikhi, i. 262, 387
śilâtala, i. 230
simaṁtonnayanam, ii. 156
siṁha, i. 220
Siṁhala, i. 301
Siṁhaladvipa, i. 233
Siṁhika (?), ii. 111
Sindh, i. 173, 198, 206, 259, 261, 270, 298, 300, 302, 310, 387 ; ii. 6, 8, 15, 48, 104, 129, 132
Sindhusâgara, i. 260
Singaldib, i. 209
Śini, i. 257
Śiprâ, i. 259
Sirvâ (?), i. 257
śishya, i. 127
śishyahitâvṛitti, i. 135
śiśira, i. 357
Śiśumâra, i. 231, 241, 242
śiśupâla, i. 165, 340, 341
sita, i. 215 ; ii. 239
Sita, i. 249
Sitâ, i. 261
śitâ, i. 178
śitadidhiti, i. 215
śitakâla, i. 357
śitâṁśu, i. 178, 215, 216
śitamayûkhamâlin, ii. 125
śitaraśmi, i. 215
Śiva, i. 131, 342, 362, 363 ; ii. 128
Śivapaura, i. 261
śivarâtri, ii. 184
Skanda, i. 118, 131 ; ii. 140
skanda-purâṇa, i. 130
skandha, a metre, i. 144
stri, i. 133
śloka, i. 127, 132, 137, 147
Śmaśrudhara, i. 301
smṛiti, i. 131, 352, 372, 373, 374, 386 ; ii. 110, 111
Sneha, i. 254
śokakṛit, ii. 128
soma, i. 215, 216, 252, 253, 342 ; ii. 103, 128
somabâra, i. 213
Somadatta, i. 239
somagraha, i. 216
Somamantra, ii. 97
Somanâtha, i. 117, 161, 165, 189, 205, 208, 261, 357, 405 ; ii. 9, 103, 104, 105, 176
soma-purâṇa, i. 130
Somaśushma, i. 398
Śona, i. 257
śoshiṇî, i. 344
sparśa, i. 42
sphuṭa, ii. 195
sphuṭâya, ii. 228
śravaṇa, i. 218 ; ii. 85, 99, 122
śrâvaṇa, i. 211, 217, 218, 358, 403 ; ii. 98, 173, 176 ; festivals, 179, 193
Śrî, i. 118, 119 ; ii. 6, 199
Śridhara, i. 403
Śrî Harsha, ii. 5
śrîmukha, ii. 127
Śriṅgâdri, i. 249
Śṛiṅgavant, i. 248
Śripâla, i. 164, 240
Śriparvata, i. 248
Śrisheṇa, i. 153, 266, 376 ; ii. 111
Śroṇi, i. 257
srûdhava (?), i. 158, 334, 336, 344, 361 ; ii. 6, 120, 192, 201–203
stâmasa (?), i. 387
Stambha, i. 394
sthânabala, ii. 225
Strîrâjya, i. 302
Subâhu, i. 394
Sûbâra, i. 209
śubha, i. 344
śubhakṛit, ii. 128

subhânu, ii. 127
Ṣuci, i. 387, 394
Suddhodana, i. 380
Sudharmâtman (?), i. 387
Sudivya (?), i. 387
śûdra, i. 101, 125, 247, 302; ii. 6, 95, 98, 136, 150, 152, 155, 157, 163, 170, 191
Sugrîva, i. 156
Suhma, i. 300; ii. 101
Suka (?), ii. 120
Sukhâ, i. 271
Sukhâpura, i. 271
śukla, ii. 127
śuklabhûmi, i. 230
śuklapaksha, i. 359
Śukra, i. 132, 215, 358, 394; ii. 121, 199
śukrabâra, i. 213
Sukṛita, i. 262
Sukṛiti, i. 394
Ṣukshetra, i. 387, 394
Ṣukti, i. 257
Ṣuktibâm (?), i. 247
Śuktimatî, i. 257
Sukûrda, i. 261
śûla, i. 119, 240
Śûladanta, i. 231
Sûlika, i. 300, 302
Sumâli, i. 231
Sumanas, i. 255
Sumantu, i. 127
Sumedhas, i. 394
Sunnâm, i. 206
śûnya, i. 178
Suprayogâ, i. 257
surâ, i. 235
Surasa, i. 257
surakshas, i. 231
Śûrasena, i. 299, 300, 302
Surâshṭra, i. 300
Surejya, ii. 127
sureṇu, i. 251
sûri, i. 217
śûrpa, i. 163
Ṣûrpakarṇa, i. 300
Śûrpakâraka, i. 300
sûrya, i. 179, 215
Śûryâdri, i. 301
sûryaputra, i. 215
Sûrya-siddhânta, i. 153
Susaṁbhâvya, i. 387
Ṣuśânti, i. 387
Śushmin, i. 254
sûtaka, i. 355
sutâla, i. 230
sutala, i. 230
Sutapas, i. 394
Sutaya, i. 394
sûtra, i. 158
suvarṇa, i. 160, 161, 162, 163, 164
Suvarṇabhûmi, i. 303
Suvarṇadvîpa, i. 210; ii. 106
suvarṇavarṇa, i. 230
svâdûdaka, i. 235
Śvamukha, i. 302
Śvâpada, i. 231
Svargabhûmi, i. 262
svargârohaṇa, i. 133
svarloka, i. 45, 232, 233, 397
svârocisha, i. 387
svârociya, i. 387
Svastikajaya, i. 231
Svât, ii. 182
svâtî, i. 218, 391; ii. 85, 99, 100, 121
Svayaṁbhû, i. 398
svayambhuva, i. 241, 387
Śveta, i. 248; ii. 142
śvetaketu, ii. 242
Śyâmâka, i. 303
Syâvabala (?), ii. 208

TAITILA, ii. 197, 199
Tâkeshar, i. 208; ii. 8
Takshaka, i. 231, 247; ii. 120
Takshaśila, i. 302
tala, i. 290
tâla, i. 167, 230
Tâlahala, i. 302
tâlaka, i. 188
Târakruti (?), i. 302
Tâlakûna (?), i. 300
Tâlikaṭa, i. 301
Tâmalipta, i. 262
Tâmaliptikâ, i. 301
Tâmara, i. 262, 300
tamas, i. 40, 237, 399
Tamasâ, i. 257
tâmasa, i. 300
tâmasakîlaka, ii. 234, 238
tâmbiru, i. 220
Tâmrâ, i. 259
Tâmraliptika, i. 299
Tâmraparṇa, i. 301
Tâmravarṇâ, i. 257, 296
Tâna, i. 203, 205, 209, 298
tanduâ, i. 204
Tânesbar, i. 117, 199, 205, 300, 308, 316, 317; ii. 103, 145, 147
Taṅgaṇa, i. 303
Tankaṇa, i. 301
tantra, i. 155, 156

Tanvat (?), i. 201
tapana, i. 178
Tâpasâśrama, i. 301
Tapasvin, i. 394
Tâpi, i. 257
Tapodhṛiti, i. 394
tapoloka, i. 232
Tapomûrti, i. 394
Taporati, i. 394
taptakumbha, i. 60
Târa (?), i. 303 ; ii. 64
Târakâksha, i. 231
taraṇa, ii. 64
târaṇa, ii. 127
târî, i. 171
târkshya-purâṇa, i. 130
Tarojanapâla, ii. 13, 14
Tarû, i. 201
Tarûpana (?), i. 300
Taskara, ii. 238
tattva, i. 44, 179
Tattvadarśica (!), i. 394
taukshika, i. 220
Tavalleshar, i. 208
Tharpura (?), i. 300
thohar (Sindhî), i. 192
Tiauri, i. 202
tikani- (?)-yâtrâ, i. 158
Tillita (?), i. 300
Tilvat, i. 201
Timingilâśana (?), i. 301
tiryagloka, i. 59
Tishya, i. 254, 372, 380
tithi, i. 179 ; ii. 194, 195, 201-203
Tobâ, i. 257
tola, i. 160, 162
trahagattata (?), ii. 192
trahi, trohi, ii. 197
Traipura, i. 300
tranjâi, ii. 182
trâsauiya, i. 344
trayam, i. 178
Trayyâruna, i. 398
tretâ, i. 372
tretâyuga, i. 253, 373, 397, 398 ; ii. 186
Tridhâman, i. 398
Tridivâ, i. 257, 262
Trigarta, i. 300, 302
triguṇa (?), i. 178
triharkasha (?), ii. 191
trihaspaka (?), ii. 191
trijagat, i. 178
trikâla, i. 178
trikaṭu, i. 178
Trikûṭa, i. 248
Trilocanapâla, ii. 13, 14
Trinetra, i. 303
triṅsaṁśaka, ii. 223
Tripavâ (?), i. 257
Tripurântika, i. 248
Tripurî, i. 301
Trisâgâ, i. 257
Triśira, i. 231
Trivikrama, i. 403
Trivṛisha, i. 398
triya, ii. 197
truṭi, i. 335 *seq.*, 337, 362, 363
Tukhâra, i. 261, 302
tulâ, i. 165, 219, 220
tulâdi, i. 357
Tumbavana, i. 301
Tumbura, i. 300
Tuṅgabhadrâ, i. 257
Turagânana, i. 302
Tûrân, i. 208
Tvashṭṛi, i. 217, 342, 358 ; ii. 117, 121, 127

UDAKA, i. 136
Udayagiri, i. 301
Udbhira, i. 300
Uddehika, i. 300
udruvaga, i. 220
Udunpûr, i. 173
udvatsara, ii. 125
Udyânamarûra, i. 262
udyoga, i. 133
Ugrabhûti, i. 135
Ujain, i. 189, 202, 259, 298, 301, 304, 308, 311, 313, 316
Ujjayinî, ii. 241
Ûlyânda (?), i. 137
Umâdevi, i. 54
Ûmmalnâra, i. 209
ûna, ii. 21
ûnarâtra, i. 354 ; ii. 21 ; universal or partial, 23, 25, 34, 37, 186, 187, 192
Uñjara (?), i. 231
Ûpakâna, i. 262
upari, i. 290
Upavaṅga, i. 301
upavâsa, ii. 172
Uraga, i. 262
Ûrdhabishau, i. 200
Ûrdhvakarṇa, i. 301
Ûrdvakuja, i. 231
Ûrja, i. 394
Urur, i. 387
urvarâ, i. 178
uśanas, i. 77, 131, 398

Ûshkârâ, i. 207
ushṇakâla, i. 357
Ushṭrakarṇa, i. 262
Uskala, i. 301
utâmasa (?), i. 387
Utkala, i. 300
utkṛiti, i. 179
Utpala, i. 157, 158, 298, 334, 336, 337, 361, 367
Utpalavinî (?), i. 257
utsarpiṇî, i. 371
Uttama, i. 398
Uttamaujas, i. 387
Uttamarṇa, i. 300
Uttânapâda, i. 241, 242
uttara, i. 290
uttarabhâdrapadâ, i. 218, 342 ; ii. 85, 86, 122, 127
uttarakhaṇḍakhâdyaka, i. 156 ; ii. 87, 90, 91
uttarakûla, i. 357
Uttarakurava, i. 302
uttaramânasa, ii. 142
Uttaranarmada, i. 300
uttaraphalgunî, i. 218 ; ii. 84, 121
uttarâshâḍhâ, i. 218 ; ii. 85, 122
uttarâyaṇa, i. 356, 357 ; ii. 169
Uvaryahâr (?), i. 200

VAḌAVÂMUKHA, i. 266, 267, 269, 272, 278, 279, 302, 307, 327 ; ii. 201
Vaḍavânala, ii. 104
Vâḍha, i. 300
Vadhra, ii. 101
vâhinî, i. 407
Vahirgira, i. 299
Vâhlîka (!), i. 300
vahnijvâla, i. 61
Vaidarbha, i. 300
Vaideśa, i. 300
vaidhṛita, ii. 204, 206, 208
Vaidika, i. 300
Vaidûrya, i. 301
Vaihand, i. 206, 259, 317
Vainyâ, i. 257
Vairahma (?), i. 344
vaiśâkha, i. 217, 218, 358, 403 ; ii. 123, 173 ; festivals, 179, 182, 186, 193
vaishṇava, i. 357
Vaishṇavî, i. 120
vaiśvânara, i. 178
Vaiśaṁpayana, i. 127
vaiśya, i. 101, 125, 247, 302 ; ii. 95, 98, 136, 155, 157, 170, 191
vaitaraṇî, i. 61, 257
Vaivasvata, i. 271, 387
Vâjasravas, i. 398
vajra, i. 119, 236, 241, 321, 360, 386 ; ii. 2, 3, 65, 203
vajrabrahmahatyâ, ii. 162
Vâka, i. 299
vakra, i. 215 ; ii. 101
Vâlikhilya, i. 395
Vallabha, i. 192, 193, 209 ; ii. 5, 6
Vallabhî, i. 192 ; ii. 6
Vâlmîki, i. 398 ; ii. 3
Vâmana, i. 129, 131, 396, 403
vâmana-purâṇa, i. 130
Vaṁśavara, i. 257
Vâṁśca (!), i. 394
vâna, i. 178, 300
Vanarâjya, i. 303
Vanaugha, i. 302
Vânavâsî, i. 301
Vanavâsika, i. 299
Vaṅga, i. 301
Vaṅgeya, i. 299
Vânupadevaś-ca, i. 387
Vaprivan, i. 398
Vapushmat, i. 394
var (?), ii. 10
vâra, i. 355
Varâha, i. 131
Varâhamihira, i. 23, 54, 117-121, 153, 157, 158, 162, 164, 166, 167, 219, 220, 266, 268, 272, 276, 297, 299, 300 *seq.*, 320, 348, 359, 391, 392 ; ii. 7, 51, 66, 70, 86, 87, 88, 89, 92, 95, 103, 107 *seq.*, 113, 115, 116, 118, 123, 145, 190, 208, 235, 239, 240
varâha-purâṇa, i. 130
Vârâhî, i. 120
Varaka, i. 394
Vardhamâna, i. 301
varga, i. 297, 298
Vâricara, i. 301
varṇa, i. 100
varsha, i. 359
varshakâla, i. 211, 357 ; ii. 94
Varuṇa, i. 217, 242, 271, 292, 342, 358, 372 ; ii. 92, 115, 122
varuṇamantra, ii. 97
Varvara, i. 261
Vasâ, ii. 241
vâsara, ii. 118
vasanta, i. 357 ; ii. 179
Vasâti, i. 302
Vasavas, ii. 122
Vasishṭha, i. 115, 131, 225, 239, 268, 280, 340, 390, 394, 398 ; ii. 66, 96

vasishtha-siddhânta, i. 153
vasu, i. 178, 291, 342, 394
Vâsudeva, i. 22, 52, 104, 107, 122, 133, 165, 199, 218, 254, 340, 341, 352, 362, 397, 398, 400 *seq.*, 401 *seq.*, 403 ; ii. 105, 137, 138, 147, 148, 175, 176, 177, 178, 180, 181, 182
Vâsuki, i. 231, 247 ; ii. 120
Vasukra, i. 126
Vasumân, i. 302
vata, ii. 170
Vatsa, i. 299, 300, 301
vâyava, i. 290, 297, 302 ; ii. 202
Vâyavamantra, ii. 97
Vâyu, i. 292 ; ii. 66, 121
vâyu-purâṇa, i. 41, 130, 168, 194, 230, 231, 232, 234, 239, 241, 248, 251, 257, 258, 271, 287, 295, 296, 299 *seq.*, 337 ; ii. 62, 63, 65, 142, 245
veda, i. 29, 31, 104, 125, 131, 132, 178, 348, 393, 396, 398 ; ii. 21, 22, 82, 95, 96, 110, 111, 131, 136, 139, 140, 152, 179
Vedabâhu, i. 394
Vedasmṛiti, i. 257, 259
Vedaśrî, i. 394
Vedavatî, i. 257
vega, i. 344
Veṇâ, i. 301
Venavyâsa, i. 398
Veṇumati, i. 259, 302
Venvâ, i. 257
Vibhâ, i. 271
vibhava, ii. 127
Vibhâvaripura, i. 271
Vicitra, i. 387
Vidarbha, i. 301
Vidâsinî, i. 259
Vidhâtṛi, i. 217, 238
Vidiśâ, i. 257, 259
vidyâdhara, i. 91, 262 ; ii. 92
vidyut, i. 42
Vidyujjihva, i. 231
vighaṭikâ, i. 334
vijaya, ii. 127
Vijayanandin, i. 156, 343 ; ii. 49, 90
Vikaca, ii. 237
vikârin, ii. 128
vikrama, ii. 127, 128
Vikramâditya, i. 189 ; ii. 5, 6, 7, 129
vikṛita, ii. 127
vilambin, ii. 128
Vimalabuddhi, i. 158
vinâḍî, i. 337
Vinatâ, i. 252, 253
Vinâyaka, i. 120, 134
Vindhya, i. 247, 248, 257, 262, 301 ; ii. 92
Vindhyamûli. i. 300
Vipaścit, i. 387
Virâj, i. 241
Virajas, i. 387, 394
Virañcana, i. 361, 362
Virâṭa, i. 133
Viriñcya, i. 342
Virocana, i. 117, 231, 396 ; ii. 11
virodhin, ii. 127
viśâkhâ, i. 218, 231, 291, 391 ; ii. 85, 121
viśâla, i. 230, 344
Viśâlâ, i. 259
Viśâlyakaraṇa, i. 254
viśasana, i. 61
visha, ii. 159
Vishṇu, i. 94, 118, 130, 131, 216, 217, 231, 242, 253, 255, 358, 365, 382, 388, 394, 397, 398, 403 ; ii. 107, 120, 121, 122
Vishṇucandra, i. 153, 266, 376 ; ii. 111
vishṇu-dharma, i. 54, 113-115 (?), 126 (?), 132, 216, 217, 218, 241, 242, 287, 288, 291, 321, 329, 331, 332, 344, 353, 354, 358, 360, 372, 379, 380, 381, 386, 387, 398 ; ii. 2, 3, 21, 64, 65, 102, 121, 140, 145 (?), 174, 175
Vishṇupada, ii. 142
vishṇu-purâṇa, i. 47, 60, 61, 63, 77, 126, 130, 131, 230, 232, 235, 237, 238, 248, 254, 255, 256, 262, 325, 387, 388, 393 ; ii. 62, 105, 131, 132
Vishṇuputra, i. 387
vishṭi, ii. 197, 199
vishuva, ii. 188
viśva, i. 179, 342
Viśvakarman, ii. 121
Viśvâmitra, i. 239, 322, 394
Viśvarûpa, ii. 238
viśvâvasu, ii. 128
viśvedevâḥ, i. 357, 358 ; ii. 122
vitala, i. 230
Vitastâ, ii. 181
vitasti, i. 167
vitta (?), i. 215
Vitteśvara, i. 156, 392
vivâhapaṭala, i. 158
Vivarṇa, i. 262
Vivasvant, i. 217

Viviṁśa, i. 254
viyat, i. 178
Viyattha, i. 259
Voḍha, i. 325
Vokkâṇa, i. 302
Vṛihaspati, i. 131, 215
Vṛika, i. 299
Vṛikavaktra, i. 231
vṛiścika, i. 220
vriścikaloka, ii. 233
Vṛisha, i. 301, 387
vṛishabha (?), ii. 127
Vṛishabadhvaja, i. 300
vṛishan, i. 220
vṛishṇi, i. 344
Vṛitraghnî (?), i. 257
vṛitta, i. 145
vahara (?), ii. 104
Vyâḍi, i. 189–191
Vyâgramukha, i. 300
vyâkaraṇa, i. 135
vyakta, i. 41
Vyâlagrîva, i. 301
Vyâna (?), ii. 121
Vyâsa, i. 44, 104, 107, 108, 126, 127, 131, 132, 134, 171, 238, 340, 341, 352, 369, 394, 397, 398
vyâsamaṇḍala, i. 238
vyastatrairâśika, i. 313
vyatipâta, ii. 204, 206, 208
Vyaya, i. 394; ii. 127

Yâdava, i. 133, 404, 405
yâhi, ii. 197
Yajna, i. 242
Yâjnavalkya, i. 128, 131, 132; ii. 174
yajnopavîta, i. 181; ii. 130, 136
yajurveda, i. 127, 128
yaksha, i. 89, 91, 92, 247, 262
Yama, i. 131, 178, 271, 291, 292, 303, 342; ii. 115, 122
Yamakoṭi, i. 267, 268, 272, 303
yamala, i. 178
Yamunâ, i. 308, 316
Yâmuna, i. 300, 302
yâmya, i. 358
Yâmyodadhi, i. 301
Yaśodâ (?), i. 382, 397, 401
Yaśovati, i. 302
yâtrâ, ii. 178
Yaudheya, i. 303
yava, i. 160, 162
Yavana, i. 153, 158, 300, 302; ii. 5
Yâvana-koṭi, i. 306
Yavasa (?), i. 261
Yayâti, ii. 174
yoga, ii. 191, 204 *seq.*
yogayâtrâ, i. 158
yojana, i. 153, 167, 168, 169, 224, 234, 236, 244 *seq.*, 265, 311; ii. 65, 67
yojanas of heaven, ii. 72, 74, 79
Yima, i. 119
Yudhishṭhira, i. 340, 341, 390, 391, 403; ii. 3
yuga, i. 298, 367, 372 *seq.*, 397; ii. 1, 2, 124; their beginnings, 186, 187
yûkâ, i. 162
Yuktasa, i. 394
yuvan, ii. 127

Zâbaj, i. 210
Zanba (?), ii. 142
Zindutuuda (?), i. 261

# INDEX II.

'Abdalkarîm Ibn 'Abi Al'aujâ', i. 264
'Abdallâh Ibn Almukaffa', i. 159
'Abd-almun'im v. Abû-Sahl, i. 5
Abû-Aḥmad Ibn Catlaghtagîn, i. 317
Abû-al'abbâs Alêrânshahrî (v. Aleranshahri), i. 6
Abû-al'aswad Al-du'alî, i. 136
Abû-alfatḥ Albustî, i. 34
Abû-alḥasan of Ahvâz, ii. 19
Abû-Bakr Al-shiblî, i. 87
Abû-Ma'shar, i. 304, 325
Abû-Sahl 'Abd-almun'im Ibn 'Alî Ibn Nûḥ Al-tiflîsî, i. 5, 7 (also under 'Abd-almun'im)
Abû-Ya'kûb of Sijistân, his book *Kashf-almaḥjûb*, i. 64
Abû-Yazîd Albistâmî, i. 88
'Aḍud-aldaula, ii. 157
Afghans, i. 208
Afrâsiâb, i. 304
Al-êrânshahrî v. Abû-al'abbâs, i. 6, 249, 326
Alexander, story of his birth, i. 96
Alexander of Aphrodisias, i. 320
Alexandria, i. 153
Alfazârî, i. 165, 303, 314, 315 ; ii. 15, 16, 17, 18, 23
Al-ḥajjâj, ii. 153
'Alî Ibn Zain of Tabaristan, i. 382
Aljâḥiẓ, i. 204
Al jaihânî, book of routes, i. 240
Alkhalîl Ibn 'Aḥmad, i. 138, 147
Al-khwârizmî, ii. 79, 114
Alkindî, ii. 200, 201
Alma'mûra, i. 21
almanac from Kashmir, i. 391
Almanṣûr, Khalif.
Al-manṣûra, i. 21, 173, 193, 205, 260, 316 ; ii. 6
Ammonius, i. 85
Aphrodisius, i. 407
Apollonius, *de causis rerum*, i. 40
Arabian astronomy (lunar stations), ii. 81, 90
Arabian metric, i. 138, 142, 144
Arabian traditions, i. 170, 185
Arabic literature, translation of Caraka, i. 159 ; Kalila and Dimna, translation from the Indian corrupt, i. 162
Arabs, i. 302 ; different forms of matrimony with them, i. 108 ; their idols, i. 123
Aratus, i. 97, 383 ; scholia on the *Phænomena*, i. 97, 384
Archimedes, i. 168
Ardashîr Ibn Bâbak, i. 100, 109
Ardiyâ, Eranian, i. 249
Aristotle, letter to Alexander, i. 124, 225, 226, 232 ; φυσικὴ ἀκρόασις, i. 320
Arjabhar, ii. 19
Arkand, i. 312, 316 ; ii. 7, 48, 49
Asclepius, i. 222
Asvira, i. 207

Babylonia, ii. 153
Bagdâd, ii. 15, 67
Balkh, i. 21, 260, 304
Barhatagin, ii. 10
Barîdish, Eranian, i. 260
Barmecides, i. 159
Barshawâr, i. 109
Barzakh, i. 63
Barzôya, i. 159
Bashshâr Ibn Burd, ii. 131
Bhatta-Shâh, i. 207
Bhattavaryân, i. 207
bist (=vishṭi), ii. 201
Bolor mountains, i. 117, 207
Bolor-Shâh, i. 206

Buddhists, i. 7, 21, 40, 91, 121, 156; their writing, 173; their cosmographic views, 249, 326; ii. 169
Bûshang, i. 299

CALENDAR of Kashmir, ii. 5, 8
Ceylon, i. 209; pearls, i. 211
chess, i. 183–185
China, ii. 104
Chinese, ii. 239
Chinese paper, i. 171
Christianity, i. 6, 8
Christians, their use of the words Father and Son, i. 38
Christian views, i. 69
Christians, i. 94; ii. 186
Christian traditions, ii. 151, 161
clepsydræ, i. 337
Commodus, Emperor, i. 123
Constantine, Emperor, ii. 161

DAIBAL, i. 208
Daizan, i. 109
Dânak, Persian, i. 163
Denars, i. 309
Dibajât (Maledives, Laccadives), i. 233; ii. 106
Dirhams, i. 160, 163, 164
diz (Persian), i. 304

EMPEDOCLES, i. 85
era of the realm of Sindh, ii. 48, 49
era of Yazdajird, ii. 48, 49
Eranian traditions, i. 249
Erânshahr, i. 54
Erichthonius, i. 407

FÂRFAZA, i. 299
farsakh, Persian, i. 167, 311; ii. 67, 68
Fulûs, i. 160
Fûsanj, i. 299

GALENUS, i. 222, 320; *de indole animæ*, i. 123; *book of speeches*, i. 95; *book of deduction*, i. 97; commentary to the Apothegms of Hippocrates, ii. 168; Protredticus, i. 34; commentary on the Aphorisms of Hippocrates, i. 35, 36; Κατὰ γένη, i. 127, 151
Gange-year, ii. 2, 7, 28, 31, 39, 44, 47, 48, 50, 53
Ghazna, i. 117, 206, 317
Ghaznin, ii. 103
*ghûr*, measure in Khwârzim, i. 166

Ghurrat-alzîjât, ii. 90
Ghuzz (Turks), ii. 168
Gilgit, i. 207
Girnagar, Eranian, i. 250
Girshâh, i. 109
Gospel, quoted, i. 4
Greek legends, i. 96
Greek philosophy, i. 7, 24, 33
Greek traditions, i. 105, 112, 143; origin of the alphabet, i. 172; on the astrolabe, i. 215, 219, 220, 222; on the Milky Way, i. 281, 289; on the first meridian, i. 304; on the chariot of war, i. 407

HARKAN, ii. 52
Hebrew, i. 36, 37, 38
Herbadh, i. 109
*Hindus*, their language, i. 17; classical and vernacular, i. 18; shortcomings of manuscript tradition, i. 18; the metrical form of composition, i. 19; their aversion to strangers, i. 20; their systems of matrimony, i. 107; the balance they use, i. 164; relation between authors (writers) and the nation at large, i. 265; their architecture, ii. 144
Hippocrates, his pedigree, i. 379
Homer, i. 42, 98
Huns, ii. 239

IBN ALMUḲAFFA', i. 264
Impilâ, name of the rhinoceros with the Negroes, i. 204
India, rainfall, i. 211, 212
Isfandiyâd, i. 193
Islam, sectarian views, i. 31, 263, 264
Ispahbad (of Kâbul), ii. 157
'Iyâs Ibn Mu'âwiya, ii. 158

JABRIYYA, a Muslim sect, i. 31
Jalam Ibn Shaibân, i. 116
Jam, i. 304
Jewish tradition on the tetragrammaton, i. 173
Jews, i. 6, 109; ii. 240
Johannes Grammaticus, refutation of Proclus, i. 36, 65, 226, 231; ii. 171
Jûn, Arabised form of *yojana*, i. 167
Jurjâu, i. 258, 305; ii. 182
Jûzajân, i. 308

KÂBUL, i. 22; its history, ii. 10, 157

Kâbul-Shâhs, ii. 10
Kâf mountain, i. 193, 249
Kaikâ'ûs, i. 304
Kaikhusrau, i. 304
Kalîla and Dimna, i. 159
Kandi (?), ii. 182
Kangdiz, i. 304
Kanz-al'iḥyâ, title of a book of the Manichæans, quoted, i. 39
kardajât, i. 245, 275 ; ii. 205
Karmatians, i. 116, 117
Kâ'ûs, i. 193
Kashmir, i. 117
ḳatâ-birds, i. 195
Khaṇḍakhâdyaka, Arabic, ii. 208
khôm, Eranian, i. 249
Khoten, i. 206
Khayâl-alkusûfaini (by Alberuni), ii. 208
Khurâsân, i. 21
Khwârizm, sea of, i. 258
Khwârizmian measures, i. 166
kirṭâs (papyrus), i. 170
Kitâb-almanshûrât (by Ptolemy), ii. 69
Kitâb-tibb-alfiyala, ii. 245
Koran, i. 4 ; Ṣûfî interpretation, i. 83, 88 ; quoted, i. 170, 222 ; sectarian interpretations, i. 263 ; quoted, i. 264 ; ii. 111, 113
Ḳulzum, i. 270
Ḳumair islands, i. 210
ḳurtaḳ, Arabic piece of dress, i. 180, 239

Laccadives, i. 210, 233
Langa (dove-country), i. 309
Langabâlûs, i. 241, 310
lavang (=clove), i. 309
Lohâniyya, i. 316
lunar stations (of the Hindus), i. 297

Mahmûd (Yamin-aldaula), i. 22, 117 ; ii. 2, 13, 103
Makrân, i. 208
Maledives, i. 210, 233
Manâ, Arabic, i. 163, 164, 166
Mânî, i. 48, 54, 55 ; his Book of Mysteries, i. 54, 264, 381 ; ii. 105, 169
Manichæans, i. 7, 39, 111, 123, 159
Miftâḥ-'ilm-alhai'a (by Alberuni), i. 277
miḳyâs, Arabic, i. 166
mithḳâl, i. 160, 161, 163, 164
Mu'âwiya, Khalif, i. 124
Muḥammad Ibn Alḳâsim, the conqueror of Sindh, i. 21, 116
Muḥammad Ibn Isḥâḳ, of Sarakhs, ii. 15, 16, 18
Muḥammad Ibn Zakariyyâ Al-râzî, i. 319
Muḥammira (Buddhists), i. 380
Muḳl, Arabic, a tree, i. 208
Mulamma', Arabic, kind of wood, i. 211
Multân, i. 121
Mu'tazila, i. 5
Myrtilus (?), i. 407

Nard, a play, i. 182
Nauroz, ii. 2
Nikâḥ-almaḳt, i. 109
Nile, sources, i. 270
nimbahr, Persian, i. 343
nimbahra, Persian, i. 214
Nimroz, i. 198
Nishâpûr, i. 305
nubbahr, ii. 225, 228, 229

Ordeals, ii. 159, 160
Oxus, i. 260

Paper, i. 171
papyrus, i. 171
Persian, i. 40 ; vazidaj = guzida, i. 158, 213, 214 ; *susmâr*, i. 241
Persian grammar, technical term, i. 19
Persian metric, i. 138
Persian traditions, i. 21, 63, 100, 109, 193, 304
Plato, i. 43, 65, 67 ; *Leges*, i. 105, 123 ; 379, 385 ; *Timæus*, i. 35, 223. 231, 322 ; *Phædo*, i. 56, 57, 65–67, 71, 76, 85, 86 ; ii. 166, 167, 171
Pontus Euxinus, i. 258
Porphyry, quoted, i. 43
Proclus, i. 57, 86
Ptolemy, Almajest, i. 226, 269 ; geography, 298, 390 ; ii. 69
Pythagoras, i. 65, 75, 85

Ramm, island, i. 210
raṭl, Arabic, i. 163
Rome, i. 306
Romulus and Remus, i. 112
Rustam, ii. 246

Sabuktagîn (Nâṣir-aldaula), i. 22

Śakakâla, ii. 46, 47, 49, 50, 51, 54, 55
Śakilkand, i. 299
Samarḳand, paper of, i. 171
Sarakhs, ii. 15
Satti, ii. 155
Seven Rishis, i. 394
Shakh (=Śaka ?), ii. 48, 49
Shamaniyya (śramaṇa), i. 21
Shapûrḳân, i. 304, 308
Shâsh, i. 298
shauḥaṭ, Arabic, kind of wood, i. 211
Shiltâs, i. 207
Shughnân-Shâh, i. 206
Sicily, i. 124
Sidâr, Arabic, piece of dress, i. 180
Sijistân, i. 198
Simonides, i. 172
Sindh, Muhammadan conquest, i. 21, 22, 165; Eranian, i. 260; mission from Sindh to Bagdad, ii. 15
Sindhind, i. 153, 332, 368; ii. 90, 191
Slavonians, ii. 167
Slavonians, sea of the, i. 258
smallpox (a wind blowing from Laṅkâ), i. 309
Socrates, i. 25, 85, 170; ii. 171
Sogdiana, i. 249
spêd-muhra, Persian, i. 328
Stoa, i. 98
Sufâla, i. 204, 211, 270; ii. 104
Sufi, explanation of the word, i. 33
Ṣûfis, i. 351
Ṣûfism, i. 8, 57, 62, 69, 76, 83, 87, 88
sukhkh, measure in Khwârizm, i. 166
susmâr, Persian, i. 241
Syria, i. 270
Syriac, *pailâsôpâ*, i. 33

Tarkîb-al'aflâk (v. Ya'ḳûb), i. 316, 353; ii. 67
Tartarus, i. 67
Tâshkand, i. 298
Tausar, i. 109
Tibet, i. 201, 206
Tibetans, ii. 10
Tirmidh, i. 260, 302
Tiz, i. 208
Tûrân, i. 208
Turks, i. 22, 206, 252, 302; ii. 10, 135, 178
Tûz, Persian, name of a tree, i. 171

Unang, i. 207
Uzain (ujain), i. 308

Vakhân-Shâh, i. 206
vellum, i. 171

Waḳwâḳ, island, i. 210

Ya'ḳûb Ibn Ṭâriḳ, his *Tarkîb-al'aflâk*, i. 169, 303, 312, 316, 353; ii. 15, 18, 23, 26, 34, 38, 44, 45, 67, 68
Yazdajird, his era, ii. 48
Yemen (distinguished from Arabia), i. 270

Zâbaj, i. 210; ii. 106
Zanj, the nations of Eastern Africa, i. 252, 270; ii. 104
Zarḳân, i. 7
Zindîk, i. 264
Zoroaster, i. 21, 91, 96
Zoroastrians (in Sogdiana), i. 249, 260; their dakhmas, ii. 167

PRINTED BY BALLANTYNE, HANSON AND CO.
EDINBURGH AND LONDON.

www.ingramcontent.com/pod-product-compliance
Lightning Source LLC
Chambersburg PA
CBHW032008300426
44117CB00008B/937
*9783337080464*